MOZART'S LIBRETTOS

MOZART'S LIBRETTOS

translated by
Robert Pack
and
Marjorie Lelash

Meridian Books
THE WORLD PUBLISHING COMPANY
Cleveland and New York

ROBERT PACK
Robert Pack is the author of two volumes of poetry—
The Irony of Joy and *A Stranger's Privilege*—
one of the co-editors of *New Poets of England and America*
(Meridian, M50), a frequent contributor to periodicals,
and a teacher of English at Barnard College.

MARJORIE LELASH
Marjorie Lelash is a young singer who has appeared
in productions of Mozart operas, among others.
Her articles and translations have appeared in *Musical
America* and the Metropolitan Opera program. She has
written free-lance musical publicity for N.C.A.C. for the
past two years.

ML
49
M83
P3

Ⅳ

AN ORIGINAL MERIDIAN BOOK
Published by The World Publishing Company
2231 West 110 Street, Cleveland 2, Ohio
First printing April 1961

43228

CONTENTS

FOREWORD

In preparing these translations, we have tried to accomplish two things: first, to present the librettos of the five major Mozart operas as readably and as dramatically as possible, finding the natural or colloquial English phrase without falling into mannerism or dullness; second, steering a middle course between literal pedestrianism and figurative flight of fancy, to make the translations correspond to the exact meanings of the German and Italian texts. These two objectives naturally conflicted to some extent, but we hope that without too much loss in textual accuracy, we have succeeded in conveying the essential spirit of these five operas.

The translations will be found opposite their equivalent texts. Thus the reader can use them to follow a recorded performance, or to refresh his memory before or after a "live" rendition of any of the operas. Cuts have been made in conformance with current practice, although this, of course, varies greatly with each conductor, and with every opera house.

Certain technical points remain to be clarified. We have kept the traditional numberings of arias and ensembles because the numbers serve as convenient listening guides. However, the system of beginning another "scene" every time a new character is introduced seems antiquated and confusing, and it has not been retained. Stage directions have been held to that minimum necessary to explain the action, and some of these directions have been revised, again, in conformance with current practice. Our texts approximate as closely as possible what our readers will actually see and hear, since this book is intended not as a scholarly work but as an attempt to make the riches of Mozart's operas more accessible to a less specialized audience.

We wish to acknowledge the invaluable assistance of Miss Joan Bonime, as well as the help of Constantin Vichey and Willie Schumann.

R. P.
M. L.

THE
ABDUCTION
FROM
THE
SERAGLIO

DIE
ENTFÜHRUNG
AUS
DEM
SERAIL

*An opera
in three acts*

*Music by
Wolfgang Amadeus Mozart
(K. 384)*

*Words by
Christoph Friedrich Bretzner,
adapted by
Gottlieb Stephanie
the Younger*

INTRODUCTION

The Abduction from the Seraglio, the earliest of Mozart's operas to continue to hold the stage today (although *Idomeneo* enjoys occasional revivals), was composed during the summer of 1781, when Mozart was twenty-five and contemplating marriage to Constanze Weber, who later became his wife. Fittingly enough, the opera's heroine is also named Constanze. Mozart poured the joy of youthful love into the old mold of the Singspiel (literally, a play with songs), augmenting its traditional form to accord with the newly fashionable preoccupation with all things Turkish—for the Turks were an ever-present threat to the Viennese. The finished product—first performed in July 1782 —is remarkable for grace, elegance, and zest, and for characters who experience the passions of love and hate simply, directly, and without sophisticated self-examination.

Mozart's impeccable taste was instinctive, not learned; from the beginning he possessed a unique melodic facility and a remarkable power to shape the right phrase for a given character or situation. He was able to join the old form and the new fashions into an expression of his own personal style—the music of *The Abduction from the Seraglio* is as unmistakably Mozart's as that of *Don Giovanni.* Never at variance with the patterns chosen by his predecessors, Mozart, rather, used them to attain his own ends. Thus he was free to achieve the serenity and coherence that were the constant characteristics of his style.

The Abduction from the Seraglio includes the conventional hero and heroine—puppets who are called upon to stand and sing incredibly difficult music incredibly well— and the sublimely noble Pasha Selim, who does not sing a note. But what will especially endear this opera to the confirmed Mozartean are the three clearly defined character parts, which anticipate many of the roles in the later operas. Blonde, the intrepid, independent servant girl who stands up for her own rights, is contrasted to Constanze, much as Susanna sets off the Countess in *The Marriage of*

10

Figaro, or Despina complements Fiordiligi in *Così fan tutte.* In the same way, Pedrillo provides a contrast to Belmonte. While his noble master is casting about for a means of rescuing the ladies from their imprisonment, it is Pedrillo who makes the plans that finally culminate in his hilarious drunken duet with Osmin. In this respect, he is a predecessor of Figaro and of Don Alfonso in *Così fan tutte.* Osmin, however, is quite unique. He bears resemblance to Leporello in *Don Giovanni* and to Bartolo in *Figaro,* but the crochety, ferocious old man is so skillfully drawn that he achieves a vivid individuality. His music is undoubtedly showy—a good basso profondo can make a sensation with his two arias—but it is also revelatory of character to a degree that Mozart was not to approach again until his later operas.

The Singspiel with its spoken dialogue offers a more relaxed atmosphere than Italian opera with the more sustained requirements of its sung recitative. This tends, however, to make the work somewhat spotty and episodic; in *The Abduction from the Seraglio* there is no real suspense until act three, and throughout, there is little welding of music and drama in the manner of the second-act finale of *Figaro* or the scene in which Don Giovanni meets his downfall. Given an uncomplicated subject, Mozart dealt with it on its own terms. He was not attempting to probe the profoundest human emotions; he was interested in the expression of happy young love, love reciprocal and serene that would triumphantly withstand peril and temptation. But he was also beginning the examination of human character and action which he continued so brilliantly in his later works.

The Abduction from the Seraglio shares many characteristics with the later operas: parallel pairs of lovers, heroic arias for an ineffectual tenor and a long-suffering soprano, a scintillant soubrette, magically balanced ensembles and duets, serenity, polish, and an immediate charm that becomes more persuasive as we become better acquainted with the opera. But *The Abduction* will always delight lovers of Mozart's music primarily because of the glow of youth and happiness that adorns it.

SYNOPSIS

ACT ONE

Constanze, her maid Blonde, and Pedrillo, the servant of Belmonte, Constanze's beloved, have been captured by pirates after a shipwreck, and all three have been sold as slaves to the wealthy Pasha Selim. As the opera begins, Belmonte arrives at the Pasha's palace but is denied entrance by the jealous old overseer, Osmin. When Osmin has left, Pedrillo delightedly greets his master, telling him that despite the Pasha's advances, Constanze has remained faithful. Constanze, who is having difficulty warding off these advances, informs the Pasha that she will suffer any torture, but she cannot love him—nothing can shake her fidelity to Belmonte. Although Osmin seeks to block their way, Pedrillo and Belmonte, whom Pedrillo has presented to the Pasha as an architect eager to enter his service, go into the palace, where they hope to arrange for the rescue of Constanze and Blonde.

ACT TWO

Blonde, who seems to have the lustful Osmin somewhat under her control, is told by Pedrillo, who loves her, that Belmonte has arrived with a ship. Overjoyed, Blonde runs off to tell Constanze the news of their impending rescue. Inducing Osmin to drink with him, Pedrillo manages to put a sleeping potion into the old man's wine, and the two pairs of lovers are thus enabled to meet and swear eternal fidelity.

ACT THREE

After many delays, the ladies' abduction is accomplished by means of ladders at their windows. At the last moment, the fugitives are apprehended by Osmin and are brought back to the Pasha, who discovers that Belmonte is the son of his greatest enemy. Nevertheless, he forgoes revenge and permits all four to depart unharmed. The opera ends with a chorus in praise of the Pasha's magnanimity and kindness.

CHARACTERS

BELMONTE, *a young Spanish nobleman*   *Tenor*
PEDRILLO, *his servant*   *Tenor*
OSMIN, *the overseer of* PASHA SELIM   *Bass*
CONSTANZE, *beloved of* BELMONTE   *Soprano*
BLONDE, *her maid, beloved of* PEDRILLO   *Soprano*
PASHA SELIM   *Speaking part*
KLAAS, *a sailor on* BELMONTE'S *ship*   *Speaking part*
A GUARD *of the* PASHA   *Speaking part*
CHORUS *of Janissaries*
Guards, a mute servant, an officer of the PASHA

The action takes place in Turkey, during the eighteenth century, in and around the palace of PASHA SELIM.

13

DIE ENTFÜHRUNG AUS DEM SERAIL

ERSTER AUFZUG

Platz vor dem Palast des BASSA *am Ufer des Meeres.* BEL-
MONTE *allein.*

1. Arie

BELMONTE: Hier soll ich dich denn sehen,
Constanze, dich mein Glück!
O Himmel, hör mein Flehen:
Gib mir die Ruh zurück!
Ich duldete der Leiden,
O Liebe, allzuviel.
Gib mir dafür nun Freuden,
Und bringe mich an's Ziel.

Dialog

Aber wie soll ich in den Palast kommen? Wie sie sehen?
Wie sprechen?
(OSMIN *erscheint mit einer Leiter. Er lehnt sie an einen
Feigenbaum vor dem Palast, steigt hinauf und nimmt Fei-
gen ab.*)

2. Arie und Duett

OSMIN: Wer ein Liebchen hat gefunden,
Die es treu und redlich meint,
Lohn es ihr durch tausend Küsse,
Mach ihr all das Leben süsse,
Sei ihr Tröster,
Sei ihr Freund.
Tralla-le-ra, tralla-le-ra.
Doch sie treu zu erhalten,
Schliess er Liebchen sorglich ein;
Denn die losen Dinger haschen
Jeden Schmetterling und naschen
Gar zu gern von fremden Wein.
Tralla-le-ra, tralla-le-ra.

BELMONTE: He, Alter, he! hört Ihr nicht? Ist hier des Bassa
Selim Palast?
(OSMIN *sieht ihn an, dreht sich herum und singt wie zuvor.*)

OSMIN: Sonderlich beim Mondenscheine,
Freunde, nehmt sie wohl in Acht:
Oft lauscht da ein junges Herrchen,
Kirrt und lockt das kleine Närrchen,
Und dann Treue gute Nacht!
Tralla-le-ra, tralla-le-ra.

ACT ONE

Before the walls of the PASHA'S *palace on the shore of the sea.* BELMONTE *is alone.*

1. Aria

BELMONTE: Here shall I see you again, Constanze, my love! O heaven, I implore you, return my peace to me! Beloved, I have endured many sorrows because my love is so great. Give me back my happiness and permit me to reach my goal!

Dialogue

But how can I get into the palace? How can I see her? How can I speak to her?

(OSMIN *enters, carrying a ladder. He puts it against a fig tree before the palace, climbs up, and begins to pick figs.*)

2. Aria and Duet

OSMIN: If you find a true and honest sweetheart, you should praise her with a thousand kisses; you should sweeten all her life, and be her comforter and friend. Tralla-le-ra! Tralla-le-ra! If she remains true to you, you must lock her up carefully to preserve her virtue, for loose women try to capture every butterfly and to sample every stranger's wine. Tralla-le-ra! Tralla-le-ra!

BELMONTE: Hey there, old man, don't you hear me? Is this the Pasha Selim's palace?

(OSMIN *sees him, turns around, and continues singing.*)

OSMIN: Often, young men attempt to entice the little fools, and then it's truly good night! Tralla-le-ra! Tralla-le-ra!

BELMONTE: Verwünscht seist du samt deinem Liede!
Ich bin dein Singen nun schon müde,
So hör doch nur ein einzig Wort!

OSMIN: Was Henker, lasst Ihr Euch gelüsten,
Euch zu ereifern, Euch zu brüsten!
Was wollt Ihr? was wollt Ihr? was wollt Ihr?
Hurtig, ich muss fort!

BELMONTE: Ist das des Bassa Selim Haus?

OSMIN: Das ist des Bassa Selim Haus.

BELMONTE: So wartet doch! Ein Wort!

OSMIN: Ich kann nicht weilen, geschwind, denn ich muss
eilen.

BELMONTE: Seid Ihr in seinen Diensten, Freund?

OSMIN: Ich bin in seinen Diensten, Freund!

BELMONTE: Wie kann ich den Pedrill wohl sprechen,
Der hier in seinen Diensten steht?

OSMIN: Den Schurken, der den Hals soll brechen!
Seht selber zu,
Wenn's anders geht!
Seht selber zu, wenn's anders geht!

BELMONTE (*für sich*): Was für ein alter grober Bengel!

OSMIN (*für sich*): Das ist just so ein Galgenschwengel.

BELMONTE: Ihr irrt, Ihr irrt, Ihr irrt, es ist ein braver
Mann.

OSMIN: So brav, so brav, so brav,
Dass man ihn spiessen kann.

BELMONTE: Ihr müsst ihn wahrlich nicht recht kennen.

OSMIN: Recht gut, ich liess ihn heut verbrennen.
Auf einen Pfahl gehört sein Kopf! (*Will fort.*)

BELMONTE: So bleibet doch!

OSMIN: Was wollt Ihr noch?

BELMONTE: Ich möchte gerne—

OSMIN (*spöttisch*): So hübsch von ferne
Um's Haus 'rum schleichen, und Mädchen stehlen?
Fort, Euresgleichen braucht man hier nicht!

BELMONTE: Ihr seid besessen,
Sprecht voller Galle
Mir so vermessen
Ins Angesicht?

BELMONTE: Be accursed with your song! I'm sick of it! Listen to one word from me.

OSMIN: What hangman let him escape? Why is he shouting so loudly? What do you want? I must be on my way!

BELMONTE: Is this the Pasha Selim's house?
OSMIN: This is the Pasha Selim's house.
BELMONTE: Wait a moment! One word!
OSMIN: I can't wait; I must hurry about my business.

BELMONTE: Are you in the Pasha's service, my friend?
OSMIN: I am in the Pasha's service, my friend.
BELMONTE: How can I speak to Pedrillo, who also serves him?
OSMIN: That scoundrel! I'll break his neck! See for yourself if I don't! See for yourself if I don't!

BELMONTE (*to himself*): What a coarse old fellow!
OSMIN (*to himself*): He's a rogue straight from the gallows!
BELMONTE: You're wrong; Pedrillo is an honest man!

OSMIN: So honest that he deserves to be killed!

BELMONTE: Perhaps you don't know him well.
OSMIN: I know him well enough to want to see him burned. His head belongs on a pike! (*Turns to go.*)
BELMONTE: Wait!
OSMIN: What do you want now?
BELMONTE: I would very much like—
OSMIN (*mocking*): How cleverly he sneaks about the house to steal our women! Go away! We don't need you here.

BELMONTE: You must be insane, to revile me so bitterly!

OSMIN: Nur nicht in Eifer—

BELMONTE: Schont Euren Geifer.

OSMIN: Ich kenn Euch schon!

BELMONTE: Lasst Euer Droh'n!

OSMIN: Marsch, geht zum Teufel!
Ihr kriegt, ich schwöre,
Sonst ohne Gnade
Die Bastonade;
Noch habt Ihr Zeit!

BELMONTE: Es ist kein Zweifel,
Ihr seid von Sinnen,
Welch ein Betragen
Auf meine Fragen!
Gebt doch Bescheid!

(OSMIN *drängt* BELMONTE *hinaus.*)

Dialog

OSMIN: Könnt ich mir doch noch so einen Schurken auf die Nase setzen, wie den Pedrillo; so einen Gaudieb, der Tag und Nacht nichts tut, als nach meinen Weibern herumzuschleichen und zu schnobern, ob's nichts für seinen Schnabel setzt. Aber ich laure ihm sicher auf den Dienst, und wohl bekomm dir die Prügelsuppe, wenn ich dich einmal beim Kanthaken kriege! Hätt er sich nur beim Bassa nicht so eingeschmeichelt, er sollte den Strick längst um den Hals haben.

(PEDRILLO *kommt herein.*)

PEDRILLO: Nun, wie steht's, Osmin? Ist der Bassa noch nicht zurück?

OSMIN: Sieh darnach, wenn du's wissen willst.

PEDRILLO: Schon wieder Sturm im Kalender? Hast du das Gericht Feigen für mich gepflückt?

OSMIN: Gift für dich, verwünschter Schmarotzer!

PEDRILLO: Was in aller Welt ich dir nur getan haben muss, dass du beständig mit mir zankst. Lass uns doch einmal Friede machen.

OSMIN: Friede mit dir? Mit so einem schleichenden, spitzbübischen Passauf, der nur spioniert, wie er mir eins versetzen kann? Erdrosseln möcht ich dich!

PEDRILLO: Aber sag nur, warum, warum?

OSMIN: Warum? Weil ich dich nicht leiden kann.

OSMIN: Now, one minute—

BELMONTE: Save your breath.

OSMIN: I know you already!

BELMONTE: Stop your droning!

OSMIN: Go to the devil, or I swear that I shall beat you without mercy! You still have time to escape!

BELMONTE: There's no doubt about it: he's out of his mind. His answers show he's quite deranged!
(OSMIN *pushes* BELMONTE *out.*)

Dialogue

OSMIN: Why should I endure another such rogue as Pedrillo, another thief who does nothing day and night—who sneaks around the women, waiting to see whether any of them will favor him! If he had not beguiled the Pasha, he would long ago have a noose around his neck!
(PEDRILLO *enters.*)

PEDRILLO: Now what is it, Osmin? Has the Pasha come back yet?

OSMIN: Look for yourself!

PEDRILLO: So we can expect a storm? Did you pick those figs for me?

OSMIN: Poison for you, damned scoundrel!

PEDRILLO: What in the world have I done to make you dislike me? Let us be friends, for once.

OSMIN: Friends? With such a sneaking, spying rogue, who always tries to play tricks on me? I should like to strangle you!

PEDRILLO: But tell me why!

OSMIN: Why? Because I dislike you!

19

3. *Arie*

OSMIN: Solche hergelauf'ne Laffen,
Die nur nach den Weibern gaffen,
Mag ich für den Teufel nicht;
Denn ihr ganzes Tun und Lassen ist,
Uns auf den Dienst zu passen,
Doch mich trügt kein solch' Gesicht.
Eure Tücken, eure Ränke,
Eure Finten, eure Schwänke
Sind mir ganz bekannt.
Mich zu hintergehen,
Müsst ihr früh aufstehen:
Ich hab auch Verstand, ich!
Ich hab auch Verstand.
Drum beim Barte des Propheten!
Ich studiere Tag und Nacht,
Dich so mit Manier zu töten,
Nimm dich wie du willst in Acht;
Nimm dich in Acht! (*Geht ab.*)

Dialog

PEDRILLO: Geh nur, verwünschter Aufpasser; es ist noch
nicht aller Tage Abend. Wer weiss, wer den andern über-
listet; und dir misstrauischem, gehässigem Menschenfeinde
eine Grube zu graben, sollte ein wahres Fest für mich sein.
(BELMONTE *kommt herein.*)

BELMONTE: Pedrillo, guter Pedrillo!

PEDRILLO: Ach mein bester Herr! Ist's möglich? Sind Sie's
wirklich? Bravo, Madame Fortuna, bravo, das heisst doch
Wort gehalten! Schon verzweifelte ich, ob einer meiner
Briefe Sie getroffen hätte.

BELMONTE: Sag, guter Pedrillo, lebt meine Constanze noch?

PEDRILLO: Lebt, und noch, hoff ich, für Sie. Seit dem
schrecklichen Tage, an welchem das Glück uns einen so
hässlichen Streich spielte und unser Schiff von den Seeräu-
bern erobern liess, haben wir mancherlei Drangsal erfahren.
Glücklicherweise traf sich's noch, dass der Bassa Selim
uns alle drei kaufte: Ihre Constanze nämlich, meine Blonde
und mich. Er liess uns sogleich hier auf sein Landhaus
bringen. Donna Constanze ward seine auserwählte Geliebte.

BELMONTE: Ah! Was sagst du?

3. Aria

OSMIN: These filthy monkeys who always leer at women! I hate them like the devil! Their aim in life is to interfere with our work, while evading their own. But I'll never be deceived by such a face as yours! I know your tricks already. You'll have to get up early to get around me— I have intelligence and understanding! By the Prophet's beard, I think of my vengeance night and day! Your slyness is in vain; I won't rest until I see you dead! (*Exits.*)

Dialogue

PEDRILLO: Go along, you accursed overseer; your time has not yet come. Who knows which of us will finally outwit the other? To dig a grave for you, you suspicious, quarrelsome misanthrope, would be a true festival for me! (BELMONTE *enters.*)

BELMONTE: Pedrillo, good Pedrillo!

PEDRILLO: Ah, my dear master! Is it possible? Can it be true? Bravo, Lady Luck, bravo, you have kept your promise! I doubted that my letters had reached you.

BELMONTE: Tell me, good Pedrillo, is my Constanze still living?

PEDRILLO: She lives, and, I hope, only for you. Since that terrible day when fate was so cruel and our ship was overtaken by pirates, we have endured many hardships. Fortunately, it happened that Pasha Selim bought all three of us as slaves—your Constanze, my Blonde, and myself. He had us brought at once to his palace. My lady Constanze was his chosen love.

BELMONTE: What are you saying?

PEDRILLO: Nun, nur nicht so hitzig! Sie ist noch nicht in die schlimmsten Hände gefallen. Der Bassa ist ein Renegat und hat noch so viel Delikatesse, keine seiner Weiber zu seiner Liebe zu zwingen; und so viel ich weiss, spielt er noch immer den unerhörten Liebhaber.

BELMONTE: Wär es möglich? Wär Constanze noch treu?

PEDRILLO: Sicher noch, lieber Herr! Aber wie's mit meinem Blondchen steht, weiss der Himmel! Das arme Ding schmachtet bei einem alten hässlichen Kerl, dem sie der Bassa geschenkt hat; und vielleicht—ach, ich darf gar nicht dran denken!

BELMONTE: Doch nicht der alte Kerl, der soeben ins Haus ging?

PEDRILLO: Eben der.

BELMONTE: Und dies ist der Liebling des Bassa?

PEDRILLO: Liebling, Spion und Ausbund aller Spitzbuben, der mich mit den Augen vergiften möchte, wenn's möglich wäre.

BELMONTE: O guter Pedrillo, was sagst du?

PEDRILLO: Nur nicht gleich verzagt! Unter uns gesagt: ich hab auch einen Stein im Brett beim Bassa. Durch mein bisschen Geschick in der Gärtnerei hab ich seine Gunst weggekriegt, und dadurch hab ich so ziemlich Freiheit, die tausend andere nicht haben würden. Da sonst jede Manns-person sich entfernen muss, wenn eine seiner Weiber in den Garten kommt, kann ich bleiben; sie reden sogar mit mir, und er sagt nichts darüber. Freilich mault der alte Osmin, besonders, wenn mein Blondchen ihrer Gebieterin folgen muss.

BELMONTE: Ist's möglich? Du hast sie gesprochen? O sag, sag! Liebt sie mich noch?

PEDRILLO: Hm! Dass Sie daran zweifeln! Ich dächte, Sie kennten die gute Constanze mehr als zu gut, hätten Proben genug ihrer Liebe. Doch damit dürfen wir uns gar nicht aufhalten. Hier ist bloss die Frage, wie's anzufangen ist, hier wegzukommen?

BELMONTE: O da hab ich für alles gesorgt! Ich hab hier ein Schiff in einiger Entfernung vom Hafen, das uns auf den ersten Wink einnimmt, und—

PEDRILLO: Now, don't be too upset! She could have fallen into worse hands. The Pasha may be a Mohammedan, but he has enough delicacy not to force any of his wives to love him, and as far as I know, in this case he has so far played the part of the rejected suitor.

BELMONTE: Is it possible? Can my Constanze still be true to me?

PEDRILLO: Certainly, dear master! But heaven only knows how it is with my Blonde. The poor thing is in the hands of an ugly old churl to whom she was presented by the Pasha, and perhaps— Ah, I don't even like to think about it!

BELMONTE: Not the same old fellow who went into the house?

PEDRILLO: That's the one.

BELMONTE: And he is the favorite of the Pasha?

PEDRILLO: Favorite, spy, and paragon of all rascals. He would kill me with his looks, if it were possible.

BELMONTE: O good Pedrillo, what is to be done?

PEDRILLO: Don't despair! Between us, the Pasha is indebted to me. I have won his favor by my skill in gardening, and so I have more freedom than anyone else. Every other male must leave when the Pasha's wives come into the garden, but I can remain; even if they speak to me, he makes no objection. Of course, old Osmin grumbles about it, especially when my Blonde is there.

BELMONTE: Is it possible that you have spoken to Constanze? Oh, tell me about it! Does she still love me?

PEDRILLO: Can you doubt it? I thought you knew Constanze better, and that you had more faith in her love. But let's not delay any longer. The only question is—how shall we all escape from here?

BELMONTE: Oh, I've taken care of that! I have a ship here at anchor—at the first signal—

PEDRILLO: Ah, sachte, sachte! Erst müssen wir die Mädels haben, ehe wir zu Schiffe gehen, und das geht nicht so husch, husch, wie Sie meinen!

BELMONTE: O lieber, guter Pedrillo, mach nur, dass ich sie sehen, dass ich sie sprechen kann! Das Herz schlägt mir vor Angst und Freude!

PEDRILLO: Pfiffig müssen wir das Ding anfangen, und rasch müssen wir's ausführen, damit wir den alten Aufpasser übertölpeln. Bleiben Sie hier in der Nähe. Jetzt wird der Bassa bald von einer Lustfahrt auf dem Wasser zurückkommen. Ich will Sie ihm als einen geschickten Baumeister vorstellen, denn Bauen und Gärtnerei sind seine Steckenpferde. Aber lieber, goldner Herr, halten Sie sich in Schranken; Constanze ist bei ihm—

BELMONTE: Constanze bei ihm? Was sagst du? Ich soll sie sehen?

PEDRILLO: Gemach, gemach ums Himmels willen, lieber Herr, sonst stolpern wir! Ah, ich glaube, dort seh ich sie schon angefahren kommen. Gehn Sie nur auf die Seite, wenn er kommt; ich will ihm entgegen gehen. (*Geht ab.*)

4. Arie

BELMONTE: Constanze! Constanze! dich wiederzusehen, dich!
O wie ängstlich, o wie feurig
Klopft mein liebevolles Herz!
Und des Wiedersehens Zähre
Lohnt der Trennung bangen Schmerz.
Schon zittr ich und wanke,
Schon zag ich und schwanke,
Es hebt sich die schwellende Brust.
Ist das ihr Lispeln?
Es wird mir so bange.
War das ihr Seufzen?
Es glüht mir die Wange.
Täuscht mich die Liebe?
War es ein Traum?
(PEDRILLO *kommt hurtig gelaufen.*)

Dialog

PEDRILLO: Geschwind, geschwind auf die Seite und versteckt! Der Bassa kommt.

(BELMONTE *versteckt sich.* CHOR *der Janitscharen kommt herein, dann* BASSA SELIM *mit* CONSTANZE.)

PEDRILLO: Speak softly! Before we can go to the ship we must rescue the ladies, and that won't be arranged as easily as you might think.

BELMONTE: O dear, good Pedrillo, let me see her, so that I may speak to her! My heart is torn between fear and joy!

PEDRILLO: We must dispatch this matter cleverly in order to outwit the old overseer. Wait here—soon the Pasha will return from a pleasure trip on the river. I will present you to him as a well-known architect, for building and gardening are his hobbies. But, dear master, you must control yourself; Constanze is with him—

BELMONTE: Constanze with him? What are you saying? Shall I see her?

PEDRILLO: Be calm, for heaven's sake, dear master, or we shall ruin everything! Ah, I believe that I see them already arriving. Wait over there; when he comes I will go to meet him. (*Exits.*)

4. Aria

BELMONTE: Constanze! Constanze! Will I now see you again? How eagerly, how passionately my loving heart is beating! Our reunion will atone for our sad parting; I am trembling and shaking; I palpitate and shiver. Can this be the end of my suffering? Is that her sigh? My pain increases. Does love deceive me? Was it all a dream?

(PEDRILLO *enters in a rush.*)

Dialogue

PEDRILLO: Hurry, hurry, go over there! The Pasha is coming!

(BELMONTE *hides.* CHORUS *of Janissaries enters, followed by* PASHA SELIM, *with* CONSTANZE.)

Die Entführung aus dem Serail

5. Chor der Janitscharen

CHOR: Singt dem grossen Bassa Lieder,
Dem grossen Bassa Lieder,
Töne feuriger Gesang,
Und vom Ufer halle wieder,
Vom Ufer halle wieder
Unsrer Lieder Jubel klang.
Weht ihm entgegen,
Kühlende Winde.
Ebne dich sanfter,
Wallende Flut.
Singt ihm entgegen,
Fliegende Chöre,
Singt ihm der Liebe Freuden ins Herz.

(CHOR *und* PEDRILLO *gehen ab.* BASSA SELIM *und* CONSTANZE *sind allein.*)

Dialog

BASSA SELIM: Immer noch traurig, geliebte Constanze? Immer in Tränen? Sieh, dieser schöne Abend, diese reizende Gegend, diese bezaubernde Musik, meine zärtliche Liebe für dich. Sag, kann nichts von allem dich endlich beruhigen, endlich dein Herz rühren? Sieh, ich könnte befehlen, könnte grausam mit dir verfahren, dich zwingen.

(CONSTANZE *seufzt.*)

Aber nein, Constanze, dir selbst will ich dein Herz zu danken haben, dir selbst!

CONSTANZE: Grossmütiger Mann! O dass ich es könnte, dass ich's erwidern könnte—aber—

BASSA SELIM: Sag, Constanze, sag, was hält dich zurück?

CONSTANZE: Du wirst mich hassen.

BASSA SELIM: Nein, ich schwöre dir's. Du weisst, wie sehr ich dich liebe, wieviel Freiheit ich dir vor allen meinen Weibern gestatte, dich wie meine einzige schätze.

CONSTANZE: O so verzeih!

6. Arie

Ach ich liebte, war so glücklich,
Kannte nicht der Liebe Schmerz,
Schwur ihm Treue, dem Geliebten,
Gab dahin mein ganzes Herz.
Doch wie schnell schwand meine Freude!
Trennung war mein banges Los,
Und nun schwimmt mein Aug in Thränen!
Kummer ruht in meinem Schoss.

5. Chorus of Janissaries

CHORUS: Sing the great Pasha's praises! Let our joyous song awaken echoes from the shore! Blow on him, cooling breezes; ebb more softly, rising wave! Sing love's joy into his heart!

(CHORUS *and* PEDRILLO *exit, leaving* PASHA SELIM *and* CONSTANZE *alone.*)

Dialogue

PASHA SELIM: Are you still sad, beloved Constanze? This beautiful evening, this charming place, this enchanting music, my tender love for you—can nothing move you or bring repose to your heart? I could force you to do my will.

(CONSTANZE *sighs.*)
But I choose to win your love only by your consent.

CONSTANZE: You are so generous! If only I could—but—

PASHA SELIM: Tell me, Constanze, what restrains you?
CONSTANZE: You will hate me.
PASHA SELIM: No, I will not. You know what freedom I give to you, more than to all my other wives, and how much I love you. You are my only beloved.
CONSTANZE: Please forgive me!

6. Aria

Ah, I loved, and I was so happy. I knew nothing of love's pain. I swore to be true to my beloved, and I gave him my whole heart. But now my joy has vanished, for I am separated from him. Now only grief reigns in my breast!

Dialog

Ach, ich sagt es wohl, du würdest mich hassen. Aber verzeih, verzeih dem liebekranken Mädchen! Du bist ja so grossmütig, so gut. Ich will dir dienen, deine Sklavin sein bis ans Ende meines Lebens, nur verlange nicht ein Herz von mir, das auf ewig versagt ist.

BASSA SELIM: Ha, Undankbare! Was wagst du zu bitten?

CONSTANZE: Töte mich, Selim, töte mich, nur zwinge mich nicht, meineidig zu werden! Noch zuletzt, wie mich der Seeräuber aus den Armen meines Geliebten riss, schwur ich aufs feierlichste—

BASSA SELIM: Halt ein, nicht ein Wort! Reize meinen Zorn nicht noch mehr. Bedenke, dass du in meiner Gewalt bist!

CONSTANZE: Ich bin es, aber du wirst dich ihrer nicht bedienen, ich kenne dein gutes, dein mitleidsvolles Herz. Hätte ich's sonst wagen können, dir das meinige zu entdecken?

BASSA SELIM: Wag es nicht, meine Güte zu missbrauchen!

CONSTANZE: Nur Aufschub gönne mir, Herr, nur Zeit, meinen Schmerz zu vergessen!

BASSA SELIM: Wie oft schon gewährt ich dir diese Bitte.

CONSTANZE: Nur noch diesmal!

BASSA SELIM: Es sei, zum letzten Male! Geh, Constanze, geh! Besinne dich eines Bessern, und morgen—

CONSTANZE (*im Abgehn*): Unglückliches Mädchen! O Belmonte, Belmonte!

BASSA SELIM: Ihr Schmerz, ihre Tränen, ihre Standhaftigkeit bezaubern mein Herz immer mehr, machen mir ihre Liebe nur noch wünschenswerter. Ha, wer wollte gegen ein solches Herz Gewalt brauchen? Nein, Constanze, nein, auch Selim hat ein Herz, auch Selim kennt Liebe!

(PEDRILLO *kommt mit* BELMONTE *herein.*)

PEDRILLO: Herr, verzeih, dass ich es wage, dich in deinen Betrachtungen zu stören!

BASSA SELIM: Was willst du, Pedrillo?

PEDRILLO: Dieser junge Mann, der sich in Italien mit vielem Fleiss auf die Baukunst gelegt, hat von deiner Macht, von deinem Reichtum gehört und kommt her, dir als Baumeister seine Dienste anzubieten.

Dialogue

Ah, I knew that you would despise me. But forgive a heart wounded by love! You are so generous, so good! I will serve you and be your slave to the end of my life. But do not ask for my heart—it is forever pledged to another.

PASHA SELIM: Ungrateful girl! What do you dare to ask me?

CONSTANZE: Kill me, Selim, kill me, but do not force me to perjure myself! For at the moment when the pirates tore me from my lover's arms, I solemnly swore—

PASHA SELIM: Stop! Not another word! Don't excite my anger any further. Remember that you are in my power!

CONSTANZE: Yes, I am, but you will not avail yourself of it; I know your good, compassionate heart. If I had no faith in you, I never would have told you my true feelings.

PASHA SELIM: Do not take advantage of my kindness!

CONSTANZE: I ask only a postponement, my Lord, to give me time to forget my pain!

PASHA SELIM: How often have I heard this plea!

CONSTANZE: Only once more!

PASHA SELIM: So be it, for the last time. Go, Constanze, think the matter over, and tomorrow—

CONSTANZE (*leaving*): I am so unhappy! O Belmonte, Belmonte!

PASHA SELIM: Her pain, her tears, her steadfastness, enchant my heart and make her love even more desirable to me. Who could use force against such a nature? No, Constanze, Selim also has a heart, and he too understands the pangs of love.

(PEDRILLO *enters, with* BELMONTE.)

PEDRILLO: My Lord, forgive me for disturbing your contemplation!

PASHA SELIM: What do you want, Pedrillo?

PEDRILLO: A young man who has industriously studied architecture in Italy has heard of your wealth, and he has come here to offer you his services.

BELMONTE: Herr, könnte ich so glücklich sein, durch meine geringen Fähigkeiten deinen Beifall zu verdienen!

BASSA SELIM: Hm! Du gefällst mir. Ich will sehen, was du kannst. (*zu* PEDRILLO) Sorge für seinen Unterhalt. Morgen werde ich dich wieder rufen lassen. (*Geht ab.*)

PEDRILLO: Ha! Triumph, Triumph, Herr! Der erste Schritt war getan.

BELMONTE: Ach, lass mich zu mir selbst kommen! Ich habe sie gesehen, hab das gute, treue, beste Mädchen gesehen! O Constanze, Constanze! Was könnt ich für dich tun, was für dich wagen?

PEDRILLO: Ha! Gemach, gemach, bester Herr! Stimmen Sie den Ton ein bisschen herab; Verstellung wird uns weit bessere Dienste leisten. Wir sind nicht in unserm Vaterlande. Hier fragen sie den Henker darnach, ob's einen Kopf mehr oder weniger in der Welt gibt. Bastonade und Strick um Hals sind hier wie ein Morgenbrot.

BELMONTE: Ach, Pedrillo, wenn du die Liebe kenntest!

PEDRILLO: Hm! Als wenn's mit unser einem gar nichts wäre. Ich habe so gut meine zärtlichen Stunden als andere Leute. Und denken Sie denn, dass mir's nicht auch im Bauche grimmt, wenn ich mein Blondchen von so einem alten Spitzbuben, wie der Osmin ist, bewacht sehen muss?

BELMONTE: O wenn es möglich wäre, sie zu sprechen—

PEDRILLO: Wir wollen sehen, was zu tun ist. Kommen Sie nur mit mir in den Garten, aber um alles in der Welt vorsichtig und fein. Denn hier ist alles Aug und Ohr.

(*Sie wollen in den Palast.* OSMIN *kommt ihnen in der Tür entgegen und hält sie zurück.*)

OSMIN: Wohin?

PEDRILLO: Hinein!

OSMIN (*zu* BELMONTE): Was will das Gesicht? Zurück mit dir, zurück!

PEDRILLO: Ha, gemach, Meister Grobian, gemach! Er ist in des Bassa Diensten.

OSMIN: In des Henkers Diensten mag er sein! Er soll nicht herein!

PEDRILLO: Er soll aber herein!

OSMIN: Kommt mir nur einen Schritt über die Schwelle—

BELMONTE: Unverschämter! Hast du nicht mehr Achtung für einen Mann meines Standes?

BELMONTE: My Lord, I would be so happy if my modest talent should find favor with you!

PASHA SELIM: You please me. I will see what you can do. (*to* PEDRILLO) See him to his lodging. Tomorrow I will summon you to me. (*He exits.*)

PEDRILLO: Triumph, my master! Our first step is accomplished.

BELMONTE: Ah, let me come to my senses! I have seen my faithful beloved! O Constanze, Constanze—for you I would dare anything!

PEDRILLO: Slowly, dear master! Lower your voice a little. Deceit will be our best weapon. We are not in our own country. Here the hangman is never idle. Beatings and hangings are as ordinary as breakfast.

BELMONTE: Ah, Pedrillo, if only you knew love!

PEDRILLO: You think people like me have no feelings? I have my tender moments, just like everybody else. Don't you think it grieves me when I see my Blonde guarded by that old rascal Osmin?

BELMONTE: Oh, if it were only possible to speak to her—

PEDRILLO: We shall see what can be done. Now come with me into the garden, and try to be crafty and discreet. The very walls have ears!
(*As they are leaving,* OSMIN *blocks the door.*)

OSMIN: Where are you going?

PEDRILLO: Inside!

OSMIN (*to* BELMONTE): You have an ugly face! Get out!

PEDRILLO: Stand back, you bully! He's in the Pasha's service.

OSMIN: In the hangman's service, rather! He won't get in here!

PEDRILLO: He will!

OSMIN: If he tries to come one step over the threshold—

BELMONTE: What impertinence! Have you no respect for a man of my position?

31

OSMIN: Ei, Ihr mögt mir vom Stande sein! Fort, fort, oder ich will euch Beine machen.

PEDRILLO: Alter Dummkopf! Es ist ja der Baumeister, den der Bassa angenommen hat.

OSMIN: Meinethalben sei er Stockmeister, nur komm er mir nicht zu nahe. Ich müsste nicht sehen, dass es so ein Kumpan deines Gelichters ist, und dass das so eine abgeredete Karte ist, uns zu überlisten. Der Bassa ist weich wie Butter, mit dem könnt ihr machen was ihr wollt, aber ich habe eine feine Nase. Gaunerei ist's um den ganzen Kram, mit euch fremden Gesindel; und ihr abgefeimten Betrüger habt lange ein Plänchen angelegt, eure Pfiffe auszuführen; aber wart ein bisschen! Osmin schläft nicht. Wär ich Bassa, ihr wär't längst gespiesst. Ja, schneid't nur Gesichter, lacht nur höhnisch in den Bart hinein!

PEDRILLO: Ereifere dich nicht so, Alter, es hilft dir doch nichts. Sieh, soeben werden wir hinein spazieren.

OSMIN: Ha, das will ich sehen!
(*Stellt sich vor die Tür.*)

PEDRILLO: Mach keine Umstände.

BELMONTE: Weg, Niederträchtiger!

7. Terzett

OSMIN: Marsch! marsch! marsch! trollt euch fort,
Sonst soll die Bastonade
Euch gleich zu Diensten steh'n.

BELMONTE: Ei, ei, ei, das wär ja Schade,
Mit uns so umzugeh'n.

OSMIN: Kommt nur nicht näher.

PEDRILLO *und* BELMONTE: Weg von der Türe.

OSMIN: Sonst schlag' ich drein!

PEDRILLO *und* BELMONTE: Wir geh'n hinein!

OSMIN: Marsch! fort, marsch! fort, marsch! fort!

PEDRILLO *und* BELMONTE: Platz! fort, Platz! fort, Platz! fort!
Wir geh'n hinein!

OSMIN: Sonst schlag ich drein!

PEDRILLO *und* BELMONTE: Platz! fort, fort, fort, fort, fort!

OSMIN: Marsch! fort, fort, fort, fort, fort!

PEDRILLO *und* BELMONTE: Wir geh'n hinein!

OSMIN: Get out, or your position will be flat on your back!

PEDRILLO: Old idiot! This man is an architect whom the Pasha has just engaged.

OSMIN: He may be the chief executioner; don't let him come near me. I see too well that he resembles you, and he, too, will plot to deceive me. The Pasha is soft as butter; one can do what one likes with him, but I have a fine nose for smelling out deception. This place is a storehouse of intrigues; you foreign trash are always plotting to carry out your tricks. But wait a while! Osmin never sleeps. If I were the Pasha, you would have been impaled long ago. Yes, you can keep on making faces. Go on, mock me if you want!

PEDRILLO: Don't excite yourself, old man, it won't do you any good. Anyway, we are going to walk in!

OSMIN: Ha, we'll see about that!
(*He stands before the door.*)

PEDRILLO: Now, don't be difficult!

BELMONTE: Out of our way, old wretch!

7. Trio

OSMIN: March! Walk away from here, or soon I'll reward you with a beating!

BELMONTE: Only a stubborn fool would behave like this!

OSMIN: Don't come any nearer.

PEDRILLO *and* BELMONTE: Get away from the gate.

OSMIN: I'll guard this gate!

PEDRILLO *and* BELMONTE: We are going in!

OSMIN: March!

PEDRILLO *and* BELMONTE: Out of our way! We are going in!

OSMIN: I'll guard this gate!

PEDRILLO *and* BELMONTE: Out of our way!

OSMIN: March!

PEDRILLO *and* BELMONTE: We are going in!

OSMIN: Marsch, marsch!
(*Stossen* OSMIN *fort und gehen hinein.*)

OSMIN: March, march!
(PEDRILLO *and* BELMONTE *push* OSMIN *aside and enter the palace.*)

Garten am Palast des BASSA SELIM*; an der Seite* OSMINS *Wohnung.* BLONDE *und* OSMIN *kommen herein.*

Dialog

BLONDE: O des Zankens, Befehlens und Murrens wird auch kein Ende! Einmal für allemal: das steht mir nicht an! Denkst du alter Murrkopf etwa eine türkische Sklavin vor dir zu haben, die bei deinen Befehlen zittert? O da irrst du dich sehr! Mit europäischen Mädchen springt man nicht so herum; denen begegnet man ganz anders.

8. Arie

Durch Zärtlichkeit und Schmeicheln,
Gefälligkeit und Scherzen
Erobert man die Herzen
Der guten Mädchen leicht.
Doch mürrisches Befehlen,
Und Poltern, Zanken, Plagen
Macht, dass in wenig Tagen
So Lieb als Treu' entweicht.

Dialog

OSMIN: Ei seht doch mal, was das Mädchen vorschreiben kann! Zärtlichkeit? Schmeicheln? Es ist mir wie pure Zärtlichkeit! Wer Teufel hat dir das Zeug in den Kopf gesetzt? Hier sind wir in der Türkei, und da geht's aus einem andern Tone. Ich dein Herr, du meine Sklavin; ich befehle, du musst gehorchen!

BLONDE: Deine Sklavin? Ich deine Sklavin? Ha, ein Mädchen eine Sklavin! Noch einmal sag mir das, noch einmal!

OSMIN (*für sich*): Ich möchte toll werden, was das Mädchen für ein starrköpfiges Ding ist. (*laut*) Du hast doch wohl nicht vergessen, dass dich der Bassa mir zur Sklavin geschenkt hat?

BLONDE: Bassa hin, Bassa her! Mädchen sind keine Ware zum verschenken! Ich bin eine Engländerin, zur Freiheit geboren und trotz jedem, der mich zu etwas zwingen will!

ACT TWO

The garden of PASHA SELIM'S *palace;* OSMIN'S *house is on one side.* BLONDE *and* OSMIN *enter.*

Dialogue

BLONDE: I wish that you'd stop your ordering and complaining! Once and forever, I'm not going to stand for it. Do you think, you old grumbler, that you have before you a Turkish slave who trembles at your every command? Oh, you are quite wrong! With European girls, men must behave in an entirely different way!

8. Aria

With tenderness and kindness, with amusement and flattery, a man may easily conquer a young girl's heart. But if he grumbles, quarrels, and torments her, after only a few days both love and fidelity will disappear!

Dialogue

OSMIN: Well now, listen to that! How this girl lays down the law for me! Tenderness? Flattery? It's not for you to tell me to be tender! What devil puts these things into your head? Here we are in Turkey, and here the custom is completely different. I'm your lord; you are my slave; I command you and you must obey!

BLONDE: I, your slave? Ha! A girl like me a slave! Say it once more, just once more!

OSMIN (*to himself*): I could go mad! What a stubborn girl this is! (*aloud*) I hope you haven't forgotten that the Pasha gave you to me as a slave?

BLONDE: Pasha this, Pasha that! Girls are not property that can be given away! I'm an Englishwoman born to liberty, and I'll defy anyone who tries to force me to do anything!

37

OSMIN (*beiseite*): Gift und Dolch über das Mädchen! Beim Mahomet, sie macht mich rasend. Und doch lieb ich die Spitzbübin, trotz ihres tollen Kopfes! (*laut*) Ich befehle dir, augenblicklich mich zu lieben!

BLONDE: Ha ha ha! Komm mir nur ein wenig näher, ich will dir fühlbare Beweise davon geben.

OSMIN: Tolles Ding! Weisst du, dass du mein bist und ich dich dafür züchtigen kann?

BLONDE: Wag's nicht, mich anzurühren, wenn dir deine Augen lieb sind.

OSMIN: Wie? Du unterstehst dich—

BLONDE: Da ist zu unterstehen! Du bist der Unverschämte, der sich zuviel Freiheit herausnimmt. So ein altes hässliches Gesicht untersteht sich, einem Mädchen wie ich, jung, schön, zur Freude geboren, wie einer Magd zu befehlen! Wahrhaftig, das stünde mir an! Uns gehört das Regiment; ihr seid unsere Sklaven und glücklich, wenn ihr Verstand genug habt, euch die Ketten zu erleichtern.

OSMIN: Bei meinem Bart, sie ist toll! Hier, hier in der Türkei?

BLONDE: Türkei hin, Türkei her! Weib ist Weib, sie sei wo sie wolle! Sind eure Weiber solche Närrinnen, sich von euch unterjochen zu lassen, desto schlimmer für sie; in Europa verstehen sie das Ding besser. Lass mich nur einmal Fuss hier gefasst haben, sie sollen bald anders werden.

OSMIN: Beim Allah, die wär imstande, uns allen die Weiber rebellisch zu machen!

BLONDE: Aufs Bitten müsst ihr euch legen, wenn ihr etwas von uns erhalten wollt; besonders Liebhaber deines Gelichters.

OSMIN: Freilich, wenn ich Pedrillo wär, so ein Drahtpüppchen wie er, da wär ich vermutlich willkommen, denn euer Mienenspiel hab ich lange weg.

BLONDE: Erraten, guter Alter, erraten! Das kannst du dir wohl einbilden, dass mir der niedliche Pedrillo lieber ist, wie dein Blasebalggesicht. Also wenn du klug wärst—

OSMIN: Sollt ich dir die Freiheit geben, zu tun und zu machen, was du wolltest, he?

OSMIN (*aside*): The devil take this girl! By Mohammed, she drives me out of my mind! And yet I love the little shrew in spite of her nonsense. (*aloud*) I order you to love me, immediately!

BLONDE: Ha, ha! Just come a little closer, and I'll give you some proofs of my love!

OSMIN: You little idiot! Do you know that you are mine, and that I can chastize you as I please?

BLONDE: Don't you dare to touch me, if you value your eyes!

OSMIN: What? You have the audacity—

BLONDE: I, the audacity! You are the shameless one who allows himself liberties. Such an ugly old creature should not dare to give orders to a girl like me—young, pretty, and born to liberty—as if I were a kitchen maid! Indeed, that would suit me better than being your servant! *I* am the mistress here; you are my slave, and all you can do is be resigned to your burden!

OSMIN: By my beard, she is mad! Here—here in Turkey?

BLONDE: Turkey here, Turkey there! A woman is a woman no matter where she is. Are your women such fools that they let themselves be subjugated? So much the worse for them! In Europe they understand these things much better. Just let me get a foothold here and things will soon be different.

OSMIN: By Allah, she would be capable of driving all our wives to a revolt!

BLONDE: You men have to plead with us for our favors, especially lovers of your kind.

OSMIN: Of course, if I were Pedrillo, or a puppet like him, then I suppose I would be acceptable. You see that I've discovered your secret.

BLONDE: You've guessed it, old man, you've guessed it! You can well imagine that I prefer the charming Pedrillo to you, old bagpipe-face, and if you were clever—

OSMIN: I suppose I would give you your freedom? To do as you please, eh?

BLONDE: Besser würdest du immer dabei fahren: denn so wirst du sicher betrogen.

OSMIN: Gift und Dolch! Nun reisst mir die Geduld! Den Augenblick hinein ins Haus! Und wenn du's wagst—

BLONDE: Mach mich nicht lachen.

OSMIN: Ins Haus, sag ich!

BLONDE: Nicht von der Stelle!

OSMIN: Mach nicht, dass ich Gewalt brauche.

BLONDE: Gewalt werd ich mit Gewalt vertreiben. Meine Gebieterin hat mich hier in den Garten bestellt; sie ist die Geliebte des Bassa, sein Augapfel, sein alles; und es kostet mich ein Wort, so hast du fünfzig auf die Fussohlen. Also geh!

OSMIN: Das ist ein Satan! Ich muss nachgeben, so wahr ich ein Muselmann bin; sonst könnte ihre Drohung eintreffen.

9. Duett

Ich gehe, doch rate ich dir,
Den Schurken Pedrillo zu meiden,
Den Schurken Pedrillo zu meiden.

BLONDE: Fort, pack dich, befiehl nicht mit mir,
Du weisst ja, ich kann es nicht leiden,
Du weisst ja, ich kann es nicht leiden.

OSMIN: Versprich mir!

BLONDE: Was fällt dir da ein!
Fort, lass mich allein!

OSMIN: Zum Henker!
Beim Allah! ich werde nicht gehen,
Bis du zu gehorchen mir schwörst.

BLONDE: Nicht so viel, das sollst du bald sehen,
Und wenn du der Grossmogul wärst.

OSMIN: O Engländer! seid ihr nicht Toren,
Ihr lasst euern Weibern den Willen!

BLONDE: Ein Mädchen zur Freiheit geboren,
Lässt nie sich als Sklavin befehlen:
Und ist auch die Freiheit verloren,
Doch bleibt sie noch Fürstin der Welt.

OSMIN: Wie ist man geplagt und geschoren,
Wenn man so ein Früchtchen erhält!

BLONDE: You would fare much better in that way. As things are now, you will certainly be deceived.

OSMIN: Poison and daggers! Now my patience has reached its end. Get into the house this moment, and if you should dare—

BLONDE: Don't make me laugh!

OSMIN: Into the house, I say!

BLONDE: I won't budge!

OSMIN: Don't make me use force!

BLONDE: I can oppose force with force. My mistress has asked me to join her in the garden. She's the Pasha's beloved, the apple of his eye. It will take only a word, and you'll have fifty strokes on the soles of your feet. Go, now!

OSMIN: She is Satan himself! By Mohammed, I have to yield, for she might make her threats come true!

9. Duet

I'll go, but I advise you to avoid that rascal Pedrillo!

BLONDE: Oh, go away; stop ordering me around! You know very well that I won't stand for it!

OSMIN: Promise me!

BLONDE: What an absurd idea! Go; leave me alone!

OSMIN: By the devil! On the contrary, I won't move a step until you swear to obey me.

BLONDE: Don't get so excited, you poor old creature! Even if you were the great Mogul himself—

OSMIN: O Englishmen, you are fools to let your wives have their own way!

BLONDE: A heart born to liberty never allows itself to be treated like a slave's, and even while conquered, it remains proud! A free heart laughs at the world.

OSMIN: What torment it is to be treated this way!

BLONDE: Nun troll dich.

OSMIN: So sprichst du mit mir?

BLONDE: Nicht anders!

OSMIN: Nun bleib ich erst hier.

BLONDE: Ein andermal, jetzt musst du gehen!

OSMIN: Wer hat solche Frechheit gesehen!

BLONDE: Es ist um die Augen geschehen
Wofern du noch länger verweilst.

OSMIN: Nur ruhig, ich will ja gern gehen,
Bevor du gar Schläge erteilst.
(OSMIN *geht ab.* CONSTANZE *kommt langsam heran.*)

Dialog

BLONDE: Wie traurig das gute Mädchen daher kommt!
Freilich tut's weh, den Geliebten zu verlieren und Sklavin
zu sein. Es geht mir wohl auch nicht viel besser; aber ich
habe doch noch das Vergnügen, meinen Pedrillo manchmal
zu sehen, ob's gleich auch mager und verstohlen genug
geschehen muss; doch wer kann wider den Strom schwim-
men!

10. Rezitativ und Arie

CONSTANZE: Welcher Kummer herrscht in meiner Seele
Seit dem Tag, da ich mein Glück verloren!
O Belmont! hin sind die Freuden,
Die ich ach! an deiner Seite kannte;
Banger Sehnsucht Leiden,
Wohnen nun dafür
In der beklemmten Brust.
Traurigkeit ward mir zum Lose,
Weil ich dir entrissen bin.
Gleich der wurmzernagten Rose,
Gleich dem Gras in Wintermoose
Welkt mein banges Leben hin.
Selbst der Luft darf ich nicht sagen
Meiner Seele bittern Schmerz.
Denn unwillig ihn zu tragen,
Haucht sie alle meine Klagen
Wieder in mein armes Herz.

Dialog

BLONDE: Ach mein bestes Fräulein, noch immer so traurig?

42

BLONDE: Now, leave me alone!

OSMIN: You dare to talk like this to me?

BLONDE: Exactly!

OSMIN: Really? I'll stay right here, then.

BLONDE: Another time, but now you must go!

OSMIN: Has there ever been such impertinence?

BLONDE: If you stay longer I'll scratch your eyes out!

OSMIN: Be quiet. I'll gladly go, before you begin to carry out your threats!

(OSMIN *exits.* CONSTANZE *comes slowly onto the stage.*)

Dialogue

BLONDE: How sad the poor girl seems! Of course it's depressing to be a slave and to lose one's beloved. But I'm not much better off myself. Although I have the pleasure of seeing my Pedrillo now and then, we can only meet in secret—but then, one has to swim with the tide!

10. Recitative and Aria

CONSTANZE: What sadness has transformed my soul since the day that fate separated us! O Belmonte! Vanished are the joys that I knew at your side! The pain of anxious longing burns in my unhappy breast. Sorrow is my fate since I was torn from your side. Like the withering rose, like the grass under winter's frost, my life dwindles away. Even to the air I cannot tell my soul's bitter pain, for I breathe it back again into my own poor heart!

Dialogue

BLONDE: O my dearest mistress! Still so sad?

CONSTANZE: Kannst du fragen, die du meinen Kummer weisst? Wieder ein Abend, und noch keine Nachricht, noch keine Hoffnung! Und morgen —ach Gott, ich darf nicht daran denken!

BLONDE: Heitern Sie sich wenigstens ein bisschen auf. Sehn Sie, wie schön der Abend ist, wie blühend uns alles entgegenlacht, wie freudig uns die Vögel zu ihrem Gesang einladen! Verbannen Sie die Grillen, und fassen Sie Mut!

CONSTANZE: Wie glücklich bist du, Mädchen, bei deinem Schicksal so gelassen zu sein! O dass ich es auch könnte!

BLONDE: Das steht nur bei Ihnen, hoffen Sie—

CONSTANZE: Wo nicht der mindeste Schein von Hoffnung mehr zu erblicken ist?

BLONDE: Hören Sie nur: ich verzage mein Lebtag nicht, es mag auch eine Sache noch so schlimm aussehen. Denn wer sich immer das Schlimmste vorstellt, ist auch wahrhaftig am schlimmsten dran.

CONSTANZE: Und wer sich immer mit Hoffnung schmeichelt und zuletzt betrogen sieht, hat alsdann nichts mehr übrig als die Verzweiflung.

BLONDE: Jedes nach seiner Weise. Ich glaube bei der meinigen am besten zu fahren. Wie bald kann Ihr Belmonte mit Lösegeld erscheinen oder uns listiger Weise entführen? Wären wir die ersten Frauenzimmer, die den türkischen Vielfrassen entkämen? Dort seh ich den Bassa.

CONSTANZE: Lass uns ihm aus den Augen gehn.

BLONDE: Zu spät. Er hat Sie schon gesehen. Ich darf aber getrost aus dem Wege trollen, er schaffte mich ohnehin fort. (*im Weggehen*) Courage, wir kommen gewiss noch in unsre Heimat!

(BASSA SELIM *kommt herein.*)

BASSA SELIM: Nun, Constanze, denkst du meinem Begehren nach? Der Tag ist bald verstrichen. Morgen musst du mich lieben, oder—

CONSTANZE: Muss? Welch albernes Begehren! Als ob man die Liebe anbefehlen könnte wie eine Tracht Schläge! Aber freilich, wie ihr Türken zu Werke geht, lässt sich's auch allenfalls befehlen. Aber ihr seid wirklich zu beklagen. Ihr kerkert die Gegenstände eurer Begierden ein und seid zufrieden, eure Lüste zu büssen.

44

CONSTANZE: Can you ask such a question—you, who know my grief? Another evening, and still no news, no hope! And tomorrow—God, I dare not even think of it!

BLONDE: But at least cheer yourself up a bit—look at this lovely evening, how everything smiles at us in its blooming, how joyfully the birds invite us to join in their song! Forget your sadness, and take courage!

CONSTANZE: How happy you are, my dear, to be so resigned to your fate! Oh, if only I could be like you!

BLONDE: That depends entirely upon yourself. Never give up hope!

CONSTANZE: Where there is not the faintest glimmer of hope?

BLONDE: Now listen to me! I never give up, no matter how grim things look, because whoever expects the worst is always the worst off!

CONSTANZE: She who deludes herself with hope, then sees too late that she is deceived, has nothing left but despair.

BLONDE: Each to his own way. I believe that one fares best by my theories. How soon can your Belmonte appear with the ransom, or arrange to abduct us? We can't be the first women who have fallen into the hands of these Turkish criminals— But there I see the Pasha.

CONSTANZE: Let us avoid him.

BLONDE: Too late. He has seen us already. But I can quietly go my own way. He would only send me away if I stayed. (*while leaving*) Have courage! I'm certain that we'll see our own country again!
(PASHA SELIM *enters.*)

PASHA SELIM: Well, Constanze, have you considered my wishes? The day is almost over. Tomorrow you must love me, or else—

CONSTANZE: I must? You cannot command love as if you were ordering a beating. But of course you Turks think that you can order anything. Really, though, you are to be pitied. You think you can satisfy your lust by imprisoning the object of your desires.

45

BASSA SELIM: Und glaubst du etwa, unsere Weiber wären weniger glücklich als in euren Ländern?

CONSTANZE: Die nichts besseres kennen!

BASSA SELIM: Auf diese Art wäre wohl keine Hoffnung, dass du je anders denken wirst.

CONSTANZE: Herr! Ich muss dir frei gestehen, denn was soll ich dich länger hinhalten, mich mit leerer Hoffnung schmeicheln, dass du dich durch mein Bitten erweichen liessest, ich werde stets so denken wie jetzt: dich verehren, aber—lieben? Nie!

BASSA SELIM: Und du zitterst nicht vor der Gewalt, die ich über dich habe?

CONSTANZE: Nicht im geringsten. Sterben ist alles, was ich zu erwarten habe, und je eher dies geschieht, je lieber wird es mir sein.

BASSA SELIM: Elende! Nein! Nicht sterben, aber Martern von allen Arten—

CONSTANZE: Auch die will ich ertragen: du schreckst mich nicht, ich erwarte alles.

11. Arie

Martern aller Arten, aller Arten
Mögen meiner warten,
Ich verlache Qual und Pein.
Nichts, nichts
Soll mich erschüttern,
Nur dann, würd' ich zittern,
Wenn ich untreu,
Untreu könnte sein.
Lass dich bewegen,
Verschone mich,
Des Himmels Segen
Belohne dich!
Doch dich rührt kein Flehen,
Standhaft, sollst du sehen,
Duld ich jede Qual und Not.
Ordne nur, gebiete,
Drohe, strafe, wüte,
Zuletzt befreit mich doch der Tod. (*Entfernt sich.*)

PASHA SELIM: And you think that our wives are less happy than those in your countries?

CONSTANZE: Those that don't know any better!

PASHA SELIM: Then there is no hope that you will ever change your way of thinking?

CONSTANZE: My Lord, I must confess to you frankly. Why should I protract this discussion any longer or deceive myself with the empty hope that you will ever be mollified by my prayers? I will always feel the way I do now. I shall always esteem you—but love you? Never!

PASHA SELIM: And you do not tremble at my power?

CONSTANZE: Not in the least. Death is all that I have to fear, and the sooner it comes, the happier I shall be.

PASHA SELIM: No, not death! But tortures of every kind—

CONSTANZE: Even those I am prepared to suffer. You cannot intimidate me!

11. Aria

All torments may await me; I laugh at torture and at pain. Nothing will move me. I tremble only at the thought of faithlessness. Let yourself be moved; spare me; let heaven's blessing reward you. But you have decided. Willingly and undismayed I choose the harshest pain or trial. Command me; order me; storm, rage, threaten; at the end, death will liberate me from my suffering! (*Exits.*)

Dialog

BASSA SELIM: Ist das ein Traum? Wo hat sie auf einmal den Mut her, sich so gegen mich zu betragen? Hat sie vielleicht Hoffnung, mir zu entkommen? Ha, das will ich verwehren! (*will fort*) Doch das ist's nicht, dann würde sie sich eher verstellen, mich einzuschläfern suchen. Ja, es ist Verzweiflung! Mit Härte richt ich nichts aus, mit Bitten auch nicht, also, was Drohen und Bitten nicht vermögen, soll die List zuwege bringen.

(BASSA SELIM *geht ab.* BLONDE *kommt allein.*)

BLONDE: Kein Bassa, keine Constanze mehr da? Sind sie miteinander eins worden? Schwerlich, das gute Kind hängt zu sehr an ihrem Belmonte! Ich bedaure sie von Grund meines Herzens. Sie ist zu empfindsam für ihre Lage. Freilich, hätt ich meinen Pedrillo nicht an der Seite, wer weiss, wie mir's ginge! Doch würd ich nicht so zärteln wie sie. Die Männer verdienen wahrlich nicht, dass man ihrethalben sich zu Tode grämt. Vielleicht würd ich muselmännisch denken.

(PEDRILLO *kommt herein.*)

PEDRILLO: Pst, pst! Blondchen! Ist der Weg rein?

BLONDE: Komm nur, komm! Der Bassa ist wieder zurück. Und meinem Alten habe ich eben den Kopf ein bisschen gewaschen. Was hast du denn?

PEDRILLO: O Neuigkeiten, Neuigkeiten, die dich entzücken werden.

BLONDE: Nun? Hurtig heraus damit!

PEDRILLO: Erst, liebes Herzens-Blondchen, lass dir vor allen Dingen einen recht herzlichen Kuss geben; du weisst ja, wie gestohlnes Gut schmeckt.

BLONDE: Pfui, pfui! Wenn das deine Neuigkeiten alle sind.

PEDRILLO: Närrchen, mach darum keinen Lärm, der alte spitzbübische Osmin lauert uns sicher auf den Dienst.

BLONDE: Nun? Und die Neuigkeiten?

PEDRILLO: Sind, dass das Ende unserer Sklaverei vor der Tür ist. Belmonte, Constanzes Geliebter, ist angekommen, und ich hab ihn unter dem Namen eines Baumeisters hier im Palast eingeführt.

BLONDE: Ah, was sagst du? Belmonte da?

Dialogue

PASHA SELIM: Is this a dream? Where does she get the courage to behave like this? Is it possible that she hopes to escape me? Ha, I shall prevent that! (*starting to leave*) But that's not her plan. She would hide her defiance, if only to quiet my suspicions. No, she is despairing; I shall accomplish nothing with harshness or entreaties, so I must use my cunning.

(PASHA SELIM *exits.* BLONDE *enters, alone.*)

BLONDE: The Pasha and Constanze gone? Could they have come to an understanding? Hardly! That noble girl is too much attached to Belmonte. I pity her from the bottom of my heart. Her position is delicate. Of course, if I didn't have Pedrillo at my side, who knows how things would go with me. But still I wouldn't pine as she does. Men certainly don't deserve that we should die of grief on their account! Perhaps I should try to look at matters like a Moslem!

(PEDRILLO *enters.*)

PEDRILLO: Blonde! Is the coast clear?

BLONDE: Oh, come in! The Pasha has come back again. And I have just given my old friend a good piece of my mind. What is wrong?

PEDRILLO: Oh, I have news that will enchant you!

BLONDE: Well then, let's have it!

PEDRILLO: First of all, my dearest sweetest Blonde, let's have a hearty kiss. You know very well how much I like forbidden fruit!

BLONDE: Is that all your news?

PEDRILLO: You little fool, don't make such noise. That old rascal Osmin must certainly be lying in wait for us.

BLONDE: Well? And your news?

PEDRILLO: Our slavery will soon be at an end. Belmonte has arrived, and I have brought him into the palace by pretending that he is an architect.

BLONDE: What did you say? Belmonte's here?

PEDRILLO: Mit Leib und Seele!

BLONDE: Ha, das muss Constanze wissen!

PEDRILLO: Hör nur, Blondchen, hör nur erst: Er hat ein Schiff hier in der Nähe in Bereitschaft, und wir haben beschlossen, euch diese Nacht zu entführen.

BLONDE: O allerliebst, allerliebst! Herzens-Pedrillo, das verdient einen Kuss! Geschwind, geschwind zu Constanze!

PEDRILLO: Halt nur, halt, und lass erst mit dir reden. Um Mitternacht kommt Belmonte mit einer Leiter zu Constanzes Fenster, und ich zu dem deinigen, und dann geht's heidi davon!

BLONDE: O vortrefflich! Aber Osmin?

PEDRILLO: Hier ist ein Schlaftrunk für den alten Schlaukopf, den misch ihm fein manierlich ins Getränk, verstehst du? Ich habe dort auch schon ein Fläschchen angefüllt. Geht's hier nicht, wird's dort wohl gehen.

BLONDE: Sorg nicht für mich! Aber kann Constanze ihren Geliebten nicht sprechen?

PEDRILLO: Sobald es vollends finster ist, kommt er hier in den Garten. Nun geh und bereite Constanze vor; ich will hier Belmonte erwarten. Leb wohl, Herzchen, leb wohl!

BLONDE: Leb wohl, guter Pedrillo! Ach, was werd ich für Freude anrichten!

(PEDRILLO *geht ab.*)

12. Arie

Welche Wonne, welche Lust
Regt sich nun in meiner Brust!
Voller Freuden will ich springen,
Ihr die frohe Nachricht bringen,
Und mit Lachen
Und mit Scherzen
Ihrem schwachen, kranken Herzen
Trost und Rettung prophezeih'n.
(*Sie eilt ab.* PEDRILLO *kommt herein.*)

Dialog

PEDRILLO: Ah, dass es schon vorbei wäre! Dass wir schon auf offner See wären, unsre Mädels im Arm und dies verwünschte Land im Rücken hätten! Doch sei's gewagt; entweder jetzt oder niemals! Wer zagt, verliert!

PEDRILLO: Body and soul!

BLONDE: I must tell my lady Constanze!

PEDRILLO: But listen, Blonde; listen to me, first. He has a ship nearby all ready for us, and we have planned to abduct both of you tonight!

BLONDE: Oh, marvelous! Darling Pedrillo, this deserves a kiss. Now, quickly, I must tell Constanze!

PEDRILLO: Wait a minute—let me tell you everything. At midnight Belmonte will come to Constanze's window with a ladder, and I to yours, and then, off we go!

BLONDE: Oh, excellent! But Osmin?

PEDRILLO: Here I have a sleeping potion for the old fox. Pour it secretly into his drink, do you understand? I have filled a little bottle for myself. If your potion doesn't work, mine will.

BLONDE: Don't worry about me; I can take care of myself. But can't Constanze see Belmonte before tonight?

PEDRILLO: As soon as it gets dark, he'll come into the garden. Now go and prepare your mistress: I'll wait here for Belmonte. Au revoir, my darling!

BLONDE: Au revoir, dearest Pedrillo! Oh, what joy I shall bring to my dear mistress!
(PEDRILLO *exits*.)

12. Aria

What happiness and joy fill my breast! Without delay I'll hurry to bring Constanze the news! With joyous laughter I'll promise a blissful future to her anxious heart!
(*She hurries out.* PEDRILLO *enters*.)

Dialogue

PEDRILLO: Oh, if only it were over! If only we were on the open sea with the girls in our arms and this God-forsaken land behind us! But we must make the attempt; it's now or never! He who hesitates is lost!

13. Arie

Frisch zum Kampfe! frisch zum Streite!
Nur ein feiger Tropf verzagt.
Sollt ich zittern?
Sollt ich zagen?
Nicht mein Leben mutig wagen?
Nein, ach nein, es sei gewagt!
(OSMIN *kommt herein.*)

Dialog

OSMIN: Ha! Geht's hier so lustig zu? Es muss dir verteufelt wohl gehen.

PEDRILLO: Ei, wer wird so ein Kopfhänger sein; es kommt beim Henker dabei nichts heraus! Das haben die Pedrillos von jeher in ihrer Familie gehabt. Fröhlichkeit und Wein versüsst die härteste Sklaverei. Freilich könnt ihr armen Schlucker das nicht begreifen, dass es so ein herrlich Ding um ein Gläschen guten alten Lustigmacher ist. Wahrhaftig, da hat euer Vater Mahomet einen verzweifelten Bock geschossen, dass er euch den Wein verboten hat. Wenn das verwünschte Gesetz nicht wäre, du müsstest ein Gläschen mit mir trinken, du möchtest wollen oder nicht. (*für sich*) Vielleicht beisst er an: er trinkt ihn gar zu gern.

OSMIN: Wein mit dir? Ja, Gift—

PEDRILLO: Immer Gift und Dolch, und Dolch und Gift! Lass doch den alten Groll einmal fahren und sei vernünftig. Sieh einmal, ein paar Flaschen Cyperwein! Ah! Die sollen mir vortrefflich schmecken!

OSMIN (*für sich*): Wenn ich trauen dürfte?

PEDRILLO: Das ist ein Wein, das ist ein Wein!
(*Er setzt sich nach türkischer Art auf die Erde und trinkt aus der kleinen Flasche.*)

OSMIN: Kost einmal die grosse Flasche auch.

PEDRILLO: Denkst wohl gar, ich habe Gift hinein getan? Ha, lass dir keine grauen Haare wachsen! Es verlohnte sich der Mühe, dass ich deinetwegen zum Teufel führe. Da sieh, ob ich trinke. Nun, hast du noch Bedenken? Traust mir noch nicht? Pfui, Osmin, sollst dich schämen! Da nimm!
(*Er gibt ihm die grosse Flasche.*)
Oder willst du die kleine?

13. Aria

Off to battle! Off to the fight! Only a coward trembles before danger. I'll never hesitate or refuse to risk my life courageously! No, no, I must brave all perils! Quickly now; I must be off!

(OSMIN *enters.*)

Dialogue

OSMIN: What's all this gaiety? You must feel strangely well!

PEDRILLO: Why be depressed all the time? No pleasure comes of that. The Pedrillos have always been lighthearted. Merriment and wine sweeten the hardest slavery. Of course, you poor devils will never understand how marvelous a little glass of wine can be. Truly, your dear father, Mohammed, should never have forbidden it to you. If it weren't for that accursed commandment, you would be able to enjoy a glass of wine with me. (*to himself*) Perhaps he'll accept; he probably likes drinking only too well!

OSMIN: Me, drink wine? With you? Poison, rather!

PEDRILLO: Always poison, poison! Let bygones be bygones. Be less fanciful for once. Look! Two bottles of Cyprus wine. I shall certainly enjoy them!

OSMIN (*to himself*): If only I could trust him!

PEDRILLO: This is a wonderful wine!
(*Sitting on the ground, he drinks from the smaller of the two bottles.*)

OSMIN: Taste the big bottle too!

PEDRILLO: Do you think that I put poison in it? Don't get gray hairs from worrying over that! It would hardly be worth my while to go to hell on your account! Look, I'm drinking! Do you still have reservations? Even now, you don't trust me? Osmin, you should be ashamed of yourself! Here have a taste!
(*He gives him the big bottle.*)
Or would you rather try the little one?

OSMIN: Nein, lass nur, lass nur! Aber wenn du mich verrätst—

PEDRILLO: Als wenn wir einander nicht weiter brauchten. Immer frisch! Mahomet liegt längst auf'm Ohr und hat nötiger zu tun, als sich um deine Flasche Wein zu bekümmern.

14. Duett

Vivat Bacchus! Bacchus lebe!
Bacchus war ein braver Mann.

OSMIN: Ob ich's wage? ob ich trinke?
Ob's wohl Allah sehen kann?

PEDRILLO: Was hilft das Zaudern?
Hinunter! hinunter!
Nicht lange, nicht lange gefragt!
(OSMIN *trinkt.*)

OSMIN: Nun wär's geschehen!
Nun wär's geschehen!
Das heiss ich, das heiss ich gewagt.

PEDRILLO *und* OSMIN: Es leben die Mädchen,
Die Blonden, die Braunen!
Sie leben, sie leben, sie leben hoch!

PEDRILLO: Das schmeckt trefflich!

OSMIN: Das schmeckt herrlich!

PEDRILLO *und* OSMIN: Ach! das heiss' ich Göttertrank!
Vivat Bacchus, Bacchus lebe,
Bacchus der den Wein erfand!
Bacchus der den Wein erfand!
Vivat Bacchus, Bacchus lebe,
Es leben die Mädchen,
Die Blonden, die Braunen,
Sie leben hoch!

Dialog

PEDRILLO: Wahrhaftig, das muss ich gestehen, es geht doch nichts über den Wein! Wein ist mir lieber, als Geld und Mädchen. Bin ich verdriesslich, mürrisch, launisch: hurtig nehm ich meine Zuflucht zur Flasche, und kaum seh ich den ersten Boden: weg ist all mein Verdruss! Meine Flasche macht mir kein schiefes Gesicht, wie mein Mädchen, wenn ihr der Kopf nicht auf dem rechten Fleck steht.

OSMIN: It doesn't matter. But if you should betray me—

PEDRILLO: As if we didn't need each other's co-operation! Go to it! Mohammed has more important things to do than to worry over your bottle of wine!

14. Duet

Long live Bacchus! He was a jolly fellow!

OSMIN: Should I dare? Should I drink? I wonder if Allah can see me now?

PEDRILLO: Why this hesitation? Forget it! Don't think so much! Don't ask so many questions!
(OSMIN *drinks*.)

OSMIN: Now it's done! Now I've swallowed it! I call this daring!

PEDRILLO *and* OSMIN: Long live the girls, the blondes and brunettes! Long live all of them!

PEDRILLO: This tastes marvelous!

OSMIN: This tastes magnificent!

PEDRILLO *and* OSMIN: Oh, I call this nectar for the gods! Long live Bacchus, who invented wine! Long live Bacchus, and long live the girls, the blondes, the brunettes! Long live all of them!

Dialogue

PEDRILLO: I must admit that there's nothing better than wine! I prefer it to money or women. When I'm in a bad humor, grumbling, moody, or ill-disposed, I always take refuge in my bottle; a few swallows later my disposition is much improved. My bottle never makes a sour face like my girl when she is out of temper. Praise the sweetness of love

Und schwatzt mir von Süssigkeiten der Liebe und des Ehestandes, was Ihr wollt: Wein auf der Zunge geht über alles!

OSMIN (*fängt bereits an, die Wirkung des Weins und des Schlaftrunks zu spüren*): Das ist wahr—Wein—Wein—ist ein schönes Getränk; und unser grosser Prophet mag mir's nicht übelnehmen- Gift und Dolch, es ist doch eine hübsche Sache um den Wein!- Nicht- Bruder Pedrillo?

PEDRILLO: Richtig, Bruder Osmin, richtig!

OSMIN: Man wird gleich so—munter —so vergnügt—so aufgeräumt. Hast du nichts mehr, Bruder?
(*Er langt auf eine lächerliche Art nach einer zweiten Flasche.*)

PEDRILLO: Hör du, Alter, trink mir nicht zu viel, es kommt einem in den Kopf.

OSMIN: Trag doch keine—Sorge, ich bin so—so—nüchtern wie möglich. Aber das ist wahr, es schmeckt—vortrefflich!

PEDRILLO (*für sich*): Es wirkt, Alter, es wirkt!

OSMIN: Aber verraten musst du mich nicht, Brüderchen—verraten—denn—wenn's Mahomet nein, nein—der Bassa wüsste—denn siehst du liebes Blondchen—ja oder nein!

PEDRILLO (*für sich*): Nun wird's Zeit, ihn fortzuschaffen! (*laut*) Nun komm, Alter, komm, wir wollen schlafen gehn!

OSMIN: Schlafen? Schämst du dich nicht? Gift und Dolch! Wer wird denn so schläfrig sein—es ist ja kaum Morgen!

PEDRILLO: Ho, ho, die Sonne ist schon hinunter! Komm, komm, dass uns der Bassa nicht überrascht!

OSMIN: Ja, ja—eine Flasche, guter Bassa, geht über alles! Gute Nacht, Brüderchen, gute Nacht.
(PEDRILLO *führt ihn hinein, kommt aber gleich wieder zurück.*)

PEDRILLO: Gute Nacht, Brüderchen, gute Nacht! Haha-haha, alter Eisenfresser, erwischt man dich so? Gift und Dolch! Du hast deine Ladung! Nur fürcht ich, ist's noch zu zeitig am Tage; bis Mitternacht sind noch drei Stunden, und da könnt er leicht wieder ausgeschlafen haben. Ach, kommen Sie, kommen Sie, liebster Herr! Unser Argus ist blind, ich hab ihn tüchtig zugedeckt.
(BELMONTE *kommt herein.*)

BELMONTE: O dass wir glücklich wären! Aber sag: ist Constanze noch nicht hier?

and matrimony as much as you like; the taste of wine surpasses everything else!

OSMIN (*beginning to feel the effects of the wine and the sleeping potion*): How true! And I hope that our great prophet will not think badly of me. Wine is a wonderful thing, isn't it, brother Pedrillo?

PEDRILLO: It's true, brother Osmin, it's true.

OSMIN: One becomes so contented—so at peace with the world! Haven't you any more?
(*He reaches for the second bottle.*)

PEDRILLO: Listen, old man, don't drink too much; it goes to one's head!

OSMIN: Don't you worry about me—I'm as so-sober as possible. But it's true it tastes—divine!

PEDRILLO (*to himself*): It's having its effect on him!

OSMIN: But don't betray me, little brother—because if Mohammed—if the Pasha—knew—because, you see, dearest Blonde—yes or no?

PEDRILLO (*to himself*): Now it's time to get rid of him! (*aloud*) Come, old man, we're going to sleep!

OSMIN: To bed? Aren't you ashamed? Hell and the devil, I'm not sleepy—it's not even morning yet!

PEDRILLO: But it's late at night. Come, or the Pasha will surprise us here!

OSMIN: Yes, a bottle, dear Pasha, surpasses everything! Good night, little brother, good night!
(PEDRILLO *pushes* OSMIN *off stage, and then quickly returns.*)

PEDRILLO: Good night, little brother, good night! Ha, ha, old fire-eater! How simple it is to trap you! Hell and the devil! Now you have your just reward! But I'm afraid that it's a little too early; there are three more hours until midnight, and by then he may have slept it off. Come here now, my dearest master; Argus is blind!
(BELMONTE *enters.*)

BELMONTE: Oh, if we could only consummate our happiness! But where is Constanze?

PEDRILLO: Eben kommt sie da den Gang herauf. Reden Sie alles mit ihr ab, aber fassen Sie sich kurz, denn der Verräter schläft nicht immer.

(CONSTANZE *und* BLONDE *kommen herein.*)

CONSTANZE: O mein Belmonte!

BELMONTE: O Constanze!

CONSTANZE: Ist's möglich? Nach so viel Tagen der Angst, nach so viel ausgestandenen Leiden, dich wieder in meinen Armen.

BELMONTE: O dieser Augenblick versüsst allen Kummer, macht mich all meinen Schmerz vergessen.

CONSTANZE: Hier will ich an deinem Busen liegen und weinen! Ach, jetzt fühl ich's, die Freude hat auch ihre Tränen.

16. Quartett

Ach Belmonte! ach mein Leben!

BELMONTE: Ach Constanze, ach mein Leben!

CONSTANZE: Ist es möglich? welch Entzücken!
Dich an meine Brust zu drücken,
Nach so vieler Tage Leid!

BELMONTE: Welche Wonne, dich zu finden!
Nun muss aller Kummer schwinden,
O wie ist mein Herz erfreut!

CONSTANZE: Sieh die Freudentränen fliessen!

BELMONTE: Holde, lass hinweg sie küssen!

CONSTANZE: Dass es doch die letzte sei.

BELMONTE: Ja, noch heute wirst du frei!

PEDRILLO: Also, Blondchen, hast's verstanden?
Alles ist zur Flucht vorhanden,
Um Schlag zwölfe sind wir da.

BLONDE: Unbesorgt, es wird nichts fehlen,
Die Minuten werd ich zählen,
Wär' der Augenblick schon da!

ALLE: Endlich scheint die Hoffnungssonne
Hell durch's trübe Firmament.
Voll Entzücken,
Freud, und Wonne
Seh'n wir unsrer Leiden End'!

PEDRILLO: She's just coming up the stairs. Discuss everything with her, but be brief because the old rascal won't sleep forever.

(CONSTANZE *and* BLONDE *enter.*)

CONSTANZE: O my Belmonte!

BELMONTE: O Constanze!

CONSTANZE: Can it be true, after so many days of longing, after such torments, that I am in your arms!

BELMONTE: This moment sweetens all my grief and banishes all my sorrows!

CONSTANZE: Here I shall weep on your bosom! Ah, now I feel it; joy, too, knows its tears.

16. *Quartet*

Ah, Belmonte! My love, my life!

BELMONTE: Ah, Constanze! My love, my life!

CONSTANZE: Is it possible that after so many days apart I can hold you to my breast?

BELMONTE: Such joy! To find you! Now all sorrows disappear.

CONSTANZE: See my tears of joy!

BELMONTE: Beloved, let me kiss them away!

CONSTANZE: They will be my last tears.

BELMONTE: Yes, today our longing is fulfilled!

PEDRILLO: Well, Blonde, do you understand me now? Everything is ready for the escape. At the stroke of midnight we shall be there.

BLONDE: Don't worry about us; we won't fail. I'll count the minutes. Oh, if only that moment were already here!

ALL: At last the sun of hope shines through the dark sky, and we see an end of our sorrows!

BELMONTE: Doch ach! bei aller Lust
Empfindet meine Brust
Noch manch geheime Sorgen.

CONSTANZE: Was ist es? Liebster, sprich:
Geschwind, erkläre dich,
O halt mir nichts verborgen!

BELMONTE: Man sagt du sei'st—

CONSTANZE: Nun weiter!

PEDRILLO: Doch Blondchen, ach! die Leiter!
Bist du wohl so viel wert?

BLONDE: Hans Narr! schnappt's bei dir über?
Ei, hättest du nur lieber
Die Frage umgekehrt!

PEDRILLO: Doch Herr Osmin—

BLONDE: Lass hören!

CONSTANZE (*zu* BELMONTE): Willst du dich nicht erklären?

BELMONTE (*zu* CONSTANZE): Ich will, doch zürne nicht,
Wenn ich nach dem Gerücht,
Das ich gehört,
Es wage, dich zitternd, bebend frage,
Ob du den Bassa liebst?

CONSTANZE: O wie du mich betrübst!

PEDRILLO (*zu* BLONDE): Hat nicht Osmin etwan,
Wie man fast glauben kann,
Sein Recht als Herr probiret
Und bei dir exerciret?
Dann wär's ein schlechter Kauf!

BLONDE (*gibt ihm eine Ohrfeige*): Da nimm die Antwort
drauf!

PEDRILLO: Nun bin ich aufgeklärt!

BELMONTE: Constanze, ach vergib!

BLONDE (*zu* PEDRILLO): Du bist mich gar nicht wert!

CONSTANZE (*zu* BELMONTE): Ob ich dir treu verblieb?

BLONDE (*zu* CONSTANZE): Der Schlingel fragt gar an,
Ob ich ihm treu geblieben?

CONSTANZE (*zu* BLONDE): Dem Belmont sagte man,
Ich soll den Bassa lieben!

PEDRILLO: Dass Blonde ehrlich sei,
Schwör ich bei allen Teufeln!

BELMONTE: But in spite of this joy, my heart is still anxious.

CONSTANZE: What is it, dearest? Speak quickly; explain yourself! Don't hide anything from me!

BELMONTE: Suppose that you—

CONSTANZE: Go on!

PEDRILLO: Blonde, I must see to the ladder! Do you really think you're worth all this trouble?

BLONDE: You fool! You should have asked that question more tactfully!

PEDRILLO: But Osmin—

BLONDE: What are you talking about?

CONSTANZE (*to* BELMONTE): Won't you explain yourself?

BELMONTE (*to* CONSTANZE): I would like to tell you. Don't be angry when I ask you this— Have you yielded to the Pasha?

CONSTANZE: Oh, how you sadden me!

PEDRILLO (*to* BLONDE): Hasn't Osmin ever used his rights over you? That would be unfortunate for me!

BLONDE (*slapping him*): Here's your answer!

PEDRILLO: Now everything is clear!

BELMONTE: Constanze, please forgive me!

BLONDE (*to* PEDRILLO): You're not worthy of me!

CONSTANZE (*to* BELMONTE): Have I been true to you!

BLONDE (*to* CONSTANZE): He dares to ask me if I have been true to him!

CONSTANZE (*to* BLONDE): Somebody has told Belmonte that I love the Pasha!

PEDRILLO: Blonde is faithful to me—I swear it by all the devils!

61

BELMONTE: Constanze ist mir treu,
Daran ist nicht zu zweifeln.

CONSTANZE *und* BLONDE: Wenn unsrer Ehre wegen
Die Männer Argwohn hegen,
Verdächtig auf uns seh,
Das ist nicht auszusteh'n.

BELMONTE *und* PEDRILLO: Sobald sich Weiber kränken,
Dass wir sie untreu denken,
Dann sind sie wahrhaft treu,
Von allem Vorwurf frei.

PEDRILLO: Liebstes Blondchen! ach verzeihe,
Sieh, ich bau auf deine Treue
Mehr jetzt als auf meinen Kopf.

BLONDE: Nein! das kann ich dir nicht schenken, nein.
Mich mit so was zu verdenken,
Mit dem alten dummen Tropf!

BELMONTE: Ach Constanze! ach mein Leben!
Könntest du mir doch vergeben,
Dass ich diese Frage tat.

CONSTANZE: Belmont! wie, du konntest glauben,
Dass man dir dies Herz kann rauben,
Das nur dir geschlagen hat?

PEDRILLO: Liebstes Blondchen! ach verzeihe!

BELMONTE: Ach verzeihe!

PEDRILLO: Ach verzeihe!

BELMONTE: Ich bereue!

PEDRILLO: Ich bereue!

CONSTANZE: Ich verzeihe deiner Reue.

BLONDE: Ich verzeihe deiner Reue.

ALLE: Wohl, es sei nun abgetan,
Es lebe die Liebe,
Nur sie sei uns teuer!
Nichts fache das Feuer der Eifersucht an,
Nichts, nichts, nichts,
Nichts fache das Feuer der Eifersucht an!

fertig gemacht?

zt will ich ein wenig um den Palast
ie's aussieht. Singen Sie indessen eins.
Abende getan; und wenn Sie da auch
, oder Ihnen begegnet, denn alle Stun-
Janitscharenwache die Runde, so hat's
ie sind das von mir schon gewohnt; es
nn man Sie so still hier fände.

h nur machen, und komm bald wieder.

tanze, wie schlägt mir das Herz! Je
k kommt, desto ängstlicher zagt meine
d wünsche, bebe und hoffe. O Liebe, sei

änen fliessen,
Geliebten hold;
e zu küssen,
ster, grösster Sold.
n zu sehen,
oll Entzücken
zu drücken,
ron' und Pracht.
iederfinden
h ganz empfinden,
ie Trennung macht.
erein.)

t auf dem Ohr; es ist alles so ruhig, so
ach der Sündflut.

lass uns sie befreien. Wo ist die Leiter?

hitzig. Ich muss erst das Signal geben.
ndert dich denn, es nicht zu tun? Mach

ht, Schlag zwölf. Gehen Sie dort an die
ie wohl acht, dass wir nicht überrascht

nur nicht! (*Geht ab.*)

BELMONTE: Constanze is true to me! I cannot doubt it!

CONSTANZE *and* BLONDE: When men suspect our honor, that is too much to bear!

BELMONTE *and* PEDRILLO: When women are insulted by our suspicions, then they are faithful to their vows!

PEDRILLO: Dearest Blonde, forgive me! Now I see that your fidelity is truer than my reason!

BLONDE: No! I cannot pardon you if you suspect me of such a thing with that stupid old idiot! I cannot tolerate that!

BELMONTE: O Constanze! O my love! If only you could forgive me!

CONSTANZE: Belmonte, how could you believe it? Could anyone steal this heart from you?

PEDRILLO: Dearest Blonde, forgive me!
BELMONTE: Oh, forgive me!
PEDRILLO: Oh, forgive me!
BELMONTE: I am sorry!
PEDRILLO: I am sorry!
CONSTANZE: I forgive you if you really feel remorse.
BLONDE: I forgive you if you really feel remorse.
ALL: Let love and forgiveness prevail! Let nothing fan the fires of jealousy. Nothing, nothing, nothing! Let nothing fan the fires of jealousy!

DRITTER AUFZUG

Platz vor dem Palast des BASSA SELIM. *Es ist Mitternacht.*
PEDRILLO *und* KLAAS, *der eine Leiter bringt, kommen herein.*

Dialog

PEDRILLO: Hier, lieber Klaas, hier leg sie indes nur nieder und hole die zweite vom Schiff. Aber nur hübsch leise, dass nicht viel Lärm gemacht wird, es geht hier auf Tod und Leben.

KLAAS: Lass mich nur machen, ich versteh das Ding auch ein bisschen; wenn wir sie nur erst an Bord haben.

PEDRILLO: Ach, lieber Klaas, wenn wir mit unsrer Beute glücklich nach Spanien kommen, ich glaube, Don Belmonte lässt dich in Gold einfassen.

KLAAS: Das möchte wohl ein bisschen zu warm aufs Fell gehn; doch das wird sich schon geben. Ich hole die Leiter. (*Geht ab.*)

PEDRILLO: Ach, wenn ich sagen sollte, dass mir's Herz nicht klopfte, so sagt ich eine schreckliche Lüge. Die verzweifelten Türken verstehn nicht den mindesten Spass; und ob der Bassa gleich ein Renegat ist, so ist er, wenn's aufs Kopfab ankommt, doch ein völliger Türke.
(KLAAS *bringt die zweite Leiter.*)
So, guter Klaas, und nun lichte die Anker und spanne alle Segel auf, denn eh eine halbe Stunde vergeht, hast du deine völlige Ladung.

KLAAS: Bring sie nur hurtig, und dann lass mich sorgen. (*Geht ab.*)

PEDRILLO: Ach, ich muss Atem holen! Es zieht mir's Herz so eng zusammen, als wenn ich's grösste Schelmstück vorhätte! Ach, wo mein Herr auch bleibt!
(BELMONTE *kommt herein.*)

BELMONTE: Pedrillo! Pedrillo!

PEDRILLO: Wie gerufen!

A square in fr[...]
night. PEDRILL[...]
ship, are bring[...]

Dialogue

PEDRILLO: Her[...]
bring the secon[...]
cause now it's [...]

KLAAS: Just let [...]
If only it were [...]
board!

PEDRILLO: Oh, [...]
our cargo intact [...]
in gold.

KLAAS: Well, tha[...]
see what happen[...]
there. (*Exits.*)

PEDRILLO: If I [...]
I would be tellin[...]
Turks have no s[...]
may be better th[...]
Turk when it con[...]
(KLAAS *brings a s[...]*)
Well now, my go[...]
sails! Before half [...]
cargo safely on b[...]

KLAAS: Bring it qu[...]

PEDRILLO: Ah, I n[...]
going to commit [...]
monte be?
(BELMONTE *enters.[...]*)

BELMONTE: Pedrill[...]

PEDRILLO: You're j[...]

BELMONTE: Ist alles[...]

PEDRILLO: Alles! Je[...]
herum spionieren, w[...]
Ich habe das so alle[...]
jemand gewahr wird[...]
den macht hier eine[...]
nichts zu bedeuten, [...]
ist fast besser, als w[...]

BELMONTE: Lass m[...]
(PEDRILLO *geht ab.[...]*)

O Constanze, Con[...]
näher der Augenbli[...]
Seele; ich fürchte u[...]
du meine Leiterin! [...]

15. Arie

Wenn der Freude T[...]
Lächelt Liebe dem [...]
Von den Wangen s[...]
Ist der Liebe, schö[...]
Ach Constanze! di[...]
Dich voll Wonne, [...]
An dies treue Herz[...]
Lohnet mir nicht [...]
Ha! dieses sel'ge [...]
Lässt innig erst m[...]
Welchen Schmerz [...]
(PEDRILLO *komm[...]*)

Dialog

PEDRILLO: Alles l[...]
stille als den Tag[...]

BELMONTE: Nun, [...]

PEDRILLO: Nicht [...]

BELMONTE: Was [...]
fort.

PEDRILLO: Eben [...]
Ecke, und geben [...]
werden.

BELMONTE: Zaud[...]

BELMONTE: Is everything ready?

PEDRILLO: Everything! I'm going to take a quick look around the palace. In the meantime, why don't you sing a little serenade? I have used that trick many times. If someone should hear you—for every hour the Janissary guards make their rounds—he won't think it unusual because everyone is accustomed to *my* singing. It will be better than having you wait here with nothing to do.

BELMONTE: I'll sing then, but be sure to come back quickly.

(PEDRILLO *exits.*)

O Constanze, Constanze, how my heart beats for you! The nearer the moment comes, the more I hesitate. I fear, I hope, I tremble. O Love, lead me onward!

15. Aria●

When the tears of joy flow, love smiles graciously upon the beloved; to kiss the tears off her cheeks is love's greatest, most beautiful reward. O Constanze! If only I might see you! Filled with joy, filled with delight, I would press you to this true heart—crown and splendor are not more to me. Oh! This blissful reunion makes me feel again so intensely what pain is caused by separation.

(PEDRILLO *enters.*)

Dialogue

PEDRILLO: Everybody is sound asleep: everything is so quiet, so still, like the day after the Flood.

BELMONTE: Well, then, let's abduct them now. Where is the ladder?

PEDRILLO: Don't be so hasty. First I must give the signal.

BELMONTE: What prevents you from doing it? Go ahead— quickly!

PEDRILLO: Just right; the stroke of twelve. Go over there and see that we are not surprised.

BELMONTE: Don't lose any time! (*Exits.*)

● This aria is generally sung here, in place of number 17.

PEDRILLO (*indem er seine Mandoline hervorholt*): Es ist doch um die Herzhaftigkeit eine erzläppische Sache. Wer keine hat, schafft sich mit aller Mühe keine an! Was mein Herz schlägt! Mein Papa muss ein Erzpoltron gewesen sein. (*fängt an*) Nun, so sei es denn gewagt!

18. Arie

Im Mohrenland gefangen war
Ein Mädchen hübsch und fein,
Sah rot und weiss, war schwarz von Haar,
Seufzt' Tag und Nacht und weinte gar,
Wollt gern erlöset sein.
Da kam aus fremdem Land daher
Ein junger Rittersmann
Den jammerte das Mädchen sehr,
Juchhe! rief er: "wag' ich Kopf und Ehr',
Wenn ich sie retten kann." (*für sich*)
Noch geht alles gut, es rührt sich noch nichts.
(BELMONTE *kommt hervor.*)

Dialog

BELMONTE: Mach ein Ende, Pedrillo.

PEDRILLO: An mir liegt es nicht, dass sie sich noch nicht zeigen. Entweder schlafen sie fester als jemals, oder der Bassa ist bei der Hand. Wir wollen's weiter versuchen. Bleiben Sie nur auf Ihrem Posten.
(BELMONTE *geht wieder fort.*)

Arie

"Ich komm zu dir in finst'rer Nacht,
Lass, Liebchen, husch mich ein;
Ich fürchte weder Schloss noch Wacht,
Holla, horch auf! um Mitternacht
Sollst du erlöset sein."
Gesagt, getan!
Glock zwölfe stand
Der tapf're Ritter da,
Sanft reicht sie ihm die weiche Hand,
Früh man die leere Zelle fand
Fort war sie hopsasa!
(BELMONTE *kommt wieder herein.*)

Dialog

Sie macht auf, Herr, sie macht auf!

BELMONTE: Ich komme, ich komme!

PEDRILLO (*taking out a mandolin*): It's a strange thing about courage. If you haven't any, no amount of effort can bring it to you. How my heart pounds! My father must have been a real coward! (*plays*) Well, let's get it over with!

18. Aria

In a Moorish land a beautiful maiden was held captive. Her skin was like roses and snow, and her hair was black as night. Every day she sighed and even wept, for she longed to be rescued. From a far land there came a young cavalier who took great pity on the maiden. He shouted: "I shall risk my life and my honor if I can only save her!" (*to himself*) Everything is going well; nobody is moving.
(BELMONTE *re-enters.*)

Dialogue

BELMONTE: That's enough, Pedrillo.

PEDRILLO: I'll end my song as soon as they show themselves. Either they are sound asleep or else the Pasha is nearby. We'll have to try it again. Now go back to your post.
(BELMONTE *exits again.*)

Aria

"I've come to you in darkest night. Let me in, my dearest, quickly! I fear neither castle nor guardsmen. Listen to me—at midnight you will be free." And so what was said was done! At the stroke of midnight the brave cavalier arrived. Tenderly the maiden gave him her soft hand. Next morning the chamber was empty; she had been borne away.
(BELMONTE *re-enters.*)

Dialogue

She's opening her window, my Lord.

BELMONTE: I'm here! I'm here!

CONSTANZE (*oben am Fenster*): Belmonte!

BELMONTE: Constanze, hier bin ich; hurtig die Leiter!

(PEDRILLO *stellt die Leiter an Constanzes Fenster*, BELMONTE *steigt hinein.*)

PEDRILLO: Was das für einen abscheulichen Spektakel macht. Es wird immer ärger, weil es nun Ernst wird. Wenn sie mich hier erwischten, wie schön würden sie mit mir abtrollen, zum Kopfabschlagen, zum Spiessen oder zum Hängen. Je nu, der Anfang ist einmal gemacht, jetzt ist's nicht mehr aufzuhalten, es geht nun schon einmal aufs Leben oder auf den Tod los!

BELMONTE (*kommt mit* CONSTANZE *unten zur Tür heraus*): Nun, holder Engel, nun hab ich dich wieder, ganz wieder! Nichts soll uns mehr trennen.

CONSTANZE: Wie ängstlich schlägt mein Herz, kaum bin ich imstande, mich aufrecht zu halten; wenn wir nur glücklich entkommen!

PEDRILLO: Nur fort, nicht geplaudert, sonst könnt es freilich schief gehen, wenn wir da lange Rat halten und seufzen!

(*Stösst* BELMONTE *und* CONSTANZE *fort.*)

Nur frisch nach dem Strande zu! Ich komme gleich nach.

(BELMONTE *und* CONSTANZE *ab.*)

Nun, Kupido, du mächtiger Herzendieb, halte mir die Leiter und hülle mich samt meiner Gerätschaft in einen dicken Nebel ein!

(*Er legt die Leiter an* BLONDES *Fenster und steigt hinauf.*)

Blondchen, Blondchen, mach auf, um Himmels willen, zaudre nicht, es ist um Hals und Kragen zu tun!

(*Es wird das Fenster geöffnet, er steigt hinein.* OSMIN *und ein schwarzer Stummer öffnen die Tür. Der Stumme gibt* OSMIN *durch Zeichen zu verstehen, dass es nicht richtig sei.*)

OSMIN: Lärmen hörtest du? Was kann's denn geben? Vielleicht Schwärmer? Geh, spioniere, bringe mir Antwort.

(*Der Stumme sieht die Leiter und erschrickt.*)

Gift und Dolch! Was ist das? Wer kann ins Haus steigen? Das sind Diebe oder Mörder. Hurtig, hole die Wache! Ich will unterdessen lauern.

(*Der Stumme ab;* OSMIN *setzt sich auf die Leiter, und nickt*

CONSTANZE (*above, at her window*): Belmonte!

BELMONTE: Constanze, here I am! Give me the ladder, quickly!
(PEDRILLO *puts the ladder against the wall, and* BELMONTE *climbs up to* CONSTANZE'S *window.*)

PEDRILLO: What a racket we are making! This is becoming really serious! If they should ever catch us here, how quickly they would drag us away to chop off our heads, to impale us, or to hang us! Well then, we've begun, and now there's no turning back. It's a matter of life and death!

BELMONTE (*coming out of the door below with* CONSTANZE): Now, dearest angel, now you're mine again! No longer shall we suffer apart.

CONSTANZE: How fearfully my heart is beating! I'm hardly able to stand. If only we can escape!

PEDRILLO: Let's not stop and talk. If we're going to hold council and sigh here, we'll never get away!

(*He pushes* BELMONTE *and* CONSTANZE *out.*)
Go toward the beach! I'll follow you in a few minutes.
(BELMONTE *and* CONSTANZE *exit.*)
Now, Cupid, you mighty thief of hearts, hold my ladder and surround me with a thick fog!

(*He puts a ladder against* BLONDE'S *window, and climbs up.*)
Blonde! Blonde, open up, for heaven's sake! Don't waste any time! This is the moment; it's now or never!
(*The window opens and he climbs in.* OSMIN, *with a black mute, opens the door. The mute signals* OSMIN *that something is amiss.*)

OSMIN: You heard a noise? What could it be? Perhaps a lover. Spy around a little and bring me an answer.
(*The mute starts as he sees the ladder.*)
Poison and daggers! What is this? Who could want to get into the palace? Thieves and murderers! Hurry, call the guard! Meanwhile, I'll keep watch.
(*The mute exits, as* OSMIN *leans back on the ladder and*

ein. PEDRILLO *kommt rückwärts wieder zum Fenster heraus-
gestiegen und will die Leiter wieder herunter.* BLONDE, *oben
am Fenster wird* OSMIN *gewahr und ruft* PEDRILLO *zu.*)

BLONDE: O Himmel, Pedrillo wir sind verloren!

PEDRILLO (*sieht sich um, und sowie er* OSMIN *gewahr wird,
stutzt er, besieht ihn und steigt wieder zum Fenster hinein*):
Ach, welcher Teufel hat sich wider uns verschworen!

OSMIN (*auf der Leiter dem* PEDRILLO *nach, ruft*): Blondchen, Blondchen!

PEDRILLO (*im Hineinsteigen zu* BLONDE): Zurück, nur zurück!

OSMIN: Wart, Spitzbube, du sollst mir nicht entkommen.
Hilfe! Hilfe! Wache! Hurtig, hier gibt's Räuber, herbei,
herbei!

(PEDRILLO *kommt mit* BLONDE *unten zur Haustür heraus,
sieht schüchtern nach der Leiter und schleicht sich dann
mit* BLONDE *darunter weg.*)

BLONDE *und* PEDRILLO: O Himmel steh uns bie, sonst sind
wir verloren!

(OSMIN *will nach.*)

OSMIN: Zu Hilfe, zu Hilfe! Geschwind!

(WACHE, *mit Fackeln, kommt herein und hält* OSMIN.)

WACHE: Halt, halt! Wohin?

OSMIN: Dorthin, dorthin.

WACHE: Wer bist du?

OSMIN: Nur nicht lange gefragt, sonst entkommen die
Spitzbuben. Seht ihr denn nicht? Hier ist noch die Leiter.

WACHE: Das sehn wir; kannst nicht du sie angelegt haben?

OSMIN: Gift und Dolch! Kennt ihr mich denn nicht? Ich
bin Oberaufseher der Gärten beim Bassa. Wenn ihr noch
lange fragt, so hilft euer Kommen nichts.

(*Ein Teil der Wache bringt* PEDRILLO *und* BLONDE *zurück.*)
Ah endlich! Gift und Dolch! Seh ich recht! Ihr beide?
Warte, spitzbübischer Pedrillo, dein Kopf soll am längsten
festgestanden sein.

PEDRILLO: Brüderchen, Brüderchen, wirst doch Spass verstehn? Ich wollt dir dein Weibchen nur ein wenig spazieren
führen, weil du heute dazu nicht aufgelegt bist. Du weisst
schon wegen des Cyperweins.

OSMIN: Schurke, glaubst du mich zu betäuben? Hier ver-

falls asleep. PEDRILLO *comes out of the window, his back toward* OSMIN, *and is about to descend.* BLONDE, *at the window, sees* OSMIN *and calls to* PEDRILLO.)

BLONDE: Heavens, Pedrillo, we are done for!

PEDRILLO (*seeing* OSMIN *and climbing back through the window*): Oh, what devil has conspired against us?

OSMIN (*awakening, turning around, and seeing* PEDRILLO): Blonde, Blonde!

PEDRILLO (*climbing back, calls to* BLONDE): Back, I say, back!

OSMIN: Wait, you rascal; you're not going to get away! Help! Help! Guards! Quickly, there are robbers here! This way! This way!
(PEDRILLO *comes out of the house with* BLONDE *and looks at the ladder. He and* BLONDE *flee.*)

BLONDE *and* PEDRILLO: May heaven be with us—or we are lost!
(OSMIN *starts to follow them.*)

OSMIN: Help, help! Quickly!
(GUARD *comes, with a torch, and stops* OSMIN.)

GUARD: Halt! Halt! Where did they go?

OSMIN: That way!

GUARD: Who are you?

OSMIN: Don't ask any more long questions, or those rascals will escape. Don't you see them? Their ladder is still here.

GUARD: I can see that, but you could very well have put it there yourself.

OSMIN: Poison and daggers! Don't you know me? I'm the chief overseer of the Pasha's gardens. If you're going to ask any more questions, you'll be of no use at all.
(*Other guards bring back* BLONDE *and* PEDRILLO.)
Finally! Can I believe my eyes? Both of you! Just wait, Pedrillo; your head has been joined to your body long enough already!

PEDRILLO: Brother, dearest brother, can't you understand a joke? I only wanted to take your sweetheart out for a walk, since tonight you are not inclined to go with her yourself—you know, on account of the Cyprus wine.

OSMIN: You liar! Did you think you could intoxicate me?

73

stehe ich keinen Spass; dein Kopf muss herunter, so wahr ich ein Muselmann bin.

PEDRILLO: Und hast du einen Nutzen dabei? Wenn ich meinen Kopf verliere, sitzt deiner um so viel fester? (*Ein anderer Teil der Wache bringt* BELMONTE *und* CONSTANZE.)

BELMONTE: Schändliche, lasst mich los!

WACHE: Sachte, junger Herr, sachte! Uns entkommt man nicht so geschwinde.

OSMIN: Sieh da, die Gesellschaft wird immer stärker! Hat der Herr Baumeister auch wollen spazieren gehen! O ihr Spitzbuben! Hatte ich heute nicht recht, dass ich dich nicht ins Haus lassen wollte? Nun wird der Bassa sehen, was für sauberes Gelichter er um sich hat.

BELMONTE: Das beiseite! Lass hören, ob mit euch ein vernünftig Wort zu sprechen ist? Hier ist ein Beutel mit Zechinen, er ist euer, und noch zweimal so viel; lasst mich los.

CONSTANZE: Lasst euch bewegen!

OSMIN: Ich glaube, ihr seid besessen? Euer Geld brauchen wir nicht, das bekommen wir ohnehin; eure Köpfe wollen wir. (*zur Wache*) Schleppt sie fort zum Bassa!

CONSTANZE *und* BELMONTE: Habt doch Erbarmen, lasst euch bewegen!

OSMIN: Um nichts in der Welt! Ich habe mir längst so einen Augenblick gewünscht. Fort, fort! (*Die Wache führt* BELMONTE *und* CONSTANZE *fort, samt* PEDRILLO *und* BLONDE.)

19. Arie

O! wie will ich triumphieren,
Wenn sie euch zum Richtplatz führen,
Und die Hälse schnüren zu.
Schnüren zu!
Hüpfen will ich, lachen, springen,
Und ein Freudenliedchen singen:
Denn nun hab ich vor euch Ruh.
Schleicht nur säuberlich und leise,
Ihr verdammten Harems-Mäuse,
Unser Ohr entdeckt euch schon:
Und eh ihr uns könnt entspringen,
Seht ihr euch in unsern Schlingen,
Und erhaschet euren Lohn.

(OSMIN *geht ab.* BASSA SELIM, *mit Gefolge, kommt herein.*)

74

Tonight I'm not in the mood for joking. As I am a Moslem, your head must come off!

PEDRILLO: And what use will you make of it? If I lose my head, will yours be more firmly fastened to your body? (*Another group of guards brings in* BELMONTE *and* CONSTANZE.)

BELMONTE: You wretches, let me go!

GUARD: Softly, young man, softly! You can't escape us that easily!

OSMIN: Look here, the company is increasing. Did my Lord architect want to go for a walk as well? O you rascals, I was right to keep you out of the palace! Now the Pasha will see what a fine group of servants he has around him!

BELMONTE: Be quiet! Let's see if we can't understand each other! Here is a purse full of ducats. It's yours, and I'll give you twice as many beside if you'll release us.

CONSTANZE: Please let us go!

OSMIN: I think you must be mad! We don't need your money; we'll get it anyway. What we want are your heads! (*to the guards*) Drag them off to the Pasha!

CONSTANZE *and* BELMONTE: Have pity!

OSMIN: Nothing in the world can change my mind. I've always longed for such a moment! Away with you—away! (*The guards lead* BELMONTE *and* CONSTANZE, PEDRILLO *and* BLONDE, *away.*)

    19. Aria

Oh, how I will rejoice when they lead you to the scaffold, when they tie the rope around your neck! I'm going to dance and laugh, jump, and sing a little song of joy! Then I'll be rid of you forever! No matter how stealthily you creep, you damned harem-mouse, we will hear you, and before you can escape us, you'll find yourself in our traps, just as you deserve!

(OSMIN *exits.* PASHA SELIM *enters, with his following.*)

Dialog

BASSA SELIM (*zu einem Offizier*): Geht, unterrichtet euch, was der Lärm bedeutet; er hat uns im Schlaf aufgeschreckt, und lasst mir Osmin kommen.

(*Der Offizier will abgehen, indem kommt* OSMIN, *zwar hastig, doch noch ein wenig schläfrig.*)

OSMIN: Herr, verzeih, dass ich es so früh wage, deine Ruhe zu stören!

BASSA SELIM: Was gibt's, Osmin, was gibt's? Was bedeutet der Aufruhr?

OSMIN: Herr, es ist die schändlichste Verräterei in deinem Palast—

BASSA SELIM: Verräterei?

OSMIN: Die niederträchtigen Christensklaven entführen uns —die Weiber. Der grosse Baumeister, den du gestern auf Zureden des Verräters Pedrillo aufnahmst, hat deine— schöne Constanze entführt.

BASSA SELIM: Constanze? Entführt? Ah, setzt ihnen nach!

OSMIN: O, s'ist schon dafür gesorgt! Meiner Wachsamkeit hast du es zu danken, dass ich sie wieder beim Schopf gekriegt habe. Auch mir selbst hatte der spitzbübische Pedrillo eine gleiche Ehre zugedacht, und er hatte mein Blondchen schon beim Kopf, um mit ihr in alle Welt zu reisen. Aber Gift und Dolch, er soll mir's entgelten! Sieh, da bringen sie sie!

(BELMONTE *und* CONSTANZE *werden von der Wache hereingeführt.*)

BASSA SELIM: Ah, Verräter! Ist's möglich? Ha, du heuchlerische Sirene! War das der Aufschub, den du begehrtest? Missbrauchtest du so die Nachsicht, die ich dir gab, um mich zu hintergehen?

CONSTANZE: Ich bin strafbar in deinen Augen, Herr, es ist wahr; aber es ist mein Geliebter, mein einziger Geliebter, dem lang schon dieses Herz gehört. O nur für ihn, nur um seinetwillen fleh ich um Aufschub. O lass mich sterben! Gern, gern will ich den Tod erdulden; aber schone nur sein Leben—

BASSA SELIM: Und du wagst's, Unverschämte, für ihn zu bitten?

CONSTANZE: Noch mehr: für ihn zu sterben!

Dialogue

PASHA SELIM (*to an officer*): Go and find out who is making that noise! It awakened me from my sleep. Let Osmin come to me.

(*The officer starts to go, when* OSMIN *comes in hurriedly, but still half-asleep.*)

OSMIN: My Lord, forgive my disturbance of your peace.

PASHA SELIM: What it is, Osmin? What does all this commotion mean?

OSMIN: My Lord, the most dangerous treason exists in your palace—

PASHA SELIM: Treason?

OSMIN: Those vile Christian slaves have tried to abduct— our women. The architect whom you employed upon the advice of the traitor Pedrillo planned to abduct—your beautiful Constanze.

PASHA SELIM: To abduct Constanze! Go after them at once!

OSMIN: It's all taken care of. Thanks to my vigilance—we caught them just in the nick of time. The rascal Pedrillo already had my Blonde by the hand and wanted to take her to the ends of the world, but—poison and daggers!— he's not going to succeed! Look; they're bringing them here!

(*Guards bring in* CONSTANZE *and* BELMONTE.)

PASHA SELIM: Oh, traitors, is this possible? False siren, was this the reason that you pleaded for a delay? My indulgence is repaid with deceit!

CONSTANZE: It is true that I am guilty in your eyes, my Lord, but it is to my lover, my only lover, that my heart has always belonged. For his sake alone I begged for this delay. Oh, let me die! I will gladly suffer death if you will only spare his life!

PASHA SELIM: And you dare, shameless woman, to implore pity for his sake?

CONSTANZE: More than that: I ask to die for him!

BELMONTE: Ha, Bassa! Noch nie erniedrigte ich mich zu bitten, noch nie hat dieses Knie sich vor einem Menschen gebeugt: aber sieh, hier lieg ich zu deinen Füssen und flehe dein Mitleid an. Ich bin von einer grossen spanischen Familie, man wird alles für mich zahlen. Lass dich bewegen, bestimme ein Lösegeld für mich und Constanze so hoch du willst. Mein Name ist Lostados.

BASSA SELIM: Was hör ich! Der Komandant von Oran, ist er dir bekannt?

BELMONTE: Das ist mein Vater.

BASSA SELIM: Dein Vater? Welcher glückliche Tag, den Sohn meines ärgsten Feindes in meiner Macht zu haben! Kann was angenehmeres sein? Wisse, Elender, dein Vater, dieser Barbar, ist schuld, dass ich mein Vaterland verlassen musste. Sein unbiegsamer Geiz entriss mir eine Geliebte, die ich höher als mein Leben schätzte. Er brachte mich um Ehrenstellen, Vermögen, um alles. Kurz, er zernichtete mein ganzes Glück. Und dieses Mannes einzigen Sohn habe ich nun in meiner Gewalt! Sage, er an meiner Stelle, was würde er tun?

BELMONTE: Mein Schicksal würde zu beklagen sein.

BASSA SELIM: Das soll es auch sein. Wie er mit mir verfahren ist, will ich mit dir verfahren. Folge mir, Osmin, ich will dir Befehle zu ihren Martern geben. (*zu der Wache*) Bewacht sie hier.

20. Duett

BELMONTE: Welch ein Geschick! O Qual der Seele!
Hat sich denn alles wider mich verschworen!
Ach! Constanze! durch mich bist du verloren,
Welch eine Pein!

CONSTANZE: Lass, ach Geliebter, lass dich das nicht quälen!
Was ist der Tod?
Ein Uebergang zu Ruh,
Und dann, an deiner Seite,
Ist er Vorgeschmack der Seligkeit.

BELMONTE: Engelsseele! Welch holde Güte!
Du flössest Trost in mein erschüttert Herz!
Du linderst mir den Todesschmerz,
Und ach! ich reisse dich ins Grab!
Ha! du solltest für mich sterben,

BELMONTE: Ah, Pasha, never before have I lowered myself to beg; never before have I knelt to any man; but now, here I lie at your feet and invoke your compassion. I belong to a noble family of Spain; they will stand credit for me. Set whatever ransom you please for Constanze and me. My name is Lostados.

PASHA SELIM: Do I hear correctly? Do you know the commander of Oran?

BELMONTE: He is my father.

PASHA SELIM: Your father? What a glorious thing to have the son of my worst enemy in my power! Could there be anything more fortunate? You wretch, your barbarous father had me exiled from my country. His fierce avarice deprived me of a beloved one whom I valued above my own life. He robbed me of honor, fortune—everything. He destroyed my happiness. And now I have this man's only son in my power. Tell me, in my place what would *he* do?

BELMONTE: My fate would indeed be unspeakable.

PASHA SELIM: That it shall be! As he has done to me, thus shall I do to you. Follow me, Osmin; I shall arrange for their torture. (*to the guards*) Watch them here!
(OSMIN *and* PASHA SELIM *exit.*)

20. Duet

BELMONTE: What torments are in store for us! Everything has conspired against us! O Constanze, because you love me you are lost!

CONSTANZE: Don't grieve over this, my beloved! What is death but a transition to eternal rest, and at your side it is a glimpse into blessedness!

BELMONTE: O soul of an angel, what sublime goodness! You bring consolation to my crushed heart! You soften death's agonies. But alas! I speed your path to the grave! You are dying for me! Constanze, can I still dare to face you, I who prepared your death?

79

Ach Constanze! kann ich's wagen,
Noch die Augen aufzuschlagen?
Ich bereite dir den Tod.

CONSTANZE: Ach! für mich gibst du dein Leben;
Ich nur zog dich in's Verderben,
Und ich soll nicht mit dir sterben?
Wonne ist mir dies Gebot.

CONSTANZE *und* BELMONTE: Ach Geliebter! dir zu leben,
War mein Wunsch und all mein Streben!
Ohne dich ist's mir nur Pein,
Länger auf der Welt zu sein.

BELMONTE: Ich will alles gerne leiden.
Weil ich dir zur Seite bin.

CONSTANZE: Mutig sterb ich, und mit Freuden,
Weil ich dir zur Seite bin.

CONSTANZE *und* BELMONTE: Um dich, Geliebter,
Geb ich gern mein Leben hin.
O welche Seligkeit!
Mit dem Geliebten sterben,
Ist seliges Entzücken,
Mit wonnevollen Blicken
Verlässt man da die Welt!
(PEDRILLO *und* BLONDE *werden von einem andern Teil der
Wache hereingeführt.*)

   Dialog

PEDRILLO: Ach, Herr, wir sind hin! An Rettung ist nicht
mehr zu denken. Man macht schon alle Zubereitungen, um
uns aus der Welt zu schaffen. Es ist erschrecklich, was sie
mit uns anfangen wollen! Ich, wie ich im Vorbeigehen
gehört habe, soll in Oel gesotten und dann gespiesst werden.
Das ist ein sauber Traktament! Ach, Blondchen, Blondchen,
was werden sie wohl mit dir anfangen?

BLONDE: Das gilt mir nun ganz gleich. Da es einmal gestor-
ben sein muss, ist mir alles recht.

PEDRILLO: Welche Standhaftigkeit! Ich bin doch von gutem
altchristlichen Geschlecht aus Spanien, aber so gleichgültig
kann ich beim Tode nicht sein! Weiss der Teufel— Gott
sei bei mir, wie kann mir auch jetzt der Teufel auf die
Zunge kommen?
(BASSA SELIM *und* OSMIN *kommen herein.*)

BASSA SELIM: Nun, Sklave! Elender Sklave! Zitterst du?
Erwartest du dein Urteil?

80

CONSTANZE: Belmonte, you risked your life for me, I drew you to your destruction; should I not die with you? Such a fate would be joyful to me!

CONSTANZE *and* BELMONTE: O noblest heart, to live for you was my only wish and desire!

BELMONTE: I shall suffer all gladly, since I am at your side.

CONSTANZE: Calmly I shall die, and joyfully, for we are united!

CONSTANZE *and* BELMONTE: For you, beloved, I gladly relinquish my life. Oh, what blessedness, to die with one's beloved! What ecstasy to leave this world with glances of mutual adoration!

(*Another group of guards brings in* PEDRILLO *and* BLONDE.)

Dialogue

PEDRILLO: Oh, master, we're all done for! There's no chance of escaping now! They're already making preparations to dispatch us from this world. It's horrible! You can't imagine what they plan to do to us! First we'll be boiled in oil, and afterward, impaled! Ah, Blonde, dear Blonde, what will they do to you?

BLONDE: I no longer care. If I have to die, it's all the same to me.

PEDRILLO: How heroic! I'm from a good old Spanish Christian family, and I cannot remain indifferent to my own death; the devil knows that. Good God, how can I speak of the devil at such a moment?

(PASHA SELIM *and* OSMIN *enter.*)

PASHA SELIM: Miserable slave, do you tremble as you await your verdict?

81

BELMONTE: Ja, Bassa, mit so vieler Kaltblütigkeit, als Hitze du es aussprechen kannst. Kühle deine Rache an mir, tilge das Unrecht, so mein Vater dir angetan; ich erwarte alles und tadle dich nicht.

BASSA SELIM: Es muss also wohl deinem Geschlechte ganz eigen sein, Ungerechtigkeiten zu begehen, weil du das für so ausgemacht annimmst? Du betrügst dich. Ich habe deinen Vater viel zu sehr verabscheut, als dass ich je in seine Fusstapfen treten könnte. Nimm deine Freiheit, nimm Constanze, segle in dein Vaterland, sage deinem Vater, dass du in meiner Gewalt warst, dass ich dich freigelassen, um ihm sagen zu können, es wäre ein weit grösser Vergnügen, eine erlittene Ungerechtigkeit durch Wohltaten zu vergelten, als Laster mit Lastern tilgen.

BELMONTE: Herr! Du setzest mich in Erstaunen—

BASSA SELIM: Das glaub ich. Zieh damit hin, und werde du wenigstens menschlicher als dein Vater, so ist meine Handlung belohnt.

CONSTANZE: Herr, vergib! Ich schätzte bisher deine edle Seele, aber nun bewundere ich—

BASSA SELIM: Still! Ich wünsche für die Falschheit, so Sie an mir begangen, dass Sie es nie bereuen möchten, mein Herz ausgeschlagen zu haben.

PEDRILLO: Herr, dürfen wir beide Unglückliche es auch wagen, um Gnade zu flehen? Ich war von Jugend auf ein treuer Diener meines Herrn.

OSMIN: Herr, beim Allah, lass dich ja nicht von dem verwünschten Schmarotzer hintergehn! Keine Gnade! Er hat schon hundertmal den Tod verdient.

BASSA SELIM: Er mag ihn also in seinem Vaterlande suchen. (*zur Wache*) Man begleite alle vier an das Schiff. (*gibt* BELMONTE *ein Papier*) Hier ist euer Passport.

OSMIN: Wie, meine Blonde soll er auch mitnehmen?

BASSA SELIM: Alter, sind dir deine Augen nicht lieb? Ich sorge besser für dich als du denkst.

OSMIN: Gift und Dolch! Ich möchte bersten.

BASSA SELIM: Beruhige dich. Wen man durch Wohltun nicht für sich gewinnen kann, den muss man sich vom Halse schaffen.

BELMONTE: Yes, Pasha, I anticipate only your cruelty. Cool your vengeance on me; cancel the injustice that my father showed to you. I expect it, and I will not reproach you.

PASHA SELIM: Injustice must be quite usual in your family, for you seem to accept it with such equanimity. You deceive yourself. I hate your father too much to follow in his footsteps. Go! Have your freedom, take Constanze, sail back to your own country, and tell your father that you were in my power, and that I have set you free. It is a far greater pleasure to reward injustice with mercy than to balance vice with vice.

BELMONTE: My Lord, you astonish me!

PASHA SELIM: I can believe that! Go now, and learn to be more humane than your father, so that I shall be compensated for my leniency.

CONSTANZE: Forgive me, my Lord! Until today I merely esteemed your noble soul, but now I stand in awe of you!

PASHA SELIM: Say no more! Although you have been false to me, I hope that you will never suffer regret for having refused my love!

PEDRILLO: My Lord, may we unfortunate ones also dare to beg for your mercy? Since my youth I have been Belmonte's faithful servant.

OSMIN: My Lord, by Allah, don't let yourself be outwitted by this accursed parasite! Show him no mercy! He has deserved his death a hundred times!

PASHA SELIM: Then let him seek it in his own country. (*to the guards*) Accompany all four of them to their ship! (*giving* BELMONTE *a piece of paper*) Here is your passport.

OSMIN: What, my Blonde will go with him too?

PASHA SELIM: Old fool, do not oppose my will! My concern for you surpasses your own judgment.

OSMIN: Poison and daggers! I could burst!

PASHA SELIM: Calm yourself. When one cannot win a woman because of one's own goodness, then it is better to let her go.

83

21. Finale

BELMONTE: Nie werd ich deine Huld verkennen,
Mein Dank bleibt ewig dir geweiht.
An jedem Ort, zu jeder Zeit
Werd ich gross und edel nennen.
Wer so viel Huld vergessen kann,
Den seh man mit Verachtung an.

ALLE: Wer so viel Huld vergessen kann,
Den seh' man mit Verachtung an.

CONSTANZE: Nie werd ich, selbst im Schoss der Liebe,
Vergessen was der Dank gebeut.
Mein Herz, der Liebe nun geweiht,
Hegt auch dem Dank geweihte Triebe.
Wer so viel Huld vergessen kann,
Den seh man mit Verachtung an.

ALLE: Wer so viel Huld vergessen kann,
Den seh man mit Verachtung an.

PEDRILLO: Wenn ich es je vergessen könnte,
Wie nah ich am Erdrosseln war,
Und all der anderen Gefahr,
Ich lief, als ob der Kopf mir brennte.
Wer so viel Huld vergessen kann,
Den seh man mit Verachtung an.

ALLE: Wer so viel Huld vergessen kann,
Den seh man mit Verachtung an.

BLONDE: Nehmt meinen Dank mit tausend Freuden.
Herr Bassa! lebt gesund und froh!
Osmin! das Schicksal will es so,
Ich muss von dir auf ewig scheiden; (*auf* OSMIN *zeigend*)
Wer so wie du nur zanken kann,
Den sieht man mit Verachtung an.

OSMIN: Verbrennen sollte man die Hunde,
Die uns so schändlich hintergeh'n;
Es ist nicht länger anzuseh'n,
Mir starrt die Zunge fast im Munde,
Um ihren Lohn zu ordnen an.
Erst geköpft, dann gehangen,
Dann gespiesst auf heisse Stangen,
Dann verbrannt, dann gebunden
Und getaucht, zuletzt geschunden!
(OSMIN *läuft voll Wut ab.*)

84

21. Finale

BELMONTE: I shall always remember your graciousness, and my gratitude shall be dedicated to you. At every place and time I shall proclaim your nobility. He who can forget such goodness must be held in contempt.

ALL: Whoever can forget such goodness must be held in contempt.

CONSTANZE: I shall always remember, even in the midst of love's pleasure, what gratitude we owe to you. My heart, though dedicated now to love, will still cherish the remembrance of your kindness! Whoever can forget such goodness must be held in contempt.

ALL: Whoever can forget such goodness must be held in contempt.

PEDRILLO: When I think how near I was to being strangled or tortured, I could run as if my head were on fire! Whoever can forget such goodness must be held in contempt.

ALL: Whoever can forget such goodness must be held in contempt.

BLONDE: My Lord Pasha, let me thank you for your hospitality, but I am really very glad that you will let me depart. (*pointing to* OSMIN) Just look at that old Osmin and tell me if anybody could ever love such a creature as that!

OSMIN: We should burn these dogs; they have deceived us miserably! It's no longer to be tolerated; my tongue starts in my mouth to order the punishment that they deserve! Hang them, then behead them, then impale them on red-hot rods, then burn them, bind them, drown them, and finally, flay them!

(OSMIN *runs out in anger.*)

CONSTANZE, BLONDE, BELMONTE, PEDRILLO: Den edlen
Mann entstellt die Rache,
Grossmütig, menschlich, gütig sein,
Und ohne Eigennutz verzeih'n,
Ist nur der grossen Seelen Sache.

CONSTANZE: Wer dieses nicht erkennen kann,
Den seh man mit Verachtung an.

CONSTANZE, BLONDE, BELMONTE, PEDRILLO: Wer dieses
nicht erkennen kann,
Den seh man mit Verachtung an.

CHOR: Bassa Selim lebe lange,
Bassa Selim glücklich lebe!
Ehre sei sein Eigentum!
Seine holde Stirn umschwebe
Jubel, Freude, Glück und Ruhm!

CONSTANZE, BLONDE, BELMONTE, PEDRILLO: Nothing is uglier than revenge. But to be humane and generous and to forgive without self-interest is the mark of a great soul!

CONSTANZE: He who would ignore the moral of this tale should be condemned.

CONSTANZE, BLONDE, BELMONTE, PEDRILLO: He who would ignore the moral of this tale should be condemned.

CHORUS: Long live Pasha Selim; may honor be his reward! Let the fame of his justice bring him endless joy!

THE
MARRIAGE
OF
FIGARO

LE
NOZZE
DI
FIGARO

*An opera
in four acts*

*Music by
Wolfgang Amadeus Mozart
(K. 492)*

*Words by
Lorenzo da Ponte*

INTRODUCTION

Although it was begun in the autumn of 1784, only three years after *The Abduction from the Seraglio, The Marriage of Figaro* reveals Mozart in possession of his full powers as an operatic composer. Like *The Abduction, Figaro,* in addition to its timeless values, has a certain topical interest. Based on *Le Mariage de Figaro,* a play by Beaumarchais which was first performed in France in 1784 and was subsequently banned in Vienna as subversive and conducive to revolution, it also marks the first collaboration of Mozart with the great librettist Lorenzo da Ponte, who was to perform for him a service similar to that which Arrigo Boito performed for Verdi a century later. By pointing out that his libretto emphasized the human conflicts of Beaumarchais's play, rather than its political overtones —that it treated the struggle between the Count and Figaro, master and servant, as a personal conflict, rather than as an incitement to revolt—Da Ponte induced Emperor Joseph II to relax his ban and permit the opera to be performed in Vienna.

For full understanding of the plot of *Figaro,* some knowledge of Beaumarchais's earlier play, *Le Barbier de Seville,* is needed. In this play, the basis of the popular opera by Rossini, Count Almaviva, with the aid of Figaro, the resourceful barber of Seville, steals the beautiful Rosina away from her elderly guardian, Bartolo. As *The Marriage of Figaro* opens, we find that Figaro has become the Count's steward, and that the Count is beginning to neglect Rosina, now the Countess, in favor of other women—among them, Figaro's intended bride, Susanna.

The situation that evolves contains all the elements essential to true comedy. The action takes place in a small, isolated world, the Count's household, but the characters belong to a highly civilized society, and they are all playing a game of skill with all their wits. Women dominate and control the action, and point the final moral: Men must learn to see their own absurdities, and to recover their lost dignity in this recognition.

Mozart has set the story in the form of the Italian *opera buffa* of his period, with recitative instead of dialogue to advance the action, which proceeds with headlong speed. Nevertheless, every character retains his musical identity throughout the long, elaborate ensembles that are necessary to further the plot.

The characters in *Figaro* are complete human beings, more human, perhaps, than any in Mozart's subsequent operas, and very different from the somewhat flat "types" of *The Abduction from the Seraglio.* Susanna, for example, is more complex than Blonde; Blonde is always the same, but Susanna's reactions vary with her companions. Her two arias indicate the range of her nature. The first is an outpouring of her youthful merriment; the second, after its opening recitative, is an expression of her deep love for Figaro. Like Blonde, Susanna has wit and vivacity, but Mozart never lets us forget that she is a young girl in love —how much so we do not know, perhaps, until her final aria. At first she is afraid of the Count, and then she is a bit contemptuous of him; she is spiteful with Marcellina, solicitous with the Countess, mocking at Cherubino's raptures, and indignant at Basilio's insinuations.

Constrasted with Susanna, and far more complex than the nobly suffering Constanze of *The Abduction,* the Countess is a woman who, though still young and still able to enjoy life and its intrigues, laments the exigencies forced on her by her husband's philandering; her first aria shows the reflective side of her nature; in her second, she reaffirms her belief in life and in love. Figaro, although his barbs against the nobility have been softened a bit by Da Ponte, remains a colorful figure; he is inventive and energetic, and like any man in love, quick to take occasion for jealousy. The Count may be selfish, but still we find him somewhat sympathetic; we cannot hate him any more than we would hate any immature and confused young man of today. The other characters—Barbarina, Marcellina, Bartolo, Don Basilio, and even Antonio and Don Curzio—are sharply delineated in the libretto and deftly characterized in the music.

With all its wealth of characterization, and its moments of serious emotion, *Figaro* is, above all, a comedy. It depicts a world ruled by reason rather than passion, one in which people discover their own failings and absurdities, and in which all complications are happily resolved by the final curtain. It is a world where only human forces are at work; there are no judgments of the characters beyond their opinions of each other, and nowhere is any divine or infernal presence suggested. The love that triumphs in this opera is wholly human; perhaps it is for this reason that many operagoers consider *The Marriage of Figaro* the most appealing of all Mozart's operas.

SYNOPSIS

ACT ONE

Figaro, Count Almaviva's steward, is about to marry Susanna, the Countess's maid. Susanna informs Figaro that their master's kind attentions toward her are not as disinterested as they seem; in fact, he would like to spend the wedding night with her, in accordance with the medieval custom. Enraged, Figaro rushes off to consider retaliation. Marcellina, an old spinster who hopes to marry Figaro, and Bartolo, a former suitor of the Countess, are determined to prevent the wedding, but Susanna makes it clear that she is not to be intimidated. No sooner has Marcellina departed, than Cherubino, a young page, comes to lament his hopeless love for the Countess. He is surprised in Susanna's room by the Count and hides behind a chair listening delightedly to his master's amorous proposals to Susanna. At the arrival of the spiteful music master, Don Basilio, the Count, in turn, conceals himself, only to emerge in a jealous rage at Basilio's gossip about the Countess and Cherubino. Discovering the page's hiding place, the Count furiously orders him to join his regiment at Seville. The act ends with Figaro's mock-heroic farewell to Cherubino, who will now exchange his effete existence for the rigors of military life.

ACT TWO

The Countess has determined to assist Figaro and Susanna, hoping to regain her husband's wayward affections. Figaro discloses a plot to ridicule his master by arranging a meeting with Cherubino, dressed as a girl, and the Countess and Susanna begin to disguise the page. As the Count's voice is heard at the door, Susanna flees to her own room, while Cherubino hides in a closet. The Count demands to know who is locked behind the closet door. The Countess replies that it is Susanna, but she refuses to open the closet for her husband's inspection. While the Count goes off to get a crowbar, Susanna releases Cherubino and locks herself into the closet in his place; the page escapes through a window. Upon returning, the Count discovers Susanna, and begs his wife's forgiveness for his suspicions. Figaro enters, anxious to begin the wedding ceremonies, but when Antonio, the gardener, appears with news that he has just seen a man jumping out of the Countess's window, the Count's suspicions are aroused anew. Figaro asserts that he himself was the unknown man. He is at first unable to cite the contents of a paper that Antonio has found under the window, but after adroit prompting by Susanna and the Countess, he correctly declares it to be the page's commission, which he claims had been given to him for sealing. The act ends in utter confusion, as Marcellina, Bartolo, and Don Basilio rush in, accusing Figaro of breach of promise, and demanding justice of the Count, to the disgust of Figaro, Susanna, and the Countess.

ACT THREE

The Countess and Susanna fabricate a new plot: Susanna is to make a rendezvous for that evening with the Count, but the Countess, dressed in Susanna's clothes, will go in her place. Meanwhile, Don Curzio, the Count's lawyer, has decided matters in Marcellina's favor—Figaro must either marry her or pay a sum of money that he owes her. In the explanations that follow it is discovered that Figaro is the long-lost son of Marcellina and Bartolo, who decide, somewhat belatedly, to get married that very day. Susanna misunderstands when she first sees the new-found mother and son embracing, but all is eventually explained, and the two couples go off to prepare for a double wedding. As soon as they are gone, Cherubino reappears with Susanna's cousin, Barbarina, who is taking him home to dress him as a girl, so that he can unobtrusively take part in the wedding festivities. Still deploring her husband's infidelities, the Countess returns to dictate a letter to Susanna, designating the place of meeting with the Count for that evening; Susanna is to give it to him with instructions to return the pin with which it is sealed. Cherubino is unmasked by Antonio as he presents a bouquet of flowers to the Countess, but Barbarina obtains his pardon by relating another of the Count's indiscretions. The wedding ceremonies finally begin, as Susanna manages to deliver her note to the Count. The act ends in general rejoicing, and a chorus in praise of the Count's benevolence.

ACT FOUR

That night, in the gardens of the castle, Barbarina laments the loss of the pin that the Count has asked her to return to Susanna, and innocently arouses Figaro's suspicions of his bride. Marcellina warns Susanna, as Figaro, after a diatribe on the infidelity of women, hides in the bushes to await his "rival." Discovering Figaro's hiding place, but pretending not to have seen him, Susanna taunts him by singing of the "lover" whom she awaits; then she conceals herself in the bushes at the opposite side of the garden. Cherubino comes to meet Barbarina and sees the Countess, disguised as Susanna. His attempts at flirtation are interrupted by the Count, who also mistakes his wife for Susanna, and behaves accordingly, finally sending her to wait for him in a summerhouse. Figaro's musings on his bride's betrayal are interrupted by Susanna, posing as her mistress. Figaro soon recognizes her, but continues the deception, pretending to be madly in love with the Countess. Susanna reveals herself; the lovers are reconciled and stage a violent love scene for the benefit of the Count, who happens to be passing at that moment. At the Count's shouts of indignation, all the characters emerge from various hiding places. When the real Countess unmasks herself, the disconcerted Count is forced to beg his wife's pardon, which is generously granted to him.

CHARACTERS

COUNT ALMAVIVA — *Baritone*

COUNTESS ALMAVIVA (ROSINA), *his wife* — *Soprano*

FIGARO, *the* COUNT'S *steward* — *Baritone or Bass-baritone*

SUSANNA, *the* COUNTESS'S *maid;*
betrothed to FIGARO — *Soprano*

CHERUBINO, *a young page* — *Soprano or Mezzo-soprano*

DON BASILIO, *the* COUNT'S *music master* — *Tenor*

DOCTOR BARTOLO, *a physician from Seville;*
formerly the COUNTESS'S *guardian* — *Bass*

MARCELLINA, *his housekeeper; formerly the*
COUNTESS'S *governess* — *Soprano or Mezzo-soprano*

ANTONIO, *the* COUNT'S *gardener;* SUSANNA'S *uncle* — *Bass*

BARBARINA, *his daughter* — *Soprano*

DON CURZIO, *a lawyer* — *Tenor*

TWO PEASANT GIRLS — *Soprano and Mezzo-soprano*

CHORUS *of peasants*

The action takes place during one day, in and around the COUNT'S *castle, near Seville, during the mid-eighteenth century.*

LE NOZZE DI FIGARO

ATTO PRIMO

Camera quasi smobiliata. FIGARO *prende la misura d' un letto;* SUSANNA *prova il suo cappello di nozze.*

1. *Duettino*

FIGARO: Cinque—dieci—venti—
Trenta—trenta sei—quarantatre.

SUSANNA: Ora sì, ch'io son contenta,
Sembra fatto in ver per me.

FIGARO: Cinque.

SUSANNA: Guarda un po', mio caro Figaro!

FIGARO: Dieci. Venti.

SUSANNA: Guarda adesso il mio cappello!

FIGARO: Quarantatre.

SUSANNA: Guarda un po', mio caro Figaro.
Guarda adesso il mio cappello!

FIGARO: Si, mio core, or è più bello.
Sembra fatto in ver per te.

SUSANNA: Guarda un po'.

FIGARO: Sì, mio core.

SUSANNA: Ora sì, ch'io son contenta.

FIGARO: Sì, mio core.

SUSANNA: Ah! il mattino alle nozze vicino,
Quant'è dolce al mio tenero sposo
Questo bel cappellino vezzoso
Che Susanna ella stessa si fè!

FIGARO: Ah! il mattino alle nozze vicino,
Quant'è dolce al tuo tenero sposo
Questo bel capellino vezzoso
Che Susanna ella stessa si fè!

Recitativo

SUSANNA: Cosa stai misurando, caro il mio Figaretto?

FIGARO: Io guardo se quel letto, che ci destina il Conte, farà buona figura in questo loco.

SUSANNA: In questa stanza?

FIGARO: Certo, a noi la cede generoso il padrone.

THE MARRIAGE OF FIGARO

ACT ONE

A half-furnished room. FIGARO *is measuring a bed;* SUSANNA *is trying on her wedding hat.*

1. Duettino

FIGARO: Five — ten — twenty — thirty — thirty-six — forty-three.

SUSANNA: Now I'm so very happy! It seems to be really made for me.

FIGARO: Five.

SUSANNA: Look at me, my dear Figaro!

FIGARO: Ten. Twenty.

SUSANNA: Now look at my hat!

FIGARO: Forty-three.

SUSANNA: Look at me, my dear Figaro. Now look at my hat!

FIGARO: Yes, my darling, now it's even prettier. It seems to be really made for you.

SUSANNA: Look at me.

FIGARO: Yes, my darling.

SUSANNA: Now I'm so very happy.

FIGARO: Yes, my darling.

SUSANNA: Ah, with our wedding day so near, how my dear fiancé loves this pretty, charming little hat that Susanna has made for herself.

FIGARO: Ah, with our wedding day so near, how my dear fiancée loves this pretty, charming little hat that Susanna has made for herself.

Recitative

SUSANNA: What are you measuring there, my dear little Figaro?

FIGARO: I'm seeing whether this bed, which our generous master has given us, will look well in this corner.

SUSANNA: In this room?

FIGARO: Surely; the Count has generously given it to us.

99

SUSANNA: Io per me te la dono.

FIGARO: E la ragione?

SUSANNA (*toccandosi la fronte*): La ragione l'ho qui.

FIGARO (*facendo lo stesso*): Perchè non puoi far, che passi un po' qui!

SUSANNA: Perchè non voglio. Sei tu mio servo, o no?

FIGARO: Ma non capisco perchè tanto ti spiacia, la più comoda stanza del palazzo.

SUSANNA: Perch'io son la Susanna, e tu sei pazzo.

FIGARO: Grazie, non tanti elogi; guarda un poco, se potria meglio stare in altro loco.

2. Duetto

Se a caso madama la notte ti chiama—
Din, din, din, din—
In due passi da quella puoi gir.
Vien poi l'occasione
Che vuolmi il padrone—
Don, don, don, don—
In tre salti lo vado a servir.

SUSANNA: Così si il mattino il caro Contino—
Din, din, don, don,
E ti manda tre miglia lontan—
Din, din, don, don—
A mia porta il diavol lo porta—
Ed ecco in tre salti—

FIGARO: Susanna pian, pian.

SUSANNA: Ed ecco—

FIGARO: Pian, pian—

SUSANNA: In tre salti—

FIGARO: Pian, pian—

SUSANNA: Din, din—

FIGARO: Pian, pian—

SUSANNA: Don, don!—

FIGARO: Pian, pian—

SUSANNA: Ascolta!

FIGARO: Fa presto!

SUSANNA: And I give my part of it back to you.

FIGARO: And your reason?

SUSANNA (*pointing to her forehead*): I have the reason here.

FIGARO (*pointing to his own forehead*): And why can't you transmit it *here?*

SUSANNA: Because I don't want to. Are you my slave or not?

FIGARO: But I don't understand why you're objecting to the most convenient room in the castle.

SUSANNA: Because I'm Susanna, and you're stupid!

FIGARO: Thank you; not so much flattery; look and see if you can find us a better place!

2. Duet

If the Countess, by chance, should call you at night—ding, ding!—just two steps from here and you'd be with her. And then, if the Count, should want *me*—dong, dong!—in three jumps I could be at his side.

SUSANNA: And so, if one morning, the dear little Count—ding, ding!—sends you three miles away—ding, ding—dong, dong!—the devil would bring him to my door—and then, in three jumps—

FIGARO: Be calm, Susanna!

SUSANNA: And then—

FIGARO: Be calm—

SUSANNA: In three jumps—

FIGARO: Be calm—

SUSANNA: Ding, ding!—

FIGARO: Be calm—

SUSANNA: Dong, dong!—

FIGARO: Be calm—

SUSANNA: Listen, now!

FIGARO: Tell me quickly.

SUSANNA: Se udir brami il resto,
Discaccia i sospetti, che torto mi fan.

FIGARO: Udir bramo il resto,
I dubbi, i sospetti gelare me fan.

SUSANNA: Discaccia i sospetti, che torto mi fan.

FIGARO: I dubbi, i sospetti gelare me fan.

Recitativo

SUSANNA: Or bene, ascolta e taci.

FIGARO: Parla, che c'è di nuovo?

SUSANNA: Il signor Conte, stanco d'andar cacciando le straniere bellezze forestiere, vuole ancor nel castello ritentar la sua sorte; n'è già di sua Consorte, bada bene, appetito gli viene.

FIGARO: E di chi dunque?

SUSANNA: Della tua Susannetta.

FIGARO: Di te?

SUSANNA: Di me medesma, ed ha speranza ch'al nobil suo progetto utilissima sia tal vicinanza.

FIGARO: Bravo! tiriamo avanti.

SUSANNA: Queste le grazie son, questa la cura ch'egli prende di te, della tua sposa.

FIGARO: O guarda un po', che carità pelosa!

SUSANNA: Chetati, or viene il meglio; Don Basilio, mio maestro di canto, e suo factotum, nel darmi la lezione me ripete ogni dì questa canzone.

FIGARO: Chi! Basilio! Oh birbante!

SUSANNA: E tu credevi, che fosse la mia dote merto del tuo bel muso?

FIGARO: Me n'era lusingato.

SUSANNA: Ei la destina per ottener da me certe mezz'ore che il diritto feudale—

FIGARO: Come! ne' i feudi suoi non l'ha il Conte abolito?

SUSANNA: Ebben, ora è pentito, e par che tenti rescattarlo da me.

FIGARO: Bravo! mi piace; che caro signor Conte; Ci vogliamo divertir, trovato avete—
(*Suona un campanella.*)
Chi suona? La Contessa.

SUSANNA: If you want me to go on, discard your nasty suspicions! They only wrong me.

FIGARO: I want to hear the rest of it, but my doubts and suspicions make my blood run cold!

SUSANNA: Discard your suspicions! They only wrong me.

FIGARO: My doubts and suspicions make my blood run cold!

Recitative

SUSANNA: Very well, now listen and be quiet!

FIGARO: Tell me. What has happened?

SUSANNA: The Count is tired of pursuing foreign beauties, and he would like to try his luck again in his own castle; but it's not his wife, you see, who has aroused his passions.

FIGARO: Who is it, then?

SUSANNA: Your own Susanna.

FIGARO: You?

SUSANNA: My own little self, and he hopes that our proximity will further his plans.

FIGARO: Delightful! We're making progress!

SUSANNA: That's his great generosity! That's why he's so considerate of you and your fiancée.

FIGARO: Look at that! What hypocrisy!

SUSANNA: One moment; now comes the best of all. Don Basilio, my singing teacher, is the Count's willing helper, and during my lessons, he incessantly pleads the Count's cause.

FIGARO: Who—Basilio? That scoundrel!

SUSANNA: And you believed that my dowry was given for *your* good looks?

FIGARO: So I flattered myself!

SUSANNA: He intended the money to win from me certain privileges that the feudal rights—

FIGARO: What! Didn't he abolish his feudal rights?

SUSANNA: Well, now he's sorry, and it seems that he'll try to restore them through me.

FIGARO: Wonderful! I'm flattered! What a generous master! He wants some amusement, and he's found—
(*A bell rings.*)
Who's ringing? The Countess.

SUSANNA: Addio, addio, Figaro bello.

FIGARO: Coraggio, mio tesoro!

SUSANNA: E tu, cervello! (*Parte.*)

3. Aria

FIGARO: Bravo, signor padrone!
Ora incomincio a capire il mistero,
E a veder schietto
Tutto il vostro progetto.
A Londra, è vero?
Voi ministro, io corriero,
E la Susanna—
Segreta ambasciatrice.
Non sarà, Figaro il dice.
Se vuol ballare, signor Contino,
Il chitarrino le suonerò, sì.
Se vuol venire nella mia scuola,
La capriola le insegnerò, sì.
Saprò—ma piano, piano—
Meglio ogni arcano
Dissimulando scoprir potrò.
L'arte schermendo,
L'arte adoprando,
Di qua pungendo, di là scherzando,
Tutte le macchine rovescierò.
(*Parte. Entrano* BARTOLO *e* MARCELLINA.)

Recitativo

BARTOLO: Ed aspettaste il giorno fissato per le nozze, a parlarmi di questo?

MARCELLINA: Io non mi perdo, dottor mio, di coraggio, per romper de' sponsali più avanzati di questo, bastò spesso un pretesto; ed egli ha meco, oltre questo contratto certi impegni—so io—basta! Conviene la Susanna atterrir, convien con arte impuntigliarla a refiutari il conte; egli per vendicarsi prenderà il mio partito, e Figaro così fia mio marito.

BARTOLO: Bene, io tutto farò. Senza riserva, tutto a me palesate. (*a parte*) Avrei pur gusto di dar in moglie la mia serva antica, a chi mi fece un dì rapir l'amica.

4. Aria

La vendetta, oh, la vendetta
E un piacer serbato ai saggi.

SUSANNA: I must go now, Figaro darling!

FIGARO: Be brave, my love!

SUSANNA: And you, be clever! (*Exits.*)

3. Aria

FIGARO: So that's your game, my Lord! Now I'm beginning to understand the mystery, and to see your plans all too clearly. So we're going to London? You as minister, I as courier, and my Susanna—as secret ambassadress. You'll never succeed—Figaro has spoken! If my friend the Count wishes to dance, I'll be the one to play the guitar. If he wishes to come to my school, I'll teach him the steps. I'll know his plans—be calm now!—it's better to uncover a secret by stealth! I'll use art to conceal art; I'll fight or cajole, and I'll bring all his plots to ruin.
(*He goes off.* BARTOLO *and* MARCELLINA *enter.*)

Recitative

BARTOLO: And you waited until the wedding day to mention this to me?

MARCELLINA: I would have courage, my dear Doctor, to break off a marriage even further advanced than this one is; a pretext is often enough; and I have one. In addition to this contract, I have with me certain pledges—enough! We must intimidate Susanna and make her resist the Count's proposals. To avenge himself, he'll take my part, and so Figaro will be forced to marry me!

BARTOLO: Good! I'll do everything, without reservations. But tell me all about it. (*aside*) How I would love to marry off Marcellina, my old servant, to the man who helped the Count to steal my Rosina from me.

4. Aria

Revenge! Ah, revenge is the satisfaction reserved for the

L'obliar l'onte, gli oltraggi
E bassezza, è ognor viltà.
Coll'astuzia, coll'arguzia
Col giudizio, col criterio
Si potrebbe, il fatto è serio;
Ma credete si farà.
Se tutto il codice
Dovessi volgere
Se tutto l'indice
Dovessi leggere,
Con un equivoco, con un sinomimo,
Qualche garbuglio si troverà.
Tutta Siviglio conosce Bartolo,
Il birbo Figaro vinto sarà. (*Parte.*)

Recitativo

MARCELLINA: Tutto ancor non ho perso; mi resta la speranza.

(SUSANNA *entra.*)

Ma Susanna si avanza; io vo' provarmi—fingiam di non vederla. (*come fra se, ma forte*) E quella buona perla la vorrebbe sposar.

SUSANNA (*a parte*): Di me favella.

MARCELLINA: Ma da Figaro alfine non può meglio sperarsi—*l'argent fait tout.*

SUSANNA: Che lingua! Manco male ch'ognun sa quanto vale.

MARCELLINA: Brava! Questo è giudizio! Con quegl'occhi modesti, con quell'aria pietosa! E poi—

SUSANNA: Meglio è partir.

MARCELLINA: Che cara sposa!

(*Tutti i due vogliono partire;* MARCELLINA *ironicamente invita* SUSANNA *a precedarla.*)

5. Duetto

Via resti servita, madama brillante.

SUSANNA: Non sono sì ardita, madama piccante.

MARCELLINA: No, prima a lei tocca.

SUSANNA: No, no, tocca a lei.

MARCELLINA e SUSANNA: Io so i dover miei,
Non fo' incivilità.

MARCELLINA: La sposa novella!

wise. To forget a shame or an insult is a weakness; I call it vile. With subtlety and craft, with wisdom and discrimination, believe me, it can be done, although it's very difficult. If I have to overturn all the codes of law, if I must read all the statutes, I'll find some loophole, some contradiction that will confuse them. All of Seville respects Doctor Bartolo! That rascal Figaro will be beaten at last! (*Exits.*)

Recitative

MARCELLINA: All is not lost; some hope remains to me. (SUSANNA *enters.*)
But Susanna is approaching; let's see what I can do—I'll ignore her completely. (*as if to herself, but loudly*) And that's the pearl of virtue that he'd like to marry!

SUSANNA (*aside*): She speaks of me.

MARCELLINA: After all, from Figaro's taste, one can't expect much—money is all that matters!

SUSANNA: How bitter! I'm glad that everyone knows her for what she is!

MARCELLINA: Well, this is wisdom! Such modest eyes! What a pious air! And yet—

SUSANNA: I'd better go.

MARCELLINA: What a sweet bride!
(*Both are about to leave;* MARCELLINA *ironically invites* SUSANNA *to go first.*)

5. Duet

I'm your servant, most brilliant of brides!

SUSANNA: I'm not so presumptuous, most learned lady!

MARCELLINA: You must precede me.

SUSANNA: No, no, after you.

MARCELLINA *and* SUSANNA: I've learned my manners; I'm never impolite!

MARCELLINA: The innocent little bride!

SUSANNA: La dama d'onore!

MARCELLINA: Del Conte la bella!

SUSANNA: Di Spagna l'amore!

MARCELLINA: I meriti!

SUSANNA: L'abito!

MARCELLINA: Il posto!

SUSANNA: L'età!

MARCELLINA: Perbacco, precipito
Se ancor resto qua.

SUSANNA: Sibilla decrepita,
Da rider mi fa!

MARCELLINA: Via resti servita.

SUSANNA: Non sono sì ardita.
(MARCELLINA *parte.*)

Recitativo

Va là, vecchia pedante, dottoressa arrogante, perchè hai
letti due libri, e seccata madama in gioventù!
(*Entra* CHERUBINO *dalla finestra.*)

CHERUBINO: Susannetta, sei tu?

SUSANNA: Son io, cosa volete?

CHERUBINO: Ah, cor mio, che accidente!

SUSANNA: Cor vostro? Cosa avvenne?

CHERUBINO: Il Conte ieri, perchè trovommi sol con Barbarina, il congedo mi diede; e se la Constessina, la mia
bella comare, grazia non m'intercede, io vado via, io non
ti vedo più, Susanna mia.

SUSANNA: Non vedete più me? Bravo! Ma dunque non più
per la Contessa secretamente il vostro cor sospira?

CHERUBINO: Ah, che troppo rispetto ella m'ispira! Felice
te, che puoi vederla quando vuoi, che la vesti il mattino,
che la sera la spogli, che le metti gli spilloni—i merletti—
ah! se in tuo loco— Cos'hai lì? Dimmi un poco.

SUSANNA: Ah, il vago nastro e la notturna cuffia di comare
sì bella.

SUSANNA: The respected old lady!

MARCELLINA: The Count's sweetheart!

SUSANNA: The sweetheart of all Spain!

MARCELLINA: Your virtue!

SUSANNA: Your manners!

MARCELLINA: Your position!

SUSANNA: Your age!

MARCELLINA: By God, I'll slap her if I stay here any longer!

SUSANNA: Decrepit old hag! She makes me laugh!

MARCELLINA: I'm your servant.

SUSANNA: I'm not so presumptuous.
(MARCELLINA *exits.*)

Recitative

Go ahead, you pedantic old woman! How can you be so arrogant just because you've read two books and were governess to my lady when she was a child?
(CHERUBINO *enters though a window.*)

CHERUBINO: Susanetta, is it you?

SUSANNA: It's I; what do you want?

CHERUBINO: Ah, my darling, what trouble!

SUSANNA: Your darling? What has happened?

CHERUBINO: Yesterday the Count, because he found me alone with Barbarina, dismissed me from his service; and if the lovely Countess, my beautiful godmother, won't intercede for me, I'll have to go away, and then I won't see you again, my dear Susanna.

SUSANNA: You won't see me again! How lovely! But then it's no longer the Countess for whom you sigh in secret?

CHERUBINO: Ah, she inspires me with too much respect. Oh, lucky you, who can see her when you want to, who dress her each morning, and undress her every evening, who fasten her pins and laces—oh, if only I were in your place — What are you holding? Let me see it!

SUSANNA: Ah, this lovely ribbon belongs to the nightcap of your beautiful godmother.

Le Nozze di Figaro

CHERUBINO: Deh, dammelo, sorella, per pietà.
(*Piglia il nastro.*)

SUSANNA: Presto quel nastro!

CHERUBINO: Oh caro, oh bello, oh fortunato nastro! Io non tel renderò che colla vita.

SUSANNA: Cos'è quest'insolenza?

CHERUBINO: Eh via, sta cheta. In ricompensa, poi, questa mia canzonetta io ti vo' dare.

SUSANNA: E che ne debbo fare?

CHERUBINO: Leggila alla padrona, leggila tu medesima, leggila a Barbarina, a Marcellina. Leggila ad ogni donna del palazzo!

SUSANNA: Povero Cherubin, siete voi pazzo?

6. *Aria*

CHERUBINO: Non so più cosa son, cosa faccio.
Or di foco, ora sono di ghiaccio.
Ogni donna cangiar di colore.
Ogni donna mi fa palpitar.
Solo ai nomi d'amore di diletto,
Mi si turba, mi s'altera il petto,
E a parlare mi sforza d'amore,
Un desio ch'io non posso spiegar.
Parlo d'amor vegliando,
Parlo d'amor sognando,
All'acqua, all'ombra, ai monti,
Ai fiori, all'erbe, ai fonti,
All'eco, all'aria ai venti,
Che il suon d'vani accenti
Portano via con se.
Parlo d'amor—
E se non ho chi m'oda,
Parlo d'amor con me.
(*Una voce di fuori.*)

Recitativo

Ah, son perduto—il Conte!

SUSANNA: Oh, me meschina!

(*Entra* IL CONTE; CHERUBINO *si nasconde in dietro d'una poltrona.*)

IL CONTE: Susanna, come sembri agitata e confusa.

110

CHERUBINO: Please give it to me, dear Susanna, for pity's sake.

(*He snatches the ribbon from her.*)

SUSANNA: Give back that ribbon!

CHERUBINO: Oh, dear, beautiful, fortunate ribbon! I'll give it up only with my life!

SUSANNA: How can you be so horrid?

CHERUBINO: Now, now, be calm; instead I'll give you this little love song of mine.

SUSANNA: And what must I do with it?

CHERUBINO: Read it to my lady, read it to yourself, read it to Barbarina, to Marcellina. Read it to every woman in the castle!

SUSANNA: Poor Cherubino, you're quite insane!

6. Aria

CHERUBINO: I know no longer what I am, or what I'm doing. First I'm like fire, then I'm like ice. Every woman makes me blush and tremble. At the very mention of love I'm troubled and excited, and when I hear of the power of love, I feel a desire I can't explain. Waking and sleeping I speak of love—to water, to shadows, to hills, to flowers, to grass, to fountains, to the echo, to the air, to the winds, so that they may carry away the burden of my vain longings. I speak of love— And if no one will listen, I'll speak of love to myself!

(*He hears a noise.*)

Recitative

Ah, I'm lost! It's the Count!

SUSANNA: Oh, I'm afraid!

(*The* COUNT *comes in;* CHERUBINO *hides behind an armchair.*)

COUNT: Susanna, you seem confused and agitated.

SUSANNA: Signor, io chiedo scusa, ma, se mai qui sorpresa
—per carità, partite!

IL CONTE: Un momento e ti lascio. Odi.

SUSANNA: Non odo nulla.

IL CONTE: Due parole. Tu sai che ambasciatore a Londre
il Re mi dichiarò. Di condur meco Figaro destinai.

SUSANNA: Signor, se osassi—

IL CONTE: Parla, mia cara, e con quel dritto ch'oggi prendi
su me, finchè tu vivi chiedi, imponi, prescrivi.

SUSANNA: Lasciatemi, Signor; dritti non prendo, non ne
vo', non ne intendo. Oh, me infelice!

IL CONTE: Ah, no, Susanna, io ti vo' far felice! Tu ben sai
quant'io t'amo; a te Basilio tutto già disse. Or senti, se per
pochi momenti meco in giardin, sull'imbrunir del giorno—
Ah, per questo favore io pagherei.

DON BASILIO (*fuori*): E uscito poco fa.

IL CONTE: Chi parla?

SUSANNA: O Dei!

IL CONTE: Esci, ed alcun non entri.

SUSANNA: Ch'io vi lasci qui solo?

DON BASILIO (*fuori*): Da madama sarà, vado a cercarlo.

IL CONTE: Qui dietro mi porrò.

SUSANNA: Non vi celate.

IL CONTE: Taci—e cerca ch'ei parta.

SUSANNA: Ohimè! che fate?
(IL CONTE *si nasconde dietro della poltrona; non vede*
CHERUBINO *chi si pose nella poltrona, e* SUSANNA *lo copre
presto con un mantello. Entra* DON BASILIO).

DON BASILIO: Susanna, il ciel vi salvi! Avreste a caso
veduto il Conte?

SUSANNA: E cosa deve far meco il Conte? Animo, uscite.

DON BASILIO: Aspettate, sentite! Figaro di lui cerca.

SUSANNA: My Lord, I ask your pardon, but if we were ever found here—for heaven's sake, please leave me!

COUNT: I'll leave you in a moment. Listen.

SUSANNA: I won't listen.

COUNT: Two words. You know that the King has appointed me as envoy to London, and that I expect to take Figaro with me.

SUSANNA: My Lord, if I dared to tell you—

COUNT: Tell me, tell me, my dear, and with the power you have over me now and as long as you live, ask me, order me, command me!

SUSANNA: Please let me go, my Lord; I don't claim this power, I don't wish it, I don't understand it. Oh, I'm so unhappy!

COUNT: Ah, no, Susanna, I want to make you happy. You know well how much I love you; Basilio has told you everything already. Listen; if for a few moments at twilight you'll join me in the garden—I'll reward you for that favor.

DON BASILIO (*outside*): He left a few minutes ago.

COUNT: Who's there?

SUSANNA: O heavens!

COUNT: Go out and stop him.

SUSANNA: And leave you alone here?

DON BASILIO (*outside*): He must be with the Countess. I'll go look for him there.

COUNT: I'll hide behind this chair.

SUSANNA: Not there!

COUNT: Quiet—and get him out of here!

SUSANNA: Oh, dear— What are you doing?

(*The* COUNT *hides behind the armchair;* CHERUBINO, *unseen by the* COUNT, *jumps into the chair, and* SUSANNA *quickly covers him with a cloak.* DON BASILIO *enters.*)

DON BASILIO: Susanna, heaven save you! Have you by any chance seen the Count?

SUSANNA: And what has the Count to do with me? You're rude; go away!

DON BASILIO: Wait, listen! Figaro is looking for him.

SUSANNA: Oh cielo! Ei cerca chi, dopo voi, più l'odia.

IL CONTE (*a parte*): Vediam come mi serve.

DON BASILIO: Io non ho mai nella moral sentito, ch'uno ch'ami la moglie odii il marito. Per dir che il Conte v'ama—

SUSANNA: Sortite, vil ministro dell'altrui sfrenatezza; io non ho d'uopo della vostra morale, del Conte, del suo amor!

DON BASILIO: Non c'è alcun male. Ha ciascun i suoi gusti. Io me credea che preferir doveste per amante, come fan tutte quantet un signor liberal, prudente e saggio, a un giovinastro, a un paggio.

SUSANNA: A Cherubino?

DON BASILIO: A Cherubino, Cherubin d'amore, ch'oggi sul far del giorno passeggiava qui intorno per entrar.

SUSANNA: Uomo maligno, un impostura è questa!

DON BASILIO: E un maligno con voi chi ha gli occhi in testa? E quella canzonetta, ditemi in confidenza—Io sono amico ed altrui nulla dico—è per voi, o per madama?

SUSANNA (*a parte*): Chi diavol glie l'ha detto?

DON BASILIO: A proposito, figlia, instruitelo meglio. Egli la guarda a tavola sì spesso, e con tanta immodestia—che s'il Conte s'accorge—e su tal punto, sapete egli è un bestia.

SUSANNA: Scellerato! E perchè andate voi tai menzogne spargendo?

DON BASILIO: Io? Che ingiustizia! Quel che compró io vendo, a quel che tutti dicono io non aggiungo un pelo. (IL CONTE *si alza da dietro la poltrona.*)

IL CONTE: Come! Che dicon tutti?

DON BASILIO (*a parte*): Oh bella!

SUSANNA (*a parte*): Oh cielo!

7. Terzetto

IL CONTE: Cosa sento! Tosto andate
E scacciate il seduttor.

DON BASILIO: In mal punto son qui giunto;
Perdonate, o mio signor.

SUSANNA: In that case, he's looking for the one man who hates him more than you do.

COUNT (*aside*): Let's see how he serves me.

DON BASILIO: I've never read in any moral tract that one who loves the wife must hate the husband. In fact, since the Count loves you—

SUSANNA: Get out of here, you horrible panderer! I have no need of your morals, of the Count, or of his love!

DON BASILIO: I meant no harm. Everyone has his own tastes. But I believed you would prefer for a lover, as most women do, a lord who is liberal, prudent, and wise to a little boy, a page.

SUSANNA: To Cherubino?

DON BASILIO: To Cherubino, the cherub of love, who was wandering about outside this room at daybreak, hoping to get in.

SUSANNA: You're a wicked man, and that's a lie!

DON BASILIO: Is everyone with eyes in his head wicked in your opinion? And that love song, tell me in confidence— I'm a friend and won't say anything to anyone— Is it for you or for the Countess?

SUSANNA (*aside*): What devil could have told him?

DON BASILIO: Next time, my dear girl, you might teach him better. At the table he looks at her so often and with such immodesty—if the Count should notice—you know, when jealous, he's like a beast.

SUSANNA: Villain! Why do you go about spreading such lies?

DON BASILIO: I? How unjust! I say what I hear, without adding a word to the common gossip.
(*The* COUNT *rises from behind the armchair.*)

COUNT: What gossip?

DON BASILIO (*aside*): Delightful!

SUSANNA (*aside*): O heavens!

7. *Trio*

COUNT: What are you saying? That seducer Cherubino must be banished at once!

DON BASILIO: I came here at an awkward moment; pardon me, my Lord.

SUSANNA: Che ruina! Me meschina!
Son oppressa dal terror!

IL CONTE: Tosto andate e scacciate il seduttor!

DON BASILIO: In mal punto son qui giunto.

SUSANNA: Che ruina!

DON BASILIO *ed* IL CONTE: Ah! già svien la poverina.
Come, oh Dio, le batte il cor.

DON BASILIO: Pian, pianin, su questo seggio.

SUSANNA: Dove sono? Cosa veggio?
Che insolenza—andate fuor!

DON BASILIO *ed* IL CONTE: Siamo què per aiutar vi (ti),
E sicuro il vostro onor.
Non turbati, o mio tesor.

DON BASILIO: Ah, del paggio quel ch'ho detto
Era solo un mio sospetto.

SUSANNA: E un'insidia, una perfidia,
Non credete all'impostor.

IL CONTE: Parta, parta il damerino.

SUSANNA *e* DON BASILIO: Poverino!

IL CONTE: Poverino! Poverino!
Ma da me sorpreso ancor!

SUSANNA: Come?

DON BASILIO: Che?

SUSANNA: Che?

IL CONTE: Da tua cugina, l'uscio ier trovai
Rinchiuso: picchio, m'apre
Barbarina paurosa fuor dell'uso.
Io, dal muso insospettito,
Guardo, cerco in ogni sito,
Ed alzando piano pianino
Il tappeto al tavolino,
(*Dimostra col mantello sulla poltrona.*)
Vedo il paggio.
Ah, cosa veggio?

SUSANNA: Ah, crude stelle!

DON BASILIO: Ah, meglio ancora!

IL CONTE: Onestissima signora!

SUSANNA: Accader no può di peggio.

IL CONTE: Or capisco come va!

SUSANNA: What a scandal! It's too much for me to bear!

COUNT: He must go at once!

DON BASILIO: I came here at an awkward moment.

SUSANNA: What a scandal!

DON BASILIO *and* COUNT: The poor girl is fainting. O God, how her heart is beating!

DON BASILIO: Let's put her gently in this armchair.

SUSANNA: Where am I? What are you doing? What insolence—go away!

DON BASILIO *and* COUNT: We are here to help you; your honor is safe. Don't worry, my darling.

DON BASILIO: What I told you about the page was only my own suspicion.

SUSANNA: It's a lie; don't believe this impostor!

COUNT: That damned page is going to leave the castle!

SUSANNA *and* DON BASILIO: Poor boy!

COUNT: Poor boy! Poor boy! But this isn't the first time that I've caught him!

SUSANNA: How?

DON BASILIO: What?

SUSANNA: Where?

COUNT: At your cousin's house—yesterday I found the door locked. I knocked and Barbarina opened, but she was very nervous. A suspicion crossed my mind; I looked, searching in every place, and drawing the tablecloth very gently from the table (*demonstrating with the cloak on the chair*) I saw Cherubino. Ah, what do I see?

SUSANNA: Good Lord!

DON BASILIO: Ah, better still!

COUNT: Most honest lady!

SUSANNA: Nothing worse could happen.

COUNT: Now I understand what's going on!

117

DON BASILIO: Così fan tutte
Le belle.

SUSANNA: Giusti Dei—
Che mai sarà?

DON BASILIO: Non c'è alcuna novità!

SUSANNA: Accader non—
Può di peggio—
Ah, no, ah, no!

DON BASILIO: Così fan tutte le belle.
Non c'è alcuna novità.
Ah, del paggio quel ch'ho detto,
Era solo un mio sospetto.

SUSANNA: Accader non può di peggio.

IL CONTE: Onestissima signora—

DON BASILIO: Così fan tutte le belle.

Recitativo

IL CONTE: Basilio, in traccia tosto di Figaro volate; io vo' che veda.

SUSANNA: Ed io che senta; andate.

IL CONTE: Restate. (*a parte a* SUSANNA) Che baldanza! e quale scusa, se la copla è evidente?

SUSANNA: Non ha d'uopo di scusa un'innocente.

IL CONTE: Ma costui quando venne?

SUSANNA: Egli era meco, quando voi qui giungeste, e me chiedâ d'impegnar la padrona a intercedergli grazia. Il vostro arrivo in scompiglio lo pose, ed allor in quel loco si nascose.

IL CONTE: Ma s'io stesso m'assisi, quando in camera entrai!

CHERUBINO: Ed allora di dietro io mi celai.

IL CONTE: E quando io là mi posi?

CHERUBINO: Allor io pian mi volsi e qui m'ascosi.

IL CONTE (*a* SUSANNA): Oh cielo! Dunque ha sentito quello che io ti dicea!

CHERUBINO: Feci per non sentir quanto potea.

IL CONTE: Oh perfidia!

DON BASILIO: Frenatevi—vien gente.

DON BASILIO: That's how all the women do it.

SUSANNA: Good God—how will it ever end?

DON BASILIO: It's nothing new!
SUSANNA: Nothing worse could happen— Ah, no, ah, no!

DON BASILIO: That's how all the women do it. It's nothing new. Ha, what I said about the page was only my own suspicion.

SUSANNA: Nothing worse could happen.
COUNT: Most honest lady—
DON BASILIO: That's how all the women do it.

Recitative

COUNT: Basilio, go and find Figaro at once; I want to see him.

SUSANNA: And *I* want him to hear this; go on!

COUNT: Wait. (*aside to* SUSANNA) What boldness! What excuse can you have when your sin is so evident?

SUSANNA: I am innocent and have no need of an excuse.

COUNT: How long has this boy been here?

SUSANNA: He was with me when you came, and he was asking me to beg Madame to intercede with you for his pardon. Your arrival completely confused him, so he hid himself in that armchair.

COUNT: But I, myself, sat in that chair when I entered the room!

CHERUBINO: And then I hid myself behind it.

COUNT: But when I placed myself there?

CHERUBINO: Then I quietly turned around and hid myself in the chair.

COUNT (*to* SUSANNA): Good God! Then he heard what I said to you!

CHERUBINO: I did whatever I could not to hear.

COUNT: I'm sure you did!

DON BASILIO: Restrain yourself—someone is coming.

119

IL CONTE (*a* CHERUBINO): E voi restate qui, picciol serpente.
(*Entra un* CORO *dei contadini, con* FIGARO, *un velo in mano.*)

8. Coro

CORO: Giovani liete, fiori spargete,
Davanti al nobile nostro Signor,
Il suo gran core vi serba intatto
D'un più bel fiore l'almo candor.

Recitativo

IL CONTE: Cos'è questa commedia?

FIGARO (*a parte a* SUSANNA): Eccoci in danza, secondami, cor mio.

SUSANNA (*a parte a* FIGARO): Non ci ho speranza.

FIGARO: Signor, non disdegnate questo del nostro affetto meritato tributo; or che aboliste un diritto si ingrato a chi ben ama.

IL CONTE: Quel dritto or non v'è più; cosa si brama?

FIGARO: Della vostra saggezza il primo frutto oggi noi coglierem: le nostre nozze si son già stabilite; or a voi tocca costei che un vostro dono illibata serbò, coprir di questa, simbolo d'onestà, candida vesta.

IL CONTE (*a parte*): Diabolica astuzia, ma fingere convien. (*forte*) Son grato, amici, ad un senso si onesto, ma non merto per questo, nè lodi, e un dritto ingiusto ne' miei feudi abolendo a natura, al dover lor dritti io rendo.

TUTTI: Evviva, evviva, evviva!

SUSANNA: Che virtù!

FIGARO: Che giustizia!

IL CONTE: A voi prometto compier la cerimonia, chiedo sol breve indugio; io voglio in faccia de' miei più fidi, e con più ricca pompa rendervi appien felici. (*a parte*) Marcellina si trovi. (*ai contadini*) Andate, amici.

CORO: Giovani liete—
(*Il* CORO *parte.*)

FIGARO: Evviva!

SUSANNA: Evviva!

DON BASILIO: Evviva!

120

COUNT (*to* CHERUBINO): And you stay here, you little serpent!
(CHORUS *of peasants enters, followed by* FIGARO, *who has a veil in his hand.*)

8. Chorus

CHORUS: Happy young people, scatter flowers before our noble Count! His great kindness preserves the purity of a bride for the one she loves.

Recitative

COUNT: What is this comedy?

FIGARO (*aside to* SUSANNA): We're making progress; follow my lead, my dear.

SUSANNA (*aside to* FIGARO): There's no hope.

FIGARO: My Lord, don't spurn this merited tribute of our affection now that you've abolished a custom so repellent to those who really love each other.

COUNT: The custom is abolished. What more do you want?

FIGARO: We would like to reap the first fruit of your generosity: our wedding is already planned; now you must place this symbol of honor on my bride's head; this chaste wedding veil.

COUNT (*aside*): Devilish cunning! but I'll pretend to agree. (*aloud*) I'm grateful, friends, for such a warm reception, but I don't deserve these tributes and praises; it's an unjust custom that I abolished; I yield my right to nature and duty.

ALL: Hurrah, hurrah, hurrah!

SUSANNA: What virtue!

FIGARO: What wisdom!

COUNT: I promise that I'll complete the ceremony. I ask only a little time; I wish to gather my vassals and to unite you with richer pomp and ceremony. (*aside*) Marcellina will be there! (*to the peasants*) Leave me now, my friends.

CHORUS: Happy young people—
(CHORUS *exits.*)

FIGARO: Hurrah!

SUSANNA: Hurrah!

DON BASILIO: Hurrah!

121

Le Nozze di Figaro

FIGARO (*a* CHERUBINO): E voi non applaudite?

SUSANNA: E afflitto, poveretto, perchè il padron lo scaccia dal castello.

FIGARO: Ah, in un giorno sì bello!

SUSANNA: In un giorno di nozze!

FIGARO (*al* CONTE): Quando ognuno v'ammira!

CHERUBINO: Perdono, mio Signor!

IL CONTE: Nol meritate.

SUSANNA: Egli è ancora fanciullo.

IL CONTE: Men di quel che tu credi.

CHERUBINO: E ver, mancai; ma dal mio labbro alfine—

IL CONTE: Ben, bene; io vi perdono; anzi farò di più: vacante è un posto d'uffizial nel reggimento mio; io scelgo voi, partite tosto, addio.

SUSANNA *e* FIGARO: Ah, fin domani sol.

IL CONTE: No, parta tosto.

CHERUBINO: A ubbidirvi, Signor, son già disposto.

IL CONTE: Via, per l'ultima volta la Susanna abbracciate. (*a parte*) Inaspettato è il colpo.
(*Partono* IL CONTE *e* DON BASILIO.)

FIGARO: Ehi, capitano, a me pure la mano. (*a parte a* CHERUBINO) Io vo' parlarti pria che tu parta. (*forte*) Addio piccolo Cherubino! Come cangia in un punto il tuo destino!

9. Aria

Non più andrai, farfallone amoroso,
Notte e giorno d'intorno girando;
Delle belle turbando il riposo,
Narcisetto, Adoncino d'amor!
Non più avrai questi bei pennacchini,
Quel cappello leggero e galante,
Quella chioma, quell'aria brillante,
Quel vermiglio donnesco color!
Fra guerrieri, poffar Bacco!
Gran mustacchi, stretto sacco,
Schioppo in spalla, sciabola al fianco,
Collo dritto, muso franco,
O un gran casco o un gran turbante,
Molto onor, poco contante!
Ed in vece del fandango,

FIGARO (*to* CHERUBINO): Why don't you cheer him?

SUSANNA: He's upset, poor little thing, because the Count has banished him from the castle.

FIGARO: Ah, on such a beautiful day!

SUSANNA: On the day of a wedding!

FIGARO (*to the* COUNT): When everyone will admire you!

CHERUBINO: My Lord, forgive me!

COUNT: You don't deserve it.

SUSANNA: He's only a child.

COUNT: You'd be surprised!

CHERUBINO: Even a child can repeat what he hears—

COUNT: Very well, I forgive you. I'll do even more than that. There's an officer's post vacant in my regiment. I appoint you to it; go at once; good-by!

SUSANNA *and* FIGARO: Let him stay here today!

COUNT: No; he must go at once.

CHERUBINO: I'm ready to obey you immediately, my Lord.

COUNT: Come, for the last time kiss Susanna. (*aside*) My strategy has succeeded.

(*The* COUNT *and* DON BASILIO *exit.*)

FIGARO: Well, Captain, shake my hand. (*aside to* CHERU-BINO) I want to speak to you alone before you go. (*aloud*) Good-by, my little Cherubino. How your destiny has changed in a moment!

9. Aria

No longer, you amorous butterfly, will you enjoy your customary boudoir excursions! No longer will you disturb the sleep of beautiful women, you Narcissus, you Adonis of love! You won't flaunt your beautiful feathers—your light and gallant cap, your curls, your brilliant air, those feminine pink cheeks! You'll live among soldiers, by Jove —with huge mustaches and a narrow bag, a gun on your shoulder and a sword at your side, a stiff neck and a frank expression, a heavy helmet or a large turban, much honor, but little pay! And instead of dancing, you'll be marching

Le Nozze di Figaro

Una marcia per il fango,
Per montagne, per valloni,
Colle nevi e i sollioni,
Al concerto di tromboni,
Di bombarde, di cannoni,
Che le palle in tutti i tuoni,
All'orecchio fan fischiar.
Cherubino all vittoria,
Alla gloria militar!

through the mud—over mountains, through valleys, in the snow and scorching sun, to the sound of trumpets, and bombardments, and cannons, and bullets thundering past your ear! Cherubino, on to glory, on to military fame!

ATTO SECONDO

La stanza della CONTESSA. LA CONTESSA *è sola.*

10. *Aria*

LA CONTESSA: Porgi amor, qualche ristoro,
Al mio duolo, a' miei sospir!
O mi rendi il mio tesoro,
O mi lascia almen morir!

Recitativo

Vieni, cara Susanna finiscimi l'istoria.
(*Entra* SUSANNA.)

SUSANNA: E già finita.

LA CONTESSA: Dunque volla sedurti?

SUSANNA: Oh, il signor Conte non fa tai complimenti colle donne mie pari; egli venne a contratto di danari.

LA CONTESSA: Ah! il crudel più non m'ama.

SUSANNA: E come poi è geloso di voi?

LA CONTESSA: Come lo sono i moderni mariti, per sistema infedeli, per genio capricciosi, e per orgoglio poi tutti gelosi. Ma se Figaro t'ama, ei sol potria.
(*Entra* FIGARO, *cantando.*)

FIGARO: La la la la la la—

SUSANNA: Eccolo. Vieni, amico, madama impaziente.

FIGARO: A voi non tocca stare in pena per questo, alfin di che si tratta? Al signor Conte piace la sposa mia; indi secretamente ricuperar vorria il diritto feudale; possibil è la cosa e naturale.

LA CONTESSA: Possibil?

SUSANNA: Natural?

FIGARO: Naturalissima e, se Susanna vuol, possibilissima.

SUSANNA: Finiscila una volta.

FIGARO: Ho già finito. Quindi prese il partito di sceglier me

126

ACT TWO

The COUNTESS's *boudoir. The* COUNTESS *is alone.*

10. Aria

COUNTESS: Is there no consolation, O God of Love, in return for my sorrows and my sighs? Either restore my dearest one's affection to me, or let me find peace in death!

Recitative

Come, dear Susanna, and finish your story.

(SUSANNA *enters.*)

SUSANNA: It's already finished.

COUNTESS: Then he hopes to seduce you?

SUSANNA: Oh, my lord Count doesn't pay such a compliment to women of the lower classes; he offered me money.

COUNTESS: Then the cruel man doesn't love me any longer!

SUSANNA: In that case, why is he so jealous?

COUNTESS: That's the custom of modern husbands; they're unfaithful by philosophy, capricious by character, and jealous as a matter of pride. But if Figaro loves you, it's possible that he can help us.

(*Enter* FIGARO *singing.*)

FIGARO: La la la la la la—

SUSANNA: Here he is! Come, my dear; the Countess is impatient.

FIGARO: There's no reason to worry about this matter. After all, what is the problem? My fiancée pleases the Count; therefore, he secretly decides to restore his feudal rights— the thing is very possible and very natural.

COUNTESS: Possible?

SUSANNA: Natural?

FIGARO: Very natural. And, if Susanna wishes, very possible.

SUSANNA: That's enough. Let's end this conversation.

FIGARO: I've already finished. That's why the Count

corriero, e la Susanna consigliera secreta d'ambasciata; e perch'ella ostinata ognor rifiuta il diploma d'onor che la destina, minaccia di protegger Marcellina; questo è tutto l'affare.

SUSANNA: Ed hai coraggio di trattar scherzando un negozio sì serio?

FIGARO: Non vi basta, che scherzando io ci pensi? ecco il progetto; per Basilio un biglietto io gli fò capitar, che l'avvertisca di certo appuntamento, che per l'ora del ballo a un amante voi deste.

LA CONTESSA: O ciel! Che sento! Ad un uom sì geloso—

FIGARO: Ancora meglio, così potrem più presto imbarazzarlo, confonderlo, imbrogliarlo, rovesciargli i progetti, empierlo di sospetti, e porgli in testa, che la moderna festa ch'ei di fare a me tenta, altri a lui faccia; onde qui perda il tempo, ivi la traccia, così, quasi ex abrupto, e senza ch'abbia fatto per frastornarci alcun disegno vien l'ora delle nozze, in faccia a lei non fia, ch'osi d'opporsi ai voti miei.

SUSANNA: E ver, ma in di lui vece s'opporrà Marcellina.

FIGARO: Aspetta, al Conte farai subito dir, che verso sera attendati in giardino; il piccol Cherubino, per mio consiglio non ancor partito, da fammina vestito, faremo che in sua vece ivi sen vada; questa è l'unica strada, onde Monsù, sorpreso da Madama sia costretto a far poi quel che si brama.

LA CONTESSA (*a* SUSANNA): Che ti par?

SUSANNA: Non c'è mal.

LA CONTESSA: Nel nostro caso?

SUSANNA: Quand'egli è persuaso—

LA CONTESSA: E dove? E il tempo?

FIGARO: Ito è il Conte alla caccia, e per qualch'ora non sarà di ritorno; io vado, e tosto Cherubino vi mando, lascio a voi la cura di vestirlo.

LA CONTESSA: E poi?

FIGARO: E poi? Se vuol ballare, Signor Contino, il chitarrino Le suonèro, sì. Le suonèro! (*Parte.*)

decided to appoint me as courier, and to consult Susanna as secret ambassadress. And because she has obstinately refused this honor, he threatens to assist Marcellina; that's the whole of the story.

SUSANNA: Have you the courage to joke about such a serious matter?

FIGARO: You should be glad that I can joke about it. Here's my plan! I'll send a note by Basilio to inform the Count of a certain rendezvous that you made this evening with a lover.

COUNTESS: O heavens! What are you saying? With such a jealous husband—

FIGARO: All the better. We'll be able to embarrass him, confound him, confuse him, overturn all his plans, fill him with suspicions, and fix it in his mind that the trick he's trying to play on me may be played on him by others. While he's losing his time and his composure, our wedding hour will come before he can oppose it.

SUSANNA: That's true, but Marcellina will oppose us in his place.

FIGARO: Wait—tell the Count that you'll wait for him in the garden toward evening. Little Cherubino—I told him not to leave yet—dressed in women's clothes, can meet him there instead of you. That's the only way that my lord, surprised by my lady, will be forced to agree to everything that we ask for.

COUNTESS (*to* SUSANNA): What do you think?

SUSANNA: It's not bad.

COUNTESS: In our situation?

SUSANNA: When Figaro's persuaded—

COUNTESS: Where? And at what time?

FIGARO: The Count has gone hunting, and won't return for several hours. I'm going to send Cherubino here at once. I leave to you the task of dressing him.

COUNTESS: And then?

FIGARO: And then? If my friend, the Count, wishes to dance, I'll be the one to play the guitar, yes! I'll be the one to play the guitar! (*Exits.*)

129

LA CONTESSA: Quanto duolmi, Susanna, che questo giovi-
notto abbia del Conte le stravaganze udito! Ah! tu non sai
—ma per qual causa mai da me stessa ei non venne?
Dov'è la canzonetta?

SUSANNA: Eccola, appunto facciam che ce la canti, Zitto;
vien gente—
(*Va alla porta.*)
E desso: avanti, signor ufficiale!
(*Entra* CHERUBINO.)

CHERUBINO: Ah non chiamarmi con nome sì fatale! Ei mi
rammenta che con abbandonar degg'io comare tanto
buona—

SUSANNA: E tanto bella!

CHERUBINO: Ah, sì, certo!

SUSANNA: Ah, sì, certo! Ipocritone, via presto la canzone,
che stamane a me deste, a madama cantate.

LA CONTESSA: Che n'è l'autor?

SUSANNA: Guardate, egli ha due brace di rossor sulla
faccia.

LA CONTESSA: Prendi la mia chitarra e l'accompagna.

CHERUBINO: Io sono sì tremante— Ma se Madama vuole—

SUSANNA: Lo vuole, sì, lo vuol, manco parole.

11. Aria

CHERUBINO: Voi che sapete che cosa è amor,
Donne, vedete s'io l'ho nel cor.
Quello ch'io provo vi ridirò.
E per me nuovo, capir nol so.
Sento un affetto pien di desir,
Ch'ora è diletto, ch'ora è martir.
Gelo, e poi sento l'alma avvampar
E in un momento torno a gelar;
Ricerco un bene fuori di me,
Non so ch'il tiene, non so cos'è,
Sospiro e gemo senza voler,
Palpito e tremo senza saper.
Non trovo pace notte nè dì,
Ma pur mi piace languir così.

130

COUNTESS: It makes me so unhappy, Susanna, that that young boy heard all the Count's indiscretions. Ah, you don't yet understand—but why didn't Cherubino come to me himself, instead of asking you to intercede for him? Where is that song that he gave you?

SUSANNA: Here it is. Now we'll make him sing it to us. Wait! someone's coming—

(*She goes to the door.*)

It's he! Come in, come in, exalted officer!

(CHERUBINO *enters.*)

CHERUBINO: Don't call me that fatal name! It reminds me that I must leave such a kind godmother—

SUSANNA: So kind and so pretty!

CHERUBINO: Oh, yes, lovely!

SUSANNA: Oh, yes, lovely! You flatterer! Now, quickly, sing the song that you gave me this morning for Madame.

COUNTESS: Who is the author?

SUSANNA: Look at him! His cheeks are like two bunches of roses!

COUNTESS: Take my guitar and accompany him.

CHERUBINO: I'm trembling with embarrassment—but if Madame wishes it—

SUSANNA: Of course she does—quickly, now, sing it!

11. Aria

CHERUBINO: Ladies, you who know the nature of love, search for it in my heart! I will tell you about my emotions; since they are new to me, I can't understand them. I feel longing full of desire that first is pleasure and then becomes pain. I freeze, and then I feel my soul aflame, and in the next moment, I turn cold again. I'm drawn by something beyond myself—I don't know how to grasp it; I don't know what it may be. Without wishing to, I sigh and groan; without knowing why, I shake and tremble. I find no rest night or day, but somehow I enjoy suffering like this.

131

Recitativo

LA CONTESSA: Bravo, che bella voce, io non sapea che cantaste sì bene.

SUSANNA: Oh, in verità egli fa tutto ben quello ch'ei fa. Presto a noi, bel soldato; Figaro v'informò—

CHERUBINO: Tutto me disse.

SUSANNA: Lasciatemi veder; andrà benissimo: siam d'uguale statura—giù quel manto.

LA CONTESSA: Che fai?

SUSANNA: Niente paura.

LA CONTESSA: E se qualcuno entrasse?

SUSANNA: Entri, che mal facciamo? La porta chiuderò, ma come poi acconciargli i capelli?

LA CONTESSA: Una mi cuffia prendi mel gabinetto, presto! (SUSANNA *parte.*)
Che carta è quella?

CHERUBINO: La patente.

LA CONTESSA: Che sollecita gente!

CHERUBINO: L'ebbi or da Basilio.

LA CONTESSA: Della fretta obliato hanno il sigillo! (SUSANNA *ritorna.*)

SUSANNA: Il sigillo di che?

LA CONTESSA: Della patente.

SUSANNA: Cospetto! Che premura! Ecco la cuffia.

LA CONTESSA: Spicciati; va bene; miserabili noi se il Conte viene!

12. Aria

SUSANNA: Venite inginocchiatvei,
Restate fermo lì.
Pian piano o via giratevi.
Bravo! va ben così.
La faccia ora volgetemi.
Olà, quegli occhi a me.
Drittìssimo guardatemi,
Madama qui non è!
La faccia ora volgetemi—
Restate fermo lì,

Recitative

COUNTESS: Bravo! What a beautiful voice! I didn't know that you sang so well.

SUSANNA: Oh, really he does everything well when he tries. Quickly, come here, handsome soldier. Figaro has told you—

CHERUBINO: Everything!

SUSANNA: Let me see. It will do nicely; we're just the same size— Take your cloak off.

COUNTESS: What are you doing?

SUSANNA: Nothing to fear.

COUNTESS: And if anyone should come in?

SUSANNA: Let him come in; what harm are we doing? I'll lock the door. But how shall we cover his hair?

COUNTESS: Take one of my bonnets out of my closet— quickly!

(SUSANNA *goes out.*)
What paper is this?

CHERUBINO: My commission.

COUNTESS: They certainly hurried the matter.

CHERUBINO: I got it just now from Basilio.

COUNTESS: In their haste they've forgotten the seal.
(SUSANNA *comes back.*)

SUSANNA: The seal on what?

COUNTESS: On the commission.

SUSANNA: Good heavens! How stupid! Here is the bonnet.

COUNTESS: Put it on—that's nice. How dreadful it would be if the Count returned now!

12. Aria

SUSANNA: Come, get down on your knees. Stay there without moving—stay there! Now you may turn yourself, slowly. Bravo! that's very good! Now turn your face in my direction. Heavens, what eyes you're making at me! Straight, now—look at me, the Countess isn't there! Now turn your face—stay there without moving; now you may turn; look at me, bravo! This collar should be higher; the eyes a bit lowered, the hands folded on your breast. Let's see how he walks, when he gets up— Look at the little rascal! How pretty he is! What a roguish glance! What

Le Nozze di Figaro

Or via giratevi,
Guardatemi, bravo!
Più alto quel colletto.
Quel ciglio un po' più basso,
Le mani sotto il petto,
Vedremo poscia il passo,
Quando sarete in piè.
Mirate il bricconcello,
Mirate quanto è bello,
Che furba guardatura,
Che vezzo, che figura.
Se l'amano le femmine,
Hanno certo il lor perchè!

Recitativo

LA CONTESSA: Quante buffonerie!

SUSANNA: Ma se ne sono io medesma gelosa! Ehi serpentello volete tralasciar d'esser sì bello?

LA CONTESSA: Finiam le ragazzate, or quelle maniche oltre il gomito gli alza, onde più agiatamente l'abito gli si adatti.

SUSANNA: Ecco.

LA CONTESSA: Più indietro, così. Che nastro è quello?

SUSANNA: E quel ch'esso involommi.

LA CONTESSA: E questo sangue?

CHERUBINO: Quel sanguel io non so come, poco pria sdrucciolanda in un sasso, la pelle io mi sgraffiai e la piaga col nastro io mi fasciai.

SUSANNA: Mostrate—non è mal; cospetto! Ha il braccio più candido del mio! Qualche ragazza—

LA CONTESSA: E segui a far la pazza? Va nel mio gabinetto e prendi un poco d'inglese taffetà ch'è sullo scrigno.
(SUSANNA *parte.*)
In quanto al nastro in ver per il colore ma spiace di privarmene.
(SUSANNA *ritorna.*)

SUSANNA: Tenete, e da legargli il braccio?

LA CONTESSA: Un altro nastro prendi insiem col nio vestito.
(SUSANNA *parte.*)

CHERUBINO: Ah, più presto m'avria quello guarito!

charm, and what a figure! If women love him, they certainly have their reasons!

Recitative

COUNTESS: What ridiculous nonsense!

SUSANNA: But I'm jealous of him myself! Oh, you little serpent, why are you so beautiful?

COUNTESS: That's enough of this childishness! Now roll up his sleeves above his elbow, then his dress will fit him better.

SUSANNA: Like this?

COUNTESS: Further; this way. What is this ribbon?

SUSANNA: It's the one that he snatched from me.

COUNTESS: And this blood?

CHERUBINO: This blood—I don't know; just before, I fell and scratched myself, and I bound the wound with this ribbon.

SUSANNA: Show me—it's not bad. Good heavens, his arm is whiter than my own—just like a girl's!

COUNTESS: Stop wasting time. Go into my closet and find some plaster that's on the dresser.

(SUSANNA *goes out.*)

As for the ribbon, really, I wouldn't like to lose it—the color is very pretty.

(SUSANNA *returns.*)

SUSANNA: Take this; it's for his arm.

COUNTESS: We need another ribbon; bring it with the dress.

(SUSANNA *goes out.*)

CHERUBINO: Ah, the first one would have cured me much more quickly!

135

LA CONTESSA: Perchè? Questo è migliore.

CHERUBINO: Allor che un nastro legò la chimoa ovver toccò la pelle d'oggetto—

LA CONTESSA: Forestiero, è buon per le ferite, non è vero? Guardate qualità ch'io non sapea!

CHERUBINO: Madama scherza, ed io frattanto parto.

LA CONTESSA: Poverin! Che sventura!

CHERUBINO: Oh me infelice!

LA CONTESSA: Or piange.

CHERUBINO: O ciel! perchè morir non lice! Forse vicino all'ultimo momento, questa bocca oseria—

LA CONTESSA: Siate saggio, cos'è questa follia?
(*Si picchia alla porta.*)
Che picchia alla mia porta?

IL CONTE (*di fuori*): Perchè chiusa?

LA CONTESSA: Il mio sposo! oh Dei! son morta. Voi qui, senza mantello, in questo stato. Un ricevuto foglio, la sua gran gelosia!

IL CONTE (*di fuori*): Cosa indugiate?

LA CONTESSA: Son sola, ah sì, son sola!

IL CONTE (*di fuori*): E a chi parlate?

LA CONTESSA: A voi, certo, a voi stesso.

CHERUBINO: Dopo quel ch'è successo—il suo furore—non trovo altro consiglio.
(CHERUBINO *corre nel gabinetto e serra la porta.*)

LA CONTESSA: Ah, mi difenda il cielo in tal periglio!
(*Apre la porta della sua stanza. Entra* IL CONTE.)

IL CONTE: Che novità! Non fu mai vostra usanza di rinchiudervi in stanza.

LA CONTESSA: E ver, ma io—io stava qui mettendo—

IL CONTE: Via mettendo—

LA CONTESSA: Certe robe, era meco la Susanna, che in sua camera è andata.

IL CONTE: Ad ogni modo voi non siete tranquilla. Guardate questo foglio!

LA CONTESSA (*a parte*): Numi! E il foglio Figaro gli scrisse.
(*V'è uno strepito nel gabinetto.*)

COUNTESS: Why? This one is wider.

CHERUBINO: But if a ribbon has bound the hair or touched the skin of someone—

COUNTESS: With whom you're casually acquainted, it's good for wounds, isn't that true? It must have qualities that I didn't know of!

CHERUBINO: Madame is joking, and yet I must go away!

COUNTESS: Poor boy! What misfortune!

CHERUBINO: Oh, I'm unhappy!

COUNTESS: You're crying!

CHERUBINO: O God! Why don't you allow me to die? Perhaps at my last gasp, my lips would dare to tell you—

COUNTESS: Get up—this is ridiculous!

(*There is a knocking at the door.*)

Who's knocking at my door?

COUNT (*outside*): Why are you locked in?

COUNTESS: My husband! O God—I'm dying! You're here, without your cloak, in this condition. That letter he received—his dreadful jealousy!

COUNT (*outside*): What are you doing?

COUNTESS: I'm alone here—oh, yes, I'm alone!

COUNT (*outside*): And to whom were you speaking?

COUNTESS: To you; certainly, to you.

CHERUBINO: After all that has happened; his anger— I can't think what to do!

(CHERUBINO *runs into a closet and locks the door.*)

COUNTESS: May heaven defend me in this peril!

(*She unlocks outer door. The* COUNT *enters.*)

COUNT: What a novelty! It was never your custom to lock yourself into your room!

COUNTESS: That's true, but I—I was here arranging—

COUNT: Arranging? Go on!

COUNTESS: Some dresses; Susanna was with me, but she has gone into her room.

COUNT: At any rate, you're upset. Look at this letter.

COUNTESS (*aside*): Heavens! It's the note that Figaro wrote to him.

(*There is a noise in the closet.*)

Le Nozze di Figaro

IL CONTE: Cos'è codesto strepito? In gabinetto qualche cosa è caduta!

LA CONTESSA: Io non intesi niente.

IL CONTE: Convien che abbiate i gran pensieri in mente.

LA CONTESSA: Di che?

IL CONTE: Là v'è qualcuno.

LA CONTESSA: Chi volete che sia?

IL CONTE: Lo chiedo a voi, io vengo in questo punto.

LA CONTESSA: Ah, sì, Susanna appunto—

IL CONTE: Che passò mi diceste alla sua stanza.

LA CONTESSA: Alla sua stanza, o quì, no vidi bene.

IL CONTE: Susanna, e donde viene che siete sì turbata?

LA CONTESSA: Per la mia cameriera?

IL CONTE: Io non so nulla, ma turbata senz'altro.

LA CONTESSA: Ah quella serva più che non turba me, turba voi stesso.

IL CONTE: E vero, è vero! e lo vedrete adesso.

(SUSANNA *entra, inosservata, dalla sua stanza, e si nasconde dietro un paravento.*)

13. Terzetto

Susanna, or via sortite,
Sortite, così vo'!

LA CONTESSA: Fermatevi!

SUSANNA (*a parte*): Cos'è, codesta lite?

LA CONTESSA: Sentite!
Sortire ella non può.

SUSANNA (*a parte*): Il paggio dove andò?

IL CONTE: E chi vietarlo or osa? chi?

LA CONTESSA: Lo vieta l'onestà.
Un abito da sposa provando ella si sta.

IL CONTE: Chiarissima è la cosa—

LA CONTESSA: Brutissima è la cosa—

IL CONTE: L'amante qui sarà—

SUSANNA (*a parte*): Capisco qualche cosa,
Veggiamo come va.

LA CONTESSA: Brutissima è la cosa,
Chi sa cosa sarà.

138

COUNT: What's that noise? Something fell down in your closet!

COUNTESS: I didn't hear anything.

COUNT: In that case, you must be thinking great thoughts!

COUNTESS: Of what?

COUNT: There's someone there.

COUNTESS: Who could it possibly be?

COUNT: I'm asking you that; *I've* just come in.

COUNTESS: Oh, yes—Susanna, of course—

COUNT: But you said that she went into her room.

COUNTESS: To her room or to that one; I didn't watch her.

COUNT: If it was Susanna, why are you so nervous?

COUNTESS: On my maid's account?

COUNT: I know nothing about that, but you're definitely upset.

COUNTESS: You're far more upset by that girl than I am.

COUNT: That's true, that's true, and I'll prove it immediately!

(SUSANNA *comes in, unobserved, from another room, and hides behind a screen.*)

13. Trio

Susanna, come out at once! Come out—I order you to!

COUNTESS: Stay in there!

SUSANNA (*aside*): What is this quarrel about?

COUNTESS: Listen! She isn't able to come out.

SUSANNA (*aside*): Where has Cherubino gone?

COUNT: And who is forbidding her to come out? Who?

COUNTESS: Her modesty forbids her. She is trying on her wedding dress.

COUNT: The matter is most clear—

COUNTESS: The matter is very sordid—

COUNT: Her lover must be there—

SUSANNA (*aside*): I'm beginning to understand. Let's see what will happen.

COUNTESS: The matter is very sordid. Who knows what may happen!

139

IL CONTE: Chiarissima è la cosa,
L'amante qui sara.
Dunque parlate almeno,
Susanna, se qui siete.

LA CONTESSA: Nemmen, nemmen, nemmeno, io v'ordino
Tacete, tacete, tacete!

IL CONTE: Consorte mia—
Guidizio!

SUSANNA: O cielo!
Un precipizio!
Un scandalo, un disordine,
Qui certo nascerà!

LA CONTESSA: Consorte mio, guidizio!

LA CONTESSA *ed* IL CONTE: Un scandalo, un disordine,
Schiviam per carità!

Recitativo

IL CONTE: Dunque voi non aprite?

LA CONTESSA: E perchè deggio le mie camere aprir?

IL CONTE: Ebben lasciate, l'aprirem senza chiave. Ehi, gente!

LA CONTESSA: Come? Porreste a repentaglio d'una dama l'onore?

IL CONTE: E vero, io sbaglio, posso senza rumore, senza scandalo alcun di nostra gente, andar io stesso prender l'occorrente. Attendete pur qui—ma perchè in tutto sia il mio dubbio distrutto, anco le porte io prima chiuderò.

LA CONTESSA: Che imprudenza!

IL CONTE: Voi la condiscendanza di venir meco avrete;
Madama, eccovi il braccio, andiamo!

LA CONTESSA: Andiamo!

IL CONTE: Susanna starà qui finchè torniamo.
(*Partono* IL CONTE *e* LA CONTESSA. SUSANNA *corre al gabinetto.*)

14. Duetto

SUSANNA: Aprite, presto aprite, è là Susanna!
Sortite, andate via di quà!

CHERUBINO: Ohimè, che scena orribile!
Che gran fatalità!

COUNT: The matter is most clear. Her lover must be there. Then, at least speak, Susanna, if you are there.

COUNTESS: No, no! I command you to be silent!

COUNT: My lady—I warn you!

SUSANNA: O heavens! What danger! A scandal, a disaster, will certainly occur!

COUNTESS: My Lord, I warn you!

COUNTESS *and* COUNT: For pity's sake, let's avoid a scandal!

Recitative

COUNT: Then you won't open the closet?

COUNTESS: And why should I?

COUNT: Well then, don't; I'll open it without keys. Servants!

COUNTESS: What? Can you rob a lady of her honor?

COUNT: That's true; I was mistaken. I can do it without noise or scandal, without disturbing any of the servants. I'll go myself to get what I need. You'll wait for me here —but, to dispel all my doubt, first I'll lock the closet door, and the door of this room.

COUNTESS: How unreasonable!

COUNT: You'll have the kindness to accompany me; Madame, here is my arm; let's go.

COUNTESS: Very well, then.

COUNT: Susanna will stay here until we return.

(COUNT *and* COUNTESS *exit.* SUSANNA *runs to the closet.*)

14. Duet

SUSANNA: Open the door quickly! It's Susanna. Come out, you must escape from this room!

CHERUBINO: Oh, what a horrible scene! What a dreadful fate!

141

SUSANNA: Di qua—di là—
Le porte son serrate—

SUSANNA e CHERUBINO: Le porte son serrate,
Che mai sarà?

CHERUBINO: Qui perdersi non giova.

SUSANNA: V'uccide, se vi trova.

CHERUBINO: Veggiamo un po' qui fuori:
Dà proprio nel giardino.

SUSANNA: Fermate Cherubino, fermate, per pietà!

CHERUBINO: Qui perdersi non giova.

SUSANNA: Fermate, Cherubino!

CHERUBINO: M'uccide, se mi trova.

SUSANNA: Tropp'alto per un salto.

CHERUBINO: Lasciami—

SUSANNA: Fermate, per pietà!

CHERUBINO: Lasciami!
Pria di nuocerle nel foco volerei.
Abbraccio te per lei. Addio!
(*Abbraccia* SUSANNA.)
Così si fa!
(*Salta dalla finestra.*)

SUSANNA: Ei va a perire, O Dei! Fermate, per pietà!
Fermate, fermate!
(*Corre alla finestra, e guarda* CHERUBINO.)

Recitativo

Oh, guarda il demonietto fugge! (*ridendo*) E
già un miglio lontano; ma non perdiamci
invano; entriam nel gabinetto; vanga poi
lo smargiasso, io qui l'aspetto!
(*Va nel gabinetto, e chinde la porta. Entrano* IL CONTE *e*
LA CONTESSA.)

IL CONTE: Tutto è come io lasciai; volete dunque aprir voi
stessa, o deggio?

LA CONTESSA: Ahimè, fermate, e ascoltatemi un poco. Mi
credete capace di mancar al dover?

IL CONTE: Come vi piace, entro quel gabinetto che v'è
chiuso vedrò!

LA CONTESSA: Sì, lo vedrete, ma uditemi tranquillo.

IL CONTE: Non è dunque Susanna?

SUSANNA: You must get out! The doors are all locked—

SUSANNA *and* CHERUBINO: The doors are all locked. What shall we do?

CHERUBINO: I'm lost if I stay here.

SUSANNA: He'll kill you if he finds you!

CHERUBINO: Perhaps I can use the window; it opens on the garden.

SUSANNA: Stop it, Cherubino, stop, for heaven's sake!

CHERUBINO: I'm lost if I stay here.

SUSANNA: Stop it, Cherubino!

CHERUBINO: He'll kill me if he finds me here.

SUSANNA: It's too high for you to jump.

CHERUBINO: Let me go—

SUSANNA: Stop, for heaven's sake!

CHERUBINO: Let me go! Rather than hurt her, I would leap through fire—I embrace you for her sake. Farewell!
(*He kisses* SUSANNA.)
Here I go!
(*He jumps out of the window.*)

SUSANNA: He'll be killed. O God! Stop, for heaven's sake! Stop, stop!
(*She rushes to the window and looks out after* CHERUBINO.)

Recitative

Oh, look at that little demon—how he's running! (*laughing*) He's already a mile away! But I must hurry; I'll take his place in the closet. When that bully, the Count, comes back here, I'll be waiting for him!
(*She goes into the closet, closing the door. The* COUNT *and* COUNTESS *enter.*)

COUNT: Everything's as I left it. Would you like to open the door, or must I?

COUNTESS: Oh, no, wait a moment, and listen to me. Do you think I would betray you?

COUNT: That's the point in question. I'm going to the closet, to find out who is locked in there!

COUNTESS: Yes, you will find him, but listen to me calmly.

COUNT: Then it isn't Susanna?

143

LA CONTESSA: No, ma invece è un oggetto, che ragion di sospetto non vi deve lasciar: per questa sera una burla innocente di farsi disponeva, ed io vi giuro che l'onor, l'onestà—

IL CONTE: Chi è dunque? Dite—l'ucciderò!

LA CONTESSA: Sentite—(*a parte*) Ah, non ho cor!

IL CONTE: Parlate.

LA CONTESSA: E un fanciullo.

IL CONTE: Un fanciul?

LA CONTESSA: Sì, Cherubino.

IL CONTE: E mi farà il destino ritrovar questo paggio in ogni loci! Come— Non è partito? Scellerati: ecco i dubbi spiegati, ecco l'imbroglio, ecco il raggiro onde m'avvertì il foglio!

15. Finale

Esci ormai, garzon malnato!
Sciagurato, non tardar!

LA CONTESSA: Ah! signore, quel furore
Per lui fammi il cor tremar!

IL CONTE: E d'opporvi ancor osate?

LA CONTESSA: No, sentite.

IL CONTE: Via, parlate.

LA CONTESSA: Giuro al ciel ch'ogni sospetto
E lo stato in che il trovate,
Sciolto il collo, nudo il petto—

IL CONTE: Sciolto il collo! nudo il petto!
Sequitate!

LA CONTESSA: Per vestir femminee spoglie—

IL CONTE: Ah, comprendo, indegna moglie,
Mi vo' tosto vendicar!

LA CONTESSA: Mi fa torto quel trasporto!
M'oltraggiate a dubitar!

IL CONTE: Qua la chiave!

LA CONTESSA: Egli è innocente!
Voi sapete.

IL CONTE: Non so niente!
Va lontan dagli occhi miei.
Un'infida, un'empia sei,
E mi cerchi d'infamar.

COUNTESS: No; but it's someone who couldn't give you reason for suspicion. We had planned an innocent joke for this evening—that's why he was here. And I swear to you that my honor—

COUNT: Who is in there? Tell me—I'll kill him!

COUNTESS: Listen—(*aside*) Ah, I haven't the courage!

COUNT: Speak.

COUNTESS: It's a young boy.

COUNT: A young boy?

COUNTESS: Yes, Cherubino.

COUNT: Is it my destiny to find that page wherever I go? What—he hasn't left for Seville yet? Rascals! Now my doubts are confirmed—that's the trick of which the letter warned me!

15. Finale

Come out here at once, you damned page!

COUNTESS: Ah, my Lord, what fury! You make me tremble for his safety!

COUNT: And you still dare to defy me?

COUNTESS: No—listen to me!

COUNT: Well, speak quickly.

COUNTESS: I swear to heaven that your suspicions are false and that the state you'll find him in—collar undone, chest naked—

COUNT: Collar undone! Chest naked! As I expected!

COUNTESS: He's dressed in women's clothes—

COUNT: Ah, I understand now, unworthy wife; I'll avenge myself at once!

COUNTESS: Your anger wrongs me! Your doubts are outrageous!

COUNT: Give me the key!

COUNTESS: He's innocent and you know it!

COUNT: I know nothing of the sort! Get out of my sight! You're unfaithful and evil, and you've conspired to disgrace me!

LA CONTESSA: Vado, sì, ma—

IL CONTE: Non ascolto.

LA CONTESSA: Ma—

IL CONTE: Non ascolto.

LA CONTESSA: Non son rea!

IL CONTE: Vel leggo in volto!
Mora, mora!

LA CONTESSA: Ah! la cieca gelosia.
Qualche eccesso gli fa far.

IL CONTE: Mora, mora e più non sia
Ria cogion del mio pemar!
(*Spada in mano,* IL CONTE *apre la porta, e trova* SUSANNA.)
Susanna!

LA CONTESSA: Susanna!

SUSANNA: Signore!
Cos'è quel stupore?
Il brando prendete,
Il paggio uccidete,
Quel paggio malnato,
Vedetelo quà.

IL CONTE (*a parte*): Che scola!

LA CONTESSA (*a parte*): Che storia è mai questa?

IL CONTE: La testa girando mi va.

SUSANNA (*a parte*): Confusa han la testa, non san come va.

LA CONTESSA: Susanna v'è là—

IL CONTE: Sei sola?

SUSANNA: Guardate! quì ascoso sarà.

IL CONTE: Guardate!

SUSANNA ed IL CONTE: Guardiano! quì ascoso sarà.
(IL CONTE *va nel gabinetto, e poi ritorna.*)

LA CONTESSA (*a parte a* SUSANNA): Susanna, son morta,
Il fiato mi manca.

SUSANNA (*a parte alla* CONTESSA): Più lieta, più franca,
Il salvo è di già.

COUNTESS: Yes, I'll go, but—

COUNT: I won't listen!

COUNTESS: But—

COUNT: I won't listen!

COUNTESS: I'm not guilty!

COUNT: I can read guilt in your face! I'll kill him, and then I'll be avenged.

COUNTESS: Ah! His jealousy is blind. It makes him go too far.

COUNT: I'll kill him, and then I'll be avenged on the deceitful cause of my suffering!
(*He draws his sword, opens the door—and finds* SUSANNA.)
Susanna!

COUNTESS: Susanna!

SUSANNA: My Lord! Why do you look so amazed? Are you brandishing your sword to kill that disobedient page? In that event, you see him right here!

COUNT (*aside*): What a shock!

COUNTESS (*aside*): How could this happen?

COUNT: My head is whirling.

SUSANNA (*aside*): They're both so confused they don't know what has happened.

COUNTESS: Susanna was there—

COUNT: You were alone there?

SUSANNA: You might look! Someone may still be hidden.

COUNT: I'll look.

SUSANNA *and* COUNT: Let's look. Someone might still be there.
(*The* COUNT *goes to the closet and then returns.*)

COUNTESS (*aside to* SUSANNA): Susanna, I'm dying; my breath is failing me.

SUSANNA (*aside to* COUNTESS): Be happy; be cheerful. He's safe by now.

IL CONTE: Che sbaglio mai presi.
Appena lo credo.
Se a torto v'offesi,
Perdono vi chiedo,
Ma far burla simile
E poi crudeltà.

SUSANNA e LA CONTESSA: Le vostre follie
Non mertan pietà.

IL CONTE (*alla* CONTESSA): Io v'amo!

LA CONTESSA: Nol dite!

IL CONTE: Vel giuro!

LA CONTESSA: Mentite!
Son l'empia, l'infida,
Che ognora v'inganna.

IL CONTE: Quell'ira, Susanna,
M'aita a calmar.

SUSANNA: Così si condanna
Chi può sospettar.

LA CONTESSA: Adunque la fede
D'un anima amante
Sì fiera mercede
Doveve sperar?

IL CONTE: Quell'ira, Susanna—

SUSANNA: Così si condanna,
Chi può sospettar. (*alla* CONTESSA)
Signora!

IL CONTE: Rosina!

LA CONTESSA: Crudele!
Più quella non sono.
Ma il misero oggetto
Del vostro abbandono
Che avete diletto
Di far disperar.

IL CONTE: Confuso, pentito,
E troppo punito.

SUSANNA: Confuso, pentito,
Son troppo punito.

LA CONTESSA: Crudele! crudele! soffrir sì gran torto.
Quest'alma non sa.

IL CONTE: Abbiate pietà, abbiate pietà!

SUSANNA: Abbiate pietà, abbiate pietà!

COUNT: What a mistake! I still don't believe it. If I wrongly offended you, I ask your pardon. But you'll admit that it's very cruel to joke in that way!

SUSANNA *and* COUNTESS: Your arrogance doesn't deserve pity.

COUNT (*to* COUNTESS): I love you!

COUNTESS: Don't speak of it!

COUNT: I swear it!

COUNTESS: You're lying! I'm evil and unfaithful, and always deceiving you!

COUNT: Susanna, help me to calm her anger!

SUSANNA: How a jealous man condemns himself!

COUNTESS: I see that my fidelity has been fittingly rewarded.

COUNT: Susanna, help me—

SUSANNA: How a jealous man condemns himself! (*to* COUNTESS) My Lady!

COUNT: Rosina!

COUNTESS: Cruel man! I'm not Rosina any more, but the miserable, abandoned object of your scorn.

COUNT: I'm confused and repentant; I've been punished already.

SUSANNA: He's confused and repentant; he's been punished already.

COUNTESS: Cruel man; my heart cannot endure such great wrongs!

COUNT: Have mercy on me!

SUSANNA: Have mercy on him!

149

Le Nozze di Figaro

IL CONTE: Ma il paggio rinchiuso?

LA CONTESSA: Fu sol per provarvi.

IL CONTE: Ma i tremiti, i palpiti?

LA CONTESSA: Fu sol per burlarvi.

IL CONTE: Ma un foglio sì barbaro?

SUSANNA e LA CONTESSA: Di Figaro è il foglio,
E a voi per Basilio.

IL CONTE: Ah, perfidì! Io voglio—

SUSANNA e LA CONTESSA: Perdono non merta
Chi agli altri nol dà.

IL CONTE: Ebben se vi piace,
Comune è la pace.
Rosina inflessibile
Con me non sarà.

LA CONTESSA: Ah, quanto Susanna,
Son dolce di core!
Di donne al furore
Chi può crederà?

SUSANNA: Cogli uomin, signora,
Girate, volgete,
Vedrete che ognora
Si cade poi là.

IL CONTE (*alla* CONTESSA): Guardatemi!

LA CONTESSA: Ingrato!

IL CONTE: Guardatemi, ho torto,
E mi pento.

SUSANNA: Da questo momento,
Quest'alma a conoscer la
A apprender potrà.

LA CONTESSA: Da questo momento,
Quest'alma a conoscer mi
A apprender potrà.

IL CONTE: Da questo momento,
Quest'alma a conoscer vi
A apprender potrà.

(*Entra* FIGARO.)

FIGARO: Signore, di fuori,
Son già i suonatori.
Le trombe sentite,
I pifferi udite;
Tra canti, tra balli

150

COUNT: But the page was locked in?

COUNTESS: It was only to test you.

COUNT: But your trembling, your nervousness?

COUNTESS: It was only to tease you.

COUNT: And that barbarous letter?

SUSANNA *and* COUNTESS: Figaro wrote it and sent it to you through Basilio.

COUNT: Ah, traitors! I'll—I'll—

SUSANNA *and* COUNTESS: You'll never be forgiven if you cannot forgive!

COUNT: Well then, if you're satisfied, we are all at peace; Rosina would never be adamant with me.

COUNTESS: Ah! How tender my heart must be, Susanna! After this, who will ever believe in women's anger?

SUSANNA: With men, my Lady, you may maneuver as much as you please, but you'll never get the better of them.

COUNT (*to* COUNTESS): Look at me!

COUNTESS: You're ungrateful!

COUNT: Look at me; I was wrong, and now I'm sorry.

SUSANNA: From this moment, perhaps he'll value his wife at her true worth.

COUNTESS: From this moment, perhaps he'll value me at my true worth.

COUNT: From this moment, perhaps I'll value my wife at her true worth.

(FIGARO *enters.*)

FIGARO: My Lord, the musicians are already outside. Hear the trumpets! Listen to the flutes! With all your servants dancing and singing, let's hurry to celebrate our wedding.

De' vostri vassalli,
Corriamo, voliamo le nozze a compir.

IL CONTE: Pian, piano, men fretta!

FIGARO: La turba m'aspetta!

IL CONTE: Pian, piano, men tretta,
Un dubbio toglietemi
In pria di partir.

SUSANNA, LA CONTESSA, FIGARO: La cosa è scabrosa—
Com'han da finir?

IL CONTE: Con arte le carte convien scopir.
Conoscete, Signor Figaro,
Questo foglio chi vergò?

FIGARO: Nol conosco.

SUSANNA: Nol conosci?

FIGARO: No!

LA CONTESSA: Nol conosci?

FIGARO: No!

IL CONTE: Nol conosci?

FIGARO: No!

SUSANNA, LA CONTESSA, IL CONTE: Nol conosci?

FIGARO: No! No! No!

SUSANNA: E nol desti a Don Basilio?

LA CONTESSA: Per recarlo—

IL CONTE: Tu c'intendi?

FIGARO: Oibò, oibò!

SUSANNA: E non sai del damerino—

LA CONTESSA: Che stasera nel giardino—

IL CONTE: Già capisci?

FIGARO: Io no lo so.

IL CONTE: Cerchi invan difesa e scusa,
Il tuo ceffo già t'accusa,
Vedo ben che vuoi mentir.

FIGARO: Mente il ceffo, io già non mento.

SUSANNA e LA CONTESSA: Il talento aguzzi invano.
Palesato abbiam l'arcano—
Non v'e nulla da ridir.

IL CONTE: Che rispondi?

FIGARO: Niente, niente!

COUNT: One moment; there's no hurry!

FIGARO: The people are waiting!

COUNT: There's no hurry; just resolve one of my doubts before we go.

SUSANNA, COUNTESS, FIGARO: The matter is very delicate— How will it end?

COUNT: Now is the time to present those papers. Do you know, Mr. Figaro, where this letter came from?

FIGARO: I know nothing about it.

SUSANNA: You don't know it?

FIGARO: No!

COUNTESS: You don't know it?

FIGARO: No!

COUNT: You don't know it?

FIGARO: No!

SUSANNA, COUNTESS, COUNT: You don't know it?

FIGARO: No! No! No!

SUSANNA: Wasn't it for Don Basilio?

COUNTESS: To give him—

COUNT: Now do you understand?

FIGARO: No. Not at all!

SUSANNA: And you don't know about the little rascal—

COUNTESS: Who this evening, in the garden—

COUNT: Now you remember?

FIGARO: Not a word.

COUNT: You're trying in vain to defend and excuse yourself; your face already accuses you, and I can easily tell that you are lying.

FIGARO: My face may lie, then, but I don't know.

SUSANNA *and* COUNTESS: Your elusiveness is in vain. We've told all the secrets—there's nothing left to joke about.

COUNT: What is your answer?

FIGARO: Nothing, nothing!

IL CONTE: Dunque accordi?

FIGARO: Non accordo!

SUSANNA: Eh, via, chetati, balordo—

SUSANNA e LA CONTESSA: Eh, via, chetati, balordo,
La burletta ha da finir.

FIGARO: Per finirla lietamente
E all'usanza teatrale,
Un'azion matrimoniale
Le faremo ora seguir.

SUSANNA, LA CONTESSA, FIGARO: Deh signor, nol contrastate,
Consolate i miei (lor) desir.

SUSANNA e LA CONTESSA: Deh signor, nol contrastate—

IL CONTE (*a parte*): Marcellina!
Marcellina! Quante tardi a comparir!
(ANTONIO, *ubriaco, entra; porta dei garofani.*)

ANTONIO: Ah, Signor! Signor!

IL CONTE: Cosa è stato?

ANTONIO: Che insolenza!
Ch'il fece? Chi fu?

SUSANNA, LA CONTESSA, IL CONTE, FIGARO: Cosa dici?
Cos'hai, cosa è nato?

ANTONIO: Ascoltate!

SUSANNA, LA CONTESSA, IL CONTE, FIGARO: Via parla di sù!

ANTONIO: Dal balcone che guarda in giardino,
Mille cose ogni di gittar veggio,
E poc'anzi può darsi di peggio,
Vidi un uom, signor mio, gittar giù.

IL CONTE: Dal balcone?

ANTONIO: Vedete i garofani!

IL CONTE: In giardino?

ANTONIO: Sì!

SUSANNA e LA CONTESSA: Figaro, all'erta!

IL CONTE: Cosa sento?

SUSANNA, LA CONTESSA, FIGARO: Costui ci sconcerta,
Quel briacone che viene a far quì?

IL CONTE: Dunque un uom! Ma dov'è gito?

ANTONIO: Ratto, ratto il birbone è fuggito;
Ed ad un tratto di vista m'uscì.

SUSANNA (*a* FIGARO): Sai che il paggio!

154

COUNT: Then you admit it?

FIGARO: I don't admit it.

SUSANNA: Don't be stupid, Figaro—

SUSANNA *and* COUNTESS: Don't be stupid, Figaro, this joke must come to an end.

FIGARO: To end it happily, according to theatrical custom, please give us your consent to get married without further delay.

SUSANNA, COUNTESS, FIGARO: Then, my Lord, don't resist us—grant us our wishes.

SUSANNA *and* COUNTESS: Then, my Lord, don't resist us—

COUNT (*aside*): Marcellina! Marcellina! How late you are. (ANTONIO, *rather drunk, enters with a flowerpot.*)

ANTONIO: Ah, my Lord!

COUNT: What has happened?

ANTONIO: How outrageous! Who has done it? Who was it?

SUSANNA, COUNTESS, COUNT, FIGARO: What are you saying? What's the matter? What has happened?

ANTONIO: Listen!

SUSANNA, COUNTESS, COUNT, FIGARO: Well, tell us, at once!

ANTONIO: Every day a thousand things are thrown down from that balcony over there, but today it was even worse —they threw out a man, my Lord!

COUNT: From the balcony?

ANTONIO: Look at the carnations!

COUNT: Into the garden?

ANTONIO: Yes!

SUSANNA *and* COUNTESS: Figaro, listen!

COUNT: Are you certain?

SUSANNA, COUNTESS, FIGARO: This drunkard will ruin us. Why has he come here?

COUNT: But the man—where did he go?

ANTONIO: Quickly, the rascal vanished; as soon as I saw him, he escaped.

SUSANNA (*to* FIGARO): It was the page!

155

FIGARO (*a* SUSANNA): So tutto lo vidi! (*ridendo*)
Ah ah ah ah!

IL CONTE: Taci là!

FIGARO: Ah ah ah ah!

ANTONIO: Cosa ridi?

FIGARO (*ad* ANTONIO): Tu sei cotto dal sorger del dì.

IL CONTE: Or ripetimi: un uom
Dal balcone?

ANTONIO: Dal balcone—

IL CONTE: In giardino?

ANTONIO: In giardino.

SUSANNA, LA CONTESSA, FIGARO: Ma signore, se in lui parla
il vino.

IL CONTE (*ad* ANTONIO): Segui pure, nè in volto vedesti?

ANTONIO: No nol vidi.

SUSANNA: Olà! Figaro—

SUSANNA *e* LA CONTESSA: Olà! Figaro ascolta!

IL CONTE: No?

ANTONIO: Nol vidi.

FIGARO (*ad* ANTONIO): Via piangione, sta zitto una volta!
Per tre soldi far tanto tumulto!
Giacchè il fatto non può stare occulto,
Sono io stesso saltato di lì.

IL CONTE: Chi? Voi stesso?

SUSANNA *e* LA CONTESSA: Che testa, che ingengo!

FIGARO: Che stupor!

ANTONIO: Chi? Voi stesso?

FIGARO: Che stupor! Che stupor!

IL CONTE: Già creder nol posso.

ANTONIO: Come mai diventasti sì grosso?
Dopo il salto non fosti così.

FIGARO: A chi salta succede così.

ANTONIO: Ch'il direbbe!

SUSANNA *e* LA CONTESSA: Ed insiste quel pazzo?

IL CONTE (*ad* ANTONIO): Tu che dici?

ANTONIO: A me parve il ragazzo.

IL CONTE: Cherubin?

FIGARO (*to* SUSANNA): I know it; I saw him. (*laughing*) Ha ha ha!

COUNT: Quiet there!

FIGARO: Ha ha ha ha!

ANTONIO: What are you laughing at?

FIGARO (*to* ANTONIO): You're drunk from dawn to midnight!

COUNT: Now repeat your story: a man jumped from the balcony?

ANTONIO: From the balcony—

COUNT: Into the garden?

ANTONIO: Into the garden.

SUSANNA, COUNTESS, FIGARO: But, my Lord, it's the wine that's speaking in him!

COUNT (*to* ANTONIO): Now continue. Did you see his face?

ANTONIO: No, I didn't see it.

SUSANNA: There! Figaro—

SUSANNA *and* COUNTESS: There! Figaro, listen!

COUNT: No?

ANTONIO: I didn't see it.

FIGARO (*to* ANTONIO): When will you stop your complaining! Such a disturbance over nothing! Now, to clarify matters, I'll admit that I, myself, jumped from that balcony.

COUNT: You?

SUSANNA *and* COUNTESS: What a brain! How clever!

FIGARO: What a surprise!

ANTONIO: It was you?

FIGARO: What a surprise, what a surprise!

COUNT: I still can't believe it.

ANTONIO: Then how have you grown so tall? When you jumped you were much smaller.

FIGARO: That's what happens to one after one jumps.

ANTONIO: Is that true?

SUSANNA *and* COUNTESS: That idiot is persistent.

COUNT (*to* ANTONIO): What do you say?

ANTONIO: He looked to me like a boy.

COUNT: Cherubino?

SUSANNA e LA CONTESSA: Maledetto, maledetto!

FIGARO: Esso appunto, da Siviglia
A cavallo qui giunto,
Da siviglia oggi forse sarà.

ANTONIO: Questo no, chè il cavallo
Io no vidi saltare di là.

IL CONTE: Che pazienza!

SUSANNA e LA CONTESSA: Come mai—
Giusto ciel, finirà!

IL CONTE: Finiam questo ballo. (*a* FIGARO)
Dunque tu?

FIGARO: Saltai giù.

IL CONTE: Ma perchè?

FIGARO: Il timor.

IL CONTE: Che timor?

FIGARO: Là rinchiuso,
Aspettando quel caro visetto,
Tippe, tappe un susurro fuor d'uso,
Voi gridaste, lo scritto biglietto,
Saltai giù dal terrore confuso,
E stravolto n'ho un nervo del piè.

ANTONIO: Vostra dunque saran queste
Carte che perdeste.

IL CONTE: Olà, porgile a me.

FIGARO: Sono in trappola.

SUSANNA e LA CONTESSA: Figaro, all'erta.

IL CONTE: Dite un po', questo foglio cos'è?

FIGARO: Tosto, tosto, n'ho tante, aspettate.

ANTONIO: Sarà forse il sommario dei debiti?

FIGARO: No, la lista degli osti.

IL CONTE: Parlate! (*ad* ANTONIO) E tu lascialo.

SUSANNA e LA CONTESSA: Lascialo e parti.

FIGARO: Lasciami e parti.

ANTONIO: Parto sì, ma se torno a trovarti—

FIGARO: Vanne, non temo di te!
(ANTONIO *parte*.)

IL CONTE: Dunque?

LA CONTESSA (*a parte a* SUSANNA): Oh ciel, la patente del paggio!

SUSANNA *and* COUNTESS: Oh, good heavens!

FIGARO: He, of course. Perhaps he returned from Seville on horseback—for he was on his way there, you know.

ANTONIO: No, no, I didn't see a horse jumping out of the window.

COUNT: I must have patience!

SUSANNA *and* COUNTESS: Great heavens—However will this end?

COUNT: Let's finish this nonsense. (*to* FIGARO) Then it was you?

FIGARO: I jumped out.

COUNT: But why?

FIGARO: I was afraid.

COUNT: Afraid of what?

FIGARO: I was locked in the closet, waiting to see my sweet little Susanna; suddenly I heard loud noises—you were shouting—I thought of the letter that I had written. I jumped out, confused with terror, and strained a muscle in my foot.

ANTONIO: Then this paper that was lost in the garden must be yours?

COUNT: Give it to me.

FIGARO: Now I'm trapped!

SUSANNA *and* COUNTESS: Figaro, listen.

COUNT: Give me some idea of what this paper concerns.

FIGARO: At once—I have so many; only wait a moment.

ANTONIO: Perhaps it's a list of his debts.

FIGARO: No, a list of the wedding guests.

COUNT: Speak out! (*to* ANTONIO) And you leave him alone.

SUSANNA *and* COUNTESS: Leave him alone and go.

FIGARO: Leave me alone and go.

ANTONIO: I'll go, yes, but the next time I find you—

FIGARO: Go on, I'm not afraid of you!

(ANTONIO *exits.*)

COUNT: Well, then?

COUNTESS (*aside to* SUSANNA): O Lord! The page's commission!

IL CONTE: Dunque?

SUSANNA (*a parte a* FIGARO): Giusti Dei, la patente!

IL CONTE: Coraggio!

FIGARO: O che testa! Ques'è la patente
Che poc'anzi il fanciullo mi diè.

IL CONTE: Per che fare?

FIGARO: Vi manca—

IL CONTE: Vi manca?

LA CONTESSA (*a parte a* SUSANNA): Il suggello.

SUSANNA (*a parte a* FIGARO): Il suggello.

IL CONTE: Rispondi!

FIGARO: E l'usanza—

IL CONTE: Su via li confondi!

FIGARO: E l'usanza di porvi il suggello.

IL CONTE: Questo birbo mi toglie
Il cervello.
Tutto, tutto è un mistero per me!

SUSANNA *e* LA CONTESSA: Si mi salvo da questa tempesta,
Più non havvi naufragio per me!

FIGARO: Sbuffa invano e la terra calpesta!
Poverino, ne sa, men di me.
(*Entrano* MARCELLINA, DON BASILIO *e* BARTOLO.)

MARCELLINA, DON BASILIO, BARTOLO: Via signor, che giusto
siete,
Ci dovete or ascoltar.

SUSANNA, LA CONTESSA, FIGARO: Son venuti a sconcertarmi.
Qual rimedio a ritrovar?

IL CONTE: Son venuti a vendicarmi.
Io mi sento a consolar.

FIGARO: Son tre stolidi, tre pazzi,
Cosa mai vengono a far?

IL CONTE: Pian, pianin senza schiamazzi,
Dica ognun quel che gli par.

MARCELLINA: Un impegno nuziale
Ha costui con me contratto,
E pretendo che il contratto
Deva meco effettuar.

COUNT: Well, then?

SUSANNA (*aside to* FIGARO): Good heavens! The commission!

COUNT: Go on.

FIGARO: Oh, how stupid of me! That's the commission that the boy gave me a while ago.

COUNT: For what purpose?

FIGARO: It lacked—

COUNT: It lacked?

COUNTESS (*aside to* SUSANNA): The seal.

SUSANNA (*aside to* FIGARO): The seal.

COUNT: Answer me!

FIGARO: It's usual—

COUNT: Go on, confound you!

FIGARO: It's usual to seal a commission.

COUNT: This rascal will drive me insane! A seal! All this is a mystery to me!

SUSANNA *and* COUNTESS: If I survive this storm, there can be no other shipwreck for me.

FIGARO: Let him rant and shake the earth! He knows less about this affair than I do!

(MARCELLINA, DON BASILIO, *and* BARTOLO *enter.*)

MARCELLINA, DON BASILIO, BARTOLO: My Lord, justice demands that you give us another hearing.

SUSANNA, COUNTESS, FIGARO: They have come to make trouble. What can we do to combat their malice?

COUNT: They have come to avenge me. I will soon be consoled.

FIGARO: They're three stupid idiots! Whatever are they doing here?

COUNT: Be quiet; without commotion, everyone will get his chance to speak.

MARCELLINA: Figaro contracted a marriage with me, and I claim that he must keep to his bargain!

SUSANNA, LA CONTESSA, FIGARO: Come? Come?

IL CONTE: Olà, silenzio, silenzio, silenzio!
Io son qui per giudicar.

BARTOLO: Io da lei scelto avvocato,
Vengo a far le sue difese,
Le legittime pretese,
Io vi vengo a palesar.

SUSANNA, LA CONTESSA, FIGARO: E un birbante!

IL CONTE: Olà, silenzio!
Io son qui per giudicar.

DON BASILIO: Io, com'uomo al mondo cognito,
Vengo qui per testimonio
Del promesso matrimonio
Con prestanza de danar.

SUSANNA, LA CONTESSA, FIGARO: Son tre matti!

IL CONTE: Olà, silenzio!
Lo vedremo, il contratto leggeremo,
Tutto in ordin deve andar.

SUSANNA, LA CONTESSA, FIGARO: Son confusa (confuso),
son stordita (stordito)!

MARCELLINA, DON BASILIO, IL CONTE, BARTOLO: Che bel
colpo! che bel caso!

SUSANNA, LA CONTESSA, FIGARO: Disperata (Disperato),
sbalordita (sbalordito).

MARCELLINA, DON BASILIO, IL CONTE, BARTOLO: E cresciuto
a tutti il naso.

SUSANNA, LA CONTESSA, FIGARO: Certo un diavol dell'inferno
Qui li ha fatti capitar!

MARCELLINA, DON BASILIO, IL CONTE, BARTOLO: Qualche
nume a noi propizio
Qui ci ha fatti capitar.

SUSANNA, COUNTESS, FIGARO: What? What's this?

COUNT: Now, then, silence! I'm here to be the judge.

BARTOLO: I'm this lady's chosen lawyer; I'm here to defend her, and I want to state that in my opinion her claim is strictly legal.

SUSANNA, COUNTESS, FIGARO: He's a scoundrel!

COUNT: Now then, silence! I'm here to be the judge.

DON BASILIO: I, a man known to the world, am here to witness that he promised her marriage, after which she lent him money.

SUSANNA, COUNTESS, FIGARO: They're all crazy.

COUNT: Now then, silence! we'll read the contract first; everything must proceed in order.

SUSANNA, COUNTESS, FIGARO: I'm confused and stupefied!

MARCELLINA, DON BASILIO, COUNT, BARTOLO: What a stroke! What a lovely case!

SUSANNA, COUNTESS, FIGARO: We're shaken and in despair.

MARCELLINA, DON BASILIO, COUNT, BARTOLO: We'll make them pay through the nose.

SUSANNA, COUNTESS, FIGARO: Surely an infernal devil is plotting against us.

MARCELLINA, DON BASILIO, COUNT, BARTOLO: A friendly fate has helped our cause!

ATTO TERZO

Una sala nel palazzo. IL CONTE *è solo.*

Recitativo

IL CONTE: Che imbarazzo è mai questo! Un foglio anonimo, la cameriera in gabinetto chiusa, la padrona confusa, un uom che salta dal balcone in giardino, un'altro appresso, che dice esser quel desso; non so cosa pensar, potrebbe forse qualcun de' miei vassalli, a simil razza è comune l'ardir! Ma la Contessa, ah, che un dubbio l'offende! Ella rispetta troppo sè stessa, e l'onor mio—l'onor! Dove, diamin, l'ha posto umano errore!

(LA CONTESSA *entra con* SUSANNA. *Restano a parte, e parlano inascoltate dal* CONTE.)

LA CONTESSA: Via, fatti core, digli che ti attenda in giardino.

IL CONTE (*fra se*): Saprò, se Cherubino era giunto a Siviglia, a tale oggetto ho mandato Basilio.

SUSANNA (*alla* CONTESSA): O cielo! e Figaro?

LA CONTESSA: A lui non dei dir nulla, in vece tua voglio andarci io medesma.

IL CONTE: Avanti sera dovrebbe ritornar.

SUSANNA: O Dio! non oso.

LA CONTESSA: Pensa ch'è in tua mano il mio riposo.

IL CONTE: E Susanna? Chi sa ch'ella tradito abbia il segreto mio—Oh, se ha parlato, gli fo sposar la vecchia.

(SUSANNA *viene avanti, e ascolta agl'ultime parole del* CONTE. LA CONTESSA *parte.*)

SUSANNA (*fra se*): Marcellina! (*al* CONTE) Signor!

IL CONTE: Cosa bramate?

SUSANNA: Mi par che siete in collera!

IL CONTE: Volete qualche cosa?

SUSANNA: Signor, la vostra sposa ha i soliti vapori e vi chiede il fiaschetto degli odori.

A hall in the castle. The COUNT *is alone.*

Recitative

COUNT: What confusion! An anonymous letter; the maid locked in the closet; the mistress unnerved; one man jumps down from the balcony into the garden; another claims that it was *he*. I don't know what to think— On the other hand, it might have been one of my servants. People like that are too bold for their own good. But the Countess? No; to doubt her is to insult her. She has too much self-respect. But, my honor? What has human error done to my honor? (*The* COUNTESS *enters with* SUSANNA. *They remain in the background and converse unheard by the* COUNT.)

COUNTESS: Come along; take courage. Tell him to wait for you in the garden.

COUNT (*to himself*): I've sent Basilio to find out whether Cherubino has really gone to Seville.

SUSANNA (*to the* COUNTESS): O heavens! And Figaro?

COUNTESS: Don't tell him anything about it. Instead of you, I'll go there myself.

COUNT: He should be back before evening.

SUSANNA: O God! I don't dare!

COUNTESS: Remember that you're doing it for me.

COUNT: And Susanna? Who knows whether she's betrayed my secret? Oh, if she has told them, I'll make Figaro marry the old woman!

(SUSANNA *comes forward and overhears the* COUNT'S *last words, as the* COUNTESS *exits*.)

SUSANNA (*to herself*): Marcellina! (*to the* COUNT) My Lord!

COUNT: What do you want?

SUSANNA: It seems that you are angry.

COUNT: Do you want something?

SUSANNA: My Lord, your wife is indisposed, and would like a flask of smelling salts.

IL CONTE: Prendete.

SUSANNA: Or vel riporto.

IL CONTE: Ah no, potete ritenerlo per voi.

SUSANNA: Per me? Questi non son mali da donne triviali.

IL CONTE: Un'amante che perde il caro sposo sul punto d'ottenerlo?

SUSANNA: Pagando Marcellina colla dote che voi mi prometteste—

IL CONTE: Ch'io vi promisi! Quando?

SUSANNA: Credea d'averlo inteso.

IL CONTE: Si, se voluto aveste intendermi voi stessa.

SUSANNA: E mio dovere, e quel di Sua Eccellenza è il mio volere.

16. Duetto

IL CONTE: Crudel! Perchè finora
Farmi languir così?

SUSANNA: Signor, la donna ognora
Tempo ha di dir così.

IL CONTE: Dunque in giardin verrai?

SUSANNA: Se piace a voi verrò.

IL CONTE: E non mi mancherai?

SUSANNA: No, non vi mancherò.

IL CONTE: Verrai?

SUSANNA: Si!

IL CONTE: Non mancherai?

SUSANNA (*preoccupata*): No!

IL CONTE: Non mancherai?

SUSANNA: No, non mancherò, no,
Non vi mancherò.

IL CONTE: Mi sento dal contento
Pieno di gioia il cor.

SUSANNA: Scusatemi se mento
Vi che intendete amor.

IL CONTE: Mi sento dal contento
Pieno di gioia il cor.
Dunque in giardin verrai—

SUSANNA: Se piace a voi verrò—

IL CONTE: Dunque verrai?

COUNT: Take it.

SUSANNA: I'll bring it back soon.

COUNT: Ah, no; you can keep it for yourself.

SUSANNA: Myself? Chambermaids don't have such illnesses.

COUNT: A chambermaid who is losing her dear husband on the point of marrying him?

SUSANNA: But I'll pay Marcellina with the dowry that you promised me—

COUNT: That I promised you? When?

SUSANNA: I believed that I understood you.

COUNT: Yes, if you yourself had wished to understand me.

SUSANNA: It is my duty, and your lordship's wishes are my own.

16. Duet

COUNT: Cruel one! Why have you made me suffer for so long?

SUSANNA: My Lord, a woman always takes her time to say yes.

COUNT: Then you'll meet me in the garden.

SUSANNA: If you wish it, I will.

COUNT: And you won't fail me?

SUSANNA: No, I won't fail you.

COUNT: You'll come?

SUSANNA: Yes!

COUNT: You won't fail.

SUSANNA (*preoccupied*): No!

COUNT: No?

SUSANNA: I won't fail you. I won't fail you.

COUNT: I'm so happy. My heart is full of joy!

SUSANNA: Forgive me if I lie, all of you who understand love.

COUNT: I'm so happy. My heart is full of joy. Then I will see you in the garden—

SUSANNA: If you wish it, I will—

COUNT: Then I will see you?

SUSANNA: No!

IL CONTE: No?

SUSANNA: Si, se piace a voi, verrò.

IL CONTE: Non mancherai?

SUSANNA: No!

IL CONTE: Dunque verrai?

SUSANNA: Si!

IL CONTE: Non mancherai?

SUSANNA: Si!

IL CONTE: Si?

SUSANNA: No, non vi mancherò.

Recitativo

IL CONTE: E perchè fosti meco stamattina si austera?

SUSANNA: Col paggio ch'ivi c'era?

IL CONTE: Ed a Basilio che per me ti parlò?

SUSANNA: Ma qual bisogno abbiam noi che un Basilio—

IL CONTE: E vero, e mi prometti poi se tu manchi, o cor mio— Ma la Contessa attenderà il fiaschetto.

SUSANNA: Eh, fu un pretesto, parlato io non avrei senza questo.

IL CONTE: Carissima!

SUSANNA: Vien gente.

IL CONTE (*fra se*): E mia senz'altro.

SUSANNA (*fra se*): Forbitevi la bocca, o signor scaltro.
(FIGARO *entra in dietro.*)

FIGARO: Ehi! Susanna, dove vai?

SUSANNA: Taci, senza avvocato hai già vinta la causa.

FIGARO: Cos'è nato?
(SUSANNA *e* FIGARO *partono.*)

IL CONTE: Hai già vinta la causa! Cosa sento! In qual laccio cadea? Perfidi, io voglio di tal modo punirvi; a piacer mio la sentenza sarà. Ma s'ei pagasse la vecchia pretendente? Pagarla! in qual maniera? E poi v'è Antonio che all'incognito Figaro ricusa di dare una nipote in matrimonio. Coltivando l'orgoglio di questo mentecatto—tutto giova a un raggiro—il colpo è fatto.

SUSANNA: No!

COUNT: No?

SUSANNA: Yes; if you wish, I will.

COUNT: You won't fail?

SUSANNA: No!

COUNT: Then I'll see you?

SUSANNA: Yes!

COUNT: You won't fail?

SUSANNA: Yes!

COUNT: Yes?

SUSANNA: No, I won't fail you.

Recitative

COUNT: But why were you so prudish with me this morning?

SUSANNA: With the page there?

COUNT: And to Basilio, who spoke to me for you?

SUSANNA: But what need have we for a Basilio?

COUNT: That's true, that's true; and you must promise me —if you disappoint me, my darling— But the Countess is waiting for the smelling salts.

SUSANNA: It was a pretext. I couldn't have spoken to you without it.

COUNT: Dearest!

SUSANNA: Someone's coming!

COUNT (*to himself*): She's mine, without a doubt.

SUSANNA (*to herself*): Don't be too sure, Mr. Conceit!
(FIGARO *enters in the background.*)

FIGARO: Eh, Susanna, where are you going?

SUSANNA: Quiet! Without a lawyer, you've already won your case!

FIGARO: What has happened?
(SUSANNA *and* FIGARO *exit.*)

COUNT: Already won your case? What does that mean? In what net am I caught? Traitors! I'll punish them, and the sentence will depend on my own pleasure. But if he should pay off the old woman? Pay her? How can he? And then there's Antonio, who'll refuse to marry his niece to an orphan like Figaro. I'll flatter the pride of that drunkard; it will aid my plot. I have decided!

17. *Aria*

Vedrò mentr'io sospiro,
Felice un servo mio!
E un ben che invan desio
Ei posseder dovrà?
Vedrò per man d'amore
Unita a un vile oggetto
Che in me destò un affetto
Che per me poi non ha?
Ah, no! Lasciarti in pace
Non vo' questo contento,
Tu non nascesti, audace,
Per dare a me tormento,
E forse ancor per ridere
Di mia infelicità!
Già la speranza sola
Delle vendette mie
Quest'anima consola,
E giubilar mi fa.

(MARCELLINA, DON CURZIO, FIGARO e BARTOLO *entrano*.)

Recitativo

DON CURZIO: E decisa la lite, o pagarla, o sposarla. Ora ammutite.

MARCELLINA: Io respiro.

FIGARO: Ed io moro.

MARCELLINA: Alfin sposa io sarò d'un uom che adoro.

FIGARO: Eccellenza! m'appello—

IL CONTE: E giusta la senteza, o pagar, o sposar—bravo, Don Curzio.

DON CURZIO: Bontà di Sua Eccellenza!

BARTOLO: Che superba sentenza!

FIGARO: In che superba?

BARTOLO: Siam tutti vendicati.

FIGARO: Io non sposerò.

BARTOLO: La sposerai.

DON CURZIO: O pagarla, o sposarla; lei t'ha prestati due mila pezzi duri.

FIGARO: Son gentiluomo e senza l'assenso dei miei nobili parenti—

IL CONTE: Dove sono? Chi sono?

17. Aria

Shall I, while I am sighing, see a servant of mine so happy? And shall he possess that which I desire? Shall I see her lovingly united to a mere peasant, who has awakened an affection she does not have for me? Ah, no! Be assured that I won't suffer such misery. You audacious villain, you won't rise up to torment me and to laugh at my unhappiness! Only the thought of vengeance consoles my spirit and makes my heart rejoice.

(MARCELLINA, DON CURZIO, FIGARO, *and* BARTOLO *come in.*)

Recitative

DON CURZIO: The matter is decided! Either marry her or pay her. Now be quiet!

MARCELLINA: I live again!

FIGARO: I'm dying!

MARCELLINA: At last I'll be the wife of the man I love!

FIGARO: Your Lordship! I appeal—

COUNT: The sentence is just. Either marry her or pay her. Bravo, Don Curzio!

DON CURZIO: Your Lordship is too kind.

BARTOLO: What a superb sentence!

FIGARO: In what respect?

BARTOLO: We're all avenged.

FIGARO: I won't marry her.

BARTOLO: You will.

DON CURZIO: Marry her, or pay the two thousand pieces of gold she lent you.

FIGARO: I'm a gentleman, and without the consent of my noble relations—

COUNT: Where are they? Who are they?

FIGARO: Lasciate ancor cercarli, dopo dieci anni io spero di trovarli.

BARTOLO: Qualche bambin trovato?

FIGARO: No, perduto, dottor, anzi rubato.

IL CONTE: Come?

MARCELLINA: Cosa?

BARTOLO: La prova?

DON CURZIO: Il testimonio?

FIGARO: L'oro, le gemme e i ricamati panni, che ne' più teneri anni mi ritrovaron addosso i masnadieri, sono gli indizii veri di mia nascita illustre: e sopratutto questo al mio braccio impresso geroglifico—

MARCELLINA: Una spatola impressa al braccio destro?

FIGARO: E a voi ch'il disse?

MARCELLINA: Oh Dio! è desso!

FIGARO: E ver, son io!

DON CURZIO: Chi?

IL CONTE: Chi?

BARTOLO: Chi?

MARCELLINA: Raffaello!

BARTOLO: E i ladri ti rapir?

FIGARO: Presso un castello.

BARTOLO (*indicando* MARCELLINA): Ecco tua madre.

FIGARO: Balia?

BARTOLO: No, tua madre.

DON CURZIO *ed* IL CONTE: Sua madre?

FIGARO: Cosa sento?

MARCELLINA (*indicando* BARTOLO): Ecco tua padre.

18. Sestetto

Riconosci in questo amplesso
Una madre, amato figlio!

FIGARO: Padre mio, fate lo stesso,
Non mi fate più arrossir.

BARTOLO: Resistenza la coscienza
Far non lascia al tuo desir.

DON CURZIO: Ei suo padre—

172

FIGARO: Let me go looking for them. Within ten years I hope to find them.

BARTOLO: You're a foundling?

FIGARO: I was lost, Doctor, or rather stolen.

COUNT: How?

MARCELLINA: What?

BARTOLO: Is there proof?

DON CURZIO: Is there evidence?

FIGARO: The gold, jewels, and the embroidered clothes that the robbers found on me—they are the true indications of my illustrious birth—but above all, this symbol branded on my arm.

MARCELLINA: A spatula branded on your right arm?

FIGARO: And who told you about it?

MARCELLINA: O God! It's he!

FIGARO: Of course, it's I.

DON CURZIO: Who?

COUNT: Who?

BARTOLO: Who?

MARCELLINA: Raffaello!

BARTOLO: And the robbers kidnapped you?

FIGARO: Near a castle.

BARTOLO (*pointing to* MARCELLINA): Then there is your mother.

FIGARO: My nurse?

BARTOLO: No, your mother.

DON CURZIO *and* COUNT: His mother?

FIGARO: Are you insane?

MARCELLINA (*pointing to* BARTOLO): And this is your father!

18. Sextet

In this embrace, my dear son, you'll recognize your mother!

FIGARO: Father, spare my blushes, and embrace me also.

BARTOLO: My conscience won't let me oppose your wishes.

DON CURZIO: He's his father—

IL CONTE: Son smarrito—

DON CURZIO: Ella sua madre!

IL CONTE: Son stordito!

DON CURZIO: L'imeneo
Non può seguir!

IL CONTE: Meglio è assai di qua partir.

MARCELLINA: Figlio amato!

DON CURZIO: Ei suo padre—
Ella sua madre!

BARTOLO: Figlio amato!

IL CONTE: Son smarrito, son stordito!

FIGARO: Parenti amati!
(SUSANNA *entra con una borsa in mano.*)

SUSANNA: Alto, alto! Signor Conte,
Mille doppie son qui pronte,
A pagar vengo per Figaro,
Ed a porlo in libertà.

DON CURZIO *ed* IL CONTE: Non sappiam com'è la cosa—
Osservate un poco là!

MARCELLINA *e* BARTOLO: Figlio amato!

FIGARO: Parenti amati!

SUSANNA: Già d'accordo con la sposa?
Guisti Dei, che infedeltà!
Lascia, iniquo!

FIGARO: No, t'arresta!
Senti, o cara, senti, senti!

SUSANNA: Senti questa!
(*Lo batte al' orecchio.*)

MARCELLINA, FIGARO, BARTOLO: E un effetto di—
Buon core.

IL CONTE: Fremo, smanio dal furore—
Il destino me la fa!

SUSANNA: Fremo, smanio dal furore—
Una vecchia me la fa!

DON CURZIO: Freme smania dal furore—
Il destino gliela fa!

MARCELLINA: Lo sdegno calmate,
Mia cara figliola.
Sua madre abbracciate
Che or vostra sarà.

174

COUNT: I'm amazed—
DON CURZIO: She's his mother!
COUNT: I'm stupefied!
DON CURZIO: The wedding cannot go on.

COUNT: I can't bear any more of this.
MARCELLINA: Beloved son!
DON CURZIO: He's his father— She's his mother!

BARTOLO: Beloved son!
COUNT: I'm amazed, I'm stupefied!
FIGARO: Beloved parents!
(SUSANNA *enters with purse in her hand.*)
SUSANNA: Wait a moment, your Lordship. I have a thousand gold pieces ready. I've come to pay for Figaro and to give him his liberty.

DON CURZIO *and* COUNT: Who knows what will happen— Let's observe it for a while!
MARCELLINA *and* BARTOLO: Beloved son!
FIGARO: Beloved parents!
SUSANNA: He's already agreed to marry her! Good heavens, what infidelity! Let me go, you villain!

FIGARO: No, wait a moment! Listen, dear! Listen!

SUSANNA: Listen to this!
(*She slaps him.*)
MARCELLINA, FIGARO, BARTOLO: That's proof of—her love.

COUNT: I'm boiling with rage— Fate is certainly against me!
SUSANNA: I'm boiling with rage— This old woman has got the better of me!
DON CURZIO: He's boiling with rage— Fate is certainly against him!
MARCELLINA: Calm your anger, my dear little daughter. Embrace Figaro's mother, who soon will be yours.

SUSANNA: Sua madre?

BARTOLO: Sua madre!

SUSANNA: Sua madre?

IL CONTE: Sua madre!

SUSANNA: Sua madre?

DON CURZIO: Sua madre!

SUSANNA: Sua madre?

MARCELLINA: Sua madre!

MARCELLINA, DON CURZIO, IL CONTE, BARTOLO: Sua madre!
Sua madre!

SUSANNA: Tua madre?

FIGARO: E quello è mio padre,
Che a te lo dirà.

SUSANNA: Suo padre?

MARCELLINA, DON CURZIO, IL CONTE, BARTOLO: Suo padre!

SUSANNA: Tuo padre?

FIGARO: E quella è mia madre
Che a te lo dirà.

DON CURZIO *ed* IL CONTE: Al fiero tormento—
Di questo momento,
Quest'anima appena resistar or sa.

SUSANNA, MARCELLINA, FIGARO, BARTOLO: Al dolce con-
tento—
Di questo momento,
Quest'anima appena resistar or sa.
(IL CONTE *e* DON CURZIO *partono.*)

Recitativo

MARCELLINA (*a* BARTOLO): Eccovi, o caro amico, il dolce
frutto del antico amor nostro.

BARTOLO: Or non parliamo di fatti sì rimoti; egli è mio
figlio, mia consorte voi siete, e le nozze farem quando
volete.

MARCELLINA: Oggi; e doppie saranno. (*a* FIGARO) Prendi
questo—il biglietto del denar che a me devi, ed è tua dote.

SUSANNA (*a* FIGARO): Prendi ancor questa borsa.

BARTOLO: E questa ancora.

FIGARO: Bravi! gittate pur, ch'io piglio ognora.

SUSANNA: His mother?

BARTOLO: His mother!

SUSANNA: His mother?

COUNT: His mother!

SUSANNA: His mother?

DON CURZIO: His mother!

SUSANNA: His mother?

MARCELLINA: His mother!

MARCELLINA, DON CURZIO, COUNT, BARTOLO: His mother! His mother!

SUSANNA: Your mother?

FIGARO: And this is my father. He'll tell you so himself.

SUSANNA: His father?

MARCELLINA, DON CURZIO, COUNT, BARTOLO: His father!

SUSANNA: Your father?

FIGARO: And this is my mother. She'll tell you so herself.

DON CURZIO *and* COUNT: My soul can hardly endure the bitter torments of this moment.

SUSANNA, MARCELLINA, FIGARO, BARTOLO: My soul can hardly endure the sweet happiness of this moment.
(*The* COUNT *and* DON CURZIO *exit.*)

Recitative

MARCELLINA (*to* BARTOLO): My darling, there is the ripe fruit of our past love affair.

BARTOLO: Let's not speak of such remote matters. He's my son; you'll be my wife, and we'll get married whenever you wish it.

MARCELLINA: Today—a double wedding! (*to* FIGARO) Take this bill for the money you owe me; it's your dowry.

SUSANNA (*to* FIGARO): Take this purse too.

BARTOLO: And this one too.

FIGARO: Thank you; money is always welcome; I'll take it all.

Le Nozze di Figaro

SUSANNA: Voliamo ad informar d'ogni avventura madama e nostro zio. Chi al par di me contenta!

FIGARO: Io!

BARTOLO: Io!

MARCELLINA: Io!

SUSANNA, MARCELLINA, FIGARO, BARTOLO: E schiatti il signor conte al gusto mio!

(*Escono tutti, ridendo.* BARBARINA *entra, con* CHERUBINO.)

BARBARINA: Andiam, bel paggio; in casa mia tutte ritroverai le più belle ragazze del castello, di tutte sarai tu certo più bello.

CHERUBINO: Ah! se il conte mi trova! Misero me! Tu sai che partito ei mi crede per Siviglia.

BARBARINA: O ve', che meraviglia! e se ti trova non sarà cosa nuova, odi: vogliamo vestirti come noi. Tutte insiem andrem poi a presentar de' fiori a madamina. Fidati, o Cherubin, di Barbarina.

(BARBARINA *e* CHERUBINO *escono. Entra* LA CONTESSA.)

19. Recitativo ed Aria

LA CONTESSA: E Susanna non vien! Sono ansiosa di saper come il conte accolse la proposta. Alquanto ardito il progetto mi par— Ad uno sposo sì vivace e geloso— Ma che mal c'è? Cangiando i miei vestiti con quelli di Susanna, e i suoi co' miei al favor della notte— Oh cielo! a qual umil stato fatale io son ridotta da un consorte crudel! che dopo avermi con un misto inaudito d'infedeltà, di gelosia, di sdegno—prima amata, indi offesa, ed alfin tradita—fammi or cercar da una mia serva aita!

Dove sono i bei momenti
Di dolcezza e di piacer?
Dove andaron i giuramenti,
Di quel labbro menzogner?
Perchè mai, se in pianti e in pene
Per me tutto si cangiò,
La memoria di quel bene
Dal mio sen non trapassò?
La memoria di quel bene non trapassò?
Ah! se almen la mia costanza
Nel languire amando ognor
Mi portasse una speranza
Di cangiar l'ingrato cor!

(LA CONTESSA *parte.* IL CONTE *ed* ANTONIO *entrano.*)

178

SUSANNA: I want to tell Madame and my uncle about what has happened. Who is as happy as I am?

FIGARO: I am!

BARTOLO: I am!

MARCELLINA: I am!

SUSANNA, MARCELLINA, FIGARO, BARTOLO: The Count is disconcerted—what a delightful spectacle!

(*They all exit, laughing.* BARBARINA *and* CHERUBINO *enter.*)

BARBARINA: Come on, handsome page! At my house you will meet the prettiest girls of the castle, but you will certainly be the most beautiful!

CHERUBINO: Ah! If the Count finds me, it will be terrible! You know that he believes I've gone to Seville.

BARBARINA: Oh, what a calamity! But if he finds you, it won't be anything new. Listen! We want to dress you like a girl. All together, we'll go to present the flowers to Madame. Trust me, Cherubino—trust Barbarina!

(BARBARINA *and* CHERUBINO *exit. The* COUNTESS *enters.*)

19. Recitative and Aria

COUNTESS: Susanna is late! I'm anxious to know how the Count received the proposal. Our plan is dangerous—my husband is so impulsive and so jealous! But what real harm is in it? I'll change clothes with Susanna in the darkness of evening— O heaven! My cruel husband has reduced me to such horrible humiliation! He's behaved with an irrational mixture of infidelity, jealousy, and scorn; he loved me at first, then he offended me, and finally betrayed me. Now he's driven me to seek my maid's assistance!

Where have they vanished, those tender moments of sweet pleasure? What has become of the promises sworn by those unfaithful lips? Everything has changed to grief and pain for me. But why does that past sweetness still possess my memory? Ah, my constant heart, whose love survives my suffering, gives me some hope of regaining my husband's affection!

(*The* COUNTESS *exits. The* COUNT *and* ANTONIO *enter.*)

Recitativo

ANTONIO: Io vi dico, signor, che Cherubino è ancora nel castello e vedete per prova il suo cappello.

IL CONTE: Ma come, se a quest'ora esser giunto a Siviglia egli dovria?

ANTONIO: Scusate, oggi Siviglia è a casa mia. Là vestissi da donna, e là lasciati ha gli altri abiti suoi.

IL CONTE: Perfidi!

ANTONIO: Andiam, e li vedrete voi.

(IL CONTE *ed* ANTONIO *partono.* LA CONTESSA *e* SUSANNA *entrano.*)

LA CONTESSA: Cosa mi narri? E che ne disse il conte?

SUSANNA: Gli si leggeva in fronte il dispetto e la rabbia.

LA CONTESSA: Piano, che meglio or lo porremo in gabbia! Dov'è l'appuntamento, che tu gli proponesti?

SUSANNA: In giardino.

LA CONTESSA: Fissiamogli un loco. Scrivi.

SUSANNA: Ch'io scriva, ma, signora—

LA CONTESSA: Eh, scrivi, dico, e tutto io prendo su me stessa: (*dettando*) Canzonetta sull'aria—

20. *Duetto*

SUSANNA (*scrive*): Sull'aria.

LA CONTESSA: Che soave zefiretto—

SUSANNA: Zefiretto—

LA CONTESSA: Questa sera spirerà—

SUSANNA: Questa sera spirerà—

LA CONTESSA: Sotto i pini del boschetto.

SUSANNA: Sotto i pini?

LA CONTESSA: Sotto i pini del boschetto.

SUSANNA: Sotto i pini del boschetto.

LA CONTESSA: Ei già il resto capirà!

SUSANNA: Certo, certo, il capirà!

Recitativo

Piegato è il foglio, or come si sigilla?

LA CONTESSA: Ecco, prendi una spilla, servirà di sigillo. Attendi, scrivi sul riverso del foglio: Rimandate il sigillo.

Recitative

ANTONIO: I'm telling you, my Lord, Cherubino is still in the castle, and here's his hat to prove it.

COUNT: But that's impossible—he should have arrived at Seville by this time.

ANTONIO: Excuse me; today Seville is my house. There they dressed him as a girl, and he's left all his clothes there.

COUNT: Traitors!

ANTONIO: Come with me, and you'll see for yourself. (*The* COUNT *and* ANTONIO *exit. The* COUNTESS *and* SUSANNA *enter.*)

COUNTESS: What are you telling me? And how did the Count react?

SUSANNA: One could read displeasure and anger in his face.

COUNTESS: Good! Now it will be easier to catch him in our trap. Where did you promise to meet him?

SUSANNA: In the garden.

COUNTESS: Let's specify a place. Write to him.

SUSANNA: I, write to him? But, my Lady—

COUNTESS: Go on; write, and I'll take all the consequences: (*dictating*) A little song to the breezes—

20. *Duet*

SUSANNA (*writing*): To the breezes—

COUNTESS: That gentle Zephyr—

SUSANNA: Zephyr—

COUNTESS: Will breathe this evening—

SUSANNA: Will breathe this evening—

COUNTESS: Among the pines in the grove—

SUSANNA: Among the pines?

COUNTESS: Among the pines in the grove.

SUSANNA: Among the pines in the grove.

COUNTESS: He'll understand the rest without being told.

SUSANNA: Certainly he'll understand!

Recitative

The letter is folded; how shall I seal it?

COUNTESS: Here, take a pin; it will serve as a seal. Listen, write on the back of the note: Return the seal!

Le Nozze di Figaro

SUSANNA: E più bizzarra di quel della patente.

LA CONTESSA: Presto, nascondi; io sento venir gente.
(*Entra il* CORO *delle contadine, poi* CHERUBINO, *travestito da rogozza, e* BARBARINA.)

21. *Coro*

CORO: Ricevete, o padroncina,
Queste rose e questi fior,
Che abbiam colti stamattina,
Per mostrarvi il nostro amor.
Siamo tante contadine,
E siam tutte poverine,
Ma quel poco che rechiamo
Ve lo diamo di buon cuor.

Recitativo

BARBARINA: Queste sono, madama, le ragazze del loco che il poco ch'han vi vengono ad offrire e vi chiedon perdon del loro ardire.

LA CONTESSA: O brave! vi ringrazio.

SUSANNA: Come sono vezzose!

LA CONTESSA: E chi è, narratemi, quell'amabil fanciulla ch'ha l'aria sì modesta?

BARBARINA: Ella è una mia cugina, e per le nozze è venuta stasera.

LA CONTESSA: Onoriamo la bella forestiera. Venite qui, datemi i vostri fiori. Come arrossì! Susanna, e non ti pare che somigli ad alcuno?

SUSANNA: Al naturale.
(*Entrano* IL CONTE *ed* ANTONIO.)

ANTONIO (*indicando* CHERUBINO): Eh cospettaccio! E questi l'uffiziale!

LA CONTESSA: Oh stelle!

SUSANNA: Malandrino!

IL CONTE (*alla* CONTESSA): Ebben, madama—

LA CONTESSA: Io sono, signor mio, irritata e sorpresa al par di voi.

IL CONTE: Ma stamane?

LA CONTESSA: Stamane, per l'odierna festa volevam travestirlo al modo stesso che l'han vestito adesso!

IL CONTE (*a* CHERUBINO): E perchè non partisti?

182

SUSANNA: This is even more complicated than the affair of Cherubino's commission!

COUNTESS: Quickly; hide it; I hear someone coming.
(*Enter* CHORUS *of peasants,* CHERUBINO, *disguised as a girl, and* BARBARINA.)

21. Chorus

CHORUS: O dear mistress, please accept these flowers which we gathered this morning to show our love for you. We're all country girls, and we're all poor, but we offer you these flowers from our hearts!

Recitative

BARBARINA: Here are the girls of the neighborhood, my Lady, who come to bring you the little that they have, and they ask your pardon for their presumption.

COUNTESS: It's lovely; I thank you.

SUSANNA: They all look so pretty!

COUNTESS: And tell me, who is that sweet girl with such a modest air?

BARBARINA: She's one of my cousins, and she came here last night for the wedding.

COUNTESS: Let's honor our pretty visitor. Come here and give me your flowers. How she blushes! Susanna, doesn't she seem to resemble someone?

SUSANNA: Absolutely!
(*The* COUNT *and* ANTONIO *enter.*)

ANTONIO (*pointing to* CHERUBINO): I knew it—that's the officer!

COUNTESS: O God!

SUSANNA: Stupid boy!

COUNT (*to the* COUNTESS): Well, Madame!

COUNTESS: My Lord, I'm just as surprised and irritated as you are.

COUNT: But, this morning?

COUNTESS: To prepare him for tonight, we dressed him this morning in the same way that they've dressed him now.

COUNT (*to* CHERUBINO): And why didn't you go to Seville?

CHERUBINO: Signor—

IL CONTE: Saprò punire la tua disubbidienza.

BARBARINA: Eccellenza! Eccellenza! Voi mi dite sì spesso qual volta m'abbracciate e mi baciate: "Barbarina, se m'ami, ti darò quel che brami!"

IL CONTE: Io dissi questo?

BARBARINA: Voi; or datemi, padrone, in sposo Cherubino; e v'amerò com'amo il mio gattino.

LA CONTESSA (*al* CONTE): Ebbene, or tocca a voi.

ANTONIO (*a* BARBARINA): Brava figliola, hai buon maestro che ti fa la scola!

IL CONTE (*fra se*): Non so qual uom, qual demone, qual dio, rivolga tutto quanto a torto mio.
(*Entra* FIGARO.)

FIGARO: Signor, se trattenete tutte queste ragazze, addio feste, addio danza!

IL CONTE: E che? Vorresti ballar col piè stravolto?

FIGARO: Eh, non mi duol più molto. Andiam, belle fanciulle.

LA CONTESSA (*a* SUSANNA): Come si caverà dall'imbarazzo?

SUSANNA: Lasciate fare a lui.

IL CONTE: Per buona sorte i vasi eran di creta!

FIGARO: Senza fallo. (*alle contadine*) Andiamo dunque, andiamo.

ANTONIO: E intanto a cavallo di galoppo a Siviglia andava il paggio.

FIGARO: Di galoppo, o di passo, buon viaggio! (*alle contadine*) Venite, o belle giovani.

IL CONTE: E a te la sua patente era in tasca rimasta?

FIGARO: Certamente, che razza di domanda!

ANTONIO (*a* SUSANNA): Via, non gli far più moti, ei non t'intende (*presenta* CHERUBINO) ed ecco che pretende che sia un bugiardo il mio signor nipote!

FIGARO: Cherubino!

ANTONIO: Or ci sei!

FIGARO: Che diamin canta?

184

CHERUBINO: My Lord!

COUNT: I'll see that you're punished for your disobedience.

BARBARINA: My Lord, my Lord! You've told me so often, when you embraced and kissed me: "Barbarina, if you'll love me, I'll give you anything you wish!"

COUNT: Did I say that?

BARBARINA: Yes, you did. Now, my Lord, let me marry Cherubino, and I will love you as dearly as my little kitten!

COUNTESS (*to the* COUNT): I see that the problem is yours.

ANTONIO (*to* BARBARINA): Well done, my daughter; you have a teacher who instructs you well!

COUNT (*to himself*): I don't know what demon is turning everything to my disadvantage!

(FIGARO *enters*.)

FIGARO: My Lord, if you delay these girls there'll be no party or dancing!

COUNT: What? Do you plan to dance with a sprained ankle?

FIGARO: It doesn't hurt me any more. Follow me, my pretty girls!

COUNTESS (*to* SUSANNA): How will he get out of this predicament?

SUSANNA: Leave it to him!

COUNT: It's lucky that the flowerpots were of clay!

FIGARO: Without a doubt. (*to the girls*) Let's go then; let's go¹

ANTONIO: And meanwhile the page was galloping toward Seville.

FIGARO: Galloping or trotting; I hope he got there! (*to the girls*) Come, pretty girls!

COUNT: And of course you had his commission in your pocket?

FIGARO: Certainly. What a question!

ANTONIO (*to* SUSANNA): Come, don't signal to him; he doesn't understand you. (*presenting* CHERUBINO) And here's the proof that my illustrious nephew is a liar!

FIGARO: Cherubino!

ANTONIO: Now you understand!

FIGARO: What story did he tell you?

185

IL CONTE: Non canta, no, ma dice ch'egli saltò stamane in su i garofani.

FIGARO: Ei lo dice—sarà—se ho saltato io, si può dare che anch esso abbia fatto lo stesso.

IL CONTE: Anch'esso?

FIGARO: Perchè no? Io non impugno mai quel che non so.

22. Finale

Ecco la marcia, andiamo!
Ai vostri posti, o belle! Ai vostri posti!
Susanna, dammi il braccio!

SUSANNA: Eccolo!
(*Escono tutti. Restano* IL CONTE *e* LA CONTESSA.)

IL CONTE: Temerari!

LA CONTESSA: Io son di ghiaccio!

IL CONTE: Contessa!

LA CONTESSA: Or non parliamo.
Ecco qui le due nozze!
Riceverle dobbiam, alfin si tratta
D'una vostra protetta.
Seggiamo.

IL CONTE: Seggiamo! (*fra se*)
E meditiam vendetta.
(*La procezione nuziale entra.* DUE CONTADINE *portano il cappello e il velo di* SUSANNA.)

DUE CONTADINE: Amanti costanti
Seguaci d'onor,
Cantate, lodate
Sì saggio signor.
A un dritto cedendo
Che oltraggia, che offende,
Ei caste vi rende
Ai vostri amator.
(SUSANNA *dà il biglietto al* CONTE.)

TUTTI: Cantiamo, lodiamo sì saggio signor—
(*Si balla;* IL CONTE *legge il biglietto.*)

IL CONTE: Eh, già, solita usanza, le donne
Ficcan aghi in ogni loco—
Ah, ah, capisco il gioco!

FIGARO (*a* SUSANNA): Un biglietto amoroso che gli diè
Nel passar qualche galante, ed era

186

COUNT: No story—only that he jumped into the carnations this morning.

FIGARO: He said that! Perhaps it's true. If I jumped, it's possible that he could have done the same thing.

COUNT: He, also?

FIGARO: And why not? I never commit myself when I don't know the facts.

22. Finale

There's the march; let's go! To your places, pretty girls! To your places! Susanna, give me your arm!

SUSANNA: Here it is!
(*All exit, except the* COUNT *and* COUNTESS.)

COUNT: The rascals!

COUNTESS: I feel as cold as ice!

COUNT: My Lady!

COUNTESS: Let's not discuss it now. Here are the two couples! We must receive them. Anyway, one of the brides is a special protégée of yours. Let's sit down.

COUNT: Very well! (*to himself*) And I'll consider my vengeance!
(*The wedding procession enters.* TWO PEASANT GIRLS *carry* SUSANNA'S *bridal hat and veil.*)

TWO PEASANT GIRLS: Constant lovers, here you may follow the path of honor. Sing the praises of such a wise lord. He yields an offensive right and now returns you chaste to your lovers!
(SUSANNA *gives the* COUNT *the note.*)

ALL: We sing the praises of our wise lord—
(*Dancing begins; the* COUNT *reads the note.*)

COUNT: Oh, now it's the custom for women to stick pins in everything—Ha, ha! Now I understand the joke!

FIGARO (*to* SUSANNA): It's a loving note that a lady has given him in passing, and it was sealed with a pin, on which

Sigillato d'una spilla, ond'egli
Si punse il dito. Il Narciso or la
Cerca—oh! che stordito!

IL CONTE: Andate, amici! e sia per questa sera
Disposto l'apparato nuziale colla
Più ricca pompa! Io vo' che sia
Magnifica la festa, e canti, e
Fochi, e gran cena, e gran ballo;
E ognuno impari, com'io tratto color
Che a me son cari.

TUTTI: Amanti costanti—

he pricked his finger. Now that Narcissus is looking for it
—oh, what stupidity!

COUNT: Go now, my friends. This evening all will be prepared to celebrate the weddings with due ceremony. It will
be a magnificent occasion, with singing, fireworks, a great
banquet and ball, so that everyone may learn how I treat
those who are dear to me.

ALL: Constant lovers—

I giardini del castello. Notte. BARBARINA *entra con una lanterna.*

23. *Aria*

BARBARINA: L'ho perduta! Me meschina!
Ah, chi sa dove sarà?
Non la trovo.
Meschinella! L'ho perduta!
E mia cugina, ed il padron,
Cosa dirà?
(*Entrano* MARCELLINA *e* FIGARO.)

Recitativo

FIGARO: Barbarina, cos'hai?

BARBARINA: L'ho perduta, cugino.

FIGARO: Cosa?

MARCELLINA: Cosa?

BARBARINA: La spilla che a me diede il padrone per recar a Susanna.

FIGARO: A Susanna, la spilla? e così, tenerella, il mestiero già sai di far tutto sì ben quel che tu fai?

BARBARINA: Cos'è? Vai meco in collera?

FIGARO: E non vedi ch'io scherzo? Osserva: (*prende una spilla da* MARCELLINA) Questa è la spilla che il conte da recare ti diede alla Susanna, e servia di sigillo a un bigliettino; vedi s'io sono instrutto.

BARBARINA: E perchè il chiedi a me quando sai tutto?

FIGARO: Avea voglia d'udir come il padrone ti diè la commissione.

BARBARINA: Che miracoli! "Tieni, fanciulla, reca questa spilla alla bella Susanna, e dille: 'questo è il sigillo dei pini.' "

FIGARO: Ah! Ah! de' pini.

BARBARINA: E ver ch'ei soggiunse; "Guarda che alcun non veda." Ma tu già tacerai.

190

The gardens of the castle. Twilight. BARBARINA *enters, with a lantern.*

23. Aria

BARBARINA: I have lost it! Ah, who knows were it might be? I can't find it! Poor me—how miserable I am! I have lost it! And my cousin and the Count— What will they say? (MARCELLINA *and* FIGARO *enter.*)

Recitative

FIGARO: Barbarina, what's the matter?

BARBARINA: I've lost it, Cousin.

FIGARO: What?

MARCELLINA: What?

BARBARINA: The pin my master gave me to return to Susanna.

FIGARO: To Susanna? The pin? And that's how discreetly you accomplish such errands?

BARBARINA: Why are you angry with me?

FIGARO: Don't you see that I'm joking? Look: (*taking a pin from* MARCELLINA) this is the pin that the Count gave you to give back to Susanna. It served as a seal for a letter; you can see that I'm well informed.

BARBARINA: Then why are you asking me, if you know all about it?

FIGARO: I was curious to know how the Count gave you the commission.

BARBARINA: What a fuss you're making! "Wait, child, return this pin to your pretty cousin Susanna and tell her: 'This is the seal of the pine grove.'"

FIGARO: Aha! The pine grove!

BARBARINA: It's true that he continued, "Take care that no one sees you." But you certainly won't tell.

191

FIGARO: Sicuramente.

BARBARINA: A te già niente preme.

FIGARO: Oh niente, niente.

BARBARINA: Addio, mio bel cugino; vo da Susanna, e poi da Cherubino (*Parte.*)

FIGARO: Madre!

MARCELLINA: Figlio!

FIGARO: Son morto.

MARCELLINA: Calmati, figlio mio!

FIGARO: Son morto, dico.

MARCELLINA: Flemma, flemma, e poi flemma: il fatto è serio, e pensar ci convien. Ma guarda un poco che ancor non sai di chi si prenda giuoco.

FIGARO: Ah! quella spilla, o madre, e quella stessa che poc'anzi ei raccolse.

MARCELLINA: E ver, ma questo al più ti porge un dritto di stare in guardia e vivere in sospetto, ma non sai se in effetto—

FIGARO: All'arte dunque! il loco del convegno so dov'è stabilito.

MARCELLINA: Dove vai, figlio mio?

FIGARO: A vendicar tutt'i mariti. Addio! (*Parte.*)

MARCELLINA: Presto avvertiam Susanna. Io la credo innocente—quella faccia, quell'aria di modestia—e caso ancora chella non fosse— Ah, quando il non ciurma personale interesse, ogni donna è portata alla difesa del suo povero sesso, da quest'uomini ingrati a torto oppresso.

24. Aria

Il capro e la capretta
Son sempre in amistà.
L'agnello all'agnelletta
La guerra mai non fa.
Le più feroce belve,
Per selve e per campagne,
Lascian le lor compagne
In pace e in libertà.
Sol noi povere femmine,
Che tanto amiam quest'uomini,
Trattate siam dai perfidi

192

FIGARO: Certainly.

BARBARINA: It doesn't concern you.

FIGARO: Oh, not at all.

BARBARINA: Good-by, my dear cousin; I'm going to see Susanna, and then to Cherubino! (*Exits.*)

FIGARO: Mother!

MARCELLINA: My son?

FIGARO: I'm dying!

MARCELLINA: Calm yourself, my dear son!

FIGARO: I'm dead, I tell you!

MARCELLINA: We must keep calm. The matter is serious and needs careful thought. But remember that you don't know yet who it is that's being made a fool of.

FIGARO: Ah, this pin, Mother, is the one his lordship picked up.

MARCELLINA: True, but that's only sufficient to put you on guard and make you suspicious. You can't really be sure that—

FIGARO: I must be clever, then! I know where the rendezvous is to be.

MARCELLINA: Where are you going?

FIGARO: To avenge all wronged husbands! Good-by! (*Exits.*)

MARCELLINA: I'll quickly warn Susanna. I believe she is innocent. She seems so sweet and modest—but still it's possible that she may be guilty. But when personal interests aren't at stake, every woman should defend her poor sex, so wrongly oppressed by ungrateful men!

24. Aria●

Among goats the sexes are always friendly. Male and female lambs don't quarrel. The most ferocious boar leaves his companions in peace and liberty in the forests and fields. Only we poor women, who love men so much, are treated by them with disdain, and even with cruelty!

(MARCELLINA *exits.* BARBARINA *enters.*)

───────────

● Usually omitted in performance.

Ognor con crudeltà!

(MARCELLINA *parte.* BARBARINA *entra.*)

Recitativo

BARBARINA: Nel padiglione a manca, ei cosi disse—è questo, è questo. E poi, se non venisse?

(*Vedendo* FIGARO.)

Son morta!

(*Esce* BARBARINA. FIGARO *entra.*)

FIGARO: E Barbarina! Chi va la?

(DON BASILIO *e* BARTOLO *entrano.*)

DON BASILIO: Son quelli che invitasti a venir.

BARTOLO: Che brutto ceffo! Sembri un conspirator! Che diamin sono quegli infausti apparati?

FIGARO: Lo vedrete fra poco. In questo stesso loco celebrerem la festa della mia sposa onesta e del feudal signor. (*Parte.*)

DON BASILIO: Hai i diavoli nel corpo!

BARTOLO: Ma che guadagni?

DON BASILIO: Nulla. Susanna piace al conte; alle d'accordo gli diè un appuntamento ch'a Figaro non piace.

(DON BASILIO *e* BARTOLO *si nascondono.* FIGARO *rientra, porta una lanterna.*)

FIGARO: Tutto è disposto; l'ora dovrebbe esser vicina; io sento gente—è dessa! non è alcun. Buia è la notte, ed io comincia omai a fare il scimunito mestiere di marito. Ingrata! Nel momento della mia cerimonia ei godeva leggendo, e nel vederlo io rideva di me senza saperlo. Ah, Susanna! Quanta pena mi costi! Con quell'ingenua faccia, con quegli occhi innocenti, chi creduto l'avria? Ah! che il fidarsi a donna è ognor follia.

26. *Aria*

Aprite un po' quegli occhi,
Uomini incauti e sciocchi;
Guardate queste femmine,
Guardate cosa son!
Queste chiamate dee
Dagli ingannati sensi,
A cui tributa incensi
La debole ragion.
Son streghe che incantano per farci penar,

Recitative

BARBARINA: In the pavilion on the left, that's what he said. It's this one! But if he shouldn't come.
(*She catches sight of* FIGARO.)
Oh, I'm afraid!
(BARBARINA *exits.* FIGARO *enters.*)

FIGARO: That was Barbarina! Who goes there?
(DON BASILIO *and* BARTOLO *enter.*)

DON BASILIO: It's those whom you invited.

BARTOLO: What an ugly expression! You look like a conspirator. What the devil are these weapons for?

FIGARO: You'll see in a minute. Hide yourselves, and don't come out until I whistle. (*Exits.*)

DON BASILIO: He's possessed by the devil.

BARTOLO: Why is he so upset?

DON BASILIO: It's nothing. Susanna pleased the Count by giving him an appointment, and that doesn't please Figaro.
(DON BASILIO *and* BARTOLO *hide.* FIGARO *re-enters, carrying a lantern.*)

FIGARO: Everything is ready; the time should be near. I hear people—it's she! No, it's no one. The night is dark. Already I'm beginning to play the foolish role of a deceived husband. Ungrateful! At the very moment of the ceremony he was reading that letter, and I laughed to see it—I laughed at myself without knowing it. O Susanna, Susanna! How much pain you've cost me. With that innocent face, those candid eyes, who would have believed it? Ah, whoever trusts in woman is gravely misguided!

26. Aria

Open your eyes a little, you foolish deluded men; look at these women; see them for what they are! These creatures, deceiving your senses, seem to you like goddesses, and your weak reason burns incense to them in tribute. They're witches enchanting us to bring us pain; they're sirens singing to make us drown; they're owls who attract us to pull out our feathers; comets that burn to extinguish our lights. They're roses with thorns; they're charming foxes; they're sweet bears; evil doves; mistresses of deceit; friends of

Sirene che cantano per farci affogar,
Civette che allettano per trarci le piume,
Comete che brillano per toglierci il lume.
Son rose spinose,
Son volpi vezzose,
Son orse benigne,
Colombe maligne,
Maestre d'inganni,
Amiche d'affanni,
Che fingono, mentono,
Amore non senton,
Non senton pietà.
No, no, no, no!
Il resto nol dico,
Già ognuno lo sa.
(FIGARO *si nasconda negli alberi.* Entrano SUSANNA, LA CON-
TESSA *e* MARCELLINA.)

Recitativo

SUSANNA: Signora! ella mi disse che Figaro verravvi.

MARCELLINA: Anzi è venuto, abbassa un po' la voce.

SUSANNA: Dunque un ci ascolta, e l'altro dee venir a cer-
carmi. Incominciam!

MARCELLINA: Io voglio qui celarmi.
(MARCELLINA *va nel padiglione.*)

SUSANNA (*alla* CONTESSA): Madama, voi tremate; avreste
freddo?

LA CONTESSA: Parmi umida la notte; io mi ritiro.

FIGARO (*fra se*): Eccoci della crisi al grande istante.

SUSANNA: Io sotto questi pini, se madama il permette, resto
a prendere il fresco una mezz'ora.

FIGARO (*fra se*): Il fresco! il fresco!

LA CONTESSA: Restaci in buon'ora. (*Parte.*)

SUSANNA (*fra se*): Il birbo è in sentinella; divertiamoci
anche noi. Diamogli la mercè de' dubbi suoi! (*forte*)
Giunse alfin il momento che godrò senza affanno in braccio
all'idol mio. Timide cure, uscite dal mio petto, a turbar
non venite il mio diletto! Oh come par che all'amoroso

trouble, pretending to love us, but it's all a lie. They don't feel pity. No, no, no, no! I won't tell you the rest; already you know it too well!

(FIGARO *hides behind the bushes.* SUSANNA, *the* COUNTESS, *and* MARCELLINA *enter.*)

Recitative

SUSANNA: My Lady! Marcellina told me that Figaro would come here.

MARCELLINA: Rather, he's here already; lower your voice a little.

SUSANNA: Then one man is listening, and the other will come to look for me. Let's begin!

MARCELLINA: I'll hide here.

(MARCELLINA *exits into pavilion.*)

SUSANNA (*to* COUNTESS): Madame, you're trembling. Are you cold?

COUNTESS: The night seems humid. I'll go in now.

FIGARO (*to himself*): Here we are at the great moment of crisis!

SUSANNA: I'll stay under these pine trees if Madame will permit me, to enjoy the cool breezes for half an hour.

FIGARO (*to himself*): The breezes! The breezes!

COUNTESS: Stay here if you like. (*Exits.*)

SUSANNA (*to herself*): The rascal is playing sentinel. I'll have my joke on him as well. I'll reward him in kind for his cruel suspicions! (*aloud*) At last the moment has come when I may freely enjoy myself in the arms of my lover. Timid fears, leave my breast, and don't disturb my pleas-

foco l'amenità del loco, la terra e il ciel risponda, come la
notte i furti miei seconda!

27. *Aria*

Deh vieni, non tardar, o gioia bella,
Vieni ove amore per goder t'appella,
Finchè non splende in ciel notturna face,
Finchè l'aria è ancor bruna, e il mondo tace.
Qui mormora il ruscel, qui scherza l'aura.
Che col dolce sussurro il cor ristaura,
Qui ridono i fioretti e l'erba è fresca,
Ai piaceri d'amor qui tutto adesca.
Vieni, ben mio, tra queste piante ascose,
Vieni, vieni! ti vo' la fronte incoronar di rose.
(*Si nasconde nei siepi e si metta il mantello della* CON-
TESSA.)

Recitativo

FIGARO: Perfida! e in quella forma meco mentia, non so
s'io veglio o dormo.
(*Entra* CHERUBINO.)

CHERUBINO: La, la, la, la, la, la, la lera!
(LA CONTESSA *entra, nel mantello della* SUSANNA.)

LA CONTESSA: Il picciol paggio.

CHERUBINO: Io sento gente—entriamo ove entrò Barbarina.
Oh, vedo qui una donna!

LA CONTESSA: Ahimè, meschina!

CHERUBINO: M'inganno! a quel cappello che nell'ombra
vegg'io parmi Susanna.

LA CONTESSA: E se il conte ora vien—sorte tiranna!

28. *Finale*

CHERUBINO: Pian, pianin, le andrò più presso,
Tempo perso non sarà.

LA CONTESSA: Ah! se il conte arriva adesso,
Qualche imbroglio accadrà.

CHERUBINO: Susanetta! Non risponde?
Colla mano il volto asconde,
Or la burlo in verità!

LA CONTESSA: Arditello, sfacciatello!
Ite presto via di qua!

198

ure! Oh, how it seems that this charming place, the earth, and the sky respond to my amorous desires! How even the darkness befriends my wishes!

27. Aria

Then come, do not be late, my darling! Come where love calls you to enjoy yourself, while there's no moon in the sky, while the air remains dark and the world is silent. Here the brook is murmuring and the breeze is playing, refreshing the heart with its sweet whisper. Here the flowers are smiling, the grass is fresh, and everything favors the pleasures of love. Join me, my darling, among these secluded trees! Come, come! I want to crown your forehead with roses!

(*She hides in the bushes opposite* FIGARO *and puts on the* COUNTESS'S *cloak.*)

Recitative

FIGARO: Traitress! And she lied like that to me! I don't know whether I'm awake or dreaming.

(CHERUBINO *enters.*)

CHERUBINO: La, la, la, la, la, la, la, la!

(*The* COUNTESS *enters, wearing* SUSANNA'S *cloak.*)

COUNTESS: It's the little page.

CHERUBINO: I hear someone. I'll go to meet Barbarina. Oh, is that she over there?

COUNTESS: How awkward!

CHERUBINO: I was wrong; from that cap I see in the darkness, it seems to be Susanna.

COUNTESS: Oh, if my husband should come now, fate would be cruel!

28. Finale

CHERUBINO: Softly, softly, I'll approach her; it won't be lost time.

COUNTESS: Ah, if the Count should suddenly appear, how horrible it would be!

CHERUBINO: Susanetta! You don't answer? Why do you hide your face with your hand? Now I'll really tease her!

COUNTESS: You're audacious and bold! Leave me alone at once!

CHERUBINO: Smorfiosa, maliziosa,
Già so perchè sei qua.
(*Entra* IL CONTE, *in dietro.*)

COUNT: Ecco qui la mia Susanna!

SUSANNA *e* FIGARO: Ecco qui l'uccellatore!

CHERUBINO: Non far meco la tiranna!

SUSANNA, IL CONTE, FIGARO: Ah! nel sen mi batte il cor!
Un'altr'uom con lei si sta!

LA CONTESSA: Via, partite, o chiamo gente!

CHERUBINO: Dammi un bacio, oh, non fai niente!

SUSANNA, IL CONTE, FIGARO: Alla voce è quegli il paggio!

LA CONTESSA: Anche un bacio!
Che coraggio!

CHERUBINO: E perchè far io non posso
Quel che il conte ognor farà?
Oh veh, che smorfie!
Sai ch'io fui dietro il sofà!

SUSANNA, IL CONTE, FIGARO: Temerario!

SUSANNA, LA CONTESSA, IL CONTE, FIGARO: Se il ribaldo
ancor sta saldo,
La faccenda guasterà.

CHERUBINO: Prendi intanto!
(IL CONTE *va tra* CHERUBINO *e* LA CONTESSA.)

LA CONTESSA: O cielo! il conte!

CHERUBINO: O cielo! il conte!

FIGARO (*fra se*): Vo' veder cosa fan là.

IL CONTE: Perchè voi non ripetete,
Ricevete questo qua!
(*Da uno sciaffa a* CHERUBINO.)

SUSANNA, LA CONTESSA, IL CONTE, FIGARO: Ah! ci ho fatto
un bel guadagno
Colla sua temerità!
(CHERUBINO *esce nel padiglione.*)

IL CONTE: Partito è alfin l'audace;
Accostati, ben mio.

LA CONTESSA (*finge la voce di* SUSANNA): Giacchè così vi
piace,
Eccomi qui, signor!

CHERUBINO: You're affected and nasty! I already know why you're here.

(*The* COUNT *enters in the background.*)

COUNT: There's my Susanna.

SUSANNA *and* FIGARO: Here comes the mighty hunter!

CHERUBINO: Don't play the fine lady with me.

SUSANNA, COUNT, FIGARO: Ah! My heart is pounding. Another man is there with her!

COUNTESS: Go; leave me, or I'll call for help!

CHERUBINO: Give me a kiss, or you won't escape!

SUSANNA, COUNT, FIGARO: The voice is Cherubino's!

COUNTESS: A kiss too! What boldness!

CHERUBINO: And why can't I follow the Count's example? Heavens, what affectation! You knew that I was behind that chair!

SUSANNA, COUNT, FIGARO: What boldness!

SUSANNA, COUNTESS, COUNT, FIGARO: If this young fool remains here any longer, he'll spoil all our plans!

CHERUBINO: Take this, meanwhile!

(*The* COUNT *steps between* CHERUBINO *and the* COUNTESS.)

COUNTESS: O heavens, the Count!

CHERUBINO: O heavens, the Count!

FIGARO (*to himself*): I want to see what they're doing over there.

COUNT: So that you don't repeat your mistake, take this from me!

(*He slaps* CHERUBINO.)

SUSANNA, COUNTESS, COUNT, FIGARO: Ah, he's caused a charming situation with his boldness and curiosity!

(CHERUBINO *exits into the pavilion.*)

COUNT: The rascal has gone at last. Come nearer, my darling.

COUNTESS (*imitating* SUSANNA): Here I am, my Lord, if it pleases you!

FIGARO (*fra se*): Che compiacente femmina,
Che sposa di buon cor!

IL CONTE: Porgimi la manina.

LA CONTESSA: Io ve la do.

IL CONTE: Carina!

FIGARO: Carina!

IL CONTE: Che dita tenerelle! che delicata pelle!
Mi pizzica, mi stuzzica,
M'empie d'un nuovo ardor!

SUSANNA, LA CONTESSA, FIGARO: La cieca prevenzione
Delude la ragione
Inganna i sensi ognor.

IL CONTE: Oltre la dote, o cara,
Ricevi ancor un brillante
Che a te porge un amante
In pegno del suo amor!

LA CONTESSA: Tutto Susanna piglia
Dal suo benefattor.

SUSANNA, IL CONTE, FIGARO: Va tutto a maraviglia,
Ma il meglio manca ancor.

LA CONTESSA: Signor, d'accese fiaccole
Io veggio il balenar.

IL CONTE: Entriam, mia bella Venere,
Andiamoci a celar!

SUSANNA e FIGARO: Mariti Scimuniti
Venite ad imparar.

LA CONTESSA: Al buio, signor mio?

IL CONTE: E quello che voglio;
Tu sai che là per leggere
Io non desio entrar!

SUSANNA e LA CONTESSA: I furbi sono in trappola,
Comincia ben l'affar.

FIGARO: La perfida lo seguita,
E vano il dubitar.

IL CONTE: Chi passa?

FIGARO (*forte*): Passa gente.

LA CONTESSA: E Figaro! Men vo!

IL CONTE: Andate, andate! Io poi verrò.
(IL CONTE e LA CONTESSA *escono da parte*.)

FIGARO (*to himself*): How very obliging! What a sweet bride!

COUNT: Give me your little hand.

COUNTESS: Here it is.

COUNT: My darling!

FIGARO: His darling!

COUNT: What tender fingers! What delicate skin! It stirs me; it teases me and fills me with new desire!

SUSANNA, COUNTESS, FIGARO: His blind infatuation robs him of reason. His senses are still deceived.

COUNT: Besides the dowry, my darling, receive also this jewel that carries the pledge of my love.

COUNTESS: Susanna gladly accepts her benefactor's gifts.

SUSANNA, COUNT, FIGARO: The plot is going beautifully, but the best is still to come.

COUNTESS: My Lord, I see lighted torches in the distance.

COUNT: Let's go in, my beautiful Venus: let's hide ourselves!

SUSANNA *and* FIGARO: Misguided husbands come here to learn!

COUNTESS: In the dark, my Lord?

COUNT: That's just what I want. You know we're not going there in order to read.

SUSANNA *and* COUNTESS: The scoundrel is in a trap; the affair progresses well.

FIGARO: The faithless creature is following him; now all doubts are in vain.

COUNT: Who's passing?

FIGARO (*aloud*): People are passing.

COUNTESS: It's Figaro! I'd better go!

COUNT: Go ahead, then! I'll follow you soon.
(COUNT *and* COUNTESS *exit, separately.*)

FIGARO: Tutto è tranquillo e placido;
Entrò la bella Venere;
Col vago Marte prendere,
Nuovo Vulcan del secolo,
In rete la potrò!

SUSANNA (*finge la voce della* CONTESSA): Ehi, Figaro!
Tacete!

FIGARO: Oh questa è la contessa!
 A tempo vi giungete;
Vedrete là voi stessa,
Il conte e la mia sposa.
Di propria man la cosa
Toccar io vi farò.

SUSANNA: Parlate un po' più basso!
Di qua non muovo il passo,
Ma vendicar mi vo'.

FIGARO (*fra se riconosce la voce di* SUSANNA): Susanna!
(*forte*)
Vendicarsi?

SUSANNA: Si!

FIGARO: Come potria farsi?

SUSANNA: L'iniquo io vo' sorprendere;
Poi so quel che farò.

FIGARO (*a parte*): La volpe vuol sorprendermi
E secondarla vo'. (*forte*)
Ah, se madama il vuole!

SUSANNA: Su via, manco parole!

FIGARO: Ah madama!

SUSANNA: Su via, manco parole!

FIGARO: Eccomi ai vostri piedi;
Ho pieno il cor di foco!
Esaminate il loco,
Pensate al traditor!

SUSANNA (*fra se*): Come la man mi pizzica!

FIGARO (*fra se*): Come il polmon mi s'altera!

SUSANNA (*fra se*): Che smania! Che furor!

FIGARO (*fra se*): Che smania! Che calor!

SUSANNA (*finge la voce della* CONTESSA): E senz'alcun
affetto?

FIGARO: Everything is calm and placid. The beautiful Venus has gone off with the charming Mars, but I, like Vulcan, will catch them in a net!

SUSANNA (*imitating the* COUNTESS): O Figaro! Be quiet!

FIGARO: Oh, that's the Countess! You've come just in time; you'll see there, with your own eyes, the Count and my bride going into the pavilion.

SUSANNA: Speak a little more softly. I won't move a step from here, yet I'll have my revenge.

FIGARO (*to himself, recognizing* SUSANNA'S *voice*): Susanna! (*aloud*) You'll have revenge?

SUSANNA: Yes!

FIGARO: How will you arrange it?

SUSANNA: The wretch will be surprised by me, then I'll know what to do!

FIGARO (*aside*): The vixen means to surprise me, and I'll play along with her scheme. (*aloud*) Ah, if Madame wishes it!

SUSANNA: Go on; I'm speechless!

FIGARO: Ah, my Lady.

SUSANNA: Go on; I'm speechless!

FIGARO: Here I am at your feet; my heart is consumed by fire! Look at this secluded place, and recall your husband's treachery!

SUSANNA (*to herself*): How my hand itches to slap him!

FIGARO (*to himself*): How my heart enjoys this relief!

SUSANNA (*to herself*): What rage, what fury I feel!

FIGARO (*to himself*): What rage, what vehemence!

SUSANNA (*imitating the* COUNTESS): But without any affection?

FIGARO: Suppliscavi il rispetto.
Non perdiam tempo in vano;
Datemi un po' la mano,
Datemi un po' la mano!

SUSANNA (*nella sua propria voce*): Servitevi, signor!
(*Lui da uno sciaffo.*)

FIGARO: Che sciaffo!

SUSANNA: E questo, e questo, e ancora questo,
E questo, e poi quest'altro.
E questo, signor scaltro!

FIGARO: O schiaffi graziosissimi!
O mio felice amor!

SUSANNA: Impara, impara, o perfido!
A fare il seduttor!

FIGARO: Pace, pace, mio dolce tesoro!
Io conobbi la voce che adoro,
E che impressa ognor serbo nel cor.

SUSANNA: La mia voce?

FIGARO: La voce che adoro.

SUSANNA e FIGARO: Pace, pace, mio dolce tesoro;
Pace, pace, mio tenero amor!
(IL CONTE *ritorna.*)

IL CONTE: Non la trovo e girai tutto il bosco.

SUSANNA e FIGARO: Quest'è il conte, alla voce il conosco.

IL CONTE: Ehi, Susanna! Sei sorda? Sei muta?

SUSANNA: Bella, bella! Non l'ha conosciuta!

FIGARO: Chi?

SUSANNA: Madama!

FIGARO: Madama?

SUSANNA: Madama!

SUSANNA e FIGARO: La commedia, idol mio, terminiamo;
Consoliamo il bizzarro amator!

FIGARO: Si, madama, voi siete il ben mio!
Un ristoro al mio cor concedete.

IL CONTE: La mia sposa? ah! senz'arme son io!

SUSANNA: Io son qui, faccio quel che volete.

IL CONTE: Ah, ribaldi, ribaldi!

FIGARO: I'll substitute respect. Let's not waste time in vain discussion; give me your hand for a moment. Give me your hand!

SUSANNA (*in her own voice*): It's at your service, Sir!
(*She slaps him.*)
FIGARO: What a blow!
SUSANNA: Take this one! And this one, and this, and then another! And this one, and still another one! And this, you scheming rascal!
FIGARO: Oh, most welcome blows! Oh, my happy love!

SUSANNA: I'll teach you, traitor, to play the seducer!

FIGARO: Peace, peace, my sweet treasure! I know the voice that I love—it is impressed upon my heart.

SUSANNA: My voice?
FIGARO: The voice I adore.
SUSANNA *and* FIGARO: Peace, peace, my sweet treasure! Peace, peace, my tender love!
(*The* COUNT *returns.*)
COUNT: I can't find her, and I've walked all through the woods!
SUSANNA *and* FIGARO: That's the Count; I know his voice.
COUNT: Oh, Susanna! Are you deaf? Can't you hear me?
SUSANNA: Lovely, lovely; he didn't recognize her!
FIGARO: Who?
SUSANNA: The Countess!
FIGARO: The Countess?
SUSANNA: The Countess!
SUSANNA *and* FIGARO: Let's conclude the comedy, my darling. Let's console this unhappy lover!
FIGARO: Yes, my Lady, you are my beloved! Won't you grant some refreshment to my heart?
COUNT: It's my wife! And I'm here without my sword!
SUSANNA: I'm here to do whatever you wish!
COUNT: Ah, disgusting, disgusting!

SUSANNA *e* FIGARO: Ah, corriamo, corriamo, mio bene,
E le pene compensi il piacer.
(IL CONTE *prende il braccio di* FIGARO.)

IL CONTE: Gente, gente, all'armi, all'armi!

FIGARO: Il padrone!

IL CONTE: Gente, gente! aiuto, aiuto!

FIGARO: Son perduto!
(SUSANNA *va nel padiglione. Entrano* DON BASILIO, DON CURZIO, BARTOLO *ed* ANTONIO.)

DON BASILIO, DON CURZIO, BARTOLO, ANTONIO: Cos'avvenne? Cos'avvenne?

IL CONTE: Il scellerato
M'ha tradito, m'ha infamato,
E con chi state a veder!

FIGARO: Son storditi, sbalorditi!

DON BASILIO, DON CURZIO, BARTOLO, ANTONIO: Son stordito, sbalordito!

FIGARO: O che scena, che piacer!

DON BASILIO, DON CURZIO, BARTOLO, ANTONIO: Non mi par che cio sia ver!

IL CONTE: Invan resistete,
Uscite, madama!
Il premio ora avete
Di vostra onestà!
(CHERUBINO *esce dal padiglione.*)
Il paggio!

ANTONIO (*prendendo* BARBARINA): Mia figlia!

FIGARO (*prendendo* MARCELLINA): Mia madre!
(SUSANNA *esce.*)

FIGARO, DON BASILIO, DON CURZIO, BARTOLO, ANTONIO: Madama!

IL CONTE: Scoperta è la trama,
La perfida è qua!

SUSANNA (*s'inginocchia*): Perdono, perdono!

IL CONTE: No, no, non sperarlo!

FIGARO: Perdono, perdono!

IL CONTE: No, no, non vo' darlo.

TUTTI: Perdono!

SUSANNA *and* FIGARO: Let's run away, my darling, and joy will repay us for our pain!

(*The* COUNT *seizes* FIGARO'S *arm.*)

COUNT: Help, help, bring weapons!

FIGARO: My master!

COUNT: Everyone, come and bear witness!

FIGARO: I'm lost!

(SUSANNA *exits into the pavilion.* DON BASILIO, DON CURZIO, BARTOLO, *and* ANTONIO *enter.*)

DON BASILIO, DON CURZIO, BARTOLO, ANTONIO: What has happened?

COUNT: This villain has betrayed me, disgraced me, and you'll see with whom!

FIGARO: I'm stupefied and bewildered!

DON BASILIO, DON CURZIO, BARTOLO, ANTONIO: We're stupefied and bewildered!

FIGARO: What a scene! What a comedy!

DON BASILIO, DON CURZIO, BARTOLO, ANTONIO: It doesn't seem that this can be true!

COUNT: Resistance is vain; come out, my Lady! Now you'll receive the reward for your fidelity.

(CHERUBINO *comes out of the pavilion.*)

The page!

ANTONIO (*bringing out* BARBARINA): My daughter!

FIGARO (*bringing out* MARCELLINA): My mother!

(SUSANNA *comes out.*)

FIGARO, DON BASILIO, DON CURZIO, BARTOLO, ANTONIO: The Countess!

COUNT: The plot is discovered; the traitress is here.

SUSANNA (*kneeling*): Forgive me, forgive me!

COUNT: No, there's no hope!

FIGARO: Forgive me, forgive me!

COUNT: I'll never forgive you.

ALL: Forgive her!

IL CONTE: No.
No, no, no, no, no, no!
(LA CONTESSA *emerge dal padiglione aposito*.)
LA CONTESSA: Almeno io per loro perdono otterrò.

IL CONTE, DON BASILIO, DON CURZIO, BARTOLO, ANTONIO:
Oh cielo, che veggio!
Deliro! Vaneggio!
Che creder non so!

IL CONTE (*s'ingaroccia*): Contessa, perdono! Perdono, perdono!

LA CONTESSA: Più docil'io sono e defico di sì.

TUTTI: Ah tutti contenti saremo così!
Questo giorno di tormenti,
Di capricci e di follia,
In contenti e in allegria
Solo amor può terminar.
Sposi! Amici! Al ballo! Al gioco!
Alle mine date foco!
Ed al suon di lieta marcia,
Corriam tutti a festeggiar!

COUNT: No. No, no, no, no, no, no!
(*The* COUNTESS *comes out of the opposite pavilion.*)

COUNTESS: Perhaps I can obtain pardon for them.

COUNT, DON BASILIO, DON CURZIO, BARTOLO, ANTONIO:
What is this? It's delirious! It's a mirage! I don't know
what to believe!

COUNT (*kneeling*): My Lady, forgive me, forgive me!

COUNTESS: My kindness prevails, and I consent to forgive
you.

ALL: Everyone will be happy now. This day of torments,
of caprices and follies, is finished—only love can end it in
happiness and gaiety. Lovers and friends! Dance and be
gay! Let joy light your faces! And to the music of a happy
march, let us hurry off to celebrate!

DON
GIOVANNI

*An opera
in two acts*

*Music by
Wolfgang Amadeus Mozart
(K. 527)*

*Words by
Lorenzo da Ponte*

INTRODUCTION

Don Giovanni was first performed at Prague in October 1787, a little more than a year after the premiere of *The Marriage of Figaro*. Although its merit has never been questioned, its essential quality is elusive—is it a comedy, a tragedy, or both? And so to this day, it has remained an enigma to both critics and operagoers. Mozart and Da Ponte may have intended this: they entitled the work a *dramma giocoso,* instead of using one of the prevailing terms, *opera buffa* or *opera seria.*

Although *Don Giovanni* includes an extraordinary range of effects, moods, and emotions, the story of the opera is simple; but the libretto, unlike that of *Così fan tutte,* has seeming inconsistencies. Donna Anna's first explanation of her seduction by Don Giovanni is absurd. She claims that she mistook the intruder for Don Ottavio, her fiancé, but what would Don Ottavio be doing at midnight in the room of a well-brought-up young lady? Her story seems to be an incoherent combination of nightmare and wish, and this mixture of dream and reality pervades the opera. While the comic impulse of *Don Giovanni* moves toward a parody of social realities, its tragic impulse intimates the darkness of human desire and fate.

The story moves from Donna Anna's tragic cries of vengeance after her father's murder, to the semicomic scene ending in Leporello's "Catalogue" aria, to the wholly comic episode of Don Giovanni's flirtation with Zerlina. But the comedy never brings complete pleasure or relief. In seeming to avoid the opera's tragic impulse, Mozart makes that impulse more obscure and more ominous.

Although the opera is dominated by Don Giovanni, it is not so much what happens to him that concerns us, but rather his effect on everyone around him. He is more than simply a character; he represents a force: the principle of sensuality. His "morality" consists of pursuing his desires and of seeking new experience; the morality of the other

214

characters demands that they resist his power. Every character in the opera questions himself, except for Don Giovanni; there is nothing inward about him; he is all thrust and motion, energy and appetite. And though he is callous and inhuman we identify ourselves with him; we feel a surge of elation when Don Giovanni defies the Statue and refuses to repent. Nevertheless, in action we would never choose to take his place, for we lack the courage to suffer his fate; we are among the bystanders—we gossip, we moralize, yet we cannot take our eyes from the awesome spectacle of Don Giovanni's downfall.

At least three of the characters do not seem really comfortable with the morality that prevails at the end of the opera—Donna Anna and Don Ottavio delay their wedding, and Donna Elvira plans to enter a convent to forget her sorrows. They and the comic characters, however, rationalize Don Giovanni's loss and attempt to exorcize him in a self-righteous sextet. For Zerlina and Masetto a measure of domestic happiness is probable—the world will go on. And Leporello, though he will find a new master, will forever be made restless by his memories—the best part of his life is over. And so, structurally and dramatically, the final sextet is necessary to the resolution of the opera.

Don Giovanni represents vitality directed toward self-gratification. Although he is Anarchy in opposition to Morality, his irrepressible good spirits are infectious; everyone in the opera is fascinated by him. But Don Giovanni's fate is not simply to be punished by eternal flames; he also suffers the endless dissatisfaction and final emptiness of self-love. There is peace perhaps in loving a single woman, but the pursuit of womankind allows no repose. For Don Giovanni the beginning and the ending of love are one; love is a game that he must ceaselessly begin, and a lie that he must unceasingly attempt to end. His love perpetuates itself only through unfulfillment, and release from this love is to be found only in death.

Leporello is the most human character in the opera. Although he envies Don Giovanni, and although he will even attempt, however ludicrously, to imitate him, he also shows fear and repugnance for Don Giovanni. He constantly threatens desertion, but his continued fidelity is assured by Don Giovanni's fascination, as well as by his bribery. Not even Don Giovanni's death can free Leporello from his vulgar appetites and dreams; he is the bridge between the formal morality of Don Ottavio and Donna Anna and the aggrandizing freedom of Don Giovanni.

Ottavio and Masetto are types often encountered in Mozart's operas. Ottavio has no ideas or direction of his own; he exists only to fulfill Donna Anna's hypocritical wish for an acceptable husband. He is a throwback to Belmonte in *The Abduction from the Seraglio* and a precursor of Tamino in *The Magic Flute*. Masetto is a conventional country bumpkin, who nevertheless displays an ineffective bravery in attempting to defy Don Giovanni.

The three women are clearly differentiated. Donna Anna's furious vengeance conceals an equally furious passion, for we know that she is obsessed by Don Giovanni throughout the opera. We are not surprised at her reluctance to marry Don Ottavio, even when the libertine has finally met his end. Donna Elvira seeks to hold Don Giovanni by the weak social chain of matrimony; when he breaks his vows, she refuses to give him up, not realizing that no woman can intimidate or bind him with any conventional tie. Nor does she completely recognize that it is precisely his fiery iconoclasm to which she so fully responds. She, like Donna Anna, may lack a sense of humor, but neither is backward in demanding her rights. Their best feminine weapons are given to them by society, and so they necessarily fail with Don Giovanni. He neither accepts marriage to Donna Elvira nor repents when Donna Anna's father completes her revenge. Zerlina is a typical Mozart soubrette, more complex than Blonde in *The Abduction from the Seraglio,* but less so than Susanna in *The Marriage of Figaro.* Zerlina is tempted by Don Giovanni's proposals, but they frighten her; actually, she is more eager for security than for adventure. And so we have a clear sense of the limitation of her love for Masetto. She cajoles him; she is tender with him; but she never will passionately love him.

The story of *Don Giovanni* is both amusing and terrifying. Because it embodies the awareness that deep within us all there is something opposed to morality and self-restraint, it never dogmatizes the need for moral reform; in a sense, the opera satirizes all moral complacency. We can note the same strain of rhetoric in certain of Donna Anna's and Donna Elvira's indignant outbursts as in Fiordiligi's arias in *Così fan tutte,* which Mozart and Da Ponte patently intended to be satirical.

Don Giovanni is comic in its parody of moral pretentiousness, but it is tragic in portraying the consequences of freedom from morality, and it is even more ultimately tragic in recognizing that there can be no end, no resolution to the war between social morality and individual desire.

R. P.

SYNOPSIS

ACT ONE

Don Giovanni's attempted seduction of Donna Anna results in a duel in which he kills the Commendatore, her father. Don Giovanni escapes unrecognized with Leporello, his servant, as Donna Anna and her fiancé, Don Ottavio, vow vengeance upon her father's murderer.

Don Giovanni next encounters an old acquaintance, Donna Elvira, whom he had seduced by a promise of marriage. He escapes while Leporello enumerates to the outraged Elvira the varied and extensive conquests of his master.

On the way to her wedding, a peasant girl, Zerlina, is accosted by Don Giovanni. Their flirtation is interrupted by Donna Elvira, who warns the girl to distrust him. Elvira also tries, with some success, to arouse the suspicions of Donna Anna and Don Ottavio. But it is not until Don Giovanni takes leave of Donna Anna that she recognizes his voice as that of the man who killed her father.

A great ball is in progress in Don Giovanni's castle, as Zerlina reassures her bridegroom, Masetto, of her affection for him. Elvira, Anna, and Ottavio, who have now joined forces, appear at the ball as masqueraders, seeking vengeance upon Don Giovanni. They prevent him from seducing Zerlina, but, sword in hand, he escapes from his accusers.

ACT TWO

Exchanging his cloak for Leporello's in order to serenade Donna Elvira's maid, Don Giovanni first entices Donna Elvira down from her balcony and then sends her off with Leporello, whom she believes to be Don Giovanni. Masetto enters. Mistaking Don Giovanni for Leporello, he is beaten after confiding his plans to murder the reprobate.

Meanwhile, Leporello cannot elude Elvira. Anna, Ottavio, Zerlina, and Masetto come upon the pair, and Elvira pleads that they spare Leporello's life, until Leporello

218

reveals his identity. In the general confusion, Leporello escapes.

Leporello rejoins Don Giovanni in a cemetery dominated by a statue of Donna Anna's father. Their laughter at the evening's events is interrupted by the foreboding voice of the Statue, which bids them leave the dead in peace. Don Giovanni, accepting the challenge, invites the Statue to dine, and this invitation is promptly accepted.

The Commendatore, as a marble statue, arrives at Don Giovanni's castle and finds Don Giovanni and Leporello carousing at dinner. Don Giovanni, refusing the Commendatore's offer of a last chance to repent, accepts his return invitation to dine. As the Commendatore exits, flames appear from all directions. Don Giovanni is engulfed by the fire. Informed by Leporello of Don Giovanni's fate, the remaining characters announce their plans: Donna Anna and Don Ottavio will postpone their wedding for a year; Donna Elvira will enter a convent; Zerlina and Masetto will go home to dinner. Leporello announces that he will seek a better master. And all rejoice at "the end of evildoers"!

CHARACTERS

DON GIOVANNI, *a nobleman*	*Bass-baritone or Baritone*
LEPORELLO, *his servant*	*Bass-baritone or Bass*
DONNA ANNA, *a lady of Seville*	*Soprano*
THE COMMENDATORE, *her father*	*Bass*
DON OTTAVIO, *betrothed to* DONNA ANNA	*Tenor*
DONNA ELVIRA, *a lady of Burgos;*	
abandoned by DON GIOVANNI	*Soprano*
ZERLINA, *a peasant girl*	*Soprano*
MASETTO, *her betrothed*	*Bass or Baritone*
CHORUS *of peasants*	
Servants, musicians, guests	

The action takes place in Seville, during the course of one day, in the middle of the seventeenth century.

DON GIOVANNI

ATTO PRIMO

Scena I

LEPORELLO *aspetta fuori dalla casa del* COMMENDATORE.

1. Introduzione

LEPORELLO: Notte e giorno faticar,
Per chi nulla sà gradir;
Piova e vento sopportar,
Mangiar male e mal dormir.
Voglio far il gentiluomo,
E non voglio più servir;
No, no, no, non voglio più servir.
Oh che caro galantuomo:
Vuol star dentro colla bella,
Ed io far la sentinella!
Ma mi par, che venga gente,
Non mi voglio far sentir, Ah!
(*Si nasconde. Entrano* DON GIOVANNI, *mascherato, e* DONNA
ANNA.)

DONNA ANNA: Non sperar, se non m'uccidi,
Ch'io ti lascio fuggir mai.

DON GIOVANNI: Donna folle, indarno gridi!
Chi son io tu non saprai.

LEPORELLO: Che tumulto! oh ciel, che gridi!
Il padron in nuovi guai.

DONNA ANNA: Gente! Servi! al traditore!

DON GIOVANNI: Taci, e trema al mio furore!

DONNA ANNA: Scelerato!

DON GIOVANNI: Sconsigliata!

DONNA ANNA: Come furia disperata
Ti saprò perseguitar.

DON GIOVANNI: Questa furia disperata
Mi vuol far precipitar.

LEPORELLO: Stà a veder ch'il malandrino
Mi farà precipitar.
(*Esce* DONNA ANNA. *Entra* IL COMMENDATORE, *spada in
mano.*)

IL COMMENDATORE: Lasciala, indegno;
Battiti meco.

DON GIOVANNI: Va, non mi degno
Di pugnar teco.

222

ACT ONE

Scene I

LEPORELLO *is waiting outside the* COMMENDATORE'S *house.*

1. Introduction

LEPORELLO: I must work night and day for someone who doesn't appreciate me; I must bear the wind and rain, scarcely eating or sleeping! I, too, would like to be a gentleman, and no longer a servant, no, no, no, no! Oh, what a worthy nobleman! You revel in there with a beautiful lady, while I have to keep watch. But I hear somebody coming, and I don't want to be seen, no, no, no, no!
(*He hides. Enter* DON GIOVANNI, *who is masked, and* DONNA ANNA.)

DONNA ANNA: Unless you kill me, don't think that you'll escape!

DON GIOVANNI: Madwoman! Your shouting is in vain! You'll never discover who I am!

LEPORELLO: What a noise—O God, what shouting! My master's in trouble again!

DONNA ANNA: Servants, come and kill the traitor!

DON GIOVANNI: Be quiet, and tremble at my fury!

DONNA ANNA: Traitor!

DON GIOVANNI: Stupid woman!

DONNA ANNA: I'll pursue you forever like a desperate Fury!

DON GIOVANNI: This raging woman will force me to do something desperate!

LEPORELLO: I'll wait here and see what this libertine expects me to do.
(DONNA ANNA *exits. The* COMMENDATORE *enters, with drawn sword.*)

COMMENDATORE: Let her go, you wretch, and fight with me!

DON GIOVANNI: Go away; it's not my custom to fight with old men.

223

IL COMMENDATORE: Così pretendi
Da me fuggir?

LEPORELLO (*a parte*): Potessi almeno
Di quà partir.

DON GIOVANNI: Misero! attendi,
Se vuoi morir.
(*Si battono.* IL COMMENDATORE *cade.*)

IL COMMENDATORE: Ah soccorso! son tradito.
L'assassino m'ha ferito,
E dal seno palpitante
Sento l'anima partir.

DON GIOVANNI: Ah! già cade il sciagurato,
Affannoso e agonizzante;
Già dal seno palpitante
Veggo l'anima partir.

LEPORELLO: Qual misfatto! qual eccesso!
Entro il sen dallo spavento
Palpitar il cor mi sento—
Io non so che far, che dir!
(IL COMMENDATORE *muore.*)

Recitativo

DON GIOVANNI (*sotto voce*): Leporello, ove sei?

LEPORELLO: Son quì per mia disgrazia; e voi?

DON GIOVANNI: Son quì.

LEPORELLO: Chi è morto—voi, o il vecchio?

DON GIOVANNI: Che domanda da bestia! il vecchio!

LEPORELLO: Bravo! due imprese leggiadre: sforzar la figlia,
ed ammazzar il padre!

DON GIOVANNI: L'ha voluto suo danno.

LEPORELLO: Ma Donn'Anna cos'ha voluto?

DON GIOVANNI: Taci! Non mi seccar, vien meco, se non
vuoi qualche cosa ancor tu—

LEPORELLO: Non vo' nulla, Signor! non parlo più.
(*Escono* DON GIOVANNI *e* LEPORELLO. *Entrano* DONNA
ANNA, DON OTTAVIO *e servi portando fiaccole.*)

DONNA ANNA: Ah, del padre in periglio! in soccorso voliam.

COMMENDATORE: Is that your excuse to avoid me?

LEPORELLO (*aside*): If only I could get away from here!

DON GIOVANNI: Miserable old man! on guard, then, since you're anxious to die!
(*They fight. The* COMMENDATORE *falls.*)
COMMENDATORE: Heaven, aid me! I'm betrayed! This assassin has struck me, and I feel that I am dying.

DON GIOVANNI: Ah, the poor old man is already dying; he's suffering and in agony. I can almost see the spirit departing from his body.

LEPORELLO: What brutality! I feel my heart shuddering within me! I don't know what to do or say.
(*The* COMMENDATORE *dies.*)

Recitative

DON GIOVANNI (*sotto voce*): Leporello, where are you?
LEPORELLO: Here I am, to my shame—and you?
DON GIOVANNI: I'm here.
LEPORELLO: Who's dead—you or the old man?
DON GIOVANNI: What a stupid question! The old man, of course.
LEPORELLO: Wonderful! Two charming projects. Seduce the daughter, and then murder the father!
DON GIOVANNI: He got what he asked for!
LEPORELLO: But Donna Anna—did she ask for what she got?
DON GIOVANNI: Be quiet! You're boring me. Come along, unless you, too, are asking for something—
LEPORELLO: I'm quite satisfied, my Lord. I won't speak another word.
(DON GIOVANNI *and* LEPORELLO *exit.* DONNA ANNA *and* DON OTTAVIO *enter, with servants carrying torches.*)

DONNA ANNA: My father is in terrible danger; I must help him.

225

DON OTTAVIO: Tutto il mio sangue verserò, se bisogna. Ma dov'è il scelerato?

DONNA ANNA: In questo loco—(*vedendo il corpo del suo padre*) Ma qual mai s'offre, oh Dei! spettacolo funesto agli occhi miei! Padre mio! mio caro padre!

DON OTTAVIO: Signore!

DONNA ANNA: Ah, l'assassino mel trucidò! Quel sangue, quella piaga—quel volto tinto e coperto del color di morte! Ei non respira più—fredde le membra! Padre mio! caro padre! padre amato! Io manco—io moro!
(*Si getta sal corpo del* COMMENDATORE.)

DON OTTAVIO: Ah soccorrete, amici, il mio tesoro! (*ai servi*) Cercatemi, recatemi qualche odor, qualche spirito. Ah non tardate! Donn'Anna, sposa, amica! Il duolo estremo la meschinella uccide.

DONNA ANNA: Ahi!

DON OTTAVIO: Già riviene! Datele nuovi adjuti.

DONNA ANNA: Padre mio!

DON OTTAVIO: Celate, allontanate agli occhi suoi quell'oggetto d'orrore. Anima mia! consolati, fa core!

2. Duetto

DONNA ANNA: Fuggi, crudele, fuggi!
Lascia che mora anch'io!
Ora ch'è morto, oh Dio!
Chi a me la vita diè!

DON OTTAVIO: Senti cor mio, deh senti!
Guardami un solo istante!
Ti parla il caro amante.
Che vive sol per te!

DONNA ANNA: Tu sei, perdon! mio bene!
L'affanno mio, le pene!
Ah, il padre mio dov'è?

DON OTTAVIO: Il padre? Lascia o cara!
La rimembranza amara:
Hai sposo e padre in me!

DONNA ANNA: Ah! vendicar, s'il puoi,
Giura quel sangue ognor!

DON OTTAVIO: Lo giuro agli occhi tuoi.
Lo giuro al nostro amor!

DON OTTAVIO: I'll gladly pour out all my blood in his defense! Where is the vile wretch?

DONNA ANNA: He was here a moment ago—(*seeing her father's body*) O God! What a horrible sight offends my eyes! Father, my dearest father!

DON OTTAVIO: Your Lordship!

DONNA ANNA: Oh, the assassin has killed him! This blood, this wound, that deadly pallor! He's steeped in the color of death! And he no longer breathes! His limbs are cold! Father! Beloved father! I'm fainting, I'm dying!
(*She throws herself upon the* COMMENDATORE'S *body.*)

DON OTTAVIO: Ah, sustain yourself, my darling! (*to the servants*) Look about—bring me some smelling salts; don't delay! Donna Anna! My bride! My beloved! Poor girl; the sudden shock has almost killed her!

DONNA ANNA: Ah!

DON OTTAVIO: She's reviving now; we must help her.

DONNA ANNA: My father!

DON OTTAVIO: Hide the corpse; take the object of such horror from her eyes. My darling, console yourself—be courageous!

2. Duet

DONNA ANNA: Leave me, cruel one! Leave me here so that I too can die, now that the one who gave me life is dead!

DON OTTAVIO: Listen, my darling, please listen. Look at me for only one moment. Your dear lover is speaking to you—he who lives only for you.

DONNA ANNA: It's you—pardon me, dear—my grief, the pain—oh, where is my dear father?

DON OTTAVIO: Your father? Forget the bitter sight, my dear; in me you will have a father and a husband as well.

DONNA ANNA: Swear to avenge his blood, however you can!

DON OTTAVIO: I swear it by your eyes—and by our love!

227

DONNA ANNA *e* DON OTTAVIO: Che giuramenti oh Dei!
Che barbaro momento!
Fra cento affanni e cento
Vammi ondeggiando il cor! (*Partono.*)

Scena II

Strada. Entrano DON GIOVANNI *e* LEPORELLO.

Recitativo

DON GIOVANNI: Orsù spicciati presto—cosa vuoi?

LEPORELLO: L'affar di cui si tratta è importante.

DON GIOVANNI: Lo credo.

LEPORELLO: Importantissimo.

DON GIOVANNI: Meglio ancora. Finiscila.

LEPORELLO: Ma giurate di non andar in collera.

DON GIOVANNI: Lo giuro sul mio onore, purchè non parli del Commendatore.

LEPORELLO: Siamo soli?

DON GIOVANNI: Lo vedo.

LEPORELLO: Nessun ci sente?

DON GIOVANNI: Via!

LEPORELLO: Vi posso dire tutto liberamente?

DON GIOVANNI: Tutto sì.

LEPORELLO: Dunque quand'è così, caro signor padrone, la vita che menate è da briccone.

DON GIOVANNI: Temerario! in tal guisa!

LEPORELLO: E il giuramento.

DON GIOVANNI: Zitto! Non si parli di giuramento, taci, o ch'io—

LEPORELLO: Non parlo più! non fiato, padron mio.

DON GIOVANNI: Così saremo amici. Or odi un poco sai tu perchè son qui?

LEPORELLO: Non ne so nulla. Ma essendo l'alba chiara, non sarebbe qualche nuova conquista: io lo devo saper per porla in lista.

DON GIOVANNI: Va là che sei 'l grand'uom! Sappi ch'io sono innamorato d'una bella dama, e son certo che m'ama. La vidi, le parlai: meco al Casino questa notte verrà; zitto mi pare sentir odor di femina.

DONNA ANNA *and* DON OTTAVIO: O God, what an oath I have sworn! What a dreadful moment! A hundred afflictions tear my heart! (*Exit.*)

Scene II

A street. Enter DON GIOVANNI *and* LEPORELLO.

Recitative

DON GIOVANNI: All right, hurry up, now— What do you want to say?

LEPORELLO: It's an important matter!

DON GIOVANNI: I believe you.

LEPORELLO: It's very important!

DON GIOVANNI: Better still. Tell me and get it over with.

LEPORELLO: Promise me not to be angry.

DON GIOVANNI: I swear it on my honor—as long as you don't mention the Commendatore.

LEPORELLO: We're alone?

DON GIOVANNI: As you see.

LEPORELLO: Nobody's listening?

DON GIOVANNI: Speak!

LEPORELLO: I can tell you all freely?

DON GIOVANNI: Yes.

LEPORELLO: Well, then, it's this way; my dear lord and master, you are leading the life of a scoundrel!

DON GIOVANNI: Idiot! How dare you?

LEPORELLO: Remember your promise!

DON GIOVANNI: I don't remember any promises. Be quiet now, or I'll—

LEPORELLO: Not a word, not a breath, dear master.

DON GIOVANNI: That's fine; then we'll be friends. Now, listen to me. Do you know why we're here?

LEPORELLO: I don't know anything about it. But since a new day is dawning, it must be some new conquest. Tell me all about it, so that I can add it to my list.

DON GIOVANNI: What a great man you are! You must know that I'm in love with a beautiful lady, and I'm certain that she loves me in return. I spoke to her; I saw her; she'll come to meet me in the summerhouse tonight. Hush! I can smell the approach of a woman!

Don Giovanni

LEPORELLO (*a parte*): Cospetto! che odorato perfetto!

DON GIOVANNI: All'aria mi par bella.

LEPORELLO (*a parte*): E che occhio, dico!

DON GIOVANNI: Ritiriamoci un poco, e scopriamo terren.

LEPORELLO (*a parte*): Già prese foco.

(DON GIOVANNI *e* LEPORELLO *in disparte. Entra* DONNA ELVIRA.)

3. *Aria*

DONNA ELVIRA: Ah chi mi dice mai,
Quel barbaro dov'è?
Che per mio scorno amai,
Che mi mancò di fè.
Ah se ritrovo l'empio,
E a me non torna ancor,
Vo' farne orrendo scempio,
Gli vo' cavar il cor!

DON GIOVANNI (*a* LEPORELLO): Udisti? Qualche bella del vago abbandonata. Poverina! Poverina! Cerchiam di consolare il suo tormento.

LEPORELLO: Così ne consolò mille e ottocento.

DON GIOVANNI: Signorina!

Recitativo

DONNA ELVIRA: Chi è là?

DON GIOVANNI: Stelle! che vedo!

LEPORELLO (*a parte*): Oh bella! Donna Elvira!

DONNA ELVIRA: Don Giovanni! Sei quì? Mostro, fellon, nido d'inganni!

LEPORELLO (*a parte*): Che titoli cruscanti! Manco male che lo conosce bene.

DON GIOVANNI: Via, cara Donna Elvira, calmate quella collera—sentite—lasciatemi parlar!

DONNA ELVIRA: Cosa puoi dire dopo azion sì nera? In casa mia entra furtivamente, a forza d'arte, di giuramenti e di lusinghe arrivi a sedurre il cor mio! m'innamori, o crudele! Mi dichiari tua sposa, e poi—mancando della terra e del ciel al santo dritto—con enorme delitto, dopo tre dì da Burgos t'allontani. M'abbandoni, mi fuggi—e lasci in preda al rimorso ed al pianto per pena forse che t'amai cotanto!

230

LEPORELLO (*aside*): Good heavens, what a perfect sense of smell!

DON GIOVANNI: From here she seems to be beautiful.

LEPORELLO (*aside*): Good Lord, what eyesight!

DON GIOVANNI: Let's retire for a while, and examine the situation.

LEPORELLO (*aside*): He's on fire already!

(DON GIOVANNI *and* LEPORELLO *hide in the background.* DONNA ELVIRA *enters.*)

3. Aria

DONNA ELVIRA: Ah, who can tell me where that wretch has gone? I loved him, to my shame, and he broke his faith to me. If I find him again, and he tries to escape, I'll make a horrible scandal; I'll tear his heart from his breast!

DON GIOVANNI (*to* LEPORELLO): You hear? This beauty's been abandoned by her lover. Poor girl! Poor girl! We'll try to console her.

LEPORELLO: Just as you've consoled all the others.

DON GIOVANNI: Signorina!

Recitative

DONNA ELVIRA: Who is it?

DON GIOVANNI: Good Lord! It's she!

LEPORELLO (*aside*): Oh, lovely! Donna Elvira!

DONNA ELVIRA: Don Giovanni! You're here? Monster! Seducer! Liar!

LEPORELLO (*aside*): What pleasant titles! One can see that she knows him well.

DON GIOVANNI: Come, dearest Elvira, calm your anger! Listen for a moment—let me speak!

DONNA ELVIRA: What can you say after such evil actions? You entered my house furtively, and with oaths and flattery, you seduced my heart and made me fall in love with you! You called me your wife, and then, disregarding all the sacred ties of heaven and earth—oh, horrible crime— you left Burgos after three days! You abandoned me and left me prey to remorse and tears, a fitting punishment for having loved you so much!

LEPORELLO (*a parte*): Pare un libro stampato!

DON GIOVANNI: Oh, in quanto a questo ebbi le mie ragioni. (*a* LEPORELLO) E vero?

LEPORELLO: E vero. (*ironicamente*) E che ragioni forti!

DONNA ELVIRA: E quali sono, se non la tua perfidia, la legerezza tua? Ma il giusto cielo vuole, ch'io ti trovassi per far le sue, le mie vendette.

DON GIOVANNI: Via, cara Donna Elvira, siate più ragionevole! (*a parte*) Mi pone a cimento costei. (*forte*) Se non credete al labbro mio, credete a questo galantuomo.

LEPORELLO: Salvo il vero.

DON GIOVANNI: Via dille un poco.

LEPORELLO (*piano*): E cosa devo dirle?

DON GIOVANNI (*forte*): Si, si, dille pur tutto.

DONNA ELVIRA (*a* LEPORELLO): Ebben, fa presto.

LEPORELLO: Madama—veramente—in questo mondo conciòsia cosa quando fosse che il quadro non è tondo— (DON GIOVANNI *parte*.)

DONNA ELVIRA: Sciagurato! Così del mio dolor gioco ti prendi? Ah voi— Stelle! l'iniquo fuggì! Misera me! dove? In qual parte?

LEPORELLO: Eh, lasciate che vada! Egli non merita ch'a lui voi più pensiate.

DONNA ELVIRA: Il scelerato m'ingannò, mi tradì!

LEPORELLO: Eh consolatevi! Non siete voi, non foste, e non sarete nè la prima, nè l'ultima. Guardate questo non piccolo libro: è tutto pieno dei nomi di sue belle. Ogni villa, ogni borgo, ogni paese è testimone di sue donnesche imprese.

4. *Aria*

Madamina!
Il catalogo è questo,
Delle belle, che amò il padron mio!
Un catalogo egli è ch'ho fatto io:
Osservate, leggete con me!
In Italia sei cento e quaranta,
In Alemagna due cento trent'una;
Cento in Francia, in Turchia novant'una,

LEPORELLO (*aside*): As if she read it from a book!

DON GIOVANNI: Oh, as to that, I had my reasons! (*to* LEPORELLO) Isn't that true?

LEPORELLO: Yes, it's true. (*ironically*) And what important reasons!

DONNA ELVIRA: And what were they if not your own perfidy and shallowness? But God willed that I should find you, to take his revenge, and my own as well!

DON GIOVANNI: Come now; be more reasonable. (*aside*) This woman will drive me insane! (*aloud*) If you won't believe it from my lips, perhaps you'll believe this gentleman.

LEPORELLO: It's the truth.

DON GIOVANNI: Go ahead, tell her the story.

LEPORELLO (*softly*): And what shall I tell her?

DON GIOVANNI (*aloud*): Yes, yes. Tell her everything.

DONNA ELVIRA (*to* LEPORELLO): Well, hurry up then!

LEPORELLO: Madame—really—in this world you must know that sometimes a square is not a circle—
(DON GIOVANNI *escapes*.)

DONNA ELVIRA: Monster! Are you laughing at my grief? And as for you—heavens! The wretch has gone! I'm miserable! Where? In what direction?

LEPORELLO: Let him go! He doesn't merit a single one of your thoughts.

DONNA ELVIRA: The scoundrel has deceived and betrayed me!

LEPORELLO: Well, console yourself. You're not the first, nor will you be the last. Look here—this good-sized book is filled with the names of his conquests: every village, every town, every country, bears witness to his triumphs of love!

4. Aria

My dear lady! This is the catalogue of the women my master has loved. It's a list that I've compiled—look at it; read it over with me! In Italy, six hundred and forty; in Germany, two hundred and thirty-one; a hundred in France; ninety-one in Turkey—but in Spain there are already a thousand and three. Among them are country girls, ladies from the city, chambermaids, countesses, baronesses, marchionesses, princesses, and women of every

Ma, ma in Ispagna, son già mille e tre!
V'han fra queste contadine.
Cameriere cittadine;
V'han Contesse, Baronesse,
Marchesane, Principesse,
E v'han donne d'ogni grado,
D'ogni forma d'ogni età.

Nella bionda, egli ha l'usanza
Di lodar la gentilezza—
Nella bruna la costanza,
Nella bianca la dolcezza!
Vuol d'inverno la grassotta
Vuol d'estate la magrotta;
E la grande, maestosa;
La piccina, ognor vezzosa.
Delle vecchie fa conquista
Per piacer di porle in lista:
Sua passion predominante
E la giovin principiante
Non si picca, se sia ricca—
Se sia brutta, se sia bella!
Purchè porti la gonnella,
Voi sapete quel che fa!

(DONNA ELVIRA *e* LEPORELLO *partono. Entrano* ZERLINA *e* MASETTO *e* CORO *di contadini.*)

5. Duetto e Coro

ZERLINA: Giovinette, che fate all'amore,
Non lasciate, che passi l'età;
Se nel seno vi bulica il core,
Il rimedio vedetelo quà!
La la la, la la la!
Che piacer, che sarà.

MASETTO: Giovinetti leggieri di testa,
Non andate girando quà e là
Poco dura dei matti la festa,
Ma per me cominciata non ha!
Lera, lera la!
Che piacer, che piacer, che sarà!
Lera la, lera la!

ZERLINA, MASETTO, CORO: Vieni, vieni, carina godiamo,
E cantiamo, e balliamo, e suoniamo!
Che piacer, che piacer, che sarà!

(*Entrano* DON GIOVANNI *e* LEPORELLO.)

class, every figure, every age! With blondes, it's his habit to praise their sweetness; with brunettes, their constancy; with old women, their tenderness. In winter he likes them plump; and in the summer, slender, tall, and majestic. But still he finds the little ones charming. He even seduces the old women, simply for the pleasure of adding them to his list. But his preference is really for the young beginners. He never thinks of whether she's rich, ugly or beautiful— as long as she wears a skirt, you know very well what he does!

(DONNA ELVIRA *and* LEPORELLO *exit. Enter* ZERLINA *and* MASETTO, *with a* CHORUS *of peasants.*)

5. Duet and Chorus

ZERLINA: You young girls who play at falling in love, don't wait for your summer to pass! If your heart is bubbling over, here you see the remedy for it! How happy we will be!

MASETTO: Lightheaded young men, don't wander from one girl to another. Your happiness will soon be over, but mine hasn't even begun! How happy we will be!

ZERLINA, MASETTO, CHORUS: Come, my darling, let's enjoy ourselves, and sing and dance and play. How happy we will be!

(DON GIOVANNI *and* LEPORELLO *enter.*)

Recitativo

DON GIOVANNI: Manco male è partita! Oh guarda, guarda, che bella gioventù! Che belle donne!

LEPORELLO (*a parte*): Tra tante per mia fe, vi sarà qualche cosa anche per me.

DON GIOVANNI: Cari amici, buon giorno! Seguitate a stare allegramente; seguitate a suonar o buona gente. C'è qualche sposalizio?

ZERLINA: Si, signore; e la sposa son io.

DON GIOVANNI: Me ne consolo. Lo sposo?

MASETTO: Io per servirla.

DON GIOVANNI: Oh bravo! per servirmi! Questo è vero parlar da galantuomo.

LEPORELLO (*a parte*): Basta che sia marito.

ZERLINA: Oh, il mio Masetto è un uom d'ottimo core!

DON GIOVANNI: Oh anch'io, vedete: voglio che siamo amici. Il vostro nome?

ZERLINA: Zerlina.

DON GIOVANNI: E il tuo?

MASETTO: Masetto.

DON GIOVANNI: Oh, caro il mio Masetto! cara la mia Zerlina, v'esibisco la mia protezione. Leporello—cosa fai là, birbone?

LEPORELLO: Anch'io caro padrone, esibisco la mia protezione.

DON GIOVANNI: Presto va con costor, nel mio palazzo conducili sul fatto: ordina ch'abbiano cioccolatte, caffè, vini, presciutti—cerca divertir tutti. Mostra loro il giardin, la galleria, le camere; in effetto fa che resti contento il mio Masetto. Hai capito?

LEPORELLO: Ho capito. Andiam.

MASETTO: Signore!

DON GIOVANNI: Cosa c'è?

MASETTO: La Zerlina senza me non può star.

LEPORELLO: In vostro loco ci starà sua eccellenza—e saprà bene fare le vostre parti.

DON GIOVANNI: Oh la Zerlina è in man d'un cavalier. Va pur; fra poco ella meco verrà.

ZERLINA: Va; non temere! nelle mani son io d'un cavaliere.

Recitative

DON GIOVANNI: Thank heaven I got rid of Elvira! Oh, look here, what charming young people. What pretty girls!

LEPORELLO (*aside*): Among so many, perhaps there may be something here for me as well!

DON GIOVANNI: My friends, good morning! Continue your amusements; go on with the music, good people. Is this a betrothal?

ZERLINA: Yes, my Lord, and I am the bride.

DON GIOVANNI: Well, well—the groom?

MASETTO: Here, at your service.

DON GIOVANNI: Oh, charming! At my service—that's really the remark of a gallant man.

LEPORELLO (*aside*): It's enough that he'll be a husband.

ZERLINA: Oh, my Masetto is very good-natured!

DON GIOVANNI: So am I; I'll show you. I think we shall all be friends. What is your name?

ZERLINA: Zerlina.

DON GIOVANNI: And yours?

MASETTO: Masetto.

DON GIOVANNI: Oh, my dear Masetto! my dearest Zerlina, I offer my protection to you. Leporello—what are you doing over there, you rascal?

LEPORELLO: I, too, dear master, was offering my protection.

DON GIOVANNI: That's enough of that; invite them all to my castle, at once. Order chocolate, coffee, wines, meat—try to amuse everybody. Show them the garden, the gallery, the rooms; in other words, be sure that you keep my dear Masetto occupied— You understand me?

LEPORELLO: I understand you. Let's go.

MASETTO: My Lord!

DON GIOVANNI: What's the matter?

MASETTO: Zerlina won't stay here without me.

LEPORELLO: His lordship will be here in your place—and he knows well how to take your part.

DON GIOVANNI: Oh, Zerlina is in a nobleman's hands. Go ahead; she'll come along soon with me.

ZERLINA: Go! Don't worry; I'm with a nobleman.

MASETTO: E per questo?

ZERLINA: E per questo non c'è da dubitar.

MASETTO: Ed io, cospetto!

DON GIOVANNI: Olà! Finiam le dispute; se subito senz'altro replicar, non te ne vai, Masetto, guarda ben, ti pentirai.

6. Aria

MASETTO: Hò capito, signor sì!
Chino il capo, e me ne vo'
Giacchè piace a voi così
Altre repliche non fo'.
Cavalier voi siete già,
Dubitar non posso affè,
Me lo dice la bontà,
Che volete aver per me. (*a* ZERLINA)
Bricconaccia! malandrina!
Fosti, ognor, la mia ruina! (*a* LEPORELLO)
Vengo, vengo. (*a* ZERLINA)
Resta! resta!
E una cosa molto onesta;
Faccia il nostro cavaliere,
Cavaliera ancora te.
(MASETTO *parte con* LEPORELLO *e il* CORO.)

Recitativo

DON GIOVANNI: Alfin siam liberati, Zerlinetta gentile da quel scioccone. Che ne dite, mio ben, so far pulito?

ZERLINA: Signore, è mio marito.

DON GIOVANNI: Chi! colui? Vi par ch'un'onest'uomo, un nobil cavalier, qual io mi vanto, possa soffrir che quel visetto d'oro, quel viso inzuccherato da un bifolcaccio vil sia strapazzato.

ZERLINA: Ma, signore, io gli diedi parola di sposarlo.

DON GIOVANNI: Tal parola non vale un zero, voi non siete fatta per esser paesana. Un'altra sorte vi procuran quegli occhi bricconcelli, quei labretti sì belli, quelle dituccia candide, e odorose, parmi toccar giuncata, e fiutar rose.

ZERLINA: Ah, non vorrei—

DON GIOVANNI: Che non vorreste?

MASETTO: And so?

ZERLINA: And so there's no cause for concern.

MASETTO: And I, damn it!

DON GIOVANNI: Very well, stop arguing. Masetto, listen to me—if you don't leave us without any more chatter, I can assure you that you'll repent it!

6. Aria

MASETTO: Yes, my Lord, I understand. I must bow to you and go away, because that pleases you, and I mustn't argue any more, no, no, no! You're a gentleman, after all, and I can't doubt your honor—you speak of the esteem that you have for me. (*to* ZERLINA) You flirt! You witch! You were always my ruin! (*to* LEPORELLO) Yes, I'm going. (*to* ZERLINA) You'll stay here! It's a very honest bargain. This nobleman will make a noblewoman out of you!

(MASETTO *exits with* LEPORELLO *and* CHORUS.)

Recitative

DON GIOVANNI: At last we're free, sweet Zerlina; that stupid idiot is gone. What do you think, my dear, didn't I manage it neatly?

ZERLINA: My Lord, he's my fiancé!

DON GIOVANNI: Who, that creature? Do you think that an honest man, a nobleman such as myself, could allow that lovely face, that sweet appearance to be wasted on such a vile scarecrow?

ZERLINA: But, my Lord, I have promised to marry him.

DON GIOVANNI: Such a promise means nothing; you weren't made to be a peasant; you're assured of a higher lot by your sparkling eyes, your beautiful lips, your white and fragrant fingers, which smell like roses and are as smooth as cream.

ZERLINA: Ah, I wouldn't like—

DON GIOVANNI: What wouldn't you like?

Don Giovanni

ZERLINA: Alfine ingannata restar. Io so che rado colle donne voi altri cavalieri siete onesti e sinceri.

DON GIOVANNI: E un'impostura della gente plebea: la nobiltà ha dipinta negli occhi l'onestà. Orsù non perdiamo tempo in quest'istante io vi voglio sposar.

ZERLINA: Voi?

DON GIOVANNI: Certo io. Quel casinetto è mio: soli saremo: e là giojello mio, ci sposeremo.

7. Duettino

La ci darem la mano,
La mi dirai di sì!
Vedi, non è lontano
Partiam, ben mio, da quì!

ZERLINA: Vorrei, e non vorrei;
Mi trema un poco il cor:
Felice, è ver sarei,
Ma può burlarmi ancor.

DON GIOVANNI: Vieni mio bel diletto!

ZERLINA: Mi fa pietà Masetto.

DON GIOVANNI: Io cangierò tua sorte.

ZERLINA: Presto, non son più forte.

DON GIOVANNI: Vieni! Vieni! La ci darem la mano,
La mi dirai di sì!

ZERLINA: Vorrei e non vorrei;
Mi trema un poco il cor.

ZERLINA e DON GIOVANNI: Andiam, andiam mio bene,
A ristorar le pene
D'un innocente amor!
(*Entra* DONNA ELVIRA.)

Recitativo

DONNA ELVIRA: Fermati, scelerato! Il ciel mi fece udir le tue perfidie; io sono a tempo di salvar questa misera innocente dal tuo barbaro artiglio.

ZERLINA: Meschina! cosa sento!

DON GIOVANNI (*a parte*): Amor, consiglio! (*a* DONNA ELVIRA) Idol mio, non vedete ch'io voglio divertirmi?

DONNA ELVIRA: Divertirti, è vero, divertirti? Io so, crudele, come tu ti diverti.

ZERLINA: To be deceived after a while. I've heard that you noblemen are seldom honest and sincere with women.

DON GIOVANNI: That's a lie invented by peasants! A nobleman's honesty is written in his eyes. Come on, let's not waste time. I'll marry you this very day.

ZERLINA: You?

DON GIOVANNI: Certainly, I. That little castle is mine. We'll be alone there, and there, my dearest jewel, we'll be married!

7. Duet

There we'll take each other's hands, and then you'll tell me "yes." See; it isn't far; let's go there together, my darling!

ZERLINA: I'd like to, and yet I'm afraid—something within me holds me back. Perhaps I would be happy—but still he may be deceiving me!

DON GIOVANNI: Come, my beautiful delight!

ZERLINA: And yet I pity Masetto.

DON GIOVANNI: Your rank will equal mine!

ZERLINA: Suddenly I'm not strong enough to resist him!

DON GIOVANNI: Come with me! Come with me!

ZERLINA: I will! My heart trembles.

ZERLINA *and* DON GIOVANNI: Together, my dearest, we'll soothe the pangs of innocent love!
(DONNA ELVIRA *enters.*)

Recitative

DONNA ELVIRA: Stop, you wretch! Heaven has sent me to refute your lies; I'm just in time to save this innocent girl from your horrible designs!

ZERLINA: What is she saying? Poor me!

DON GIOVANNI (*aside*): God of Love, inspire me now! (*to* DONNA ELVIRA) My dearest, don't you see that I'm merely amusing myself?

DONNA ELVIRA: Amusing yourself? How interesting! I know well, cruel man, what your amusements are!

241

ZERLINA: Ma, signor cavaliere, è ver quel ch'ella dice?

DON GIOVANNI: La povera infelice è di me innamorata, e per pietà deggio fingere amore, ch'io son per mia disgrazia uom di buon core.

8. *Aria*

DONNA ELVIRA: Ah fuggi il traditor,
Non lo lasciar più dir!
Il labbro è mentitor,
Fallace il ciglio.
Da miei tormenti impara
A creder a quel cor,
E nasca il tuo timor
Dal mio periglio!
(*Partono* DONNA ELVIRA *e* ZERLINA.)

Recitativo

DON GIOVANNI: Mi par ch'oggi il demonio si diverta d'opporsi ai miei piacevoli progressi, vanno mal tutti quanti.
(*Entrano* DONNA ANNA *e* DON OTTAVIO.)

DON OTTAVIO: Ah! ch'ora, idolo mio, son vani i pianti! Di vendetta si parli. Oh, Don Giovanni!

DON GIOVANNI (*a parte*): Mancava questo in ver!

DONNA ANNA: Amico! a tempo vi ritroviam! Avete core, avete anima generosa?

DON GIOVANNI (*a parte*): Sta a vedere ch'il diavolo gli ha detto qualche cosa? (*forte*) Che domanda! perchè?

DONNA ANNA: Bisogno abbiamo della vostra amicizia.

DON GIOVANNI (*a parte*): Respiro. (*forte*) Comandate: i congiunti, i parenti; questa man, questo ferro, i beni, il sangue spenderò per servirvi. Ma voi, bella Donn'Anna, perchè così piangete? Sì crudele chi fu, ch'osò la calma turbar del viver vostro?
(*Entra* DONNA ELVIRA.)

DONNA ELVIRA: Ah ti ritrovo ancor, perfido mostro. (*a* DONNA ANNA)

9. *Quartetto*

Non ti fidar, o misera!
Di quel ribaldo cor!
Me già tradì quel barbaro—
Ti vuol tradir ancor.

242

ZERLINA: But, my Lord, is she telling the truth?

DON GIOVANNI: This poor unhappy lady is madly in love with me, and from pity I pretend to love her in return. I'm far too sympathetic for my own good!

8. *Aria*

DONNA ELVIRA: Ah, flee from this traitor! Don't let him say another word! His lips are lying; his glances are deceitful! Learn from my suffering to distrust his heart, and let your fear be born of my danger!

(DONNA ELVIRA *and* ZERLINA *exit.*)

Recitative

DON GIOVANNI: It seems that the devil amuses himself today by impeding the progress of my pleasures; everything has gone badly.

(DONNA ANNA *and* DON OTTAVIO *enter.*)

DON OTTAVIO: Since tears are in vain, my darling, let's think of vengeance. Oh, Don Giovanni!

DON GIOVANNI (*aside*): This is all I need!

DONNA ANNA: My Lord! We meet most opportunely! Have you a noble heart, and a generous soul?

DON GIOVANNI (*aside*): Let's see if the devil has told her anything. (*aloud*) What a question! Why do you ask me?

DONNA ANNA: We have need of your friendship.

DON GIOVANNI (*aside*): What a relief! (*aloud*) Command me! My vassals, relatives, this hand, this sword, my possessions, my blood, will flow to serve you. But you, beautiful Donna Anna, why are you weeping? Who is the villain who has dared to disturb your life's serenity?

(DONNA ELVIRA *enters.*)

DONNA ELVIRA: Ah, here you are again, perfidious monster! (*to* DONNA ANNA)

9. *Quartet*

Unhappy girl, don't trust in this barbarous man's ribald heart! He has betrayed me already—and he'll betray you as well.

DONNA ANNA *e* DON OTTAVIO: Cieli! che aspetto nobile!
Che dolce maestà!
Il suo dolor, le lagrime
M'empiono di pietà.

DON GIOVANNI: La povera ragazza
E pazza, amici miei:
Lasciatemi con lei!
Forse si calmerà.

DONNA ELVIRA (*a* DONNA ANNA): Ah non credete al perfido!

DON GIOVANNI (*a* DONNA ANNA *e* DON OTTAVIO): E pazza;
non badate.

DONNA ELVIRA (*a* DONNA ANNA *e* DON OTTAVIO): Restate,
oh Dei! restate.

DONNA ANNA *e* DON OTTAVIO: A chi si crederà?

DONNA ANNA, DON OTTAVIO, DON GIOVANNI: Certo moto
d'ignoto tormento
Dentro l'alma girare mi sento,
Che mi dice per quella infelice
Cento cose che intender non sa.

DONNA ELVIRA: Sdegno, rabbia, dispetto, spavento
Dentro l'alma girare mi sento,
Che mi dice di quel traditore
Cento cose che intender non sa.

DON OTTAVIO: Io di quà non vado via,
Se non so com'è l'affar.

DONNA ANNA: Non ha l'aria di pazzia
Il suo tratto, il suo parlar.

DON GIOVANNI (*a parte*): Se men vada, si potria
Qualche cosa sospettar.

DONNA ELVIRA: Da quel ceffo si dovria
La ner'alma giudicar.

DON OTTAVIO (*a* DON GIOVANNI): Dunque quella?

DON GIOVANNI: E pazzarella.

DONNA ANNA (*a* DONNA ELVIRA): Dunque quegli?

DONNA ELVIRA: E un traditore.

DON GIOVANNI: Infelice!

DONNA ELVIRA: Mentitore! Mentitore!

DONNA ANNA *e* DON OTTAVIO: Incomincio a dubitar.

DONNA ANNA *and* DON OTTAVIO: Heavens! What a noble manner! What sweet majesty! Her grief and tears move me to pity.

DON GIOVANNI: This poor girl is crazy, my friends! Leave me alone with her, and perhaps I can persuade her to calm herself.

DONNA ELVIRA (*to* DONNA ANNA): Ah, don't believe this traitor!

DON GIOVANNI (*to* DONNA ANNA *and* DON OTTAVIO): She's crazy; don't listen to her!

DONNA ELVIRA (*to* DONNA ANNA *and* DON OTTAVIO): Stay with me—O God! Stay with me!

DONNA ANNA *and* DON OTTAVIO: Whom can we believe?

DONNA ANNA, DON OTTAVIO, DON GIOVANNI: I feel a torment in my soul that secretly reveals to me a hundred things about this poor unhappy girl that I don't yet understand.

DONNA ELVIRA: I feel scorn, rage, spite, and fear turning within my soul, telling me a hundred things about this libertine that I don't yet understand!

DON OTTAVIO: I won't leave this place until I know the true state of affairs!

DONNA ANNA: Her bearing and speech are not those of a madwoman.

DON GIOVANNI (*aside*): If I leave them now, they may begin to suspect something.

DONNA ELVIRA: You may judge his black soul from his expression!

DON OTTAVIO (*to* DON GIOVANNI): Then, this lady—

DON GIOVANNI: Is insane.

DONNA ANNA (*to* DONNA ELVIRA): Then, this man—

DONNA ELVIRA: Is a traitor!

DON GIOVANNI: Poor girl!

DONNA ELVIRA: Liar, liar!

DONNA ANNA *and* DON OTTAVIO: I'm beginning to doubt his word.

DON GIOVANNI (*a* DONNA ELVIRA): Zitto, zitto, che la gente
Si raduna a noi d'intorno:
Siate un poco più prudente—
Vi farete criticar.

DONNA ELVIRA: Non sperarlo, a scelerato!
Ho perduta la prudenza—
Le tue colpe ed il mio stato
Voglio a tutti palesar.

DONNA ANNA *e* DON OTTAVIO: Quegli accenti sì sommessi!
Quel cangiarsi di colore
Sono indizj troppo espressi
Che mi fan determinar.
(DONNA ELVIRA *parte*.)

Recitativo

DON GIOVANNI: Povera sventurata! i passi suoi voglio seguir,
non voglio che faccia un precipizio. Perdonate, belissima
Donn'Anna; se servirvi poss'io, in mia casa v'aspetto.
Amici, addio! (*Parte*.)

DONNA ANNA: Don Ottavio, son morta.

DON OTTAVIO: Cos'è stato?

DONNA ANNA: Per pietà soccorretemi!

DON OTTAVIO: Mio ben, fate coraggio!

DONNA ANNA: Oh Dei! Quegli è il carnefice del padre mio!

DON OTTAVIO: Che dite?

DONNA ANNA: Non dubitate più. Gli ultimi accenti che
l'empio proferì, tutta la voce richiama nel cor mio di quel-
l'indegno, che nel mio appartamento—

DON OTTAVIO: Oh ciel! possibile, Che sotto il sacro manto
d'amicizia—Ma come fu? Narratemi lo strano avvenimento.

DONNA ANNA: Era già alquanto avanzata la notte, quando
nelle mie stanze, ove, soletta mi trovai per sventura, entrar
io vidi in un mantello avvolto un uom, ch'al primo istante
avea preso per voi; ma riconobbi poi ch'un inganno era il
mio.

DON OTTAVIO: Stelle! Seguite.

DONNA ANNA: Tacito a me s'appressa, e mi vuol abbracciar;
sciogliermi cerco, ei più mi stringe, io grido; non viene
alcun; con una mano cerca d'impedire la voce, e coll'altra
m'afferra stretta così, che già mi credo vinta.

DON GIOVANNI (*to* DONNA ELVIRA): Be quiet, or a crowd will gather. Be a little more prudent—you're making a spectacle of yourself!

DONNA ELVIRA: Don't hope to escape me, you scoundrel! I've lost all my prudence— I'll publish my wrongs and your misdeeds to all the world!

DONNA ANNA *and* DON OTTAVIO: His whispers and expressions incline me to decide in her favor!
(DONNA ELVIRA *exits.*)

Recitative

DON GIOVANNI: Poor unhappy woman! I'll follow her so that she won't do anything desperate. Forgive me, most beautiful Donna Anna; I'll await your commands at my castle. My friends, good morning! (*Exits.*)

DONNA ANNA: Don Ottavio, I'm dying!

DON OTTAVIO: What has happened?

DONNA ANNA: For heaven's sake, help me!

DON OTTAVIO: My darling, take courage!

DONNA ANNA: O God! That was the man who murdered my father!

DON OTTAVIO: What are you saying?

DONNA ANNA: I can't doubt it any longer. The last words that the villain spoke, his very voice recalled to my heart that wretch who came to my apartments—

DON OTTAVIO: O heavens! is it possible that under the sacred cloak of friendship— But what did he do then? Tell me the whole story!

DONNA ANNA: It was already late at night when unfortunately I found myself alone in my rooms. I saw a man come in, wrapped in a cloak; at first I mistook him for you, but I soon realized that I was deceived!

DON OTTAVIO: Good Lord! Go on.

DONNA ANNA: He quietly approached me and attempted to embrace me. I tried to escape him; he held me closer. I screamed, but nobody came. He put a hand on my mouth and held me so tightly that I believed myself conquered.

DON OTTAVIO: Perfido! e alfin?

DONNA ANNA: Alfine il duol, l'orrore dell'infame attentato accrebbe si la lena mia; che a forza di svincolarmi, torcermi, e piegarmi, da lui mi sciolsi.

DON OTTAVIO: Ohimè! respiro!

DONNA ANNA: Allora rinforzo i stridi miei, chiamo soccorso —fugge il fellon, arditamente il seguo fin nella strada per fermarlo; e sono assalitrice d'assalita. Il padre v'accorre, vuol conoscerlo, e l'indegno; che del povero vecchio era più forte. Compiè il misfatto suo col dargli morte.

10. Aria

Or sai chi l'onore rapir a me volse,
Chi fu il traditore, ch'il padre mi tolse.
Vendetta ti chieggo—la chiede il tuo cor.
Rammenta la piaga del misero seno—
Rimira di sangue coperto il terreno,
Se 'l cor in te langue d'un giusto furor. (*Parte.*)

Recitativo

DON OTTAVIO: Come mai creder deggio di sì nero delitto capace un cavaliere! Ah di scoprire il vero ogni mezzo si cerchi, io sento in petto e di sposo, e d'amico il dover che mi parla: Disingannarla voglio, o vendicarla.

11. Aria

Dalla sua pace la mia dipende—
Quel ch'a lei piace vita mi rende;
Quel che le incresce morte mi da;
S'ella sospira, sospiro anch'io;
E mia quell'ira, quel pianto è mio—
E non ho bene se non l'ha.
(DON OTTAVIO *parte. Entrano* DON GIOVANNI *e* LEPORELLO.)

Recitativo

LEPORELLO: Io deggio ad ogni patto per sempre abbandonar questo bel matto. Eccolo qui: guardate con quell'indifferenza se ne viene.

DON GIOVANNI: Leporellino mio, va tutto bene?

LEPORELLO: Don Giovannino mio, va tutto male.

DON GIOVANNI: Come? va tutto male?

DON OTTAVIO: Wretch! And then?

DONNA ANNA: Finally the dread and horror of the infamous attack increased my strength, and by twisting and struggling I tore myself away.

DON OTTAVIO: Thank heaven!

DONNA ANNA: Then I screamed more loudly, calling for help. The criminal tried to escape, and I followed him into the street, becoming the pursuer of my assailant. My father ran to me, and tried to unmask the wretch, who was stronger than the poor old man. Then he completed his crime by killing my father!

10. Aria

Now you know who tried to steal my honor, and who was the traitor that tore my beloved father from me. I ask for vengeance; your heart must also demand it. Remember the wound gaping in my father's breast! Recall his blood that covered the ground if ever you are tempted to forget your just anger at his murder! (*Exits.*)

Recitative

DON OTTAVIO: How can I believe that a nobleman could be guilty of such a black crime? I will not rest until I discover the truth. I feel a friend's and a lover's duty within my breast which says to me: "You must undeceive her or avenge her!"

11. Aria

My peace depends on her peace. Everything that pleases her gives new life to me. When she is injured, it brings me pain. If she sighs, then I sigh as well. I share her wrath and tears, and while she is sad, I can have no happiness!

(DON OTTAVIO *exits.* DON GIOVANNI *and* LEPORELLO *enter.*)

Recitative

LEPORELLO: In any case, I must leave this madman's service. Here he is now—look at him, with what indifference he behaves!

DON GIOVANNI: Well, my dear Leporello, does all go well?

LEPORELLO: My very dear Don Giovanni, everything is going badly.

DON GIOVANNI: What do you mean?

LEPORELLO: Vado a casa, come voi m'ordinaste, con tutta quella gente.

DON GIOVANNI: Bravo!

LEPORELLO: A forza di chiacchere, di vezzi, e di bugie, ch'ho imparato sì bene a star con voi, cerco d'intrattenerli.

DON GIOVANNI: Bravo!

LEPORELLO: Dico mille cose a Masetto per placarlo, per trargli dal pensier la gelosia.

DON GIOVANNI: Ma bravo, in conscienza mia!

LEPORELLO: Faccio che bevano e gli uomini e le donne; son già mezzo ubbriachi. Altri canta, altri scherza—Altri seguita a ber—in sul più bello chi credete che capiti?

DON GIOVANNI: Zerlina!

LEPORELLO: Bravo! e con lei chi venne?

DON GIOVANNI: Donna Elvira.

LEPORELLO: Bravo! e disse di voi.

DON GIOVANNI: Tutto quel mal ch'in bocca le venia!

LEPORELLO: Ma bravo, in conscienza mia!

DON GIOVANNI: E tu cosa facesti?

LEPORELLO: Tacqui.

DON GIOVANNI: Ed ella?

LEPORELLO: Seguì a gridar.

DON GIOVANNI: E tu?

LEPORELLO: Quando mi parve, che già fosse sfogata, dolcemente fuor dell'orto la trassi, e con bell'arte chiusa la porta a chiave io me n'andai, e sulla via soletta io la lasciai.

DON GIOVANNI: Bravo! Bravo! arcibravo! L'affar non può andar meglio; incominciasti, io saprò terminar. Troppo mi premono queste contadinotte: le voglio divertir finchè vien notte.

12. *Aria*

Finch'han del vino
Calda la testa,
Una gran festa,
Fa preparar:
Se trovi in piazza,
Qualche ragazza,
Teco ancor quella

LEPORELLO: I went home, as you ordered me, with all those people.

DON GIOVANNI: Bravo!

LEPORELLO: By chattering, by flattery and lies, which I have learned to do so well by being near you, I tried to detain them.

DON GIOVANNI: Bravo!

LEPORELLO: I said a thousand things to Masetto to please him, to soothe his jealousy.

DON GIOVANNI: Bravo! By my conscience!

LEPORELLO: I made them drink, and the men and women were half-drunk already. Some sang, some joked—some continued with their drinking. At the height of this confusion, who do you think arrived?

DON GIOVANNI: Zerlina!

LEPORELLO: Bravo! And who do you think came with her?

DON GIOVANNI: Donna Elvira!

LEPORELLO: Bravo! And they spoke of you.

DON GIOVANNI: Everything evil that they could think of!

LEPORELLO: Bravo, by my conscience!

DON GIOVANNI: And you, what were you doing?

LEPORELLO: I was silent.

DON GIOVANNI: And Elvira?

LEPORELLO: She continued to accuse you.

DON GIOVANNI: And you?

LEPORELLO: When she appeared to be calmer, I gently led her outside to the orchard, and I very artfully locked the door with my own key, leaving her all alone on the street.

DON GIOVANNI: Bravo, bravo! More than bravo! It couldn't have been done better. You've begun well; now I'll be able to finish the matter. These country girls tempt me so much that I wish to entertain them all night long!

12. Aria

While they are flushed with wine; prepare everything for a great party! If you find some girls in the village square, bring them along with you. Let the dancing be without special order—let there be minuets; let there be country dances—let the dancers do whatever dances they please. And I, on the other hand, among so many, can make love to whomever I please. Ah,

Don Giovanni

Cerca menar;
Senz'alcun ordine,
La danza sia,
Ch'il minuetto,
Che la follia
Chi l'Alemana,
Farai ballar;
Ed io frattanto,
Dall'altro canto,
Con questa e quella,
Vo' amoreggiar.
Ah la mia lista,
Doman mattina,
D'una decina deve aumentar.
(*Partono* DON GIOVANNI *e* LEPORELLO. *Entrano* ZERLINA *e* MASETTO.)

Recitativo

ZERLINA: Masetto, senti un pò! Masetto, dico!

MASETTO: Non mi toccar.

ZERLINA: Perchè?

MASETTO: Perfida! il tatto sopportar dovrei d'una mano infedele?

ZERLINA: Ah, no! taci, crudele, io non merto da te tal trattamento.

MASETTO: Come! ed hai l'ardimento di scusarti? Star sola con un uom; abbandonarmi il dì delle mie nozze—porre in fronte a un villano d'onore questa marca d'infamia! Ah, se non fosse se non fosse lo scandalo, vorrei—

ZERLINA: Ma se colpa io non ho—ma se da lui ingannata rimasi? E poi che temi? Tranquillati, mia vita! Non mi toccò la punta delle dita. Non me lo credi, ingrato? Vien qui, sfogati, ammazzami—fa pur tutto di me quel che ti piace! Ma poi, Masetto poi, ma poi fa pace.

13. *Aria*

Batti, batti, o bel Masetto,
La tua povera Zerlina;
Starò qui come agnellina,
Le tue botte ad aspettar.
Lascierò stracciarmi il crine;

by tomorrow morning a dozen names must be added to my list!

(DON GIOVANNI *and* LEPORELLO *exit.* ZERLINA *and* MASETTO *enter.*)

Recitative

ZERLINA: Masetto, listen to me! Masetto, I want to explain!

MASETTO: Don't touch me!

ZERLINA: Why not?

MASETTO: Slut! How can you ask me? Who could bear the touch of an unfaithful hand?

ZERLINA: Ah, no, don't say any more; I don't deserve such treatment from you!

MASETTO: What? And you have the audacity to argue with me? You were alone with that man; you abandoned me on our wedding day—and you planted the infamous horns on the forehead of an honest man! Ah, if only there would be no scandal, I would—

ZERLINA: But if it wasn't my fault—if I was deceived by him? Anyway, what are you afraid of? Be calm, my darling! He didn't even touch the tip of my finger. Don't you believe me? Ungrateful! Come here, strike me, kill me— do anything you please to me! But then, my dear Masetto, then let's be friends again.

13. Aria

Beat me, dear Masetto, beat your poor Zerlina! I'll stand here like a little lamb, awaiting your blows. I'll let you pull my hair out; I'll let you tear my eyes out, and even then I'll kiss your dear hands! Ah, I see that you haven't the heart to do it! Peace, peace, my darling—we'll pass our

253

Lascierò stracciarmi gli occhi;
E le care tue manine
Lieta poi saprò baciar.
Ah! lo vedo, non hai core!
Pace, pace, o mia!
In contenti, ed allegria,
Notte e dì vogliam passar.

Recitativo

MASETTO: Guarda un pò, come seppe questa strega sedurmi! Siamo pure i deboli di testa!

DON GIOVANNI (*di dentro*): Sia preparato tutto a una gran festa.

ZERLINA: Ah, Masetto, Masetto! odi la voce del monsù cavaliere!

MASETTO: Ebben, che c'è?

ZERLINA: Verrà.

MASETTO: Lascia che venga.

ZERLINA: Ah! se vi fosse un buco da fuggir—

MASETTO: Di cosa temi? Perchè diventi pallida? Ah, capisco! Capisco, bricconcella! Hai timor, ch'io comprenda com'è tra voi passata la faccenda.

14. Finale

Presto, presto! pria ch'ei venga
Por mi vò da qualche lato:
V'è una nicchia, qui celato
Cheto, cheto, mi vo' star

ZERLINA: Senti, senti! dove vai!
Ah, non t'asconder, o Masetto!
Se ti trova, poveretto,
Tu non sai quel che può far.

MASETTO: Faccia, dica quel che vuole.

ZERLINA: Ah! non giovan le parole!

MASETTO: Parla forte e qui t'arresta.

ZERLINA: Che capriccio ha nella testa?

MASETTO (*a parte*): Capirò se m'è fedele,
E in qual modo andò l'affar.
(*Si nasconde.*)

ZERLINA: Quell'ingrato, quel crudele
Oggi vuol precipitar.

DON GIOVANNI (*di dentro*): Su svegliatevi da bravi!

days and nights in happiness! Yes, yes, yes, we'll be happy day and night!

Recitative

MASETTO: Just look at how this little witch can get around me. Men are all weak in the head!

DON GIOVANNI (*off-stage*): Let everything be prepared for a huge celebration!

ZERLINA: Ah, Masetto, Masetto, that's the voice of Don Giovanni!

MASETTO: And what about it?

ZERLINA: He's coming here!

MASETTO: Well, let him.

ZERLINA: Ah, if there were only a hole for us to hide in—

MASETTO: What are you afraid of? Why are you so pale? Ah, I understand, you traitress! You're afraid that I'll discover how things are between you!

14. Finale

Quickly, quickly, before he gets here, I'll place myself to one side. Here's a secluded spot— I'll silently hide myself here.

ZERLINA: Come back! Where are you going? Ah, don't hide yourself here, Masetto! If he finds you, you poor thing, you don't know what he will do!

MASETTO: Let him do and say what he likes!

ZERLINA: Your boasting is all in vain!

MASETTO: Speak louder, and stay right here!

ZERLINA: What nonsense is in your head?

MASETTO (*aside*): I'll learn if she's faithful to me, and exactly what has happened!
(*He hides.*)

ZERLINA: How cruel! How suspicious! Now he's sure to do something rash!

DON GIOVANNI (*off-stage*): Continue your celebration!

Su coraggio, o buona gente.
Vogliam star allegramente!
Vogliam ridere e scherzar.
Alla stanza della danza. (*ai servi*)
Conducete tutti quante;
Ed a tutti in abbondanza
Gran rinfreschi fate dar—

CORO (*di dentro*): Su, svegliatevi da bravi!
Su coraggio, o buona gente.
Vogliam star allegramente!
Vogliam ridere e scherzar—

ZERLINA: Tra questi alberi celata,
Si può dar che non mi veda.
(*Entra* DON GIOVANNI.)

DON GIOVANNI: Zerlinetta mia garbata!
Ti ho già vista—non scappar!

ZERLINA: Ah! lasciatemi andar via!

DON GIOVANNI: No, no, resta, gioja mia!

ZERLINA: Se pietade avete in core—

DON GIOVANNI: Sì, ben mio, son tutto amore.
Vieni un poco, in questo loco,
Fortunata io ti vo' far.

ZERLINA (*a parte*): Ah! s'ei vede il sposo mio,
So ben io quel che può far.

DON GIOVANNI (*vede* MASETTO, *che emerge dal suo nascondiglio*): Masetto!

MASETTO: Sì, Masetto!

DON GIOVANNI: E chiuso là perchè?
La bella tua Zerlina—
Non può la poverina
Più star senza di te.

MASETTO: Capisco, sì signore.

DON GIOVANNI: Adesso fate core!
I suonatori udite,
Venite omai con me!

ZERLINA *e* MASETTO: Si, si facciamo core,
Ed a ballar cogli altri
Andiamo tutti tre.
(ZERLINA, MASETTO *e* DON GIOVANNI *partono.* DONNA ANNA,
DONNA ELVIRA *e* DON OTTAVIO *entrano, in maschera.*)

Good people, amuse yourselves! I want you to be happy; I want you to laugh and dance. (*to servants*) Lead everyone into the ballroom and give them all the refreshments that they can eat!

CHORUS (*off-stage*): Continue your celebration! Amuse yourselves, good people! Be happy, laugh—

ZERLINA: Perhaps he won't find me here among these secluded trees.
(DON GIOVANNI *enters.*)

DON GIOVANNI: My sweet Zerlina, I've already seen you! You can't escape from me!

ZERLINA: Ah, let me go away!

DON GIOVANNI: No, no, stay with me, my darling!

ZERLINA: If you have any pity in your heart—

DON GIOVANNI: Yes, my dear, my heart is full of love. Come into this arbor for a moment, and I'll make you very happy.

ZERLINA (*aside*): Ah! If he should ever see Masetto, I know very well what he would do!

DON GIOVANNI (*seeing* MASETTO, *who has emerged from his hiding place*): Masetto!

MASETTO: Yes, Masetto!

DON GIOVANNI: You were hidden there—but why? Your pretty Zerlina, poor girl, won't stay here another moment without you.

MASETTO: I understand, my Lord.

DON GIOVANNI: Well, then, let's be cheerful! Listen to the music, and come inside with me!

ZERLINA *and* MASETTO: Yes, yes, let's be cheerful, and go inside to dance with the others!
(ZERLINA, MASETTO, *and* DON GIOVANNI *exit.* DONNA ANNA, DONNA ELVIRA, *and* DON OTTAVIO *enter, masked.*)

DONNA ELVIRA: Bisogna aver coraggio,
O cari amici miei;
E i suoi misfatti rei
Scoprir potremo allor.

DON OTTAVIO: L'amica dice bene—
Coraggio aver conviene. (*a* DONNA ANNA)
Discaccia, o vita mia!
L'affanno ed il timor.

DONNA ANNA: Il passo e periglioso,
Può nascer qualche imbroglio;
Temo pel caro sposo—
E per noi temo ancor.
(LEPORELLO *apre una finestra dal palazzo.*)

LEPORELLO: Signor, guardate un poco!
Che maschere galanti!

DON GIOVANNI (*di dentro*): Falle passar avanti,
Di che ci fanno onor.

DONNA ANNA, DONNA ELVIRA, DON OTTAVIO: Al volto, ed alla voce
Si scopre il traditore.

LEPORELLO: Zi! Zi! signore maschere!

DONNA ANNA *e* DONNA ELVIRA (*a* DON OTTAVIO): Via rispondete.

DON OTTAVIO: Cosa chiedete?

LEPORELLO: Al ballo, se vi piace
V'invita il mio signor.

DON OTTAVIO: Grazie di tanto onore.
Andiam, compagne belle.

LEPORELLO (*a parte*): L'amico anche su quelle
Prova farà d'amor.
(*Chinde la finestra.*)

   Trio

DONNA ANNA *e* DON OTTAVIO: Protegga il giusto cielo
Il zelo del mio cor!

DONNA ELVIRA: Vendichi il giusto cielo
Il mio tradito amor!
(*Partono* DONNA ANNA, DONNA ELVIRA *e* DON OTTAVIO.)

   Scena III

Sala da ballo nel palazzo di DON GIOVANNI. DON GIOVANNI, LEPORELLO, ZERLINA, MASETTO, *suonatori, servi, contadini e contadine.*

DONNA ELVIRA: We must be courageous now, my dear friends; only then can we uncover all his black crimes!

DON OTTAVIO: Our friend is right—we must have courage. (*to* DONNA ANNA) Try to dispel your grief and fear!

DONNA ANNA: Our situation is dangerous, and the danger increases. I'm afraid for both of you, and for myself as well.
(LEPORELLO *opens a window of the palace.*)

LEPORELLO: My Lord, look out there— I see three gallant maskers!

DON GIOVANNI (*off-stage*): Call to them and invite them to the ball.

DONNA ANNA, DONNA ELVIRA, DON OTTAVIO: I recognize the traitor's voice!

LEPORELLO: Pst! My Lord maskers!

DONNA ANNA *and* DONNA ELVIRA (*to* DON OTTAVIO): Go and speak to him.

DON OTTAVIO: What did you ask me?

LEPORELLO: If it pleases you, my master invites you to his ball.

DON OTTAVIO: Thank you; we would be honored. Shall we go, my fair companions?

LEPORELLO (*aside*): My master can also give these ladies a proof of his love.
(*He closes the window.*)

Trio

DONNA ANNA *and* DON OTTAVIO: My heaven protect my heart's resolution!

DONNA ELVIRA: May heaven avenge my betrayed love!
(DONNA ANNA, DONNA ELVIRA, *and* DON OTTAVIO *exit.*)

Scene III

The ballroom of DON GIOVANNI'S *palace.* DON GIOVANNI, LEPORELLO, ZERLINA, MASETTO, *musicians, servants, and guests.*

DON GIOVANNI: Riposate, vezzose ragazze!

LEPORELLO: Rinfrescatevi, bei giovinetti.

DON GIOVANNI *e* LEPORELLO: Tornerete a far presto le pazze,
Tornerete a scherzar e ballar!

DON GIOVANNI: Ehi caffè!

LEPORELLO: Cioccolatte!

MASETTO: Ah, Zerlina, giudizio!

DON GIOVANNI: Sorbetti!

LEPORELLO: Confetti!

ZERLINA *e* MASETTO (*a parte*): Troppo dolce comincia la scena,
In amaro potria terminar.

DON GIOVANNI: Sei pur vaga, brillante Zerlina!

ZERLINA: Sua bontà!

MASETTO (*a parte*): La briccona fa festa!

LEPORELLO (*fra le ragazze*): Sei pur cara, Giannotta, San-drina!

MASETTO (*a parte*): Tocca pur, che ti cada la testa!

ZERLINA (*a parte*): Quel Masetto mi par stralunato.
Brutto, brutto si fa quest'affar.

DON GIOVANNI *e* LEPORELLO (*a parte*): Quel Masetto mi par stralunato.
Qui bisogna cervello adoprar.

MASETTO (*a parte*): La briccona mi fa disperar!
(*Entrano* DONNA ANNA, DONNA ELVIRA *e* DON OTTAVIO.)

LEPORELLO: Venite pur avanti,
Vezzose mascherette.

DON GIOVANNI: E aperto a tutti quanti,
Viva la libertà.

DONNA ANNA, DONNA ELVIRA, DON OTTAVIO: Siam grati a tanti segni
Di generosità.

DON GIOVANNI (*ai musicisti*): Ricominciate il suono!
Tu accoppia i ballerini. (*a* LEPORELLO)
Meco tu dei ballare. (*a* ZERLINA)
Zerlina, vien pur quà.

LEPORELLO: Da bravi via! ballate.

DON GIOVANNI: You must rest now, you charming girls!

LEPORELLO: Have something to eat, you handsome young men!

DON GIOVANNI *and* LEPORELLO: Soon you'll resume your dancing and amusements!

DON GIOVANNI: Here, some coffee!

LEPORELLO: Chocolate, here!

MASETTO: Ah, Zerlina, be careful!

DON GIOVANNI: Sherbets!

LEPORELLO: Candy!

ZERLINA *and* MASETTO (*aside*): This evening is beginning so sweetly, but it may end in bitterness!

DON GIOVANNI: You're so charming, my dazzling Zerlina!

ZERLINA: You're so kind!

MASETTO (*aside*): The flirt is enjoying herself!

LEPORELLO (*among the girls*): You're so sweet, Gianotta, Sandrina!

MASETTO (*aside*): Take care; I may cut off his head!

ZERLINA: Masetto is quite insane. (*aside*) This affair is becoming very ugly!

DON GIOVANNI *and* LEPORELLO (*aside*): Masetto is quite insane. Now we must use our brains!

MASETTO (*aside*): The girl is driving me to distraction! (*Enter* DONNA ANNA, DONNA ELVIRA, *and* DON OTTAVIO.)

LEPORELLO: Come forward, noble maskers!

DON GIOVANNI: This ballroom is open to all; you're at liberty to enter.

DONNA ANNA, DONNA ELVIRA, DON OTTAVIO: We thank you for such generosity.

DON GIOVANNI (*to the musicians*): Continue to play! (*to* LEPORELLO) You organize the dances. (*to* ZERLINA) You must dance with me, Zerlina; come over here.

LEPORELLO: That's fine, now go on dancing.

Don Giovanni

DONNA ELVIRA (*a* DONNA ANNA): Quell'è la contadina.

DONNA ANNA: Io moro!

DON OTTAVIO: Simulate!

DON GIOVANNI *e* LEPORELLO (*a parte*): Va bene in verità!

MASETTO (*ironicamente*): Va bene in verità?

DON GIOVANNI (*a* LEPORELLO): A bada tien Masetto!

LEPORELLO (*a* MASETTO): Non balli, poveretto.

DON GIOVANNI: Il tuo compagno io sono,
Zerlina, vien pur quà.

LEPORELLO (*a* MASETTO): Vien quà, Masetto caro!
Facciam quel ch'altri fa.

MASETTO: No, no, ballar non voglio.

LEPORELLO: Eh balla, amico mio.

MASETTO: No!

LEPORELLO: Sì, caro Masetto!

DONNA ANNA (*a parte*): Resister non poss'io.

DON OTTAVIO *e* DONNA ELVIRA: Fingete per pietà!

MASETTO: Ballare no, non voglio!

LEPORELLO: Balla, amico mio,
Facciam quel ch'altri fa.

DON GIOVANNI (*a* ZERLINA): Vieni con me, mia vita?

MASETTO (*a* LEPORELLO): Lasciami! Ah, no! Zerlina!

DON GIOVANNI: Vieni, vieni!

ZERLINA (DON GIOVANNI *la mena nel un altra stanza*): Oh,
Numi! son tradita!

LEPORELLO: Qui nasce una rovina.

DONNA ANNA, DONNA ELVIRA, DON OTTAVIO (*a parte*): L'iniquo da se stesso,
Nel laccio se ne va.

ZERLINA (*di dentro*): Gente! ajuto! Ajuto gente!

MASETTO: Ah, Zerlina!

ZERLINA (*di dentro*): Scelerato!

DONNA ANNA, DONNA ELVIRA, DON OTTAVIO: Ora grida da
quel lato!

ZERLINA (*di dentro*): Scelerato!

262

DONNA ELVIRA (*to* DONNA ANNA): That's the country girl.

DONNA ANNA: I'm dying!

DON OTTAVIO: Take courage!

DON GIOVANNI *and* LEPORELLO (*aside*): It's really going well!

MASETTO (*ironically*): It's really going well?

DON GIOVANNI (*to* LEPORELLO): Hold Masetto back!

LEPORELLO (*to* MASETTO): You're not dancing, poor boy.

DON GIOVANNI: I'm your partner, Zerlina; come here with me!

LEPORELLO (*to* MASETTO): Come here, dear Masetto! Do as the others are doing.

MASETTO: No, no, I don't want to dance!

LEPORELLO: Dance, my friend!

MASETTO: No!

LEPORELLO: Yes, dear Masetto!

DONNA ANNA (*aside*): I can't stand it any longer!

DONNA ELVIRA *and* DON OTTAVIO: Pretend, for heaven's sake!

MASETTO: I don't want to dance!

LEPORELLO: Dance, my friend. Do as the others are doing.

DON GIOVANNI (*to* ZERLINA): Come with me, my darling! Come, come!

MASETTO (*to* LEPORELLO): Let me go! Ah, no! Zerlina!

DON GIOVANNI: Come with me!

ZERLINA (*as* DON GIOVANNI *forces her into an adjoining room*): O God! I'm betrayed!

LEPORELLO: That's how he ruins them all.

DONNA ANNA, DONNA ELVIRA, DON OTTAVIO (*aside*): The wretch is falling into our trap.

ZERLINA (*off-stage*): Help me, somebody!

MASETTO: Ah, Zerlina!

ZERLINA (*off-stage*): Let me go!

DONNA ANNA, DONNA ELVIRA, DON OTTAVIO: Her voice is coming from that room!

ZERLINA (*off-stage*): You villain!

DONNA ANNA, DONNA ELVIRA, DON OTTAVIO: Ah gittiamo giù la porta!

ZERLINA (*di dentro*): Soccorretemi! Son morta!

DONNA ANNA, DONNA ELVIRA, DON OTTAVIO, MASETTO: Siam qui per tua difesa!

(MASETTO *rompe la porta dell' altra stanza;* DON GIOVANNI *ritorna, spada in mano, traendo* LEPORELLO. ZERLINA *corre a* MASETTO.)

DON GIOVANNI (*indicando* LEPORELLO): Ecco il birbo che t'ha offesa.
Ma da me la pena avrà! Mori iniquo!

LEPORELLO: Ah cosa fate?

DON GIOVANNI: Mori, dico!

DON OTTAVIO (*spada in mano*): Nol sperate, nol sperate!

DONNA ANNA, DONNA ELVIRA, DON OTTAVIO: L'empio crede con tal frode nasconder l'empietà.
(*Cavonsi le maschere.*)

DON GIOVANNI: Donna Elvira!

DONNA ELVIRA: Sì, malvagio!

DON GIOVANNI: Don Ottavio!

DON OTTAVIO: Sì, signore!

DON GIOVANNI (*a* DONNA ANNA): Ah, credete—

DONNA ANNA, DONNA ELVIRA, ZERLINA, DON OTTAVIO, MASETTO: Traditore, traditore!

ZERLINA: Tutto, tutto già si sa!

DONNA ANNA, DONNA ELVIRA, ZERLINA, DON OTTAVIO, MASETTO: Tutto tutto già si sa! Tutto! (*a* DON GIOVANNI)
Trema, trema, scelerato!
Saprà tosto il mondo intero
Il misfatto orrendo e nero
La tua fiera crudeltà!

DON GIOVANNI *e* LEPORELLO: E confusa la mia testa,
Non so più quel ch'io mi faccia,
E un orribile tempesta,
Minacciando, oh Dio, mi va!
Non mi perdo (si perde) o mi confondo (si confonde),
Se cadesse ancora il mondo,
Nulla mai temer mi fa!

DONNA ANNA, DONNA ELVIRA, DON OTTAVIO: Let's break the door down!

ZERLINA (*off-stage*): Save me! Help me! I'm dying!

DONNA ANNA, DONNA ELVIRA, DON OTTAVIO, MASETTO: We'll save you!

(MASETTO *breaks down the door to the inner room.* DON GIOVANNI *emerges, sword in hand, dragging* LEPORELLO. ZERLINA *runs out to* MASETTO.)

DON GIOVANNI (*pointing to* LEPORELLO): Here's the rascal who attacked her, but I'll see that he gets his just punishment! Die, you wretch!

LEPORELLO: Ah, what are you doing?

DON GIOVANNI: Die, I say!

DON OTTAVIO (*drawing his sword*): You'll never escape!

DONNA ANNA, DONNA ELVIRA, DON OTTAVIO: This scoundrel believes that he can conceal his crimes by such a transparent scheme!
(*They unmask.*)

DON GIOVANNI: Donna Elvira!

DONNA ELVIRA: Yes, you monster!

DON GIOVANNI: Don Ottavio!

DON OTTAVIO: Yes, it's I!

DON GIOVANNI (*to* DONNA ANNA): Ah, believe me—

DONNA ANNA, DONNA ELVIRA, ZERLINA, DON OTTAVIO, MASETTO: Traitor! Traitor!

ZERLINA: Everything is known to us!

DONNA ANNA, DONNA ELVIRA, ZERLINA, DON OTTAVIO, MASETTO: Everything is known! Everything! (*to* DON GIOVANNI) Now, vile wretch, it is your turn to tremble! Soon the whole world will know of your horrid and black crimes and your harsh cruelty!

DON GIOVANNI *and* LEPORELLO: My thoughts are whirling! The situation is out of control. O God, what a horrible tempest threatens! But I do not (he does not) lack courage. Let the heavens fall; I (he) will defy them.

Don Giovanni

DONNA ANNA, DONNA ELVIRA, ZERLINA, DON OTTAVIO, MA-
SETTO: Odi il tuon della vendetta,
Che ti fischia intorno intorno,
Sul tuo capo in questo giorno
Il suo fulmine cadrà!
(DON GIOVANNI *si scappa*.)

DONNA ANNA, DONNA ELVIRA, ZERLINA, DON OTTAVIO, MASETTO: Hear the thunder of vengeance that approaches, threatening you; soon its lightning will fall upon your head!
(DON GIOVANNI *escapes*.)

ATTO SECONDO

Scena I

Strada. A lato la casa di DONNA ELVIRA. *Entrano* DON GIO-
VANNI *e* LEPORELLO.

15. Duetto

DON GIOVANNI: Eh via, buffone,
Non mi seccar.

LEPORELLO: No no, padrone,
Non vo'restar.

DON GIOVANNI: Sentimi, amico—

LEPORELLO: Vò andar, vi dico.

DON GIOVANNI: Ma che ti ho fatto,
Che vuoi lasciarmi?

LEPORELLO: Oh niente affatto!
Quasi ammazzarmi,
Ed io non burlo,
Ma voglio andar.

DON GIOVANNI: Va, che sei matto.

LEPORELLO: Non vò restar.

Recitativo

DON GIOVANNI: Leporello!

LEPORELLO: Signore?

DON GIOVANNI: Vien quì, facciamo pace. (*da una borsa*)
Prendi!

LEPORELLO: Cosa?

DON GIOVANNI: Quattro doppie.

LEPORELLO: Oh sentite, per questa volta la ceremonia
accetto; ma non vi ci avvezzate—non credeste di sedurre i
miei pari come le donne, a forza di denari.

DON GIOVANNI: Non parliam più di ciò. Ti basta l'animo
di far quel ch'io ti dico?

LEPORELLO: Purchè lasciam le donne.

DON GIOVANNI: Lasciar le donne! Pazzo! Lasciar le donne!

268

Scene I

A street. At one side, the house of DONNA ELVIRA. *Enter* DON GIOVANNI *and* LEPORELLO.

15. Duet

DON GIOVANNI: Be quiet, you idiot; stop annoying me!

LEPORELLO: No, no, my master, I won't stay with you any longer!

DON GIOVANNI: Listen to me, my friend—

LEPORELLO: I want to go, I tell you!

DON GIOVANNI: What have I done to make you wish to leave?

LEPORELLO: Oh, nothing important—you've almost murdered me, that's all!

DON GIOVANNI: Don't be stupid—it was all only a joke.

LEPORELLO: I won't stay with you any longer!

Recitative

DON GIOVANNI: Leporello!

LEPORELLO: My Lord?

DON GIOVANNI: Come, let's make peace. (*giving him money*) Take this!

LEPORELLO: What is it?

DON GIOVANNI: Four gold pieces.

LEPORELLO: Well, for this time, I'll accept your bribe— but don't flatter yourself that you can cajole a man like me, as you do the women, with money!

DON GIOVANNI: Let's not discuss it any more. Have you the courage now to do whatever I ask?

LEPORELLO: As long as you give up the women.

DON GIOVANNI: Give up the women? Are you insane? Give

269

Sai ch'esse per me son necessarie più del pan che mangio,
Più dell'aria che spiro!

LEPORELLO: E avete core d'ingannarle poi tutte?

DON GIOVANNI: E tutto amore. Chi a una sola è fedele verso
l'altra è crudele. Io, ch'in me sento si esteso sentimento, vo
bene a tutte quante. Le donne poi, che calcolar non sanno,
il mio buon natural chiamano inganno.

LEPORELLO: Non ho veduto mai naturale più benigno! Orsù
cosa vorreste?

DON GIOVANNI: Odi! Vedesti tu la cameriera di Donna
Elvira?

LEPORELLO: Io no.

DON GIOVANNI: Non hai veduto qualche cosa di bello caro
il mio Leporello! Ora io con lei vo tentar la mia sorte, ed
ho pensato, giacchè siam verso sera, per aguzzarle meglio
l'appetito, di presentarmi a lei col tuo vestito.

LEPORELLO: E perchè non poteste presentarvi col vostro?

DON GIOVANNI: Han poco credito con gente di tal rango gli
abiti signorili Sbrigati via!

LEPORELLO: Signor, per più ragioni—

DON GIOVANNI: Finiscila, non soffro opposizioni.
(*Si cambiano vestiti.* DONNA ELVIRA *viene alla finestra, e
guarda fuori; si diventa buio.*)

16. Terzetto

DONNA ELVIRA: Ah taci, ingiusto core!
Non palpitarmi in seno!
E un empio, è un traditore
E colpa aver pietà.

LEPORELLO (*a* DON GIOVANNI): Zitto! di Donna Elvira.
Signor, la voce io sento.

DON GIOVANNI (*a* LEPORELLO): Cogliere io vo'il momento!
Tu fermati un po'là. (*si metto dietro* LEPORELLO)
Elvira idolo mio!

DONNA ELVIRA: Non è costui l'ingrato?

DON GIOVANNI: Si vita mia, son io,
E chiedo carità.

DONNA ELVIRA: Numi! che strano effetto
Mi si risveglia in petto!

up the women! You know that I need them more than the food I eat, more than the very air I breathe!

LEPORELLO: And even so, you have the heart to deceive them?

DON GIOVANNI: You don't understand my love for them. Whoever is faithful to one woman only betrays the rest. The bounty of my love embraces all womankind. But women, confused by my good nature, call it deceit!

LEPORELLO: I've never seen such good nature and such kindness! Now, what do you want of me?

DON GIOVANNI: Listen! Have you seen Donna Elvira's maid?

LEPORELLO: I? No.

DON GIOVANNI: You've never seen anything so beautiful, my dear Leporello. Now I'd like to try my luck with her, and I've been thinking that since it's near evening, I'll present myself to her in your clothing.

LEPORELLO: And why can't you appear in your own clothes?

DON GIOVANNI: With people of her rank, to be a gentleman bears no credit. Come, take your cloak off!

LEPORELLO: My Lord, for many reasons—

DON GIOVANNI: Don't delay me! I want no opposition! (*They exchange cloaks.* DONNA ELVIRA *comes to the window and looks out, as it becomes dark.*)

16. Trio

DONNA ELVIRA: Be silent, foolish heart! Do not tremble in my breast! He's unfaithful and a traitor; it would be sinful to pity him!

LEPORELLO (*to* DON GIOVANNI): Quiet, my Lord, I hear Donna Elvira's voice.

DON GIOVANNI (*to* LEPORELLO): I want to seize the moment! You stay there for a while. (*placing himself behind* LEPORELLO) My darling Elvira!

DONNA ELVIRA: Can it be that ungrateful man?

DON GIOVANNI: Yes, my love, it's I, and I beg for your pity!

DONNA ELVIRA: Heavens, what a strange feeling rises in my breast!

LEPORELLO (*a parte*): State a veder la pazza!
Ch'ancor gli crederà.

DON GIOVANNI: Discendi, o gioia bella!
Vedrai che tu sei quella,
Che adora l'alma mia,
Pentito io sono già!

DONNA ELVIRA: No! non ti credo, o barbaro!

DON GIOVANNI: Ah, credimi, o m'uccido!

LEPORELLO (*a parte*): Se seguitate, io rido.

DON GIOVANNI: Idolo mio, vien quà!

DONNA ELVIRA: Dei, che cimento è questo!
Non so s'io vado, o resto;
Ah proteggete voi
La mia credulità!

DON GIOVANNI (*a parte*): Spero che cada presto!
Che bel colpetto è questo!
Più fertile talento
Del mio no non si da.

LEPORELLO (*a parte*): Già quel mendace labbro!
Torna a sedur costei;
Deh proteggete, oh dei!
La sua credulita!
(DONNA ELVIRA *chinde la finestra.*)

Recitativo

DON GIOVANNI: Amico, che ti par?

LEPORELLO: Mi par ch'abbiate un'anima di bronzo.

DON GIOVANNI: Va là, che sè il gran gonzo! Ascolta bene; quando costei qui viene, tu corri ad abbracciarla, falle quattro carezze, fingi la voce mia, poi con bell'arte cerca teco condurla in altra parte.

LEPORELLO: Ma signor—

DON GIOVANNI: Non più repliche!

LEPORELLO: E se poi mi conosce?

DON GIOVANNI: Non ti conoscerà, se tu non vuoi—Zitto! ell'apre—ehi giudizio.
(*Si nasconde indietro, e ascolta. Entra* DONNA ELVIRA.)

DONNA ELVIRA (*vede* LEPORELLO): Eccomi a voi!

DON GIOVANNI (*a parte*): Vediamo che farà.

LEPORELLO (*aside*): Just look at that foolish woman; she's ready to trust him again!

DON GIOVANNI: Come down here, my darling! You'll see that my heart adores you; I'm already penitent.

DONNA ELVIRA: No, I don't trust you, cruel one!

DON GIOVANNI: Ah, believe me! Or I shall kill myself!

LEPORELLO (*aside*): If he goes on with this, I'll laugh out loud!

DON GIOVANNI: My darling, come here!

DONNA ELVIRA: What a strange situation! I don't know whether I should go with him or stay here! Ah, heaven protect my trusting heart!

DON GIOVANNI (*aside*): I hope she'll yield quickly! This was a fortunate stroke! My talents are beyond emulation.

LEPORELLO (*aside*): Again his lying lips deceive her! Ah, heaven protect her trusting heart!
(DONNA ELVIRA *closes the window.*)

Recitative

DON GIOVANNI: Well, my friend, how does it look?

LEPORELLO: It looks to me as if you have a heart of stone!

DON GIOVANNI: There now, don't be so prudish! Listen carefully; when she comes down here you must hurry and embrace her, give her three or four kisses, imitate my voice, and with similar deceptions, manage to lead her away from here with you.

LEPORELLO: But, my Lord!

DON GIOVANNI: Don't waste time in arguments!

LEPORELLO: And if she should recognize me?

DON GIOVANNI: She won't if you don't wish her to— Look! She's coming—be quiet!
(*He hides upstage, listening.* DONNA ELVIRA *enters.*)

DONNA ELVIRA (*seeing* LEPORELLO): Here I am, my love!

DON GIOVANNI (*aside*): Let's see what he can do.

273

LEPORELLO (*a parte*): Che bell'imbroglio!

DONNA ELVIRA: Dunque creder potrò, ch'i pianti miei abbian vinto quel cor? dunque pentito l'amato Don Giovanni al suo dovere, e all'amor mio ritorna?

LEPORELLO (*finge la voce di* DON GIOVANNI): Si, carina!

DONNA ELVIRA: Crudele! se sapeste Quante lagrime, e quanti sospiri voi mi costate!

LEPORELLO: Io, vita mia!

DONNA ELVIRA: Voi.

LEPORELLO: Poverina! quanto mi dispiace!

DONNA ELVIRA: Mi fuggirete più?

LEPORELLO: No, muso bello!

DONNA ELVIRA: Sarete sempre mio?

LEPORELLO: Sempre!

DONNA ELVIRA: Carissimo!

LEPORELLO: Carissima! (*a parte*) La burla mi da gusto!

DONNA ELVIRA: Mio tesoro!

LEPORELLO: Mia venere!

DONNA ELVIRA: Son per voi tutta foco!

LEPORELLO: Io tutto cenere!

DON GIOVANNI (*a parte*): Il birbo si riscalda.

DONNA ELVIRA: E non m'ingannerete?

LEPORELLO: No, sicuro.

DONNA ELVIRA: Giuratelo!

LEPORELLO: Lo giuro a questa mano, che bacio con trasporto, e a quei bei lumi!

DON GIOVANNI (*finge d'insequirli*): Ih, eh, ah, ih—sei morto!

DONNA ELVIRA *e* LEPORELLO: Oh Numi! (*Fugono.*)

DON GIOVANNI: Ih, eh, ah, ih! Par che la sorte mi secondi. Veggiamo; le finestre son queste: ora cantiamo.

17. Canzonetta

Deh vieni alla finestra,
O mio tesoro,
Deh vieni a consolar,

LEPORELLO (*aside*): What a situation!

DONNA ELVIRA: May I then believe that my tears have conquered your heart? Now, repentant, my beloved Don Giovanni is returning to his duty and his love?

LEPORELLO (*imitating* DON GIOVANNI'S *voice*): Yes, my darling!

DONNA ELVIRA: Cruel one! If you only knew how many tears and sighs you've cost me!

LEPORELLO: I, treasure of my life?

DONNA ELVIRA: You!

LEPORELLO: Poor girl! How sorry I am!

DONNA ELVIRA: You won't leave me again?

LEPORELLO: No, my sweetheart!

DONNA ELVIRA: You'll always be mine?

LEPORELLO: Always!

DONNA ELVIRA: My darling!

LEPORELLO: My dearest! (*aside*) This game is to my taste!

DONNA ELVIRA: My treasure!

LEPORELLO: My Venus!

DONNA ELVIRA: My heart is flaming with love!

LEPORELLO: I'm one huge furnace!

DON GIOVANNI (*aside*): The rascal is warming up!

DONNA ELVIRA: And you're not deceiving me?

LEPORELLO: No, of course not.

DONNA ELVIRA: Swear it to me!

LEPORELLO: I swear it by this hand, which I kiss with ecstasy, and by those beautiful eyes!

DON GIOVANNI (*pretending to chase them*): Ih, eh, ah—I'll kill you!

DONNA ELVIRA *and* LEPORELLO: O heavens! (*Exit.*)

DON GIOVANNI: Ih, eh, ah, ha, ha, ha! It seems that fortune is auspicious; soon I shall see. These are her windows; now to my song.

17. Canzonetta

Come here to your window, O my treasure! Come to console my tears! If you deny me, I will die here before your eyes! Your mouth is sweeter than honey; your heart is

Il pianto mio.
Se neghi a me di dar qualche ristoro;
Davanti agli occhi tuoi, morir vogl'io.
Tu ch'hai la bocca dolce,
Più del miele.
Tu che il zucchero porti in mezzo al core;
Non esser gioja mia con me crudele,
Lasciate almen veder mio bell'amore!

Recitativo

V'è gente alla finestra; forse è dessa. Zi! Zi!
(*Entra* MASSETO, *e contadini armati.*)

MASETTO: Non ci stanchiamo; il cor mi dice che trovarlo dobbiamo.

DON GIOVANNI (*a parte*): Qualcuno parla.

MASETTO: Fermatevi—mi pare ch'alcuno qui si mova.

DON GIOVANNI (*a parte*): Se non fallo, è Masetto.

MASETTO: Chi va là? Non risponde. Animo, schioppo al muso: Chi va là?

DON GIOVANNI (*a parte*): Non è solo, ci vuol giudizio. (*forte*) Amici! (*a parte*) Non mi voglio scoprir. (*forte*) Sei tu, Masetto?

MASETTO: Appunto quello! e tu?

DON GIOVANNI: Non mi conosci? Un servo son io di Don Giovanni—

MASETTO: Leporello! Servo di quell'indegno cavaliere?

DON GIOVANNI: Certo, di quel briccone.

MASETTO: Di quell'uom senz'onore, ah dimmi un poco, dove possiam trovarlo; lo cerco con costor per trucidarlo.

DON GIOVANNI (*a parte*): Bagatelle! (*forte*) Bravissimo Masetto. Anch'io con voi m'unisco per fargliela a quel birbo di padrone; ma udite un pò qual è la mia intenzione.

18. Aria

Metà di voi quà vandano,
E gli altri vadan là!
E pian pianin lo cerchino,
Lontan non sia di quà, no!
Se un uom e una ragazza passegian per la piazza
Se sotto a una finestra

made of sugar! Don't be cruel to me, my dearest. Let me see your face, my beautiful love!

Recitative

There's somebody at the window; it may be she. Pst! Pst! (MASETTO *enters, with armed villagers.*)

MASETTO: Don't give up; I know that we will find him.

DON GIOVANNI (*aside*): I hear a voice!

MASETTO: Stop! It seemed to me that somebody moved.

DON GIOVANNI (*aside*): If I don't mistake him, it's Masetto.

MASETTO: Who goes there? He doesn't answer. Aim your guns! Who goes there?

DON GIOVANNI (*aside*): He's not alone; I must be careful. (*aloud*) My friends! (*aside*) I don't want to be found out. (*aloud*) Is it you, Masetto?

MASETTO: Me myself! And who are you?

DON GIOVANNI: You don't know me? I'm the servant of Don Giovanni.

MASETTO: Leporello? Servant of that unworthy nobleman?

DON GIOVANNI: Yes, of that rascal!

MASETTO: Of that man without honor? Ah, only tell me where we can find him! I'm looking for him with these friends, in order to kill him.

DON GIOVANNI (*aside*): Nonsense! (*aloud*) That's wonderful, Masetto. I'll join you, and help you kill that rascal, my master. But listen—I have a plan.

18. Aria

Half of you go this way; and the other half, that way! Look for him silently; he can't be far from here, no! If you see a man and a girl walking on the square, if you hear love-making under a window, then strike—it will be my master. He's wearing a hat with white feathers; a heavy cloak covers his back; a sword hangs at his side. Go, hurry up!

Fare all'amor sentite
Ferite, pur ferite, il mio padron sarà.
In testa egli ha un cappello,
Con candidi pennacchi,
Addosso un gran mantello
E spada al fianco egli ha.
Andata, fate presto! (*a* MASETTO) Tu sol verrai con me.
Noi far dobbiam il resto, e già vedrai cos'e.
(*I contadini partono.*)

Recitativo

Zitto! lascia ch'io senta. Ottimamente! Dunque dobbiamo ucciderlo?

MASETTO: Sicuro.

DON GIOVANNI: E non ti basteria rompergli l'ossa—Fracassargli le spalle?

MASETTO: No, no! voglio ammazzarlo! Vò farlo in cento brani.

DON GIOVANNI: Hai buone arme?

MASETTO: Cospetto! Ho pria questo moschetto; e poi questa pistola.

DON GIOVANNI: E poi?

MASETTO: Non basta?

DON GIOVANNI: Eh, basta certo. Or prendi questa per la pistola, (*battendolo*) questa per il moschetto.

MASETTO: Ahi! ahi! La testa mia!

DON GIOVANNI: Taci, o t'uccido! Questa per l'ammazzarlo— Questa per farlo in brani. Villano, mascalzon, ceffo da cani! (*Parte.*)

MASETTO: Ahi, ahi! La testa mia! Ahi, ahi, le spalle! E il petto!
(*Entra* ZERLINA, *con una lanterna.*)

ZERLINA: Di sentire mi parve la voce di Masetto.

MASETTO: Oh Dio! Zerlina! Zerlina mia, soccorso!

ZERLINA: Cos'è stàto?

MASETTO: l'iniquo, il scelerato mi ruppe l'ossa, e i nervi.

ZERLINA: O poveretta me! chi?

MASETTO: Leporello, o qualche diavol che somiglia a lui.

(*to* MASETTO) Only you will remain here with me. We'll do the rest, and you'll soon learn what that will be.
(*The villagers exit.*)

Recitative

Be quiet, let me listen. Good; nobody's coming. Then you want to kill him?

MASETTO: Certainly!

DON GIOVANNI: And it won't be enough if you merely break his bones—wrench his shoulders?

MASETTO: No! I want to kill him and cut him into a hundred pieces!

DON GIOVANNI: Have you good weapons?

MASETTO: Of course! First have this musket; and then, this pistol.

DON GIOVANNI: And then?

MASETTO: Isn't that enough?

DON GIOVANNI: Oh, it's enough. Now take that for the pistol (*beating him*) and that for the musket!

MASETTO: Oh, my poor head!

DON GIOVANNI: Be quiet, or I'll kill you! Take this for killing him—and this for the hundred pieces! You ill-bred dog! (*Exits.*)

MASETTO: Oh, oh! My head! Oh, oh, my shoulders, my chest!
(ZERLINA *enters, with a lantern.*)

ZERLINA: Is that Masetto's voice?

MASETTO: O God! Zerlina! My Zerlina, help me!

ZERLINA: What has happened?

MASETTO: The wretch, the villain, has torn my flesh from my bones!

ZERLINA: Oh, poor dear! But who has done this?

MASETTO: Leporello, or a devil who greatly resembled him!

ZERLINA: Crudel! non tel diss'io, che con questa tua pazza gelosia ti ridurresti a qualche brutto passo. Dove ti duole?

MASETTO: Quì.

ZERLINA: E poi?

MASETTO: Quì e ancora quì.

ZERLINA: E poi non ti duol altro?

MASETTO: Duolmi un poco questo piè, questo braccio, e questa mano.

ZERLINA: Via via, non è gran mal, s'il resto è sano. Vientene meco a casa. Purchè tu mi prometta d'essere men geloso, io, io ti guarirò, caro il mio sposo.

19. Aria

Vedrai carino,
Se sei buonino,
Che bel rimedio,
Ti voglio dar.
E naturale,
Non da disgusto,
E lo speziale,
Non lo so far, nò.
E un certo balsamo,
Che porto addosso,
Dare tel posso,
S'il vuoi provar!
Saper vorresti?
Dove mi stà? (*mettendo la mano sal core*)
Sentilo battere
Toccami quà!
(ZERLINA e MASETTO *partono. Entrano* LEPORELLO e DONNA ELVIRA).

Recitativo

LEPORELLO: Di molte faci il lume s'avvicina, o mio ben; stiamo qui un poco, finchè da noi si scosta.

DONNA ELVIRA: Ma che temi, adorato il mio sposo?

LEPORELLO: Nulla, nulla. Certi riguardi—Io vò veder, s'il lume è già lontano. (*a parte*) Ah come da costei liberarmi? (*forte*) Rimanti, anima bella!

DONNA ELVIRA: Ah, non lasciarmi!

ZERLINA: Cruel one! Haven't I told you that your insane jealousy would get you into trouble? Where does it hurt you?

MASETTO: Here.

ZERLINA: Where else?

MASETTO: Here, and also here.

ZERLINA: Is that all?

MASETTO: My foot hurts me a little, this arm, and this hand.

ZERLINA: Come, come, it's not so bad if the rest is well. Now come home with me. If you'll promise me to be less jealous, I myself will cure you, my darling!

19. Aria

Come, my dearest; if you're good, I'll give you the best of all remedies. It's a natural cure, and no chemist can make it. It's a certain balsam that I carry with me. I can give it to you if you'd like to try it. Would you like to know where it is? (*putting her hand on her heart*) Listen to it beating; touch me here!

(ZERLINA *and* MASETTO *exit.* LEPORELLO *and* DONNA ELVIRA *enter.*)

Recitative

LEPORELLO: The lights of many torches surround us, my darling. We can hide here, and they will never see us.

DONNA ELVIRA: But why are you afraid, my adored one?

LEPORELLO: It's really nothing—only certain precautions. I'll see how far away they are. (*aside*) How can I get rid of her? (*aloud*) Wait there, my love!

DONNA ELVIRA: Ah, don't leave me!

Don Giovanni

20. Sestetto

Sola, sola, in bujo loco,
Palpitar il cor mi sento!
E m'assale un tal spavento,
Che mi sembra di morir.

LEPORELLO: Più che cerco men ritrovo
Questa porta sciagurata.
Piano, piano—l'ho trovata,
Ecco il tempo di fuggir.

(LEPORELLO *si nasconde.* DON OTTAVIO *e* DONNA ANNA
entrano.)

DON OTTAVIO: Tergi il ciglio, o vita mia!
E da calma al tuo dolore!
L'ombra omai del genitore
Pena avrà de tuoi martir.

DONNA ANNA: Lascia almen alla mia pena
Questo piccolo ristoro,
Sol la morte, o mio tesoro—
Il mio pianto può finir!

DONNA ELVIRA (*a parte*): Ah, dov'è lo sposo mio?

LEPORELLO (*a parte*): Se mi trova, son perduto.

DONNA ELVIRA *e* LEPORELLO: Una porta là vegg'io,
Cheta, cheta io vò partir!

(*Entrano* ZERLINA *e* MASETTO.)

ZERLINA *e* MASETTO: Ferma briccone! Dove ten vai?

DONNA ANNA *e* DON OTTAVIO: Ecco il fellone! Com'era quà?

DONNA ANNA, ZERLINA, DON OTTAVIO, MASETTO: Ah! mora
il perfido,
Che m'ha tradito!

DONNA ELVIRA: E mio marito!
Pietà! pietà!

DONNA ANNA, ZERLINA, DON OTTAVIO, MASETTO: E Donna
Elvira
Quello ch'io vedo?
Appena il credo?

DONNA ELVIRA: Pietà!

DONNA ANNA, ZERLINA, DON OTTAVIO, MASETTO: No, no!
Morrà!

LEPORELLO: Perdon, perdono!

20. Sextet

All alone in this dark place, I feel my heart pounding in my breast, and I tremble so that I fear that I'm going to die.

LEPORELLO: I'm searching for that damned gate, but I still can't find it. At last—here it is! Now it's safe for me to hide!
(LEPORELLO *hides.* DON OTTAVIO *and* DONNA ANNA *enter.*)

DON OTTAVIO: Dry your eyes, my darling, and calm your grief. Even your father's spirit would feel pain at your grief.

DONNA ANNA: Leave me to my sorrow; I can find no consolation. Only death can end my tears.

DONNA ELVIRA (*aside*): Ah, where is my husband?

LEPORELLO (*aside*): If she sees me, I'm lost.

DONNA ELVIRA *and* LEPORELLO: Here is the door; I'll quietly escape from this place!
(*Enter* ZERLINA *and* MASETTO.)

ZERLINA *and* MASETTO: Stop, you rascal! You can't escape us!

DONNA ANNA *and* DON OTTAVIO: Here's the murderer! Why is he here?

DONNA ANNA, ZERLINA, DON OTTAVIO, MASETTO: Let the wretch die! He has betrayed us!

DONNA ELVIRA: He is my husband! Have pity!

DONNA ANNA, ZERLINA, DON OTTAVIO, MASETTO: This woman is Donna Elvira! I can hardly believe it!

DONNA ELVIRA: Have pity!

DONNA ANNA, ZERLINA, DON OTTAVIO, MASETTO: No, no! He must die!

LEPORELLO: Forgive me, ladies and gentlemen! I'm not

Signori miei;
Quell'io non sono,
Sbaglia costei.
Viver lasciatemi
Per carità!

DONNA ANNA, DONNA ELVIRA, ZERLINA, DON OTTAVIO, MA-
SETTO: Dei! Leporello!
Che inganno è questo!
Stupida resto.
Che mai sarà!

TUTTI: Mille torbidi pensieri
Mi s'aggiran per la testa!

LEPORELLO: Se mi salvo in tal tempesta,
E un prodigio in verità!

DONNA ANNA, DONNA ELVIRA, ZERLINA, DON OTTAVIO, MA-
SETTO: Che giornata, o stelle, è questa—
Che impensata novità?
(DONNA ANNA *parte*.)

Recitativo

ZERLINA: Dunque quello sei tu che il mio Masetto poco fà
crudelmente maltrattasti?

DONNA ELVIRA: Dunque tu m'ingannasti, o scellerato, spac-
ciandoti con me da Don Giovanni?

DON OTTAVIO: Dunque tu in questi panni venisti quì per
qualche tradimento!

ZERLINA: A me tocca punirlo!

DONNA ELVIRA: Anzia me!

DON OTTAVIO: No, no, à me!

MASETTO: Accoppatela meco tutti trè!

21. Aria

LEPORELLO: Ah, pietà, signori miei!
Dò ragione a voi a lei.
Mà il delitto, mio non è,
Il padron con prepotenza l'innocenza mi rubò.
Donna Elvira! Compatite! Già capite come andò.
Dì Masetto non sò nulla, (*accennando* DONNA ELVIRA) vel
dirà questa fanciulla.
E un'oretta circumcirca che con lei girando vo. (*a* DON
OTTAVIO)
Ah voi, signore, non dico niente,

Don Giovanni; you've made an error. Please let me live, for pity's sake!

DONNA ANNA, DONNA ELVIRA, ZERLINA, DON OTTAVIO, MASETTO: Heavens! Leporello! What trick is this? I'm amazed! Whatever will happen?

ALL: A thousand dark thoughts are running through my head.

LEPORELLO: If I'm saved from this tempest it will really be a miracle!

DONNA ANNA, DONNA ELVIRA, ZERLINA, DON OTTAVIO, MASETTO: What a day of darkness! O heavens—what new deceit!

(DONNA ANNA *exits.*)

Recitative

ZERLINA: Then it was you who cruelly beat my Masetto!

DONNA ELVIRA: Then it was you who deceived me, you scoundrel, pretending to be Don Giovanni!

DON OTTAVIO: And you came here in his clothing, intending to deceive us all!

ZERLINA: It's my duty to punish him.

DONNA ELVIRA: No, it's mine!

DON OTTAVIO: No, no, it's mine!

MASETTO: I'll help all of you to kill him!

21. Aria

LEPORELLO: Ah, have pity, good people! You're all very right to be angry, but the crimes weren't mine. My master robbed me of my innocence. Donna Elvira, tell them! You know what happened. I don't know anything about Masetto, as this young lady (*pointing to* DONNA ELVIRA) can tell you. It was a peculiar situation; she thought she was going for a walk with him. (*to* DON OTTAVIO) And you, my Lord! I can't say a word. Certainly my fear, my ill-fortune —it was light outside—and dark inside—I couldn't find —the door—the wall—I took myself off—I hid over there

285

Don Giovanni

Certo timore, certo accidente—
Di fuori chiaro—di dentro oscuro—
Non c'è riparo—la porta—il muro—io—me—ne—vo'—
Da quel lato—poi qui celato—l'affar si sà,
Oh, si sa! Mà, s'io sapeva, fuggia per quà! (*Parte.*)

Recitativo

DONNA ELVIRA: Ferma, perfido, ferma!

MASETTO: Il birbo ha l'ali ai piedi!

ZERLINA: Con qual arte si sottrasse l'iniquo!

DON OTTAVIO: Amici miei, dopo eccessi si enormi, dubitar non possiam, che Don Giovanni non sia l'empio uccisore del padre di Donn'Anna. In questa casa per poche ore fermatevi—un ricorso vò far a chi si deve; e in pochi istanti vendicarvi prometto; cosi vuole dover, pietade, affetto.

(DONNA ELVIRA, ZERLINA e MASETTO *partono.*)

22. Aria

Il mio tesoro intanto
Andate, andate a consolar,
E del bel ciglio il pianto
Cercate di asciugar.
Ditele che i suoi torti
A vendicar io vado.
Che sol di stragi e morti
Nunzio vogl'io tornar.

(DON OTTAVIO *parte. Entra* DONNA ELVIRA.)

Recitativo

DONNA ELVIRA: In quale eccessi. oh, Numi! in quali misfatti orribili, tremendi, è avvolto il sciagurato! Ah no! non puote tardar l'ira del cielo. La giustizia tardar! Sentir già parmi la fatale saetta, che gli piomba sul capo—aperto veggio il baratro mortal—Misera Elvira! Che contrasto d'affetti in sen ti nasce! Perchè questi sospiri, e queste ambascie?

23. Aria

Mi tradì quell'alma ingrata,
Infelice oh Dio! mi fa!
Ma, tradita e abbandonata,
Provo ancor per lui pietà
Quando sento il mio tormento,
Di vendetta il cor favella;
Ma se guardo il suo cimento,
Palpitando il cor mi va. (*Parte.*)

286

—you'll understand! But if I had known, I would have run the other way! (*Exits.*)

Recitative

DONNA ELVIRA: Stop, wretch, stop!

MASETTO: The rascal has wings on his feet!

ZERLINA: How cleverly he escaped us!

DON OTTAVIO: My friends, after such a scene, who can doubt that Don Giovanni is the evil murderer of Donna Anna's father? Wait in her house for a few hours. I'll go to the authorities, and in a short time she'll be avenged. Duty, pity, and affection demand it.

(DONNA ANNA, ZERLINA, *and* MASETTO *exit.*)

22. Aria

Go to my love, meanwhile, and console her. Try to dry her beautiful eyes. Tell her that I will avenge her wrongs. Nothing can stop me from completing her revenge!

(DON OTTAVIO *exits.* DONNA ELVIRA *enters.*)

Recitative

DONNA ELVIRA: O God, to what crimes and excesses has he descended! Ah, no! heaven will not delay its wrath or its justice! Already I can feel the fatal lightning that will fall upon his head. Already I can see the last abyss opening. Wretched Elvira! What a conflict of emotions contends in your breast! Why are you sighing? Why are you so unhappy?

23. Aria

That ungrateful man has betrayed me! Oh, God, he has ruined my happiness! But, although he's betrayed me and abandoned me, I still feel pity for him. When I suffer my torments, my heart cries out for vengeance, but when I hear his voice, my heart murmurs of love. (*Exits.*)

Scena II

Recinto murato, in mezzo al quale si vede la statua del COMMENDATORE. DON GIOVANNI, *salendo il muro; indi* LEPORELLO.

Recitativo

DON GIOVANNI: Ah! ah! ah! questa è buona! or lasciala cercar: Che bella notte! E più chiara del giorno, sembra fatta per gir a zonzo, a caccia di ragazze. Vediam s'è tardi? Ah, no! Ancor non son le due di notte. Avrei voglia un pò di saper com'è finito l'affar tra Leporello e Donna Elvira; s'egli ha avuto giudizio—

LEPORELLO (*dietro il muro*): Alfin vuole ch'io faccia un precipizio!

DON GIOVANNI: E desso! Oh, Leporello!

LEPORELLO: Chi mi chiama?

DON GIOVANNI: Non conosci il padron?

LEPORELLO: Così nol conoscessi!

DON GIOVANNI: Come? birbo!

LEPORELLO: Ah, siete voi? Scusate!

DON GIOVANNI: Cos'è stato?

LEPORELLO: Per cagion vostra io fui quasi accoppato.

DON GIOVANNI: Ebben, non era questo un onore per te?

LEPORELLO: Signor, vel dono!

DON GIOVANNI: Via, via, vien quà! Che belle cose ti deggio dir!

LEPORELLO: Ma cosa fate quì?

DON GIOVANNI: Vien dentro, e lo saprai. Diverse istorielle, che accadute mi son dacchè partisti, ti dirò un'altra volta; or la più bella ti vò solo narrar.

LEPORELLO: Donnesca, al certo.

DON GIOVANNI: C'è dubbio! Una fanciulla, bella, giovin, galante, per la strada incontrai; le vado appresso, la prendo per la man—fuggir mi vuole; dico poche parole, ella mi piglia—sai per chi?

LEPORELLO: Non lo so.

DON GIOVANNI: Per Leporello!

LEPORELLO: Per me?

DON GIOVANNI: Per te!

LEPORELLO: Va bene!

Scene II

A cemetery with a statue of the COMMENDATORE. DON
GIOVANNI *leaps over the wall, to meet* LEPORELLO.

Recitative

DON GIOVANNI: Ha, ha! This is amusing! Now let her look
for me. What a beautiful night! It's brighter than the day
—perfect for making love! I wish I knew what is happen-
ing between Leporello and Elvira; if only he is clever—

LEPORELLO (*behind the wall*): I think he wants to get me
in trouble!

DON GIOVANNI: He's there! O Leporello!

LEPORELLO: Who's calling me?

DON GIOVANNI: Don't you know your master?

LEPORELLO: No, I don't know him!

DON GIOVANNI: What? You rascal!

LEPORELLO: Ah, is it you, Sir? Excuse me!

DON GIOVANNI: Tell me what has happened.

LEPORELLO: I've been almost killed for your sake.

DON GIOVANNI: I'd say that that was an honor for you.

LEPORELLO: I return that honor to you, Sir!

DON GIOVANNI: Come nearer! I have a delightful tale to
tell you!

LEPORELLO: But what are you doing here?

DON GIOVANNI: Come in here and I'll tell you. Things have
happened—but I'll discuss it with you another time. Now
I only want you to know the funniest story.

LEPORELLO: About a woman, of course.

DON GIOVANNI: Can you doubt it? I met a pretty young girl
in the street; I went near her and took her hand—she tried
to escape; I said a few words to her; she took me for—
Do you know for whom?

LEPORELLO: I don't know.

DON GIOVANNI: For Leporello!

LEPORELLO: For me?

DON GIOVANNI: For you.

LEPORELLO: Good enough!

289

DON GIOVANNI: Per la mano essa allora mi prende.

LEPORELLO: Ancora meglio.

DON GIOVANNI: M'accarezza, m'abbraccia—"Caro il mio Leporello! Leporello, mio caro!" Allor m'accorse ch'era qualche tua bella.

LEPORELLO (*a parte*): Oh, maledetto!

DON GIOVANNI: Dell'inganno approfitto; non so come mi riconosce, grida, sento gente, a fuggire mi metto, e pronto pronto per quel muretto in questo loco io monto.

LEPORELLO: E mi dite la cosa con tal indifferenza?

DON GIOVANNI: Perchè no?

LEPORELLO: Ma se fosse costei stata mia moglie?

DON GIOVANNI (*ridendo*): Meglio ancora!

LA STATUA DEL COMMENDATORE: Di rider finirai pria dell'Aurora!

DON GIOVANNI: Chi ha parlato?

LEPORELLO: Ah! qualch'anima sarà dall'altro mondo, che vi conosce a fondo.

DON GIOVANNI: Taci, sciocco! Chi va la?

LA STATUA DEL COMMENDATORE: Ribaldo, audace! lascia ai morti la pace!

LEPORELLO: Ve l'hò detto!

DON GIOVANNI: Sarà qualcun di fuori, che si burla di noi— Ehi! del Commendatore non è questa la statua? Leggi un poco quell'iscrizion!

LEPORELLO: Scusate, non hò imparato a leggere a raggi della luna.

DON GIOVANNI: Leggi, dico!

LEPORELLO (*legge*): "Dell'empio, chi mi trasse al passo estremo, qui attendo la vendetta." Udiste? io tremo!

DON GIOVANNI: O' vecchio buffonissimo! Digli che questa sera l'attendo a cena meco.

LEPORELLO: Che pazzia! Ma mi par— Oh, Dei! mirate che terribili occhiate egli ci da! Par vivo—par che senta—e che voglia parlar!

DON GIOVANNI: Orsù va àl o qui t'ammazzo! E poi ti seppellisco!

LEPORELLO: Piano, piano, signore—ora ubbidisco.

DON GIOVANNI: Then she took me by the hand.

LEPORELLO: The story is improving.

DON GIOVANNI: She caressed and embraced me. "O my dear Leporello! Leporello, my dear!" Then I thought it must be one of your mistresses.

LEPORELLO (*aside*): Damn you!

DON GIOVANNI: I profited by the deceit! I don't know how she recognized me; she screamed; I heard footsteps, and I fled and quickly leaped over this wall.

LEPORELLO: And can you tell me that with such indifference?

DON GIOVANNI: Why not?

LEPORELLO: But if she had been my wife?

DON GIOVANNI (*laughing*): Better still!

STATUE OF THE COMMENDATORE: By dawn your laughter will be ended.

DON GIOVANNI: Who spoke?

LEPORELLO: It must have been a spirit from the other world, one who knows you well.

DON GIOVANNI: Be quiet, rascal! Who was it?

STATUE OF THE COMMENDATORE: Audacious ribald! Leave the dead in peace!

LEPORELLO: I told you so!

DON GIOVANNI: It's somebody in the street making a joke of us— Isn't that the Commendator's statue? Read me that inscription!

LEPORELLO: Excuse me, but I've never learned to read by moonlight.

DON GIOVANNI: Read, I tell you!

LEPORELLO (*reading*): "Revenge awaits the villain who killed me." Do you hear that? It makes me shiver!

DON GIOVANNI: Oh, stupid old man! Tell him that I will await him at dinner this evening.

LEPORELLO: What madness! It seems— O God! look at his horrible eyes! He seems to be alive—and listening—he's going to speak.

DON GIOVANNI: Hurry; go over there, or I'll kill you and bury you here!

LEPORELLO: Be calm, my Lord—I'll obey you!

24. *Duetto*

O statua gentilissima
Del gran Commendatore—
Padron, mi trema il core;
Non posso terminar.

DON GIOVANNI: Finiscila, o nel petto
Ti metto questo acciar.

LEPORELLO (*a parte*): Che impiccio! che capriccio!
Io sentomi gelar!

DON GIOVANNI (*a parte*): Che gusto, che spassetto!
Lo voglio far tremar.

LEPORELLO: O, statua gentilissima,
Benchè di marmo siate—
Ah, padron mio! mirate!
Che seguita a guardar.

DON GIOVANNI: Mori, mori!

LEPORELLO: No, no—attendete! (*alla* STATUA)
Signore, il padron mio—
Badate ben, non io—
Ah! ah! che scena è questa!
(LA STATUA *china la testa.*)
Oh, ciel! chinò la testa!

DON GIOVANNI: Va là che sei un buffone!

LEPORELLO: Guardate! Guardate ancor, padrone!

DON GIOVANNI: E che deggio guardar?

LEPORELLO: Colla marmorea testa
Ei fa così così.

DON GIOVANNI (*alla* STATUA): Parlate, se potete,
Verrete a cena?

LA STATUA DEL COMMENDATORE: Si!

LEPORELLO: Mover mi posso appena—
Mi manca, oh Dei, la lena!
Per carità partiamo:
Andiamo via di quà!

DON GIOVANNI: Bizzarra è inver la scena—
Verrà il buon vecchio a cena
A prepararla andiamo,
Partiamo via di quà.

(DON GIOVANNI *e* LEPORELLO *partono. Entrano* DONNA ANNA
e DON OTTAVIO.)

24. Duet

Oh, most honorable statue of the great Commendatore—
Master! My heart is trembling! I cannot finish!

DON GIOVANNI: Go on, or I'll kill you with this sword!

LEPORELLO (*aside*): What a disastrous caprice! I feel my blood run cold.

DON GIOVANNI (*aside*): What an original amusement! I like to make him tremble.

LEPORELLO: Oh, most honorable statue, even though you're made of marble—ah, Master, look at him! He's staring straight at me!

DON GIOVANNI: Die, then!

LEPORELLO: No, no—wait! (*to the* STATUE) My Lord, my master—you understand, not I—wishes to dine with you this evening! Ah, ah, ah! What a scene of madness!
(*The* STATUE *nods its head.*)
O heavens, he's nodding his head!

DON GIOVANNI: You're a stupid buffoon!

LEPORELLO: Look! Look again, my Lord!

DON GIOVANNI: And what must I look at?

LEPORELLO: With his marble head he nods at us just like this!

DON GIOVANNI (*to the* STATUE): Speak if you can! Will you dine with me?

STATUE OF COMMENDATORE: Yes!

LEPORELLO: I can hardly move—my strength is gone. For pity's sake, let's escape from this place!

DON GIOVANNI: This truly is strange—the good old man accepts my invitation. Let's go and make sure that dinner is prepared for him.
(DON GIOVANNI *and* LEPORELLO *exit.* DONNA ANNA *and* DON OTTAVIO *enter.*)

Recitativo

DON OTTAVIO: Calmatevi, idol mio, di quel ribaldo vedrem puniti in breve i gravi eccessi, vendicati sarem.

DONNA ANNA: Ma il padro, oh Dio!

DON OTTAVIO: Convien chinar il ciglio al volere del ciel. Respira, o cara. Di tua perdita amara fia domani, se vuoi, dolce compenso questo cor, questa mano, ch'il mio tenero amor!

DONNA ANNA: Oh Dei! che dite, in sì tristi momenti?

DON OTTAVIO: E che? vorresti con indugi novelli accrescer le mie pene? Crudele!

DONNA ANNA: Crudele! ah no, mio ben. Troppo mi spiace allontanarti un ben che lungamente la nostr'alma desia—mà il mondo—oh Dio! Non sedur la costanza del sensibil mio core! Abbastanza per te mi parla amore.

25. Aria

Non mi dir, bell'idol mio,
Che son io crudel con te;
Tu ben sai quant'io t'amai,
Tu conosci la mia fè.
Calma, calma il tuo tormento,
Se di duol non vuoi ch'io mora!
Forse un giorno il cielo ancora
Sentirà pietà di me.
(DONNA ANNA e DON OTTAVIO *partono*.)

Scena III

Gran sala del palazzo di DON GIOVANNI. *Una mensa preparata per mangiare. Entrano* DON GIOVANNI *e* LEPORELLO.

26. Finale

DON GIOVANNI: Già la mensa è preparata—
Voi suonate, amici cari!
Già che spendo i miei danari,
Io mi voglio divertir!
Leporello, presto in tavola!

LEPORELLO: Son prontissimo a servir.
(*I musicisti suonano;* LEPORELLO *serve*.)
Bravi! *Cosa Rara!*

DON GIOVANNI: Che ti par del bel concerto?

Recitative

DON OTTAVIO: Calm yourself, my darling. We'll soon see the great crimes of that wretch punished and avenged.

DONNA ANNA: But my father, O God!

DON OTTAVIO: We must abide by God's will. Be comforted, my dear. Your loss is bitter, but I will try to recompense it by my hand, my heart, and my tender love.

DONNA ANNA: O God! What are you saying at such a sad time?

DON OTTAVIO: Well then? Will you add to my unhappiness with fresh refusals? Cruel one!

DONNA ANNA: Cruel one? Ah, no, my darling! I don't enjoy denying you something that both of us have long desired. But the world's conventions—O God! Even they can't change the constancy of my faithful heart! Let it be enough that my love is unchanging!

25. Aria

Do not tell me, my darling, that I am cruel to you! You know very well how much I love you—you know my unchanging faith. Calm your torments, if you don't wish me to perish of sorrow! Perhaps some day heaven will take pity on me.

(DONNA ANNA *and* DON OTTAVIO *exit.*)

Scene III

A large room in DON GIOVANNI'S *palace. A meal is laid out, ready to be eaten.* DON GIOVANNI *and* LEPORELLO *enter.*

26. Finale

DON GIOVANNI: Already the meal is prepared— Play your music, dear friends! If I spend my money, I want to be entertained! Leporello, come to the table!

LEPORELLO: I'm delighted to serve you!
(*The band plays while* LEPORELLO *serves.*)
Bravo! That's from *Cosa Rara!*

DON GIOVANNI: What do you think of the music?

295

LEPORELLO: E conforme al vostro merto.

DON GIOVANNI: Ah che piatto saporito!

LEPORELLO: Ah che barbaro appetito!
Che bocconi di gigante!
Mi par proprio di svenir.

DON GIOVANNI: Piatto!

LEPORELLO: Servo!
(*La musica continua.*)
Fra *I due Litiganti!*

DON GIOVANNI: Versa il vino.
Eccellente marzimino!

LEPORELLO (*a parte*): Questo pezzo di fagiano.
Piano piano vò inghiottir.

DON GIOVANNI (*a parte*): Sta mangiando quel marrano!
Fingerò di non capir.
(*Ora la musica è di* Le Nozze di Figaro *di Mozart.*)

LEPORELLO: Questa poi la conosco pur troppo!

DON GIOVANNI: Leporello!

LEPORELLO: Padron mio!

DON GIOVANNI: Parla schietto, mascalzone!

LEPORELLO: Non mi lascia una flessione
Le parole preferir.

DON GIOVANNI: Mentre io mangio, fischia un poco.

LEPORELLO: Non sò far.

DON GIOVANNI: Cos'è?

LEPORELLO: Scusate!
Sì eccellente è il vostro cuoco,
Che lo volli anch'io provar!
(*Entra* DONNA ELVIRA.)

DONNA ELVIRA (*a* DON GIOVANNI): L'ultima prova
Dell'amor mio
Ancor vogl'io
Fare con te.
Più non rammento
Gl'inganni tuoi,
Pietate io sento.

DON GIOVANNI e LEPORELLO (*a parte*): Cos'è? cos'è?

DONNA ELVIRA: Da te non chiede
Quest'alma oppressa
Della sua fede
Qualche mercè.
(*S'inginocchia.*)

LEPORELLO: It conforms to your own merits.

DON GIOVANNI: Ah, what a delicious meat pie!

LEPORELLO: Ah, what a huge appetite! What gigantic mouthfuls! It takes my breath away!

DON GIOVANNI: More pie!

LEPORELLO: Here it is!

(*The music continues.*)

That's from *I Due Litiganti!*

DON GIOVANNI: Pour the wine! Excellent!

LEPORELLO (*aside*): While he isn't looking I'll swallow down this piece of pheasant!

DON GIOVANNI (*aside*): The rascal is eating! I'll pretend not to notice.

(*Now the music is from Mozart's* Marriage of Figaro.)

LEPORELLO: I've heard that tune once too often!

DON GIOVANNI: Leporello!

LEPORELLO: My Lord!

DON GIOVANNI: Speak clearly, you rascal!

LEPORELLO: I have a cold that won't let me speak clearly.

DON GIOVANNI: While I'm eating, whistle a little.

LEPORELLO: I can't!

DON GIOVANNI: Why not?

LEPORELLO: Excuse me! Your cook is so excellent that I wanted to sample his art!

(DONNA ELVIRA *enters.*)

DONNA ELVIRA (*to* DON GIOVANNI): I want to give you the ultimate proof of my love. I no longer resent your deceit; I only pity you!

DON GIOVANNI *and* LEPORELLO (*aside*): What is this?

DONNA ELVIRA: This unhappy soul expects no gratitude for her fidelity!

(*She kneels.*)

DON GIOVANNI: Mi maraviglio!
Cosa volete?
Se non sorgete
Non resto in piè.

DONNA ELVIRA: Ah, non deridere
Gli affanni miei!

LEPORELLO (*a parte*): Quasì da piangere
Mi fa costei!

DON GIOVANNI: Io ti derido!
Cielo! perchè?
Che vuoi, mio bene?

DONNA ELVIRA: Che vita cangi!

DON GIOVANNI: Brava!

DONNA ELVIRA: Cor perfido!

DON GIOVANNI: Lascia ch'io mangi;
E se ti piace,
Mangia con me.

DONNA ELVIRA: Restati barbaro,
Nel lezzo immondo,
Esempio orribile
D'iniquità!

DON GIOVANNI: Vivan le femmine!
Viva il buon vino!
Sostegno e gloria
D'umanità!

LEPORELLO (*a parte*): Se non si muove
Al suo dolore,
Di sasso ha il core,
O cor non hà!

DONNA ELVIRA (*esce precipitosamente*): Ah!

DON GIOVANNI: Che grido è questo mai?
Va a veder che cos'è stato!

LEPORELLO (*va alla porta*): Ah!

DON GIOVANNI: Che grido indiavolato!
Leporello, che cos'è?

LEPORELLO (*ritorna*): Ah, signor, per carità,
Non andate fuor di quà!
L'uom di sasso, l'uomo bianco—
Ah, padrone, io gelo, io manco!

DON GIOVANNI: I'm astounded! What do you want? If you won't get up, I'll have to kneel as well.

DONNA ELVIRA: Ah, don't ridicule my grief!

LEPORELLO (*aside*): She almost makes me cry!

DON GIOVANNI: I, ridicule you? Heavens, why? What do you ask of me, my dear?

DONNA ELVIRA: I want you to change your way of life!
DON GIOVANNI: Brava!
DONNA ELVIRA: Evil heart!
DON GIOVANNI: Let me continue with my supper, and if you like, you are welcome to join me.

DONNA ELVIRA: Stay there, you wretch; everyone will despise you as a horrible example of depravity!

DON GIOVANNI: Long live the women! Long live good wine! Forever may they sustain and exalt humanity!

LEPORELLO (*aside*): If he isn't moved by her grief, his heart is made of stone!

DONNA ELVIRA (*rushing out*): Ah!!!

DON GIOVANNI: Why is she screaming? Go out and see what has happened!

LEPORELLO (*going to the door*): Ah!!!

DON GIOVANNI: What an infernal cry! Leporello, what did she see?

LEPORELLO (*returning*): Ah, my Lord, for pity's sake, don't go out there! There's a man of stone, a white man— ah, my master, I'm freezing, I'm fainting! If you could see his size. If you could hear his footstep—ta, ta, ta, ta!

299

Se vedeste che figura.
Se sentiste come fa—
Ta, ta, ta, ta!

DON GIOVANNI: Non capisco niente affatto.
Tu sei matto in verità!

LEPORELLO: Ah sentite!
(*Si batte alla porta.*)

DON GIOVANNI: Qualcun batte.
Apri!

LEPORELLO: Io tremo!

DON GIOVANNI: Apri, dico!

LEPORELLO: Ah!

DON GIOVANNI: Matto!
Per togliermi d'intrico
Ad aprir io stesso andrò!

LEPORELLO: Non vò più veder l'amico,
Pian pianin si m'asconderò.
(*Si nasconde sotto la tavola. Entra la statua del* COMMENDA-
TORE.)

IL COMMENDATORE: Don Giovanni, a cenar teco
M'invitasti—e son venuto!

DON GIOVANNI: Non l'avrei giammai creduto,
Mà farò quel che potrò!
Leporello, un'altra cena
Fa che subito si porti!

LEPORELLO: Ah, padron, siam tutti morti!

DON GIOVANNI: Vanne dico!

IL COMMENDATORE: Ferma un pò!
Non si pasce di cibo mortale
Chi si pasce di cibo celeste;
Altre cure, più gravi di queste,
Altra bram aquaggiù mi guidò!

DON GIOVANNI: Parla dunque—che chiedi? che vuoi?

LEPORELLO: La terzana d'avere mi sembra,
E le membra fermar più non so.

IL COMMENDATORE: Parlo, ascolta! più tempo non ho!

DON GIOVANNI: Parla, parla! ascoltando ti sto.

IL COMMENDATORE: Tu m'invitasti a cena,

DON GIOVANNI: I don't understand a word you're saying. Are you insane?

LEPORELLO: Ah, listen!
(*Somebody knocks at the door.*)

DON GIOVANNI: Someone's knocking! Open the door!

LEPORELLO: I'm frozen with terror.

DON GIOVANNI: Open, I say!

LEPORELLO: Ah!

DON GIOVANNI: Fool! To clarify this mystery I'll open the door myself.

LEPORELLO: I can't bear to look at him any more: I'll quietly hide!
(*He hides. The marble statue of the* COMMENDATORE *enters.*)

COMMENDATORE: Don Giovanni! You invited me to dinner—and here I am!

DON GIOVANNI: I would never have believed it, but I'll continue to act out the play! Leporello, another setting! Bring it immediately!

LEPORELLO: Ah, dear master, we're all dead!

DON GIOVANNI: Go, I command you!

COMMENDATORE: No, remain here! I have no need of earthly food, I who feast on heavenly substance; other concerns, more urgent, have brought me here!

DON GIOVANNI: Speak then— What do you ask? What do you demand?

LEPORELLO: I seem to have a fever, and I cannot move my limbs.

COMMENDATORE: I'll speak, and you must listen! I have very little time!

DON GIOVANNI: Speak then! I'm listening to you.

COMMENDATORE: You invited me to dinner. Now you, too,

Don Giovanni

Il tuo dover or sai;
Rispondimi: verrai
Tu a cenar meco?

LEPORELLO: Oibò! oibò! tempo non hà—scusate!

DON GIOVANNI: A torto di viltate
Tacciato mai sarò!

IL COMMENDATORE: Risolvi!

DON GIOVANNI: Ho già risolto.

IL COMMENDATORE: Verrai?

LEPORELLO: Dite di no!

DON GIOVANNI: Ho fermo il core in petto;
Non ho timor: verrò!

IL COMMENDATORE: Dammi la mano in pegno!

DON GIOVANNI: Eccola. Ohimè!
Che gelo è questo mai!

IL COMMENDATORE: Pentiti, cangia vita.
E l'ultimo momento!

DON GIOVANNI: No, no—ch'io non mi pento,
Vanne lontan da me!

IL COMMENDATORE: Pentiti, scelerato!

DON GIOVANNI: No, vecchio infatuato!

IL COMMENDATORE: Pentiti!

DON GIOVANNI: No!

IL COMMENDATORE: Sì!

DON GIOVANNI: No! No!

IL COMMENDATORE: Ah tempo più non v'è!
(IL COMMENDATORE parte. Fiamme di sottera.)

DON GIOVANNI: Da qual tremore insolito
Sento assalir gli spiriti!
Dond'escono quei vortici
Di foco pien d'orror?

CORO (di sottera): Tutto a tue colpe è poco,
Vieni c'è un mal peggior!

DON GIOVANNI: Chi l'anima mi lacera!
Chi m'agita le viscere!
Che strazio ohimè! che smania
Che inferno! che terror!

LEPORELLO: Che ceffo disperato!
Che gesti di dannato!

know your duty. Answer: Will you come to dine with me?

LEPORELLO: Oh, no, he hasn't time—please excuse him!

DON GIOVANNI: Nobody will ever accuse me of the crime of cowardice!

COMMENDATORE: Resolve, then!

DON GIOVANNI: I've already decided.

COMMENDATORE: Will you come, then?

LEPORELLO: Tell him no!

DON GIOVANNI: My heart is firm in my breast. I have no fear: I'll come!

COMMENDATORE: Give me your hand in pledge!

DON GIOVANNI: Take it! Oh, what a chill I feel!

COMMENDATORE: Repent! Change your way of life! It's your last chance!

DON GIOVANNI: No, no—I will never repent! Go—don't torment me!

COMMENDATORE: Repent, vile scoundrel!

DON GIOVANNI: No, you insane old man!

COMMENDATORE: Repent!

DON GIOVANNI: No!

COMMENDATORE: Yes!

DON GIOVANNI: No! no!

COMMENDATORE: Now there is no more time!
(*The* COMMENDATORE *exits. Flames appear from below.*)

DON GIOVANNI: This is a new terror. Spirits surround me! From where do those whirlwinds come? Those horrible flames?

CHORUS (*from below*): There is little enough punishment for your sins. There are worse pains yet to come!

DON GIOVANNI: What tears my soul? What rends my body? What pains, ah, God! Ah, what misery!

LEPORELLO: A desperate face! He is damned! What shouts! What lamentations!

Che gridi! che lamenti!
Come mi fa terror!

DON GIOVANNI: Ah!!!

(*E perso nelle fiamme. Entrano* DONNA ANNA, DONNA EL-
VIRA, ZERLINA, DON OTTAVIO *e* MASETTO.)

DONNA ANNA, DONNA ELVIRA, ZERLINA, DON OTTAVIO, MA-
SETTO: Ah dove'è il perfido,
Dov'è l'indegno!
Tutto il mio sdegno
Sfogar io vo'.

DONNA ANNA: Solo mirandolo
Stretto in catene
Alle mie pene
Calma darò!

LEPORELLO: Più non sperate
Di ritrovarlo!
Più non cercarte!
Lotano andò.

DONNA ANNA, DONNA ELVIRA, ZERLINA, DON OTTAVIO, MA-
SETTO: Cos'è? favella!
Via, presto, sbrigati!

LEPORELLO: Venne un colosso—
Mà se non posso!
Trà fume e fuoco—
Badate un poco—
L'uomo di sasso—
Fermate il passo—
Giusto là sotto—
Diede il gran botto—
Giusto là il diavolo se'l trangugiò!

DONNA ANNA, DONNA ELVIRA, ZERLINA, DON OTTAVIO, MA-
SETTO: Stelle! che sento!

LEPORELLO: Vero è l'evento.

DONNA ANNA, DONNA ELVIRA, ZERLINA, DON OTTAVIO, MA-
SETTO: Ah, certo è l'ombra
Che l'(m')incontrò!

DON OTTAVIO (*a* DONNA ANNA): Or che tutti, o mio tesoro,
Vendicati siam del cielo,
Porgi, porgi a me un ristoro,
Non mi far languire ancor!

DONNA ANNA: Lascia, o caro, un anno ancora,

DON GIOVANNI: Ah!!!
(*The flames engulf him.* DONNA ANNA, DONNA ELVIRA, ZER-
LINA, DON OTTAVIO, *and* MASETTO *enter.*)

DONNA ANNA, DONNA ELVIRA, ZERLINA, DON OTTAVIO,
MASETTO: Ah, where is the criminal? We want to bend him
to our wrath!

DONNA ANNA: To see him bound in chains would comfort
my misery!

LEPORELLO: Don't expect to see him again; I don't know
where he is. He's gone far away.

DONNA ANNA, DONNA ELVIRA, ZERLINA, DON OTTAVIO,
MASETTO: Where is he? Tell us! Quickly, let us know!

LEPORELLO: A giant came here—but I can't describe him!
There were flames and smoke—the man was made of stone
—he walked into this room, and then—then the devil
dragged my master down below!

DONNA ANNA, DONNA ELVIRA, ZERLINA, DON OTTAVIO,
MASETTO: Heavens! What is he saying?
LEPORELLO: That's exactly how it happened.

DONNA ANNA, DONNA ELVIRA, ZERLINA, DON OTTAVIO,
MASETTO: Ah, that must have been the ghost that I saw.

DON OTTAVIO (*to* DONNA ANNA): Now that all are avenged
by heaven, my darling, give me some comfort—don't let
me languish forever!

DONNA ANNA: Let me wait another year, my darling, until

Don Giovanni

Allo sfogo del mio cor!
Al desio chi t'adora,
Ceder deve un fido amor.

DON OTTAVIO: Al desio di chi m'adora,
Ceder deve un fido amor.

DONNA ELVIRA: Io men vado in un ritiro a finir la vita mia.

ZERLINA e MASETTO: Noi, a casa andiamo, a cenar in compagnia!

LEPORELLO: Ed io vado all'osteria a trovar padron miglior.

ZERLINA, LEPORELLO, MASETTO: Resti dunque quel birbon con Proserpina e Pluton!
E noi tutti, o buona gente ripetiam allegramente l'antichissima canzon!

TUTTI: Questo è il fin di chi fà mal!
E de'perfidi la morte alla vita è sempre ugual!

my heart is ready. Your faithful love will yield to the desire of the woman who adores you.

DON OTTAVIO: My faithful love will yield to the desire of the woman I adore.

DONNA ELVIRA: I'll retire to a convent to end my life.

ZERLINA *and* MASETTO: We'll go home to have our dinner!

LEPORELLO: And I'll go to the inn to find a better master!

ZERLINA, LEPORELLO, MASETTO: Let that evil one remain in hell, with Proserpina and Pluto! And all of us meanwhile will repeat the oldest of songs!

ALL: This is the end of evildoers! The fate of sinners is always equal to their crimes!

COSÌ
FAN
TUTTE

An opera
in two acts

Music by
Wolfgang Amadeus Mozart
(K. 588)

Words by
Lorenzo da Ponte

INTRODUCTION

Così fan tutte was first produced in Vienna in January 1790, the third and final collaboration of Mozart and Da Ponte. Da Ponte's brilliant libretto is his only original work of the three; the wager that forms the basis of the plot was said to have been suggested by a contemporary incident. If *The Marriage of Figaro* marks the peak of Mozart's warmly realistic comedy, *Così fan tutte* is surely the ultimate comedy of artificiality. In its hard, glittering surface, it can be likened to the plays of Congreve. A work of wisdom and sophistication, and of impeccable stylistic grace, *Così fan tutte* portrays the coming-of-age of four utterly immature young people. The explicit theme is love and the fidelity of women, but actually, Don Alfonso's defense of reason and compromise might be applied in many other situations, and it provides a philosophical basis rare among operatic works.

The purpose of the opera may best be illustrated by examining its contrived, symmetrical structure. There are six characters: two pairs of young lovers, contrasted with Don Alfonso, the unembittered philosopher, and Despina, the worldly-wise maid. At the beginning, Don Alfonso may seem to be a disgruntled cynic when his sane admonitions are contrasted with the ravings of the wildly romantic younger men, but when we meet the ladies whom they characterize as paragons of virtue, we begin to see that Don Alfonso is simply being realistic. In *Così fan tutte,* the principal function of the characters is to fit into the general pattern, but it is also true that each possesses a definite individuality. Dorabella may be shallower than Fiordiligi, Ferrando more rhapsodical than Guglielmo, but all four young people share one common characteristic—they make no allowances for anything less than perfection in the ones they love. Don Alfonso deplores this attitude toward life; he knows that human beings cannot live up to such expectations, and he chooses to impart this knowledge by a joke that will give a maximum of instruction with a minimum of lasting pain.

Despina, utterly charming and utterly unscrupulous, is Don Alfonso's structural counterpart. She is a less elegant personification of his attitude toward life—make the best of every situation, and get what you can out of it! Newer to the art of deception, she does not recognize the officers in their Albanian disguises, but once she becomes part of the plot she makes it clear that Don Alfonso has found a worthy fellow conspirator.

Così fan tutte is one of those unusual works of art in which the original purpose of the creators is totally apparent in the final product. We feel no confusion or counterpull; all is harmony and coherence. Unique for its music and libretto, the opera must also be regarded philosophically; it shows us a means of coming to terms with life, a philosophical approach that Mozart and Da Ponte, typical of the age of reason, found most effective. "Don't expect too much of people," they advise us, "and you'll never be disappointed." This is a philosophy that requires balance, self-confidence, and a sense of humor, and it is impossible for those incapable of severe self-examination. *Così fan tutte* does not attempt to present a flattering picture of humanity, nor one that is noble, but a true one.

For this reason, perhaps, *Così fan tutte,* in spite of its delightful music and engaging comedy, will never be quite as popular as the warmly human *Marriage of Figaro* or the challenging, enigmatic *Don Giovanni.* But a small group of its admirers will always regard it as the most perfect of Mozart's operas, ironically expressive of the quintessence of a philosophy and of an age.

SYNOPSIS

ACT ONE

In a tavern in Naples, two young officers, Ferrando and Guglielmo, sing the praises of their sweethearts, Fiordiligi and Dorabella. The officers' older friend, Don Alfonso, claims that a faithful woman has never existed, and never will, and he offers to prove his theory if the young men will follow his orders for the next twenty-four hours. The officers agree to a wager that they see no prospect of losing, and cheerfully propose a toast to the God of Love.

That morning, as Fiordiligi and Dorabella await their lovers, Don Alfonso arrives with bad news—the first link in his plot. The officers have been suddenly ordered off to war, he says, but they are permitted one last farewell before they go. To the young men's great delight, the ladies appear to be inconsolable.

Don Alfonso then enlists the aid of Despina, the sisters' maid, telling her that her mistresses need diversion in their loneliness. He presents the two officers, now fantastically disguised as noblemen from Albania. Despina pronounces them too grotesque to be taken seriously; the ladies are horrified at this invasion of their privacy, and Fiordiligi indignantly dismisses the "Albanians" from the house. When Ferrando and Guglielmo jubilantly demand their money from Don Alfonso, he recommends patience: the twenty-four hours have not yet run their course.

As the ladies bewail their solitude, the two "Albanians" rush in, proclaiming that they are dying of unrequired love, and have taken poison to hasten the process. Don Alfonso suggests a doctor, and returns with Despina, who is disguised as a worker of miracles, able to cure all ailments with a magnet. The men suddenly recover, and proclaim their love. From the very vehemence of the ladies' denials, it is evident that their resolve is beginning to weaken.

ACT TWO

After listening to Despina's worldly advice, the ladies conclude that they can amuse themselves with the newcomers

312

without absolute infidelity to their lovers. In a joyous duet, each sister selects the other's former sweetheart to concentrate her attentions upon. First Dorabella succumbs to Guglielmo's ardent wooing; with somewhat more resistance, Fiordiligi yields to Ferrando's impassioned pleas.

Don Alfonso explains to the outraged young men that their sweethearts are no better or worse than all women: men must accept the instability of women, and love them anyway. As the ladies are about to marry their new suitors, Don Alfonso announces that the two officers have just returned from the battlefield. The "Albanians" hide, and a few minutes later, Ferrando and Guglielmo enter, clad in their officer's uniforms. Almost immediately they discover a false marriage contract, complete with signatures, as well as Despina, dressed, this time, as a notary. Explanations follow, and Dorabella and Fiordiligi, in spite of their resentment of the joke that has been played upon them, have no choice but to forgive and forget. All join in a chorus praising the man who is guided by reason; he will accept good and ill fortune alike, with philosophic calm.

CHARACTERS

FERRANDO, *an officer in love with* DORABELLA   *Tenor*
GUGLIELMO, *an officer in love with* FIORDILIGI   *Baritone*
DON ALFONSO, *the officers' older friend*   *Bass or Baritone*
FIORDILIGI ⎱ *two sisters of Ferrara,*   *Soprano*
DORABELLA ⎰ *living in Naples*   *Soprano or Mezzo-soprano*
DESPINA, *the sisters' maid*   *Soprano*
CHORUS *of soldiers, peasants, and servants*

The action takes place within the space of twenty-four hours, in and around FIORDILIGI *and* DORABELLA'S *house in Naples, during the mid-eighteenth century.*

COSÌ FAN TUTTE

Scena I

Una taverna a Napoli. DON ALFONSO, FERRANDO *e* GUGLIELMO *bevono.*

1. Terzetto

FERRANDO: La mia Dorabella
Capace non è,
Fedel quanto bella
Il cielo la fè!

GUGLIELMO: La mia Fiordiligi
Tradirmi non sa,
Uguale in lei credo
Costanza e beltà!

DON ALFONSO: Ho i crini già grigi,
Ex cathedra parlo
Ma tali litigi
Finiscano quà.

FERRANDO *e* GUGLIELMO: No, detto ci avete
Ch'infid'esser ponno
Provar cel'dovete,
Se avete onestà.

DON ALFONSO: Tai prove lasciamo—

FERRANDO *e* GUGLIELMO: No, no le vogliamo:
O fuori la spada,
Rompiam l'amistà!

DON ALFONSO: O pazzo desire!
Cercar de scoprire
Quel mal che trovato
Meschini ci fa.

FERRANDO *e* GUGLIELMO: Sul vivo mi tocca,
Chi lascia di bocca
Sortire un accento
Che torto le fa.

Recitativo

GUGLIELMO: Fuor la spada! sciegliete qual di noi più vi piace.

DON ALFONSO: Io son uomo di pace, e duelli non fo, se non a mensa.

ACT ONE

Scene I

A tavern in Naples. DON ALFONSO, FERRANDO, *and* GU-GLIELMO *are drinking.*

1. Trio

FERRANDO: My Dorabella is incapable of deceit. Heaven made her as faithful as she is beautiful!

GUGLIELMO: My Fiordiligi could never betray me! I know that her constancy equals her beauty!

DON ALFONSO: I'm older than you are; your experience doesn't compare with mine. But we'll finish this argument here and now.

FERRANDO *and* GUGLIELMO: No! Whoever has intimated that our sweethearts might be unfaithful must prove it to us if he has any honor.

DON ALFONSO: Let's forget about such proofs—

FERRANDO *and* GUGLIELMO: No, no, we demand them! Or else draw your sword, for our friendship is at an end!

DON ALFONSO: I warn you, don't insist! It will only make you miserable. He who looks for trouble is always bound to find it.

FERRANDO *and* GUGLIELMO: When anyone utters a word that might wrong my sweetheart it's a matter of life and death to me!

Recitative

GUGLIELMO: Draw your sword! Choose whichever of us you like!

DON ALFONSO: I'm a peaceful man, and I don't use steel except at dinner.

317

FERRANDO: O battervi, o dir subito, perchè d'infedeltà la nostre amanti sospettate capaci.

DON ALFONSO: Cara semplicità, quanto mi piace!

FERRANDO: Cessate di scherzar, o giuro al cielo—

DON ALFONSO: Ed io, giuro alla terra, non scherzo, amici miei: solo saper vorrei che razza d'animali son queste vostre belle, se han come tutti noi carne, ossa, e pelle, se mangian come noi, se veston gonne, alfin, se dee, se donne son.

FERRANDO e GUGLIELMO: Son donne; ma son tali, son tali!

DON ALFONSO: E in donne pretendete di trovar fedeltà? Quanto mi piaci mai, semplicità!

2. Terzetto

E la fede delle femmine
Come l'araba Fenice,
Che vi sia, ciascum lo dice,
Dove sia,
Nessun lo sa.

FERRANDO: La fenice è Dorabella.

GUGLIELMO: La fenice è Fiordiligi.

DON ALFONSO: Non è questa, non è quella,
Non fu mai, non vi sarà.

Recitativo

FERRANDO: Scioccherie di poeti!

GUGLIELMO: Scempiaffini di vecchi!

DON ALFONSO: Or bene, udite, ma senza andar in collera: qual prova avete voi, che ognor contanti vi sien le costre amanti; chi vi fè sicurtà, che invariabili sono i lor cori?

FERRANDO: Lunga esperienza—

GUGLIELMO: Nobil educazion—

FERRANDO: Pensar sublime—

GUGLIELMO: Analogia d'umor—

FERRANDO: Disinteresse—

GUGLIELMO: Immutabil carattere—

FERRANDO: Promesse—

GUGLIELMO: Proteste—

FERRANDO: Giuramenti—

318

FERRANDO: Either accept our challenge or tell us at once why you believe that our sweethearts are capable of infidelity!

DON ALFONSO: What sweet simplicity! How very charming!

FERRANDO: Stop your joking, or I swear by heaven—

DON ALFONSO: And I swear by the earth. I'm not joking, my friends. I would only like to know what kind of creatures these ladies are; if they're made of bone, flesh, and skin; if they eat like us; if they wear skirts; in a word, if they're goddesses or women.

FERRANDO *and* GUGLIELMO: They're women, but such women, such women!

DON ALFONSO: And you expect to find fidelity in women? How delightfully naïve!

2. Trio

Women's faith is like the Phoenix of Arabia; everyone tells you that it exists, but nobody can tell you where to find it.

FERRANDO: Dorabella is a model of faith.

GUGLIELMO: So is Fiordiligi!

DON ALFONSO: You're both wrong; a faithful woman has never existed and never will!

Recitative

FERRANDO: Ridiculous poetic nonsense!

GUGLIELMO: You're becoming senile!

DON ALFONSO: Very well; now listen to me, but without losing your tempers. What proof have you that your sweethearts will always be faithful to you? How do you know that their hearts will never change?

FERRANDO: Long experience—

GUGLIELMO: Noble education—

FERRANDO: Sublime thoughts—

GUGLIELMO: Great respect for love—

FERRANDO: Careful observation—

GUGLIELMO: Unshakable principles—

FERRANDO: Promises—

GUGLIELMO: Protestations—

FERRANDO: Oaths—

DON ALFONSO: Piani, sospir, carezze, svenimenti. Lasciatemi un po' ridere!

FERRANDO: Cospetto! finite di deriderci?

DON ALFONSO: Pian piano; e se toccar con mano oggi vi fo che come l'altre sono?

GUGLIELMO: Non si può dar!

FERRANDO: Non è!

DON ALFONSO: Giochiam?

FERRANDO: Giochiamo.

DON ALFONSO: Cento zecchini.

GUGLIELMO: E mille, se volete.

DON ALFONSO: Parola.

FERRANDO: Parolissima.

DON ALFONSO: E un cenno, un motto, un gesto, giurate di non far di tutto questo alle vostre Penelopi?

FERRANDO: Giuriamo.

DON ALFONSO: Da soldati d'onore?

GUGLIELMO: Da soldati d'onore.

DON ALFONSO: E tutto quel farete ch'io vi dirò di far?

FERRANDO: Tutto!

GUGLIELMO: Tuttissimo!

DON ALFONSO: Bravissimi!

FERRANDO e GUGLIELMO: Bravissimo! Signor Don Alfonsetto! A spese vostre or ci divertiremo. E de' cento zecchini, che faremo?

3. *Terzetto*

FERRANDO: Una bella serenata
Far io voglio alla mia dea.

GUGLIELMO: In onor di Citerea
Un convito io voglio far.

DON ALFONSO: Sarò anch'io de' convitati?

FERRANDO e GUGLIELMO: Ci sarete, sì, Signor!

TUTTI: E che brindis replicati
Far vogliamo al Dio d'amor. (*Escono.*)

Scena II

La casa delle due sorelle. FIORDILIGI *e* DORABELLA *guardano i ritratti dagli amanti.*

DON ALFONSO: Tears, sighs, caresses, swoonings! Let me laugh for just a moment!

FERRANDO: Good God! Will you ever stop laughing at us?

DON ALFONSO: Be calm. Suppose that today I could make you certain that they're just like all the others?

GUGLIELMO: You couldn't do it!

FERRANDO: It isn't true!

DON ALFONSO: Shall we bet?

FERRANDO: Certainly.

DON ALFONSO: A hundred gold pieces?

GUGLIELMO: Or a thousand if you like.

DON ALFONSO: On my word of honor.

FERRANDO: Absolutely!

DON ALFONSO: And you swear not to disclose our bet to the ladies by a nod, a motion, a gesture?

FERRANDO: We swear.

DON ALFONSO: On your honor as soldiers?

GUGLIELMO: On our honor as soldiers.

DON ALFONSO: And you'll do everything that I ask you to do?

FERRANDO: Everything!

GUGLIELMO: Absolutely everything!

DON ALFONSO: Bravissimi!

FERRANDO *and* GUGLIELMO: Bravissimo! Dear little Don Alfonso! We'll amuse ourselves at your expense! Now, how shall we spend those hundred gold pieces?

3. Trio

FERRANDO: I will see that my goddess is beautifully serenaded!

GUGLIELMO: I'll hold a banquet in honor of Venus!

DON ALFONSO: Will I be among the guests?

FERRANDO *and* GUGLIELMO: You'll be there of course, my Lord!

ALL: We'll all drink endless toasts to the God of Love! (*Exit.*)

Scene II

The sisters' house. FIORDILIGI *and* DORABELLA *are admiring their lovers' portraits.*

4. Duetto

FIORDILIGI: Ah guarda, sorella,
Se aspetta più nobile si può ritrovar.

DORABELLA: Osserva tu un poco
Osserva che coco ha ne' sguardi,
Se fiamme, se dardi non sembran scoccar.

FIORDILIGI: Si vede un sembiante
Guerriero ed amante.

DORABELLA: Si vede una faccia
Che aletta, che aletta,
E minaccia.

FIORDILIGI e DORABELLA: Io sono felice!
Se questo mio core
Mai cangia desio,
Amore, mi faccia vivendo penar.

Recitativo

FIORDILIGI: Mi par, che stamattina volontieri farei la pazzarella. Ho un certo foco, un certo pizzicor entro le vene
—quando Guglielmo viene—se sapessi, che burla gli vo far.

DORABELLA: Per dirti il vero, qualche cosa di nuovo anch'io
nell'alma provo: io giurerei, che lontane non siam da gli
Imenei.

FIORDILIGI: Dammi la mano: io voglio astrologarti: uh,
che bell'Emme! e questo un Pi: va bene: Matrimonia
Presto.

DORABELLA: Affè, che ci avrei gusto.

FIORDILIGI: Ed io non ci avrei rabbia.

DORABELLA: Ma che diavol vuol dir che i nostri sposi ritardano a venir?
(*Entra* DON ALFONSO.)

FIORDILIGI: Eccoli!

DORABELLA: Non son essi; è Don Alfonso, l'amico lor.

FIORDILIGI: Ben venga il Signor Don Alfonso.

DON ALFONSO: Riverisco.

DORABELLA: Cos'è? Perche quì solo? Voi piangete? Parlate
per pietà! Che cosa è nato? L'amante—

FIORDILIGI: L'idol mio—

DON ALFONSO: Barbaro fato!

322

4. Duet

FIORDILIGI: Look here, sister! Could one ever find a more sensitive mouth or a more noble expression?

DORABELLA: Just look at this picture! What fire glows in his eyes! How they flame and sparkle!

FIORDILIGI: Here you see the portrait of a lover and a warrior!

DORABELLA: Here is a face that at once attracts and threatens me!

FIORDILIGI *and* DORABELLA: I'm so very happy! If my heart ever changes, may the God of Love take revenge upon me!

Recitative

FIORDILIGI: Really, I feel a little giddy this morning. I have a certain restlessness, a rather ticklish feeling— When Guglielmo comes here—who knows what joke I'll play on him?

DORABELLA: To tell the truth, I also feel a little different this morning. I could swear that our wedding day will come very soon!

FIORDILIGI: Give me your hand; I'll tell your fortune! Oh, what a lovely *M*! And here's a *P*—that means you'll be married quickly!

DORABELLA: I wouldn't object to that.

FIORDILIGI: It wouldn't make me unhappy, either.

DORABELLA: But why on earth are our fiancés so late? (*Enter* DON ALFONSO.)

FIORDILIGI: Here they are!

DORABELLA: No, it's Don Alfonso, their friend.

FIORDILIGI: We're honored, dear Don Alfonso!

DON ALFONSO: The honor is mine.

DORABELLA: What is it? Why are you alone here? Why are you weeping? Tell us, for heaven's sake! What has happened? My beloved—

FIORDILIGI: My Guglielmo—

DON ALFONSO: Fate has been cruel!

323

5. *Aria*

Vorrei dir, e cor non ho,
Balbettando il labbro va—
Fuor la voce uscir non può—
Ma mi resta mezza quà.
Che farete?
Che farò?
Oh che gran fatalità!
Dar di peggio non si può, ah non si può
Ho di voi, di lor pietà.

Recitativo

FIORDILIGI: Stelle! per carità, Signor Alfonso, non ci fate morir.

DON ALFONSO: Convien armarvi, figlie mie, di costanza.

DORABELLA: Oh Dei! qual male è addivenuto mai, qual caso rio? Forsè e morto il mio bene?

FIORDILIGI: E morte il mio?

DON ALFONSO: Morti non son, ma poco men che morti.

DORABELLA: Feriti?

DON ALFONSO: No.

FIORDILIGI: Ammalati?

DON ALFONSO: Neppur.

FIORDILIGI: Che cosa dunque?

DON ALFONSO: Al marzial campo ordin regio li chiama.

FIORDILIGI e DORABELLA: Ohimè! Che sento!

FIORDILIGI: E partiran?

DON ALFONSO: Sul fatto!

DORABELLA: E non v'è modo d'impedirlo?

DON ALFONSO: Non v'è.

FIORDILIGI: Ne un solo addio?

DON ALFONSO: Gli infelici non hanno coraggio di vedervi; ma se voi lo bramate, son pronti.

DORABELLA: Dove son?

DON ALFONSO: Amici, entrate!
(*Entrano* GUGLIELMO *e* FERRANDO.)

5. *Aria*

I really ought to tell you, but I don't have the heart—my lips tremble; my voice is not at my command—I have a lump in my throat. What will happen? What will you do? Oh, what a great disaster! Nothing worse could have occurred—I pity them, and I pity you!

Recitative

FIORDILIGI: Heavens! For pity's sake, Don Alfonso, don't frighten us to death!

DON ALFONSO: You must arm yourselves with courage, my dear girls.

DORABELLA: O God, what evil fate! What a dreadful catastrophe! Is my darling dead?

FIORDILIGI: And mine?

DON ALFONSO: Dead? No, not yet. But they're little better than dead.

DORABELLA: Wounded?

DON ALFONSO: No.

FIORDILIGI: Ill?

DON ALFONSO: Not really.

FIORDILIGI: Then what has happened?

DON ALFONSO: The King's orders have called them to the battlefield.

FIORDILIGI *and* DORABELLA: O heavens, how horrible!

FIORDILIGI: And when do they leave?

DON ALFONSO: This moment!

DORABELLA: Isn't there any way to save them?

DON ALFONSO: I'm afraid not.

FIORDILIGI: Can't we say good-by?

DON ALFONSO: The poor things haven't the courage to face you. But if you insist, they're ready.

DORABELLA: Where are they?

DON ALFONSO: My friends, you may come in now.
(*Enter* GUGLIELMO *and* FERRANDO.)

6. Quintetto

GUGLIELMO: Sento, o Dio!
Che questo piede
E restio nel girle avante.

FERRANDO: Il mio labbro palpitante
Non più detto pronunziar.

DON ALFONSO: Nel momenti i più terribili
Sua virtù l'eroe palesa.

FIORDILIGI e DORABELLA: Or ch'abbiam la nuova intesa,
A voi resta a fare il meno;
Fate core,
A entrambe in seno,
Immergeteci l'acciar.

FERRANDO e GUGLIELMO: Idol mio! la sorte incolpa sti deggio abbandonar!

DORABELLA: Ah no no, non partirai!

FIORDILIGI: No crudel, non tene andrai!

DORABELLA: Voglio pria cavarmi il core.

FIORDILIGI: Pria ti vo morire ai piedi.

FERRANDO (a parte a DON ALFONSO): Cosa dici?

GUGLIELMO (a parte a DON ALFONSO): Te n'avveddi?

DON ALFONSO (a parte a FERRANDO e GUGLIELMO): Saldo amico, finem lauda!

TUTTI: Il destin così defrauda,
Le speranze de' mortali,
Ah, chi mai fra tanti mali,
Chi mai puo la vita amar?

Recitativo

FERRANDO: O cielo! questo è il tamburo funesto, che a divider mi vien dal mio tesoro.

DON ALFONSO: Ecco amici, la barca.

FIORDILIGI: Io manco.

DORABELLA: Io moro.
(Entrano i soldati e contadini.)

8. Coro

Bella vita militar!
Ogni dì si cangia loco,
Oggi molto, doman poco,
Ora in terra ed or sul mar.

6. Quintet

GUGLIELMO: My feet are powerless to move!

FERRANDO: My lips cannot speak!

DON ALFONSO: A hero's courage shines forth even in life's blackest moments!

FIORDILIGI *and* DORABELLA: Now that we have heard the sad news, you must end our misery. Take courage, and plunge your swords into our breasts!

FERRANDO *and* GUGLIELMO: My darling! Only cruel fate could make me leave you!

DORABELLA: Ah, no, no, you mustn't leave me!

FIORDILIGI: No, cruel one, I won't let you go!

DORABELLA: I'll tear my own heart first!

FIORDILIGI: I'll die right here at your feet!

FERRANDO (*aside to* DON ALFONSO): What do you say now?

GUGLIELMO (*aside to* DON ALFONSO): Are you listening?

DON ALFONSO (*aside to* FERRANDO *and* GUGLIELMO): Softly, my friends; he who laughs last always laughs best!

ALL: So destiny betrays the hopes of mortals. In the midst of such tragedy, how is it possible to regard life with any kindness?

Recitative

FERRANDO: Heavens, there is the funeral drum that divides me from my beloved!

DON ALFONSO: There is the boat, my friends.

FIORDILIGI: I'm fainting!

DORABELLA: I'm dying!

(*A group of soldiers and peasants enter.*)

8. CHORUS

A soldier's life is joyous! What pleasure to be able to travel from place to place—today everything—tomorrow nothing. Sometimes we go by land and sometimes by sea. The music of horns and trumpets, the bursting of bombs and cannon

Il fragor di trombe e pifferi,
La sparar di schioppi, e bombe,
Forza accresce al braccio, e all' anima
Vaga sol di trionfar.
Bella vita militar!

Recitativo

DON ALFONSO: Non v'è più tempo, amici, andar conviene,
ove il destino, anzi il dover v'invita.

FIORDILIGI: Mio cor—

DORABELLA: Idolo mio—

FERRANDO: Mio ben—

GUGLIELMO: Mia vita—

FIORDILIGI: Ah per un sol momento—

DON ALFONSO: Del vostro reggimento già è partita la barca,
raggiungerla convien coi pocchi amici che su legno più lieve
attendendo vi stanno.

FERRANDO *e* GUGLIELMO: Abbracciami, idol mio!

FIORDILIGI *e* DORABELLA: Muojo d'affano.

9. Quintetto

FIORDILIGI: Di scrivermi ogni giorno!
Giurami, vita mia!

DORABELLA: Due volte ancora tu
Scrivimi, se puoi.

FERRANDO: Sii certa, sii certa,
O cara!

GUGLIELMO: Non dubitar,
Non dubitar, mio bene!

DON ALFONSO (*a parte*): Io crepo se non rido.

FIORDILIGI: Sii costante a me sol!

DORABELLA: Serbati fido!

FERRANDO: Addio!

GUGLIELMO: Addio!

FIORDILIGI *e* DORABELLA: Addio!

FIORDILIGI, DORABELLA, FERRANDO, GUGLIELMO: Mi si divide il cor,
Bell' idol mio!
Addio!
(*Escono* FERRANDO *e* GUGLIELMO.)

balls, gives strength to our arms and to our spirits! A soldier's life is joyous!

Recitative

DON ALFONSO: There's no more time, my friends, you must go where destiny and duty call you!

FIORDILIGI: My darling!

DORABELLA: My dearest!

FERRANDO: My sweetest!

GUGLIELMO: My life!

FIORDILIGI: Ah, only for a moment!

DON ALFONSO: Your regiment's ship is already gone; you must go with some people who are waiting for you with a smaller boat.

FERRANDO *and* GUGLIELMO: Kiss me, my darling!

FIORDILIGI *and* DORABELLA: I'm dying of grief!

9. Quintet

FIORDILIGI: Swear to write to me every day!

DORABELLA: Or twice a day if you can!

FERRANDO: I'll certainly do it, my darling!

GUGLIELMO: Don't doubt me, my dearest!

DON ALFONSO (*aside*): If I don't laugh at them, I shall burst!

FIORDILIGI: Be true to me only!

DORABELLA: Keep your faith!

FERRANDO: Good-by!

GUGLIELMO: Good-by!

FIORDILIGI *and* DORABELLA: Good-by!

FIORDILIGI, DORABELLA, FERRANDO, GUGLIELMO: O my love, my heart is torn with grief!

(FERRANDO *and* GUGLIELMO *exit*.)

Recitativo

DORABELLA: Dove son?

DON ALFONSO: Son partiti.

FIORDILIGI: Oh dipartenza crudelissima amara!

DON ALFONSO: Fate core, carissime figliuole; guardate, da lontano vi fan cenno con mano i cari sposi.

FIORDILIGI: Buon viaggio, mia vita!

DORABELLA: Buon viaggio!

FIORDILIGI: Oh Dei! come veloce se ne va quella barca! già sparisce! già non si vede più. Deh faccia il cielo ch'abbia prospero corso.

DORABELLA: Faccia che al campo giunga con fortunati auspici.

DON ALFONSO: E a voi salvi gli amanti, e a me gli amici.

10. Terzettino

FIORDILIGI, DORABELLA, DON ALFONSO: Soave sia il vento,
Tranquilla sia l'onda,
Ed ogni elemento
Benigno risponda
Ai nostri desir!
(FIORDILIGI *e* DORABELLA *partono.*)

Recitativo

DON ALFONSO: Non son cattivo comico! va bene; al concertato loco i due campioni di Ciprigna, e di Marte mi staranno attendendo; or senza indugio, raggiungerli conviene. Quante smorfie, quante buffonerie! Tanto meglio per me, cadran più facilmente: questa razza di gente è la più presta a cangiarsi d'umore. Oh poverini! per femmina giocar cento zecchini?

10A. Aria

Nel mare solca,
E nell' arena semina,
E il vago vento
Spera in rete accogliere
Chi fonda sue speranze
In cor di femmina.
(*Esce* DON ALFONSO. *Entra* DESPINA, *chi porta di cioccolatte.*)

Recitative

DORABELLA: Where are they?

DON ALFONSO: They've gone.

FIORDILIGI: Oh, most cruel, most bitter departure!

DON ALFONSO: Take heart, my dearest daughters! Look, they're waving to you from far away.

FIORDILIGI: Good fortune to my darling!

DORABELLA: Good fortune!

FIORDILIGI: O God! How quickly they're disappearing in that boat! It has already vanished. May heaven protect them on their journey!

DORABELLA: I pray that they will arrive at the battlefield refreshed and courageous!

DON ALFONSO: May heaven protect your lovers, and my friends!

10. Trio

FIORDILIGI, DORABELLA, DON ALFONSO: May the winds blow gently and the waves be calm—may every element look benignly on our desires!

(FIORDILIGI *and* DORABELLA *exit.*)

Recitative

DON ALFONSO: I'm not a bad actor; it's going very well. These two disciples of Venus and of Mars will be awaiting me at the appointed place. Now I must go to meet them, without delaying. What sighs—what languishings! What ridiculous nonsense! So much the better for me—they'll be tempted that much more easily. The more sighs and tears, the more vulnerable women become to a change of lovers. Those poor boys—to bet a hundred gold pieces on woman's fidelity!

10A. Aria

One might as well try to plow the sea or cultivate the desert, or to catch the wild wind in a net, as to trust the heart of a woman!

(DON ALFONSO *exits. Enter* DESPINA, *with a tray of hot chocolate.*)

Recitativo

DESPINA: Che vita maledetta è il far la cameriera! Dal mattino alla sera si fa, si suda, si lavora, e poi di tanto, che si fa, nulla è per noi. E mezza ora, che sbatto, il cioccolatte è fatto, ed a me tocca restar ad odorarlo a secca bocca? Non è forse la mia come la vostra? o garbate Signore, che a voi dessi l'essenza e a me l'odore? per Bacco, vo assagiarlo: com' è buono! Vien gente! oh ciel! son le padrone. (FIORDILIGI *e* DORABELLA *entrano.*) Madame, ecco la vostra collazione. Diamine! cosa fate?

FIORDILIGI *e* DORABELLA: Ah!

DESPINA: Che cosa è nato?

FIORDILIGI: Ov' è un acciaro!

DORABELLA: Un veleno, dov è!

DESPINA: Padrone, dico!

DORABELLA: Ah scostati! paventa il tristo affetto d'un disperato affetto. Chiudi quelle fenestre—odio la luce—odio l'aria che spiro—odio me stessa! Chi schernisce il mio duol? chi mi consola? Deh fuggi, per pietà! fuggi, lasciami sola.

11. *Aria*

Smanie implacabili,
Che m'agitate,
Entro quest' anima
Più non cessate,
Finchè l'angoscia
Mi fa morir.
Esempio misero
D'amor funesto,
Darò all' Eumenidi,
Se viva resto
Col suono orribile
De' miei sospir.

Recitativo

DESPINA: Signora Dorabella, Signora Fiordiligi, ditemi, che cosa è stato?

DORABELLA: Oh terribil disgrazia!

DESPINA: Sbrigatevi in buon' ora.

Recitative

DESPINA: A chambermaid has a thankless life! From morning until evening, I work, I slave, I labor, and I get nothing out of it for myself! The chocolate has been ready for half an hour, and I have to stand here and smell it while my mouth is watering! Why aren't I as good as they are? O my dear Ladies, who apportioned you the substance and me the aroma? By heaven, I'm going to taste it! Oh, how lovely! I hear someone coming—O Lord, here are my ladies!

(FIORDILIGO *and* DORABELLA *enter.*)

My Ladies, here's your breakfast. What on earth has happened?

FIORDILIGI *and* DORABELLA: Ah!

DESPINA: What can it be?

FIORDILIGI: Give me a dagger!

DORABELLA: I'm going to take poison!

DESPINA: What is it, my Ladies?

DORABELLA: Out of my sight! Respect the madness of a desperate love! Close all the windows—I hate the light—I hate the air I breathe—I hate myself! Who will comfort my grieving? Who will console me? Then leave me, I beg you—leave me to my sorrow!

11. Aria

Horrible agony that tortures me—consume my soul until I expire! I'm the miserable victim of a tragic love. While I still am living I'll frighten the Furies themselves with the horrible sound of my groans and sighs!

Recitative

DESPINA: My lady Dorabella, my lady Fiordiligi, tell me what has happened!

DORABELLA: Oh, horrible misfortune!

DESPINA: Tell me at once!

FIORDILIGI: Da Napoli partiti sono gli amanti nostri.

DESPINA: Non c'è altro? ritorneran.

DORABELLA: Chi sa!

DESPINA: Come, chi sa? dove son iti?

DORABELLA: Al campo di battaglia.

DESPINA: Tanto meglio per loro: li vedrete tornar carchi d'alloro. Ma non parliam di ciò, sono ancor vivi, e vivi torneran; ma son lontani, e più tosto che invani pianti perdere tempo, pensate a divertivi.

FIORDILIGI: Divertirci?

DESPINA: Sicuro e quel ch è meglio far all' amor come assassine, e come faranno al campo i vostri cari amanti.

DORABELLA: Non offender così quelle alme belle, di fedeltà, d'intatto amore esempi.

DESPINA: Via, via, passaro i tempi da spacciar queste favole ai bambini.

12. Aria

In uomini, in soldati,
Sperare fedeltà?
In uomini sperare fedeltà?
In soldati sperare fedeltà,
Non vi fate sentir per carità!
Di pasta simile son tutti quanti:
Le fronde mobili, l'aure incostanti
Han più degli uomini stabilità.
Mentite lagrime,
Fallaci sguardi,
Voci ingannevoli,
Vezzi bugiardi,
Son le primarie
Lor qualità.
In noi non amano che il cor diletto,
Poi ci dispregiano, neganci affetto,
Nè val da' barbari chieder pietà.
Paghiam, o femmine, d'ugual moneta
Questa malefica razza indiscreta;
Amiam per comodo, per vanità.
(FIORDILIGI e DORABELLA *escono e* DESPINA *ritorna alla sua stanza. Entra* DON ALFONSO.)

FIORDILIGI: Our lovers have left Naples.

DESPINA: That's all? They'll come back.

DORABELLA: Who knows?

DESPINA: What do you mean? Where have they gone?

DORABELLA: To the battlefield.

DESPINA: So much the better for them; you'll see them next covered with laurels! But let's not speak of that; they're still alive, and they'll be alive when they come back; and rather than wasting your time in idle tears, you must think of amusing yourselves.

FIORDILIGI: Amusing ourselves?

DESPINA: Certainly! And, more than that, you must make love to others, just as your dear lovers are doing at the front!

DORABELLA: Don't cast aspersions on those beautiful, faithful souls; they are veritable models of fidelity.

DESPINA: Come, now—let's not tell each other fairy tales!

12. Aria

You expect fidelity in men? In soldiers? Don't let anyone hear you, for heaven's sake! Men are all alike: fluttering leaves and inconstant winds have much more stability! Lying tears, false glances, deceiving promises, charming lies—those are their most usual tricks! They only use us for their pleasure, then they despise us, denying us any affection. It does no good to expect pity from these monsters! My Ladies, men are evil and indiscreet; let's pay them in their own coin—let's make love for convenience and vanity, just as they do!

(FIORDILIGI *and* DORABELLA *exit, as* DESPINA *returns to her own room.* DON ALFONSO *enters.*)

Recitativo

DON ALFONSO (*lo stesso*): Che silenzio! che aspetto di tristezza spirano queste stanze! Poverette! non han già tutto il torto: bisogna consolarle; infin che vanno i due creduli sposi, com' io loro commisi, a mascherarsi, pensiam cosa può farsi—temo un po' per Despina—quella furba potrebbe riconoscerli; potrebbe rovesciarmi le macchine, vedremo—se mai farà bisogno un regaletto a tempo, un zechinetto per una cameriere è un gran scongiuro—(*forte*) Despinetta!

DESPINA (*dalla sua stanza*): Chi batte?

DON ALFONSO: Oh!

(*Entra* DESPINA.)

DESPINA: Ih!

DON ALFONSO: Despina mia, di te bisogno avrei.

DESPINA: Ed io niente di voi.

DON ALFONSO: Ti vo fare del ben.

DESPINA: A una fanciulla un vecchio come lei non può far nulla.

DON ALFONSO: Parla piano ed osserva.
(*Le mostra un pezzo d'oro.*)

DESPINA: Me lo dona?

DON ALFONSO: Sì, se meco sei buona.

DESPINA: E che vorebbe? è loro il mio giulebbe.

DON ALFONSO: Ed oro avrai; ma ci vuol fedeltà.

DESPINA: Non c'è altro? son quà.

DON ALFONSO: Prendi ed ascolta. Sai, che le tue padrone han perduti gli amanti.

DESPINA: Lo so.

DON ALFONSO: Tutti i lor pianti, tutti deliri loro ancor tu sai.

DESPINA: So tutto.

DON ALFONSO: Or ben; se mai per consolarle un poco, e trar, come diciam, chiodo per chiodo, tu ritrovassi il modo, da metter in lor grazia due soggetti di garbo che vorrieno prova, già mi capisci. C'e una mancia pe te di venti scudi, se li fai riuscir.

Recitative

DON ALFONSO (*to himself*): What silence! What a tragic atmosphere permeates these rooms! Poor girls! The joke is only beginning; now we must try to console them. Meanwhile, I'll bring in their lovers, disguised as I directed them. But I'm a bit apprehensive about Despina—that vixen might recognize them and upset all my plans. Let's see. If I ever need to bribe her, a little money is always persuasive to a chambermaid. (*aloud*) Despinetta!

DESPINA (*from her room*): Who's knocking?

DON ALFONSO: I!

(DESPINA *enters.*)

DESPINA: You?

DON ALFONSO: My dear Despina, I have great need of your assistance.

DESPINA: And I have no need of yours.

DON ALFONSO: I only want to do you a favor.

DESPINA: At your age you can do no favors for young girls like me!

DON ALFONSO: Be quiet, and look at this.

(*He shows her a gold piece.*)

DESPINA: Is that for me?

DON ALFONSO: Yes, if you'll be kind to me.

DESPINA: Well, what would you like? Perhaps I can help you.

DON ALFONSO: You may keep the money; all I ask is your co-operation.

DESPINA: Nothing else? I'm ready!

DON ALFONSO: Take it then, and listen. You know that your mistresses have temporarily lost their lovers.

DESPINA: I know it.

DON ALFONSO: You've seen their tears and their extravagant grief?

DESPINA: I certainly have!

DON ALFONSO: Well then, if you had a chance to console them a little, and to replace one nail with another, as the saying goes, I'm sure that you'd be glad to do it. I know two charming young men who would like to try their luck. You understand me? If you'll help them, I'll give you twenty gold pieces.

DESPINA: Non mi dispiace questa proposizione. Ma con quelle buffone basta, udite: son giovani? son belli? e sopra tutto hanno una buona borsa i vostri concorrenti?

DON ALFONSO: Han tutto quello che piacer può alle donne di giudizio. Li vuoi veder?

DESPINA: E dove son?

DON ALFONSO: Son lì: li posso far entrar?

DESPINA: Direi di si.

(*Entrano* FERRANDO *e* GUGLIELMO *travestiti da albinasi.*)

13. *Sestetto*

DON ALFONSO: Alla bella Despinetta
Vi presento, amici miei;
Non dipende che da lei,
Consolar il vostro cor.

FERRANDO *e* GUGLIELMO: Per la man,
Che lieto io bacio,
Per quei rai di grazia pieni,
Fa che volga a me sereni
I begli occhi il mio tesor.

DESPINA (*fra se, ridendo*): Che sembianze!
Che vestiti!
Che figure!
Che mustacchi!
Io non so, se son Vallacchi?
O se Turchi son costor?
Vallacchi, Turchi,
Turchi, Vallacchi?

FERRANDO *e* GUGLIELMO: Or la cosa è appien decisa,
Se costei non ci ravissa
Non c'è più nesun timor.

DON ALFONSO (*a* DESPINA): Che ti par di quell' aspetto?

DESPINA: Per parlarvi schietto, schietto,
Hanno un muso fuor dell' uso,
Vera antidoto d'amor!
Che figure, che mustacchi!

FIORDILIGI *e* DORABELLA (*da lontano*): Ehi, Despina! olà Despina!

DESPINA: Le padrone.

DON ALFONSO (*a* DESPINA): Ecco l'istante!
Fa con arte:

DESPINA: I don't dislike your proposition. But those stupid women! Only tell me—are your friends young, handsome, and above all, rich?

DON ALFONSO: They are all that could please a woman of discrimination. Would you like to see them?

DESPINA: But where are they?

DON ALFONSO: They're waiting outside. May they come in?

DESPINA: I don't see why not.

(FERRANDO *and* GUGLIELMO *enter, disguised as Albanians.*)

13. Sextet

DON ALFONSO: I present you, my friends, to the lovely Despinetta. She certainly can help you to console the pangs of your love.

FERRANDO *and* GUGLIELMO: I kiss your hands, and I hope that I can induce your mistresses' beautiful eyes to look kindly upon us!

DESPINA (*to herself, laughing*): What appearances! What costumes! What figures! What mustaches! I don't know if these creatures came from Rumania or from Turkey!

FERRANDO *and* GUGLIELMO: Now the matter is decided; if Despina can't recognize us, there's no longer any reason for fear!

DON ALFONSO (*to* DESPINA): Well, what do you think of them?

DESPINA: To speak frankly, the strangeness of their appearance would be an antidote to love!

FIORDILIGI *and* DORABELLA (*off-stage*): Eh, Despina, where are you, Despina?

DESPINA: My Ladies!

DON ALFONSO (*to* DESPINA): This is the crucial moment! Manage it craftily; I'll leave you alone.

Io quì m'ascondo.
(DON ALFONSO *parte. Entrano* FIORDILIGI *e* DORABELLA.)

FIORDILIGI *e* DORABELLA: Ragazzaccia tracotante!
Che fai lì con simil gente?
Falli uscire immantinente,
O ti so pentir con lor.

DESPINA, FERRANDO, GUGLIELMO: Ah, Madame! perdonate!
Al bel piè languir mirate
Due meschin, di vostro merto,
Spasimanti adorator.

FIORDILIGI *e* DORABELLA: Giusti numi! cosa sento?
Dell' enorme tradimento,
Chi fu mai l'indegno autor?

DESPINA, FERRANDO, GUGLIELMO: Deh calmate, quello
sdegno.

FIORDILIGI *e* DORABELLA: Ah, che più non ho ritegno!
Tutta piena ho l'alma in petto
Di dispetto e di terror!

DESPINA, FERRANDO, GUGLIELMO: Mi da un poco di sos-
petto,
Quella rabbia e quel furor!
Qual diletto è a questo petto,
Quella rabbia e quel furor!
(DON ALFONSO *entra.*)

Recitativo

DON ALFONSO: Che susurro! che strepito, che scompiglio è
mai questo! siete pazze, care le mie ragazze? volete sollevar
il vicinato? cosa avete? ch' è nato?

DORABELLA: Oh ciel! mirate uomini in casa nostra?

DON ALFONSO: Che male c'è?

FIORDILIGI: Che male? in questo giorno? dopo il caso funesto?

DON ALFONSO: Stelle! sogno, o son desto? amici miei, miei
dolcissimi amici! Voi quì? come? perchè? quando! in qual
modo? Numi! quanto ne godo! (*a parte a* FERRANDO *e*
GUGLIELMO) Secondatemi.

FERRANDO: Amico Don Alfonso!

GUGLIELMO: Amico caro!

DON ALFONSO: Oh, bella improvisata!

(DON ALFONSO *exits.* FIORDILIGI *and* DORABELLA *enter.*)

FIORDILIGI *and* DORABELLA: Presumptuous girl! What are you doing here with people of that sort? Make them leave this instant, or you'll be sorry and so will they!

DESPINA, FERRANDO, GUGLIELMO: Ah, my ladies, pardon us! You see two unhappy men, passionate adorers of your virtues, languishing at your beautiful feet!

FIORDILIGI *and* DORABELLA: Heavens! What is this? Who is responsible for this horrible outrage?

DESPINA, FERRANDO, GUGLIELMO: Please calm your anger!

FIORDILIGI *and* DORABELLA: Now I can't control myself any longer! My whole soul is filled with horror and disdain!

DESPINA, FERRANDO, GUGLIELMO: I suspect this rage and fury; it doesn't quite ring true!
(DON ALFONSO *enters.*)

Recitative

DON ALFONSO: What noise! What a racket! What confusion! Have you gone insane, my dear girls? Do you want to call in all the neighborhood? What has happened? Tell me!

DORABELLA: O God! Look for yourself! Strange men in our house of sorrow!

DON ALFONSO: What harm is there in that?

FIORDILIGI: What harm? Today! After our tragic parting!

DON ALFONSO: Good heavens! Am I awake or dreaming? My friends, my dearest friends! Are you really here? How? Why? By land or sea? Good Lord, this is wonderful. (*aside to* FERRANDO *and* GUGLIELMO) Bear me out.

FERRANDO: My friend Don Alfonso!

GUGLIELMO: My dearest friend!

DON ALFONSO: Oh, happy surprise!

341

DESPINA: Li conoscete voi?

DON ALFONSO: Se li conosco! questi sono i più dolci amici ch'io m'abbia in questo mondo, e vostri ancor saranno.

FIORDILIGI: E in casa mia che fanno?

GUGLIELMO: Ai vostri piedi due rei, due delinquenti, ecco Madame! Amor—

FIORDILIGI: Numi! che sento?

FERRANDO: Amor, il nume, sì possente per voi, qui ci conduce.

GUGLIELMO: Vista appena la luce di vostre fulgidissime pupille—

FERRANDO: Che alle vive faville—

GUGLIELMO: Farfallette amorose e agonizzanti—

FERRANDO: Vi voliamo davanti—

GUGLIELMO: Ed ai lati ed a retro!

FERRANDO e GUGLIELMO: Per implorar pietade in flebil metro!

FIORDILIGI: Stelle! che ardir!

DORABELLA: Sorella! che facciamo?

14. Recitativo ed Aria

FIORDILIGI: Temerari, sortite fuori di questo loco! e non profani l'alito infausto degli infami detti nostro cor, orecchio, en nostri affetti! Invan per voi, per gli altri invan si cerca le nostre alme sedur: l'intatta fede che per noi già si diede ai cari amanti saprem loro serbar infino a morte, a dispetto del mondo e della sorte.
Come scoglio immoto resta
Contra i venti e la tempesta,
Così ognor quest' alma è forte
Nella fede e nell' amor.
Con noi nacque quello face,
Che ci piace, e ci consola;
E potrà la morte sola,
Far che cangi affetto il cor.
Rispettate, anime ingrate,
Questo esempio di costanza,
E una barbara speranza

Recitativo

FERRANDO: Ah, non partite!

342

DESPINA: Do you know these people?

DON ALFONSO: Do I know them? They are the dearest friends that I have in this world, and they will be your friends as well.

FIORDILIGI: But what are they doing in our house?

GUGLIELMO: Two rude and unworthy men kneel at your feet! Love—

FIORDILIGI: Heavens! What are you saying?

FERRANDO: Love, that overwhelming force, drove us here.

GUGLIELMO: As soon as we beheld the eloquence of your radiant eyes—

FERRANDO: They flashed flames—

GUGLIELMO: We were transformed into amorous, agonized butterflies—

FERRANDO: We flew before you—

GUGLIELMO: And fluttered back and forth!

FERRANDO *and* GUGLIELMO: We implore your pity in sweet, poetic measures!

FIORDILIGI: Heavens! What boldness!

DORABELLA: Sister, what shall we do?

14. Recitative and Aria

FIORDILIGI: Audacious intruders, leave this house immediately! Don't profane this unfortunate hearth with your infamous words! Spare our hearts, our ears, and our affections! It is vain for you or anyone else to attempt to seduce our souls! We shall keep the faith that we have pledged to our dear lovers until the hour of our death, in spite of all the world, and fate's adversity!

I stand firm as a rock against all winds and tempests! My soul will always be strong in faith and in love. My constancy consoles my grief, and only death can change my heart's affection. You, ungrateful creatures, must respect my example of fidelity—let it extinguish your false audacious hopes!

Recitative

FERRANDO: You must not leave us!

GUGLIELMO: Ah, barbara restate! (*a parte a* DON ALFONSO)
Che vi pare?

DON ALFONSO (*a parte*): Aspettate! (*forte*) Per carità ragazze, non mi fate più far trista figura.

DORABELLA: E che pretendereste?

DON ALFONSO: Eh nulla; ma mi pare che un pocchin di dolcezza—alfin son galant uomini e sono amici miei.

FIORDILIGI: Come! e udire dovrei?

GUGLIELMO: Le nostre pene e sentirne pietà! A voi davanti spirar vedrete i più fedeli amanti.

15. Aria

Non siate ritrosi
Occhietti vezzosi,
Due lampe amorosi
Vibrate un po' quà.
Felici rendeteci
Amate con noi,
E noi felicissimi
Faremo anche voi.
Guardate, toccate,
Il tutto osservate:
Siam forti e ben fatti,
E come ognun vede,
Sia merto, sia caso,
Abbiamo bel piede,
Bell' occhio, bel naso,
Guardate bel piede,
Osservate bell'occhio,
Toccate bel naso,
Il tutto osservate:
E questi mustacchi
Chiamare si possono
Trionfi degli uomini,
Penacchi d'amor,
(*Escono* FIORDILIGI, DORABELLA *e* DESPINA; GUGLIELMO
continua, ridendo.)
Trionfi,
Penacchi, mustacchi!

16. Terzetto

DON ALFONSO: E voi ridete?

GUGLIELMO: Ah, cruel ones, do not go! (*aside to* DON ALFONSO) What do you say now?

DON ALFONSO (*aside*): Wait a little longer! (*aloud*) For pity's sake, my dear girls, don't behave like the tragic Muses!

DORABELLA: And what would you like us to do?

DON ALFONSO: Oh, nothing in particular; only I thought that you might be polite—after all, these two gentlemen are my friends.

FIORDILIGI: What! And must we listen to their proposals?

GUGLIELMO: If you knew how we are suffering, you would pity us. You'll see us die here before you, we who love you so faithfully!

15. Aria

Don't be so prudish; return our loving glances with your beautiful eyes! We'll all be so happy! Love us, and we'll all be ecstatic with joy! Look at us, touch us, observe us carefully. We're strong and virile. Anyone can see that we possess every merit—beautiful feet, lovely eyes, charming noses! And one might call these mustaches the triumph of masculinity, a symbol of love!

(FIORDILIGI, DORABELLA, *and* DESPINA *exit.* GUGLIELMO *goes on, laughing.*)

A triumph! A symbol! Mustaches!

16. Trio

DON ALFONSO: And you can laugh at this?

FERRANDO *e* GUGLIELMO: Certo, ridiamo.

DON ALFONSO: Ma cosa avete?

FERRANDO *e* GUGLIELMO: Già lo sappiamo—

DON ALFONSO: Ridete piano.

FERRANDO *e* GUGLIELMO: Parlate invano.

DON ALFONSO: Se vi sentissero,
Se vi scoprissero,
Si guasterebbe tutto l'affar,
Si guasterebbe
Tutto l'affar.

FERRANDO *e* GUGLIELMO: Ah che dal ridere,
L'alma dividere,
Ah, ah, ah, ah, ah, ah, ah, ah,
Ah, che le viscere
Sento scoppiar.

DON ALFONSO: Mi fa da ridere
Questo lor ridere,
Ma so che in piangere
Dee terminar.

Recitativo

Si può sapere un poco la cagion di quel riso?

GUGLIELMO: Oh cospettaccio, non vi pare che abbiam giusta ragione, il mio caro padrone?

FERRANDO: Quanto pagar volete, e a monte è la scommessa?

DON ALFONSO: Intanto silenzio e ubbidienza fino a doman mattina.

GUGLIELMO: Siamo soldati, e amiam la disciplina.

DON ALFONSO: Or bene: andate un poco ad attendermi entrambi in giardinetto, co là vi manderò gli ordini miei.

GUGLIELMO: Ed oggi non si mangia?

FERRANDO: Cosa serve: a battaglia finita fia la cena per noi più saporita.
(*Escono* DON ALFONSO *e* GUGLIELMO.)

17. Aria

Un' aura amorosa
Del nostra tesoro
Un dolce ristoro

346

FERRANDO *and* GUGLIELMO: Of course we're laughing!

DON ALFONSO: But what's so amusing?

FERRANDO *and* GUGLIELMO: Already we know—

DON ALFONSO: Don't laugh so loudly!

FERRANDO *and* GUGLIELMO: That your sarcasm was misguided.

DON ALFONSO: Be quiet! If they overhear you, the whole affair will be spoiled!

FERRANDO *and* GUGLIELMO: My heart will burst from laughing! Ha, ha! My sides are splitting!

DON ALFONSO: Their laughter makes me laugh in turn, for it must end in tears!

Recitative

Won't you tell me the reason for this laughter?

GUGLIELMO: Oh, good Lord, doesn't it seem to you that we have good reason, my dear fellow conspirator?

FERRANDO: When will you pay us and call off the bet?

DON ALFONSO: You promised silence and obedience until tomorrow morning.

GUGLIELMO: We're soldiers, and we're used to discipline.

DON ALFONSO: Very well; go for a walk now, and wait for me together in that little garden. There I'll give you my further instructions.

GUGLIELMO: Then we'll have no dinner?

FERRANDO: Not today. Tomorrow, when the bet is won, we'll relish the banquet even more fully!

(DON ALFONSO *and* GUGLIELMO *exit.*)

17. Aria

The sweet ambiance of love will bring delightful consolation to my soul! When the heart is nourished with fond dreams of love, no other joy is needed.

Al cor porgerà.
Al cor che nudrito
Da speme, d'amore,
D'un esca migliore
Bisogna non ha.
(*Esce* FERRANDO. *Entrano* FIORDILIGI *e* DORABELLA.)

18. *Finale*

FIORDILIGI *e* DORABELLA: Ah! che tutta in un momento
Si cangiò la sorte mia,
Ah, che un mar pien di tormento,
E la vita omai per me.
Finchè meco il caro bene
Mi lasciar le ingrate stelle,
Non sapea cos' eran pene,
Non sapea languir cos' è—no!

FERRANDO *e* GUGLIELMO (*dall interno*): Si mora, sì, si mora,
Onde appagar le ingrate.

DON ALFONSO (*dall interno*): C'è una speranza ancora,
Non fate, oh dei, non fate!

FIORDILIGI *e* DORABELLA: Stelle, che grida orribili!

FERRANDO *e* GUGLIELMO: Lasciatemi!

DON ALFONSO: Aspettate!
(*Entrano i tre uomini.*)

FERRANDO *e* GUGLIELMO: L'arsenico mi liberi
Di tanta crudeltà.

FIORDILIGI *e* DORABELLA: Stelle, un velen fu quello?

DON ALFONSO: Veleno buono e bello,
Che ad essi in pochi istanti
La vita toglierà.

FIORDILIGI *e* DORABELLA: Il tragico spettacolo
Gelare il cor mi fa!

FERRANDO *e* GUGLIELMO: Barbare, avvicinatevi:
D'un disperato affetto
Mirate il tristo effetto
E abbiate almen pietà.

FIORDILIGI, DORABELLA, FERRANDO, DON ALFONSO, GUGLI-
ELMO: Ah! che del sole il raggio
Fosco per me diventa.
Tremo, le fibre e l'anima

348

(FERRANDO *exits.* FIORDILIGI *and* DORABELLA *enter.*)

18. Finale

FIORDILIGI *and* DORABELLA: Ah! How everything has changed in the space of an hour! Life is now like a stormy ocean for me! While my dear lover was near me, I never knew the meaning of suffering or pain!

FERRANDO *and* GUGLIELMO (*off-stage*): Only our death can appease these ungrateful women!

DON ALFONSO (*off-stage*): There's still a ray of hope. O God—don't do it!

FIORDILIGI *and* DORABELLA: Heavens, what horrible cries!

FERRANDO *and* GUGLIELMO: Leave us to our tragic destinies!

DON ALFONSO: Wait a moment!
(*The three men enter.*)

FERRANDO *and* GUGLIELMO: Arsenic will liberate us from their cruelty!

FIORDILIGI *and* DORABELLA: Heavens! Have they really taken poison?

DON ALFONSO: A most effective poison, one that will take their lives in a matter of minutes!

FIORDILIGI *and* DORABELLA: This tragic sight freezes my heart!

FERRANDO *and* GUGLIELMO: Cruel women, look at us! You'll see the effect of a desperate passion, and perhaps at last you'll be moved by pity!

FIORDILIGI, DORABELLA, FERRANDO, DON ALFONSO, GUGLIELMO: The sun's light is darkening! I'm trembling—my nerves and spirit are faltering—my tongue and lips cannot form a word!

349

Par che mancar si senta,
Nè può la lingua o il labbro
Accenti articolar.

DON ALFONSO: Giacchè a morir vicini
Sono quei meschinelli
Pietade almeno a quelli
Cercate di mostrar.

FIORDILIGI e DORABELLA: Gente, accorrete, gente!
Nessuno, o dio, ci sente!
Despina! Despina!

DESPINA (*dall interno*): Chi mi chiama?

FIORDILIGI e DORABELLA: Despina! Despina!
(*Entra* DESPINA.)

DESPINA: Cosa vedo!
Morti i meschini io credo,
O prossimi a spirar.

DON ALFONSO: Ah che pur troppo è vero:
Furenti, disperati
Si sono avvelenati,
Oh amore singolar!

DESPINA: Abbandonar i miseri
Saria per voi vergogna,
Soccorrerli bisogna.

FIORDILIGI e DORABELLA: Cosa possiam mai far?

DESPINA: Soccorrerli bisogna.
Di vita ancor dan segno,
Colle pietose mani
Fate un po lor sostegno. (*a* DON ALFONSO)
E voi con me correte:
Un medico un antidoto
Voliamo a ricercar.
(DESPINA e DON ALFONSO *partono*.)

FIORDILIGI e DORABELLA: Dei! che cimento è questo!
Evento più funesto
Non si potea trovar!

FERRANDO e GUGLIELMO (*a parte*): Più bella comediola
Non si potea trovar!

FIORDILIGI e DORABELLA: Sospiran gl'infelici!

FIORDILIGI: Che facciamo?

DORABELLA: Tu che dici?

DON ALFONSO: Poor boys, now that they're so near to death, you might at least show them some pity!

FIORDILIGI *and* DORABELLA: Help! Somebody, help us! O God, nobody hears us! Despina! Despina!

DESPINA (*off-stage*): Who's calling me?

FIORDILIGI *and* DORABELLA: Despina! Despina!

(DESPINA *enters.*)

DESPINA: What on earth! The poor things seem to be dead, or very near it!

DON ALFONSO: Ah, that's only too true; they were in a fury of despair; they poisoned themselves! Oh, what a strange, desperate love!

DESPINA: It would be shameful to abandon these poor wretches; we must help them!

FIORDILIGI *and* DORABELLA: Whatever can we do?

DESPINA: They still seem to be breathing. We must support them gently. (*to* DON ALFONSO) And you must come with me to find a doctor or an antidote!

(DESPINA *and* DON ALFONSO *exit.*)

FIORDILIGI *and* DORABELLA: God! What a dreadful situation! One couldn't imagine a more tragic sight!

FERRANDO *and* GUGLIELMO (*aside*): One couldn't find a funnier comedy anywhere!

FIORDILIGI *and* DORABELLA: The poor things are sighing!

FIORDILIGI: What shall we do?

DORABELLA: What do you say?

351

FIORDILIGI: In momenti si dolenti
Chi potria li abbandonar?

DORABELLA: Che figure interessanti!

FIORDILIGI: Possiam farci un poco avanti.

DORABELLA: Ha fredissima la testa.

FIORDILIGI: Fredda, fredda è ancora questa.

DORABELLA: Ed il polso?

FIORDILIGI: Io non gliel' sento.

DORABELLA: Questo batte lento, lento.

FIORDILIGI e DORABELLA: Ah se tarda ancor l'aita,
Speme più non v'è di vita.

FERRANDO e GUGLIELMO (*a parte*): Più domestiche e trat-
tabili
Sono entrambe diventate,
Sta a veder
Che lor pietade
Va in amore a terminar.

FIORDILIGI e DORABELLA: Poverini, poverini!
La lor morte
Mi farebbe lagrimar.
(*Entra* DON ALFONSO, *con* DESPINA, *travestita da medico.*)

DON ALFONSO: Eccovi il medico,
Signore belle.

FERRANDO e GUGLIELMO (*a parte*): Despina in maschera,
Che trista pelle!

DESPINA: Salvete amabiles
Bones puelles.

FIORDILIGI e DORABELLA: Parla un linguaggio
Che non sappiamo.

DESPINA: Come comandano dunque parliamo,
So il greco e l'arabo,
So il turco e il vandalo,
La sveco e il tartaro
So ancor parlar.

DON ALFONSO: Tanti linguaggi per se conservi, per se con-
servi.
Quei miserabili per ora osservi,
Preso hanno il tossico, che si può far?

FIORDILIGI e DORABELLA: Signor Dottore, che si può far?

FIORDILIGI: We can't leave them alone at such a critical moment!

DORABELLA: They have very interesting faces!

FIORDILIGI: We can go a little nearer.

DORABELLA: This one's head is cold as ice.

FIORDILIGI: So is this one's.

DORABELLA: And the pulses?

FIORDILIGI: I don't feel it.

DORABELLA: His is beating very slowly.

FIORDILIGI *and* DORABELLA: Ah, if only help would come! There will soon be no hope!

FERRANDO *and* GUGLIELMO (*aside*): They have become so intimate and maternal. Now let's see if their pity will turn into love!

FIORDILIGI *and* DORABELLA: Poor things! If they should die, I would feel dreadful!

(*Enter* DON ALFONSO, *with* DESPINA, *who is disguised as a doctor.*)

DON ALFONSO: Here's the doctor, noble ladies!

FERRANDO *and* GUGLIELMO (*aside*): Despina disguised; what a joke!

DESPINA: Salvete amabiles bones puelles.

FIORDILIGI *and* DORABELLA: He speaks a strange language that we don't understand.

DESPINA: I'll speak whatever language you command me to. I know Greek and Arabic, Turkish and Vandal, Swedish and Tartaric; I can speak them all.

DON ALFONSO: Keep your languages to yourself for the present. Please examine these miserable young men. They've taken poison; what can you do for them?

FIORDILIGI *and* DORABELLA: Most honored Doctor, what can be done?

DESPINA: Saper bisognami
Pria la cagione
E quindi l'indole
Della pozione;
Se calda
O frigida,
Se poca
O molta
Se in una volta,
Ovvere in più.

FIORDILIGI, DORABELLA, DON ALFONSO: Preso han l'arsenico,
signor Dottore,
Quì dentro il bebbero.
La causa e amore
Ed in un sorso sel mandar giù.

DESPINA: Non vi affannate,
Non vi turbate,
Ecco una prova di mia virtù.
(*Prenda un magnete dalla sua manica, e l'agita sopra i due uomini.*)

FIORDILIGI, DORABELLA, DON ALFONSO: Egli ha di un ferro
La man fornita.

DESPINA: Questo è quel pezzo
Di calamita
Pietra Mesmerica,
Ch' ebbe l'origine
Nell' Alemagna,
Che poi sì celebre
Là in Francia fù.
(GUGLIELMO *e* FERRANDO *si muovono le braccia.*)

FIORDILIGI, DORABELLA, DON ALFONSO: Come si muovono,
Torcono, scuotono,
In terra il cranio
Presto percuotono.

DESPINA (*gesticola col magnete*): A lor la fronte
Tenete sù.

FIORDILIGI *e* DORABELLA: Eccoci pronte.

DESPINA: Tenete forte,
Coraggio!
Or liberi
Siete da morte.

DESPINA: First I must know the cause, and then the nature of the poisoning. Was it warm or cold? A little or much? Was it one dose or several?

FIORDILIGI, DORABELLA, DON ALFONSO: They've taken arsenic, Doctor; they drank it right here, driven by disappointed love; they swallowed it down in one gulp!

DESPINA: Don't disturb yourselves— Now I will reveal my scientific skill!
(*She takes a magnet from her sleeve, and waves it over the two young men.*)

FIORDILIGI, DORABELLA, DON ALFONSO: He has a huge piece of iron in his hand!

DESPINA: This is a piece of Doctor Mesmer's magnetic stone. It was first discovered in Germany, and then became celebrated in France as well.
(GUGLIELMO *and* FERRANDO *move their arms.*)

FIORDILIGI, DORABELLA, DON ALFONSO: How they're moving, turning and twisting! Their heads are inclining toward the ground!

DESPINA (*gesturing with the magnet*): Now hold their heads up!

FIORDILIGI *and* DORABELLA: Here, they're ready!

DESPINA: Hold them tightly, tightly, tightly; have courage! Now they will both be saved from death!

FIORDILIGI, DORABELLA, DON ALFONSO: Attorno guardano:
Forze riprendono:
Ah questo medico vale un Perù.

FERRANDO *e* GUGLIELMO (*fingono di ravvivare*): Dove son!
Che loco è questo?
Chi è colui? color chi sono?
Son di Giove innanzi al trono?
Sei tu Palla, o Citerea?
No tu sei l'alma mia dea;
Ti ravviso al dolce viso:
E alla man ch'or ben conosco
E che sola è il mio tesor.

DESPINA *e* DON ALFONSO: Son effetti acor del tosco,
Non abbiate alcun timor.

FIORDILIGI *e* DORABELLA: Sàra ver, ma tante smorfie
Fanno torto al nostro onor.

FERRANDO *e* GUGLIELMO (*a parte*): Dalla voglia che ho di ridere,
Il polmon mi scoppia ognor. (*forte*)
Per pietà, bell' idol mio!
Volgi a me le luci liete!

FIORDILIGI *e* DORABELLA: Più resister non poss' io!

FERRANDO *e* GUGLIELMO (*s'saltano subito*): Dammi un bacio, o mio tesoro,
Un sol bacio, o qui mi moro!

FIORDILIGI *e* DORABELLA: Stelle, un bacio?

DESPINA *e* DON ALFONSO: Secondate
Per effetto di bontate.

FIORDILIGI *e* DORABELLA: Ah, che troppo si richiede
Da una fida onesta amante
Oltraggiata è la mia fede,
Oltraggiato è questo cor.

DESPINA *e* DON ALFONSO (*a parte*): Un quadretto più giocondo
Non si vide in tutti il mondo,
Quel che più mi fa da ridere
E quell' ira e quel furor.

FIORDILIGI *e* DORABELLA: Disperati, attossicati,
Ite al diavol quanti siete;
Tardi in ver vi pentirete
Se più cresce il mio furor.

FIORDILIGI, DORABELLA, DON ALFONSO: See them stirring; they're regaining their strength! Ah, this doctor is worth his weight in gold!

FERRANDO *and* GUGLIELMO (*pretending to revive*): Where am I? What place is this? Who is he? And who are you? Am I before the throne of Jupiter? Are you Athena or Venus? No, you are the goddess of my soul! Once again I see your lovely face, and by your beloved touch I recognize my love!

DESPINA *and* DON ALFONSO: It's the influence of poison; don't listen to what they say.

FIORDILIGI *and* DORABELLA: That may be true, but such passion wrongs our honor!

FERRANDO *and* GUGLIELMO (*aside*): My chest is going to burst from holding back my laughter! (*aloud*) Have pity! Let your beautiful eyes shine upon us!

FIORDILIGI *and* DORABELLA: I can't bear it any longer!

FERRANDO *and* GUGLIELMO (*suddenly leaping up*): Give me a kiss! O my darling! Only one kiss, and then I can die!

FIORDILIGI *and* DORABELLA: Heavens, a kiss?

DESPINA *and* DON ALFONSO: Go ahead; it's only kindness!

FIORDILIGI *and* DORABELLA: Ah, that's too much to ask of an honest woman! My heart and my soul are outraged by your request!

DESPINA *and* DON ALFONSO (*aside*): One couldn't find a more amusing scene in all this world! How their raging makes me laugh!

FIORDILIGI *and* DORABELLA: Take your poison to the devil. You'll repent it if you try my patience any longer!

DESPINA *e* DON ALFONSO: In poch' ore lo vedrete
Per virtù del magnetismo
Finire quel parossismo,
Torneranno al primo umor.

FERRANDO *e* GUGLIELMO (*a parte*): Un quadretto più gio-
condo
Non s'è visto in questo mondo,
Ma non so se finta o vera
Sia quell' ira
E quel furor.

DESPINA *and* DON ALFONSO: You'll see that in no time the magnet will end their spasms. They'll be just as good as new.

FERRANDO *and* GUGLIELMO (*aside*): One couldn't find a more amusing scene in all this world! But I'm beginning to doubt whether their rage is real or feigned!

ATTO SECONDO

Una stanza nella casa a delle due sorelle. DESPINA *aiuta*
FIORDILIGI *e* DORABELLA *a vestirsi.*

Recitativo

DESPINA: Andate là, che siete due bizarre ragazze!

FIORDILIGI: Oh cospettaccio! cosa pretenderesti?

DESPINA: Per me nulla.

FIORDILIGI: Per chi dunque?

DESPINA: Per voi.

DORABELLA: Per noi?

DESPINA: Per voi. Siete voi donne, o no?

FIORDILIGI: E per questo?

DESPINA: E per questo dovere far da donne.

DORABELLA: Ciò è?

DESPINA: Tratter l'amore en bagatelle. Le occasioni belle
non negliger giammai! cangiar a tempo, a tempo esser costanti, coquettizar con grazia, prevenir la disgrazia sì comune a chi si fida in uomo, mangiar il fico, e non gittare il
pomo.

FIORDILIGI (*a parte*): Che diavolo! (*forte*) Tai cose falle
tu, se n'hai voglia.

DESPINA: Io già le faccio. Ma vorrei che anche voi per
gloria del bel sesso faceste un po' lo stesso!

19. Aria

Una donna a quindici anni
Dee saper ogni gran moda,
Dove il diavolo ha la coda,
Cosa è bene, e mal cos' è,
Dee saper le maliziette,
Che innamorano gli amanti,
Finger riso, finger pianti,

ACT TWO

A room in the sisters' house. DESPINA *is helping* FIORDILIGI *and* DORABELLA *to dress.*

Recitative

DESPINA: Well, you are certainly two very strange girls!

FIORDILIGI: For goodness' sake, what do you expect of us?

DESPINA: For myself—nothing.

FIORDILIGI: For whom, then?

DESPINA: For you!

DORABELLA: For us?

DESPINA: Yes, for you. Are you women or not?

FIORDILIGI: Isn't that quite evident?

DESPINA: Well, if you are women, you must behave like women!

DORABELLA: Which means?

DESPINA: You must realize that love should not be serious. Never reject a chance to have some fun! There are times when you must be changeable and times when you must be constant. You must know how to flirt gracefully, always avoiding the common disgrace of those who trust in men. In short, you must know how to have your cake and eat it at the same time!

FIORDILIGI (*aside*): How outrageous! (*aloud*) You may do those things if you want to.

DESPINA: That's how I always do them. But for the honor and glory of our sex, I would like you both to follow my example!

19. Aria

By the time a girl is fifteen she must know the ways of the world! She must know where the devil's tail is, what is good and what is bad! She must learn the little lies that fascinate a lover, how to feign laughter or tears, and how to invent plausible excuses! She must be able to deal with a hundred suitors at the same time; she must speak to a thousand with her eyes; she must give hope to all men

Inventar i bei perchè.
Dee in un momento
Dar retta a cento,
Colle pupille
Parlar con mille,
Dar speme a tutti,
Sien belli o brutti,
Saper nascondersi,
Senza confondersi,
Senza arrossire,
Saper mentire,
E qual regina
Dall' alto soglio
Col posso e voglio farsi ubbidir. (*a parte*)
Par ch'abbian gusto
Di tal dottrina, (*forte*)
Viva Despina
Che sa servir! (*Parte.*)

Recitativo

FIORDILIGI: Sorella, cosa dici?

DORABELLA: Io son stordita dallo spirto infernal di tal ragazza.

FIORDILIGI: Ma credimi è una pazza. Ti par che siamo in caso di seguir suoi consigli?

DORABELLA: Oh certo se tu pigli pel rovescio il negozio.

FIORDILIGI: Anzio io lo piglio per il suo vero dritto: Mai nostri cori?

DORABELLA: Restano quel che sono; per divertirsi un poco, e non morire della malinconia non si manca di fè, sorella mia.

FIORDILIGI: Questo è ver.

DORABELLA: Dunque, per intenderci bene, qual vuoi scieglier per te de' due Narcisi?

FIORDILIGI: Decidi tu, sorella.

DORABELLA: Io già decisi.

20. Duetto

Prenderò quel brunettino,
Che più lepidò mi par.

FIORDILIGI: Ed intanto io col biondino
Vo un po ridere e burlar.

whether they're handsome or ugly, and know how to hide her plans without confusion, and to lie without blushing! With these talents she'll be obeyed like a queen on the highest throne. (*aside*) It seems that my advice appeals to them! (*aloud*) Trust in Despina—I'll be your guide! (*Exits.*)

Recitative

FIORDILIGI: Sister, what do you say?

DORABELLA: I'm amazed at that girl's diabolical cynicism!

FIORDILIGI: I think she's crazy. Does she believe that we'll follow her advice?

DORABELLA: Certainly not—if you undertake to stop the whole business.

FIORDILIGI: I estimate it at its true value. And our devotion?

DORABELLA: We're still devoted. To amuse oneself a little and not to die of melancholy is not the same as breaking one's faith, my dear sister.

FIORDILIGI: There is some truth in that.

DORABELLA: Well, then? Let's understand each other—which gentleman is your choice?

FIORDILIGI: You decide it, sister.

DORABELLA: I have decided!

20. Duet

I'll take that sweet little dark one; he seems more vivacious to me.

FIORDILIGI: And I will laugh and joke with the nice little blond one.

DORABELLA: Scherzosetta ai dolci detti
Io di quel risponderò.

FIORDILIGI: Sospirando i sospiretti
Io dell' altro imiterò.

DORABELLA: Mi dirà, "ben mio, mi moro."

FIORDILIGI: Mi dirà, "mio bel tesoro!"

FIORDILIGI e DORABELLA: Ed intanto che diletto,
Che spassetto io proverò!
(*Entrano* FERRANDO *e* GUGLIELMO *con* DON ALFONSO *e* DES ·
PINA.)

21. Duetto

FERRANDO e GUGLIELMO: Secondate, aurette amiche,
Secondate i miei desiri,
E portate i miei sospiri
Alla dea di questo cor.
Voi, che udiste mille volte
Il tenor delle mie pene;
Ripetete al caro bene,
Tutto quel che udiste allor.

Recitativo

FIORDILIGI e DORABELLA: Cos' è tal mascherata?

DESPINA (*a* FERRANDO *e* GUGLIELMO): Animo, via, coraggio: aveta perso l'uso della favella?

FERRANDO: Io tremo, e palpito dalla testa alle piedi.

GUGLIELMO: Amor lega la membra a vero amante.

DON ALFONSO: Da brave incorraggiteli.

FIORDILIGI: Parlate!

DORABELLA: Liberi dite pur quel che bramate!

FERRANDO: Madama—

GUGLIELMO: Anzi madame—

FERRANDO: Parla pur tu.

GUGLIELMO: No, no, parla pur tu.

DON ALFONSO: Oh! cospetto del diavolo! lasciate tali smorfie del secolo passato: Despinetta, terminiam questa festa, fa tu con lei, quel ch'io farò con questa.
(*Prende la mano di* DORABELLA; DESPINA *prende la mano di* FIORDILIGI.)

DORABELLA: I'll parody his sweet speeches.

FIORDILIGI: I'll mock his sighs.

DORABELLA: Mine will say: "My dearest, I'm dying!"

FIORDILIGI: Mine will say: "My darling, you're so beautiful!"

FIORDILIGI *and* DORABELLA: And, in any case, how amusing it will be!

(FERRANDO *and* GUGLIELMO *enter with* DON ALFONSO *and* DESPINA.)

21. *Duet*

FERRANDO *and* GUGLIELMO: Echo my desires, friendly breezes, and carry my sighs to the goddess of my heart! You who have heard the story of my suffering a thousand times, repeat it once again to my dear love!

Recitative

FIORDILIGI *and* DORABELLA: What is the meaning of this performance?

DESPINA (*to* FERRANDO *and* GUGLIELMO): Hurry, speak up now! Have you lost the use of your tongues?

FERRANDO: I'm trembling from head to foot.

GUGLIELMO: Emotion paralyzes the limbs of a true lover.

DON ALFONSO: Dear ladies, please encourage them.

FIORDILIGI: Speak!

DORABELLA: You may tell us whatever you like!

FERRANDO: Dear lady!

GUGLIELMO: Or rather, both dear ladies!

FERRANDO: You tell them.

GUGLIELMO: No, you.

DON ALFONSO: Oh, the devil! Leave such bashfulness to our grandparents. Despinetta, let's end this farce; you speak for the ladies; I'll speak for my friends.

(*He takes* DORABELLA'S *hand;* DESPINA *takes* FIORDILIGI'S *hand.*)

22. *Quartetto*

La mano a me date,
Movetevi un pò! (*ai due giovani uomini*)
Se voi non parlate,
Per voi parlerò. (*a* FIORDILIGI *e* DORABELLA)
Perdono vi chiede
Un schiavo tremante,
V'offese, lo vede,
Ma solo un istante;
Or pena, ma tace!

FERRANDO *e* GUGLIELMO: Tace!

DON ALFONSO: Or lasciavi in pace!

FERRANDO *e* GUGLIELMO: In pace!

DON ALFONSO: Non può quel che vuole,
Vorrà, quel che può.

FERRANDO *e* GUGLIELMO: Non può quel che vuole,
Vorrà quel che può.

DON ALFONSO: Su! via! rispondete!
Guardate, e ridete?

DESPINA: Per voi la risposta (*risponde per le donne*)
A loro darò.
Quello ch'e stato, è stato,
Scordiamci del passato.
Rompasi omai quel laccio,
Segno di servitù;
A me porgete il bracio:
Nè sospirate più.

DESPINA *e* DON ALFONSO (*a parte*): Per carità partiamo,
Quel che san far veggiamo,
Le stimo più
Del diavolo,
S'ora non cascan giù. (*Partono.*)

Recitativo

FIORDILIGI: Oh che bella giornata!

FERRANDO: Caldetta anzi che no.

DORABELLA: Che vezzosi arboscelli!

GUGLIELMO: Certo, certo: son belli: han più foglie che
frutti.

FIORDILIGI: Quel viali come sono leggiadri; volete passeggiar?

22. Quartet

Give me your hand; now, try to respond gracefully. (*to the two young men*) If you won't speak to these ladies, I'll find the words for you. (*to* FIORDILIGI *and* DORABELLA) A trembling slave begs for your pardon. It is true that I offended you, but only for a moment. Now I will gladly suffer in silence!

FERRANDO *and* GUGLIELMO: In silence!

DON ALFONSO: I'll leave you in peace!

FERRANDO *and* GUGLIELMO: In peace!

DON ALFONSO: If you desire it, I'll disappear from your sight.

FERRANDO *and* GUGLIELMO: If you desire it, I'll disappear from your sight.

DON ALFONSO: Come on, then! Answer me! You're watching? And smiling?

DESPINA: I'll supply their answer. (*replying for the ladies*) What is past is finished; let's forget all about it. Now we must sever the bonds of a former love which has become only slavery. Give me your hands and don't grieve any longer!

DESPINA *and* DON ALFONSO (*aside*): Let's leave them all together; we'll see what will happen. I'll respect them more than the devil himself if they can resist temptation now! (*Exit.*)

Recitative

FIORDILIGI: Oh, what a beautiful day!

FERRANDO: It's a little warm.

DORABELLA: What charming arbors!

GUGLIELMO: Yes, yes, the trees are pretty, but they have more leaves than fruit.

FIORDILIGI: What interesting pathways; would you like to walk?

367

FERRANDO: Son pronto, o cara, ad ogni vostro cenno.

FIORDILIGI: Troppa grazia!

FERRANDO (*a parte a* GUGLIELMO): Eccoci alla gran crisi.

FIORDILIGI: Cosa gli avet detto?

FERRANDO: Eh gli raccomandai di divertirla bene.

(FIORDILIGI *e* FERRANDO *partono.*)

DORABELLA: Passeggiamo anche noi?

GUGLIELMO: Come vi piace. Ahimè!

DORABELLA: Che cosa avete?

GUGLIELMO: Io mi sento si male, si male, anima mia, che mi par di morire.

DORABELLA (*a parte*): Non otterà nientissimo. (*forte*) Saranno rimasigli del velen che beveste.

GUGLIELMO: Ah che un veleno assai più forte io bevo in què' crudi e focosi mongibelli amorosi!

DORABELLA: Sarà veleno calido; fatevi un poco fregeo.

GUGLIELMO (*le offerte una medaglia col suo quadro*): Questa picciola offerta d'accettare degnatevi.

DORABELLA: Un core?

GUGLIELMO: Un core; è simbolo di quello ch'arde, languisce e spasima per voi.

DORABELLA: L'accetto.

GUGLIELMO (*a parte*): Infelice Ferrando! (*forte*) Oh che diletto!

23. *Duetto*

Il core vi dono,
Bell'idolo mio;
Ma il vostro vo'anch'io,
Via datelo a me.

DORABELLA: Mel date, lo prendo,
Ma il mia non vi rendo,
Invan me'l chiedete,
Più meco non è.

GUGLIELMO: Se teco non l'hai,
Perchè batte quì?

DORABELLA: Se a me tu lo dai,
Che mai balza lì?

FERRANDO: I'm ready to do your slightest bidding, dear.

FIORDILIGI: You're very kind.

FERRANDO (*aside to* GUGLIELMO): This is the critical moment.

FIORDILIGI: What did you say to him?

FERRANDO: I was only wishing him a pleasant walk.
(FIORDILIGI *and* FERRANDO *exit.*)

DORABELLA: Shall we walk, too?

GUGLIELMO: As you wish—O God!

DORABELLA: What is the matter?

GUGLIELMO: I feel so ill—so ill, my darling, that I think I'm going to die!

DORABELLA (*aside*): That won't get him anywhere! (*aloud*) It must be the after effects of the poison.

GUGLIELMO: Ah, but I drank a stronger poison from your beautiful eyes!

DORABELLA: Oh, what intoxicating poison! You should walk in the fresh air!

GUGLIELMO (*offering her a locket with his picture*): Will you deign to accept this small present?

DORABELLA: A heart?

GUGLIELMO: A heart, symbolic of this one that languishes and beats for you!

DORABELLA: I'll accept it.

GUGLIELMO (*aside*): Poor Ferrando! (*aloud*) Oh, I'm delighted!

23. Duet

I give you my heart, my beautiful goddess, but I desire yours in return. Come, give it to me.

DORABELLA: I'll accept the gift of your heart, but I can't return my own. You ask me for it in vain; it's no longer in my possession.

GUGLIELMO: If your heart is gone, why does it beat here?

DORABELLA: If your heart is mine, what do I feel beating here?

DORABELLA *e* GUGLIELMO: E il mio coricino,
Che più non è meco,
Ei venne a star teco,
Ei batte così.

GUGLIELMO: Qui lascia che metta.

DORABELLA: Ei qui non può star.

GUGLIELMO: T'intendo, furbetta.

DORABELLA: Che fai?

GUGLIELMO: Non guardar.

DORABELLA: Nel petta un Vesuvio d'avere mi par!

GUGLIELMO (*a parte*): Ferrando meschino! possibil non par. (*forte*)
L'occhietta a me gira.

DORABELLA: Che brami?

GUGLIELMO: Rimira, rimira,
Se meglio può andar.

DORABELLA *e* GUGLIELMO: Oh cambio felice,
Di cori e d'affetti!
Che nuovi diletti,
Che dolce penar!

(*Partono* DORABELLA *e* GUGLIELMO. *Entrano* FIORDILIGI *e* FERRANDO.)

Recitativo

FERRANDO: Barbara! perchè fuggi?

FIORDILIGI: Ho visto un aspide, un' idra, un basilisco!

FERRANDO: Ah! crudel, ti capisco! L'aspide, l'idra, il basilisco, e quanto i Libici deserti han di più fiero, in me solo tu vedi.

FIORDILIGI: E vero, è vero. Tu vuoi tormi la pace.

FERRANDO: Ma per farti felice.

FIORDILIGI: Cessa di molestarmi!

FERRANDO: No ti chiedo ch'un guardo!

FIORDILIGI: Partiti!

FERRANDO: Non sperarlo, se pria gli occhi men fieri a me non giri. O ciel! ma tu mi guardi e poi sospiri? (*Parte.*)

FIORDILIGI: Ei parte—senti—ah no—partir si lasci, so tolga ai sguardi miei l'infausto oggetto della mia debolezza. A qual cimento il barbaro mi pose! Un premia e questo ben

DORABELLA *and* GUGLIELMO: It must be my own heart which is now beating in your breast.

GUGLIELMO: Now let me put this locket on you.

DORABELLA: You mustn't put it there.

GUGLIELMO: I understand you, you vixen.

DORABELLA: What are you doing?

GUGLIELMO: Don't look!

DORABELLA: Vesuvius seems to be erupting in my breast!

GUGLIELMO (*aside*): Poor Ferrando; I wouldn't have believed it! (*aloud*) Now, open your eyes.

DORABELLA: Where shall I look?

GUGLIELMO: Look down there. Isn't it better that way?

DORABELLA *and* GUGLIELMO: Oh, happy change of heart! What new delight I feel, what sweet pain!
(DORABELLA *and* GUGLIELMO *exit*. FERRANDO *and* FIORDILIGI *enter*.)

Recitative

FERRANDO: Cruel one! Why do you shun me?

FIORDILIGI: I've seen an asp, a hydra, a basilisk!

FERRANDO: Ah, now I understand you! You see in me all the fiercest animals of the jungle!

FIORDILIGI: It's true, I confess it. You're trying to destroy my peace.

FERRANDO: But only to make you happy.

FIORDILIGI: Stop pursuing me!

FERRANDO: I ask only a kind glance!

FIORDILIGI: Leave me!

FERRANDO: No, never! First you must turn your beautiful eyes to mine. O God! You look at me and then you sigh? (*Exits*.)

FIORDILIGI: He's gone! Come back! No—let him go—let the unhappy object of my weakness be concealed from my sight. He has plunged me into a horrible dilemma!

371

dovuto a mie colpe; In tale istante dovea di nuovo amante,
i sospiri ascoltar? l'altrui querele dovea volger in gioco?
Ah, questo core a ragione condanni, o giusto amare! Io
ardo e l'ardor mio non e più effetto d'un amor virtuoso: è
smania, affanno, rimorso, pentimento, leggerezza, perfidia,
e tradimento!

25. Aria

Per pietà, ben mio, perdona,
All'error d'un alma amante
Fra quest' ombre, e queste piante
Sempre ascoso, oh Dio, sarà.
Svenerà quest'empia voglia
L'ardir mio, la mia costanza,
Perderà la rimembranza,
Che vergogna e orror mi fa.
A chi mai mancò di fede
Questo vano ingrato cor?
Si dove a miglior mercede,
Caro bene, al tuo candor!
(FIORDILIGI *parte. Entrano* GUGLIELMO *e* FERRANDO.)

Recitativo

FERRANDO: Amico, abbiamo vinto!

GUGLIELMO: Un ambo, o un terno?

FERRANDO: Una cinquinta, amico; Fiordiligi è la modestia
in carne.

GUGLIELMO: Niente meno?

FERRANDO: Nientissimo; sta attento e ascolta come fù. Mi
dissaccià superba, mi maltratto, mi fugge, testimonio ren-
dendomi e messaggio, che una femmina ell'è senza pa-
raggio.

GUGLIELMO: Bravo tu, bravo io, brava la mia Penelope!
Lascia un po ch'io ti obbracci per si felice augurio, o mio
fido mercurio.

FERRANDO: E la mia Dorabella? Come s'è diportata? Oh non
ho neppur dubbio assai conosco quella sensibil alma.

GUGLIELMO: Eppur un dubbio parlando ti a quattr'occhi,
non saria mal, se tu l'avessi!

FERRANDO: Come?

GUGLIELMO: Dico così per dir. (*a parte*) Avrei piacere d'in-
dotrarglila pilola.

But I surely deserved as much for my foolishness! At such a sad time I should never have listened to the pleas of a new lover! Should I have treated it all as a joke? No— truly my heart is guilty. Gods of Love! I am aflame, and my love is not virtuous! It is madness, suffering, remorse, repentance, perfidy, and finally—betrayal!

25. Aria

For pity's sake, my Guglielmo, grant me pardon for the errors of a loving soul. O God, they will be hidden forever among my tears and sorrows. Let my future constancy obscure the memory of this evil desire that has caused me such horror and shame. How could this vain, ungrateful heart have broken its promises? My darling, you deserved better recompense for your fidelity!

(FIORDILIGI *exits*. GUGLIELMO *and* FERRANDO *enter*.)

Recitative

FERRANDO: My friend, we've won the bet!

GUGLIELMO: Doubly or triply?

FERRANDO: Five times over, my friend; Fiordiligi is modesty personified.

GUGLIELMO: Nothing less?

FERRANDO: Exactly; listen and you'll hear what happened. She dismissed me proudly; she rebuffed me, fled from me, giving me proof that she's a woman beyond emulation.

GUGLIELMO: Good for you, good for me, good for Fiordiligi. Let me embrace you for your good fortune.

FERRANDO: And my Dorabella? How did she behave? But I have no doubt— I know that faithful soul too well.

GUGLIELMO: And yet a doubt might enter your mind, if I may speak to you frankly.

FERRANDO: What?

GUGLIELMO: Oh, I was only joking. (*aside*) I wish there were some way to make it easier for him!

FERRANDO: Stelle, cesse elle forse alle lunsinghe tue?

GUGLIELMO: Certo! anzi in prova di suo amor, di sua fede questo bel ritrattino ella mi diede.

FERRANDO: Il mio ritrato! Ah perfida!

GUGLIELMO: Ove vai?

FERRANDO: A trarle il cor dal scellerato petto, e a vendicar, il mio tradito affetto.

GUGLIELMO: Fermati!

FERRANDO: No, mi lascia!

GUGLIELMO: Sei tu pazzo? vuoi tu precipitarti per una donna, che non val due soldi? (*a parte*) Non vorrei, che facesse qualche corbelleria!

FERRANDO: Numi! tante promesse e lagrime, e sospiri, e giuramenti in sì pocchi momenti come l'empia obliò!

GUGLIELMO: Per Bacco io non lo so!

FERRANDO: Che fare or deggio! a qual partito, A qual idea mi appiglio? Abbi di me pietà, dammi consiglio!

GUGLIELMO: Amico, non saprei qual consiglia a te dar!

FERRANDO: Barbara! ingrata! in un giorno! in pocch'ore!

GUGLIELMO: Certo un caso quest'è da far stupore.

26. Aria

Donne mie, la fate a tanti!
A tanti, a tanti, a tanti, a tanti!
Che se il ver vi deggio dir,
Se si lagnano gli amanti,
Li commincio a compatir.
Io vo bene al sesso vostro,
Lo sapete, ognun lo sà,
Ogni giorno ve lo mostro,
Vi do segno d'amistà.
Ma quel farla a tanti e tanti,
A tanti e tanti,
M'avvilisce in verità.
Mille volte il brando presi,
Per salvar il vostro onor,
Mille volte vi difesi
Colla bocca, e più col cor.

FERRANDO: Heavens! Did she yield to your advances? But now—you are joking—she loves only me.

GUGLIELMO: Certainly. And in proof of her love and her faith she gave me this charming little portrait of you.

FERRANDO: My portrait! Ah, the traitress!

GUGLIELMO: Where are you going?

FERRANDO: To tear her heart from her breast, and to avenge my betrayed affection!

GUGLIELMO: Stop!

FERRANDO: No, let me go!

GUGLIELMO: Are you insane? You're going to such trouble for a woman who isn't worth two pennies? (*aside*) I wouldn't want him to do anything rash!

FERRANDO: Heavens, so many promises, tears, sighs, oaths —how could she have forgotten them in so short a time?

GUGLIELMO: Don't ask me!

FERRANDO: Where shall I go now? What shall I do? What comfort can I find? Have pity on me! Give me some advice.

GUGLIELMO: My friend, I don't know what advice to give you.

FERRANDO: She's cruel, ungrateful! Forgotten in a day— in an hour!

GUGLIELMO: It's certainly most amazing!

26. *Aria*

My dear ladies, must you eternally behave this way? Really, I begin to understand why your lovers complain about you. I adore your sex: you know it; everyone knows it. I show it every day. I constantly give you pledges of my devotion. But now this eternal behavior of yours is beginning to disgust me. I've drawn my sword a thousand times to avenge your honor. A thousand times I've defended you, believing my own words. But really, again and again, your behavior is most offensive! You're charming; you're lovable. Heaven gave you your beauty, and graces encircle you from head to foot. But, over and over, the way that you treat men

Ma quel farla a tanti e tanti,
A tanti e tanti,
E un vizietto seccator.
Siete vaghe, siete amabili,
Più tesori il ciel vi diè;
E le grazie vi circondano,
Dalla testa sino ai piè.
Ma, ma, ma la fate a tanti e tanti,
A tanti e tanti,
Che credibile non è.
Ma la fate a tanti a tanti,
A tanti a tanti, a tanti,
Che se gridano gli amanti,
Hanno certo un gran perchè.
(*Entra* DON ALFONSO.)

Recitativo

DON ALFONSO: Bravo! questa è costanza.

FERRANDO: Andate, o barbaro, per voi misero sono.

DON ALFONSO: Via se sarte buono vi tornerò l'antica calma. Udite: Fiordiligi a Guglielmo si conserva fedel, e Dorabella infedel a voi fù.

FERRANDO: Per mia vergogna.

GUGLIELMO: Caro amico, bisogna far delle differenze in ogni cosa, ti pare che una sposa mancar possa a un Guglielmo? Intanto mi darete cinquanta zecchinetti.

DON ALFONSO: Volontieri: pria però di pagar vo che facciamo qualche altra esperanza. Venite; io spero mostravi ben che folle è quel cervello, che sulla frasca ancor vende l'uccello.

(DON ALFONSO, FERRANDO *e* GUGLIELMO *escono. Entrano* DESPINA *e* DORABELLA.)

DESPINA: Ora vedo che siete una donna di garbo.

DORABELLA: Invan, Despina, di resister tentai.

DESPINA: Corpo di satanasso, questo vuol dir saper! tanto di raro noi povere ragazze abbiamo un po di bene, che bisogna pigliarlo allor ch'ei viene. Ma ecco la sorella, che ceffo!

(*Entra* FIORDILIGI.)

FIORDILIGI: Sciagurate! ecco per colpa vostra in che stato

is unbelievable! If your lovers find cause for complaint they most certainly have their reasons!
(DON ALFONSO *enters.*)

Recitative

DON ALFONSO: Well! That's fidelity for you!

FERRANDO: Leave me alone; you're the cause of all my misery!

DON ALFONSO: If you'll be calm, your peace will be restored. Listen; Fiordiligi has proved herself true to Guglielmo, while Dorabella was unfaithful to you.

FERRANDO: To my shame.

GUGLIELMO: Dear friend, we must always make allowances in everything. Do you think a woman could ever fail a Guglielmo? Meanwhile, I'd like my fifty gold pieces.

DON ALFONSO: Gladly. But before paying, I want to make one more test. Come along; I hope to show you how unwise it is to count your chickens before they're hatched!
(DON ALFONSO, FERRANDO, *and* GUGLIELMO *exit.* DESPINA *and* DORABELLA *enter.*)

DESPINA: Now I see that you're really behaving as a woman should!

DORABELLA: I couldn't resist him, Despina.

DESPINA: Good heavens, we women have so little chance to amuse ourselves that we must take it as it comes. But here's your sister. What a frown!
(FIORDILIGI *enters.*)

FIORDILIGI: Little wretch, it's your fault that I find myself

377

mi trovo! Ma non so, come mai si può cangiar in un sol giorno un core.

DORABELLA: Che domanda ridicola! siam donne! e poi tu com' hai fatto!

FIORDILIGI: Io saprò vincermi.

DESPINA: Voi non saprete nulla.

FIORDILIGI: Farò, che tu lo veda.

DORABELLA: Credi sorella, è meglio che tu ceda! (*Parte.*)

FIORDILIGI: Despina! Despina!

DESPINA: Cosa c'è!

FIORDILIGI: Tieni un po questa chiave e senza replica, senza replica alcuna, prendi nel guardaroba, e quì mi porta due spade, due cappelli, e due vestiti de nostri sposi.

DESPINA: E che volete fare?

FIORDILIGI: Vanne, non replicare.

DESPINA (*a parte*): Comanda in abregè donna Arroganza.

FIORDILIGI: Vanne, sei cavalli di posta voli un servo ordinar, di a Dorabella che parlar le vorrei.

DESPINA: Sarà servita. (*a parte*) Questa donna mi par di senno uscita. (*Parte.*)

FIORDILIGI: L'abito di Ferrando sarà buono per me.

29. Duetto

Fra gli amplessi, in pochi istanti,
Giungero del fido sposo,
Sconosciuta a lui davanti
In quest' abito verrò.
Oh che gioja il suo bel core
Proverà nel ravvisarmi!
(FERRANDO *entra inapproviso;* GUGLIELMO *e* DON ALFONSO *si nascondono in dietro.*)

FERRANDO: Ed intanto di dolore
Meschinello, io mi morrò!

FIORDILIGI: Cosa veggio!
Son tradita!
Deh, partite!

FERRANDO: Ah no, mia vita:

in this situation. I don't understand how a heart can change in a single day!

DORABELLA: What a silly question; we're women! How was your stroll?

FIORDILIGI: I know how to resist temptation!

DESPINA: Don't be too sure of that!

FIORDILIGI: You'll see that I'm in earnest.

DORABELLA: Believe me, sister, you'd do better to yield! (*Exits.*)

FIORDILIGI: Despina! Despina!

DESPINA: What's the matter?

FIORDILIGI: Take this key, and without questions, without telling anyone, go to the wardrobe trunk and find two swords, two hats, and two uniforms that belong to our fiancés.

DESPINA: What will you do with them?

FIORDILIGI: Go; don't argue with me!

DESPINA (*aside*): My Lady Arrogance is on her high horse!

FIORDILIGI: Get me a horse, and a servant to ride with me. And tell Dorabella that I would like to speak to her.

DESPINA: My lady shall be served. (*aside*) I think she's gone insane! (*Exits.*)

FIORDILIGI: The hat and uniform will disguise me beyond recognition.

29. Duet

Soon I shall be with my faithful lover again. At first he won't know me in that uniform, but then how happy he will be to see me again!
(FERRANDO *enters suddenly, as* GUGLIELMO *and* DON ALFONSO *hide upstage.*)

FERRANDO: And meanwhile I'll die of grief!

FIORDILIGI: Who is this? I'm betrayed! Please leave me!

FERRANDO: Ah no, my darling! Kill me, instead, with this

Con quel ferro di tua mano
Questo cor tu ferirai,
E se forza oh Dio non hai,
Io la man ti reggerò.

FIORDILIGI: Taci, ahimè! son abbastanza
Tormentata ed infelice!

FERRANDO: Ah che omai la sua costanza—

FIORDILIGI: Ah, che omai la mia costanza—

FIORDILIGI e FERRANDO: A quei sguardi, a quel che dice,
Incomincia a vacillar.

FIORDILIGI: Sorgi, sorgi!

FERRANDO: Invan lo credi.

FIORDILIGI: Per pietà, da me che chiedi?

FERRANDO: Il tuo cor, o la mia morte.
Cedi cara!

FIORDILIGI: Ah non son, non son più forte!
Dei, consiglio!

FERRANDO: Volgi a me pietoso il ciglio,
In me sol trovar tu puoi
Sposo, amante, a più, se vuoi,
Idol mio, più non tardar.

FIORDILIGI: Giusto ciel!
Crudel! hai vinto.
Fa di me quel che ti par!

FIORDILIGI e FERRANDO: Abbracciamci, o caro bene,
E un conforto a tante pene
Sia languir di dolce affetto,
Di diletto sospirar.

(*Partono* FIORDILIGI *e* FERRANDO. GUGLIELMO *emerge dal suo nascondiglio.*)

Recitativo

GUGLIELMO: Oh poveretto me! cosa ho veduto! cosa ho sentito mai!

(DON ALFONSO *emerge dal suo nascondiglio.*)

DON ALFONSO: Per carità! silenzio!

GUGLIELMO: Mi pelerei la barba! mi graffierei la pelle! e darei colle corna entro le stelle, fu quella Fiordiligi? la Penelope, l'Artemisia del secolo! briccona, assassina furfante, ladra, cagna!

380

sword. If you haven't the courage, I myself will guide your hand!

FIORDILIGI: O God! Don't talk like that— I've suffered enough unhappiness already!
FERRANDO: Ah, her constancy is beginning to fail—
FIORDILIGI: Ah, my constancy is beginning to fail—
FIORDILIGI *and* FERRANDO: Judging from glances and sighs.

FIORDILIGI: Go away!
FERRANDO: I won't leave you!
FIORDILIGI: For pity's sake, what do you want of me?
FERRANDO: Either your heart, or my own death. Yield, my darling!
FIORDILIGI: Ah, I'm not strong enough! God, assist me!

FERRANDO: Turn your eyes upon me, out of pity; only in me will you find the husband of your fondest dreams. My dearest, don't hesitate!

FIORDILIGI: O God! Cruel one, you have conquered! I will do whatever you desire.

FIORDILIGI *and* FERRANDO: Kiss me, O my darling, and let sweet affection and sighs of pleasure comfort us for so much suffering and pain!
(FIORDILIGI *and* FERRANDO *exit.* GUGLIELMO *comes out of his hiding place.*)

Recitative

GUGLIELMO: Oh, what shame! What have I seen? What have I heard!
(DON ALFONSO *comes out of his hiding place.*)

DON ALFONSO: Be quiet, for heaven's sake!

GUGLIELMO: I'll tear my hair out! I'll pull my skin off! I'm forever branded with the cuckold's horns! Was that Fiordiligi, the chaste, virtuous Penelope? Wretch! Vixen! Liar! Slut!

DON ALFONSO: Lasciamolo sfogar.
(*Entra* FERRANDO.)

FERRANDO: Ebben!

GUGLIELMO: Dov'è!

FERRANDO: Chi? la tua Fiordiligi?

GUGLIELMO: La mia Fior, Fior di diavolo, che strozzi lei prima e dopo me!

FERRANDO: Tu vedi bene, v'han delle differenze in ogni cosa, un poco di più merto—

DON ALFONSO: Dunque restate celibi in eterno.

FERRANDO e GUGLIELMO: Mancheran forse donne ad uomin come noi?

DON ALFONSO: Non c'è abbondanza d'altro. Ma l'altre, che faran, se ciò fer queste? in fondo voi le amate queste vostre cornacchie spennacchiate.

FERRANDO e GUGLIELMO: Ah pur troppo! Pur troppo!

DON ALFONSO: Ebben pigliatele com' elle son. Frattanto un' ottava ascoltatte:felicissimi voi, se la imparete.

30. *Aria*

Tutti accusan le donne,
Ed io le scuso,
Se mille volte al dì cangiano amore,
Altri un vizio lo chiama,
Ed altri un uso, ed a me par
Neccesità del core.
L'amante che si trova al fin deluso
Non condanni l'altrui, ma il proprio errore:
Giàcche giovani, vecchie, e belle e brutte,
Ripetete con me: Così fan tutte!

FERRANDO, GUGLIELMO, DON ALFONSO: Così fan tutte!
(*Partono* DON ALFONSO, FERRANDO e GUGLIELMO. *Entra* DESPINA, *con* CORO *dei servi.*)

31. *Finale*

DESPINA: Fate presto, o cari amici,
Alle faci il foco date,
E la mensa preparate
Con ricchezza e nobiltà!
Delle nostre padroncine
Gl'imenei son già disposti:

DON ALFONSO: Let him rave.
(FERRANDO *enters.*)

FERRANDO: Well, now?

GUGLIELMO: Where is she?

FERRANDO: Who? Your Fiordiligi?

GUGLIELMO: My Fiordiligi can go to the devil! Let him take her, and then me!

FERRANDO: You must understand that we must always make allowances in everything. All women are the same.

DON ALFONSO: Then both of you intend to remain celibate?

FERRANDO *and* GUGLIELMO: Men like us are irresistible to women.

DON ALFONSO: I don't doubt it. But what makes you think you will suffer less at the hands of others? At the bottom of your hearts you still love your unfaithful sweethearts.

FERRANDO *and* GUGLIELMO: Ah, yes, beyond reason! Beyond reason!

DON ALFONSO: Well then, accept them as they are. And now listen to a sermon. Perhaps you can learn something from it!

30. Aria

Everyone condemns women for being so changeable, but I excuse them for it. Others call it a custom or a vice, but to me it seems a necessity of the heart. The lover who at the end finds himself deceived should blame only his own folly; for the young, the old, the beautiful, even the ugly—repeat this now with me: They all do it!

FERRANDO, GUGLIELMO, DON ALFONSO: They all do it!
(DON ALFONSO, FERRANDO, *and* GUGLIELMO *exit.* DESPINA *enters with a* CHORUS *of servants.*)

31. Finale

DESPINA: Hurry up, my dear friends; light all the candles, and see that the supper is ready; prepare it all with richness and grace! We must await the celebration, and the music must begin as soon as our dear mistresses appear!

E voi gite ai vostri posti
Finchè i sposi vengon quà.

CORO: Facciam presto, o cari amici,
Alle faci il foco diamo,
E la mensa preparate
Con ricchezza e nobiltà.
(*Entra* DON ALFONSO.)

DON ALFONSO: Bravi, bravi!
Ottimamente!
Che abbondanza, che eleganza!
Una mancia conveniente
L'un e l'altro a voi darà.
Le due coppie omai si avvanzano,
Fate plauso al loro arrivo,
Lieto canto e suon giulivo
Empia il ciel d'ilarità.

DESPINA *e* DON ALFONSO: La più bella comediola
Non s'è vista, o si vedrà. (*Partono.*)

CORO: Benedetti i doppi conjugi,
E le amabili sposine:
Splenda lor il ciel benefico,
Ed a guisa di galline
Sien di figli ognor prolifiche
Che le agguaglino in beltà.
(*Entrano* FIORDILIGI, DORABELLA, FERRANDO *e* GUGLIELMO.)

FIORDILIGI, DORABELLA, FERRANDO, GUGLIELMO: Come par
che qui prometta
Tutto gioja e tutto amore!
Della cara Despinetta
Certo il merito sarà.
Radoppiate il lieto suono,
Replicate il dolce canto,
E noi qui seggiamo intanto
In maggior giovialità.

CORO: Beneditti i doppi conjugi— (*Esce.*)

FERRANDO *e* GUGLIELMO: Tutto, tutto, o vita mia,
Al mio foco, or ben rispende!

FIORDILIGI *e* DORABELLA: Pel mio sangue l'allegria
Cresce, cresce e sì diffonde!

FERRANDO *e* GUGLIELMO: Sei pur bella!

FIORDILIGI *e* DORABELLA: Sei pur vago!

FERRANDO *e* GUGLIELMO: Che bei rai!

CHORUS: Yes, we'll hurry to light the candles, and prepare a rich and noble supper.
(DON ALFONSO *enters.*)

DON ALFONSO: Bravo! You've done well! What abundance! What elegance! I shall see that you're suitably rewarded. Now the two couples will enter; cheer them as they come in. Let the sound of rejoicing fill the air with happiness.

DESPINA *and* DON ALFONSO: The best part of the comedy will now be seen. (*Exit.*)
CHORUS: God bless the brides and bridegrooms, may heaven rain its joys upon them, and may they have many children just as handsome as they are!
(FIORDILIGI, DORABELLA, FERRANDO, *and* GUGLIELMO *enter.*)

FIORDILIGI, DORABELLA, FERRANDO, GUGLIELMO: Now it seems that everything promises us joy and love! Certainly we must thank Despina, who has made all this possible. Let the happy chorus continue, and we will sit here and listen, in the greatest happiness!

CHORUS: God bless the brides and bridegrooms— (*Exits.*)
FERRANDO *and* GUGLIELMO: Now everything responds to my love!
FIORDILIGI *and* DORABELLA: My happiness is infinite!

FERRANDO *and* GUGLIELMO: You're so beautiful!
FIORDILIGI *and* DORABELLA: You're so charming!
FERRANDO *and* GUGLIELMO: What beautiful eyes!

FIORDILIGI *e* DORABELLA: Che bella bocca!

TUTTI: Tocca e bevi,
Bevi e tocca,
Tocca, bevi,
Tocca, tocca, bevi, bevi, tocca!

FIORDILIGI, DORABELLA, FERRANDO: E nel tuo, nel mio bicchiero
Si sommerga ogni pensiero,
E non resti più memoria
Del passatto ai nostri cor.

GUGLIELMO (*a parte*): Ah, bevessero del tossico
Questa volpi senza onor!
(*Entra* DON ALFONSO, *con* DESPINA *travestita da notajo.*)

DON ALFONSO: Miei Signori, tutto è fatto;
Col contratto nuziale
Il notajo è sulle scale
E ipso facto qui verrà.

FIORDILIGI, DORABELLA, FERRANDO, GUGLIELMO: Bravo,
bravo! passi subito.

DON ALFONSO: Vò a chiamarlo:
Eccolo quà.

DESPINA: Augurandovi ogni bene,
Il notajo Beccavivi
Coll' usata a voi sen viene
Notariale dignità!
E il contratto stipulato
Colle regole ordinarie,
Nelle forme giudiziarie,
Pria tossendo, poi sedendo
Clara voce leggerà.

FIORDILIGI, DORABELLA, FERRANDO, GUGLIELMO: Bravo,
bravo, in verità!

DESPINA: Per contratto da me fatto
Si congiunge in matrimonio
Fiordiligi con Sempronio,
E con Tizio Dorabella,
Sua legitima sorella,
Quelle Dame ferraresi,
Questi nobili albinesi,
E per dote e contradote—

FIORDILIGI *and* DORABELLA: What beautiful mouths!

ALL: Let's drink and toast one another!

FIORDILIGI, DORABELLA, FERRANDO: And let all thought be submerged in our glasses, and never again shall we recall the past.

GUGLIELMO (*aside*): Ah, I wish we could all drink poison! Those unfaithful sluts!

(DON ALFONSO *enters, with* DESPINA *disguised as a notary*.)

DON ALFONSO: My Lords, everything is done; the lawyer has arrived with the marriage contract, and he'll be here at once.

FIORDILIGI, DORABELLA, FERRANDO, GUGLIELMO: Let him come in!

DON ALFONSO: I'll call him. Here he is.

DESPINA: Wishing you every joy, the lawyer Beccavivi has come to lead you into the dignity of the married state. Here's the contract, stipulated according to the ordinary forms and the judicial rules. First I'll cough, then I'll sit down and read it aloud to you.

FIORDILIGI, DORABELLA, FERRANDO, GUGLIELMO: Very well, go on, quickly!

DESPINA: By this contract that I've drawn up, I hereby join you in matrimony! Fiordiligi with Sempronio, Tizio with Dorabella, the former's legitimate sister. These are ladies of Ferrara, those are nobles from Albania, and as for the dowries and the gifts—

FIORDILIGI, DORABELLA, FERRANDO, GUGLIELMO: Cose note, cose note!

Vi crediamo,
Ci fidiamo, soscriviam,
Date pur quà!

DESPINA *e* DON ALFONSO: Bravi, bravi, in verità!

CORO (*da lontano*): Bella vita militar!
Ogni dì si cangia loco,
Oggi molto, e doman poco,
Ora in terra ed or sul mar.

FIORDILIGI, DORABELLA, DESPINA, FERRANDO, GUGLIELMO: Che rumor! che canto è questo!

DON ALFONSO: State cheti; io vò a guardar. (*va alla finestra*)
Misericordia!
Numi del cielo!
Che caso orribile!
Io tremo! io gelo!
Gli sposi vostri—

FIORDILIGI *e* DORABELLA: Lo sposo mio!

DON ALFONSO: In questo istante
Tornaro, o Dio, ed alla riva
Sbarcano già!

FIORDILIGI, DORABELLA, FERRANDO, GUGLIELMO: Cosa mai sento!
Barbara stelle! in tal momento,
Che si farà?

FIORDILIGI *e* DORABELLA: Presto partite!
Presto fuggite!

DESPINA, FERRANDO, GUGLIELMO, DON ALFONSO: Ma se li veggono?
Ma se li incontrano?

FIORDILIGI *e* DORABELLA: Là, àl celatevi, per carità!
(*Escono* FERRANDO *e* GUGLIELMO.)
Numi! soccorso!
Numi consiglio!
Chi dal periglio ci salverà?
Chi?

DON ALFONSO: Rasserenatevi,
Ritranquillatevi!
In me fidatevi,
Ben tutto andrà.

FIORDILIGI *e* DORABELLA: Mille barbari pensieri

FIORDILIGI, DORABELLA, FERRANDO, GUGLIELMO: It's all noted! We believe you, and we'll all sign it now; give it to us!

DESPINA *and* DON ALFONSO: Everything is going well!
CHORUS (*off-stage*): A soldier's life is joyous! What pleasure to be able to travel from place to place—today everything—tomorrow nothing. Sometimes we go by land and sometimes by sea!
FIORDILIGI, DORABELLA, DESPINA, FERRANDO, GUGLIELMO: What's that song? I've heard it before!
DON ALFONSO: Be quiet; I'll go and see. (*going to window*) Good Lord, this is horrible! I'm trembling! I'm dizzy! Your former fiancés—

FIORDILIGI *and* DORABELLA: Our former fiancés?
DON ALFONSO: They've come home again, and they're disembarking at this moment!

FIORDILIGI, DORABELLA, FERRANDO, GUGLIELMO: What are you saying? How horrible! Now what can we do?

FIORDILIGI *and* DORABELLA: Leave us at once! You must escape!
DESPINA, FERRANDO, GUGLIELMO, DON ALFONSO: But if they come here? If we meet them?

FIORDILIGI *and* DORABELLA: You must hide yourselves somewhere.
(FERRANDO *and* GUGLIELMO *exit.*)
Heaven help us! Fate, assist us! Who will save us from this peril?

DON ALFONSO: Reassure yourselves! Be calm! Trust in me, and all will go well.

FIORDILIGI *and* DORABELLA: A thousand horrible thoughts

Tormentando il cor mi vanno,
Se discoprono l'inganno,
Ah, di noi che mai sarà!

(DESPINA *si nasconde setto una tavola. Entrano* FERRANDO
e GUGLIELMO, *vestiti da soldati, come prima.*)

FERRANDO *e* GUGLIELMO: Sani e salvi agli amplessi amorosi,
Delle nostre fidissime amanti,
Ritorniamo di gioja esultanti,
Per dar premio alla lor fedeltà.

DON ALFONSO: Giusti Numi! Guglielmo! Ferrando!
O che giubilo! qui,
Come,
E quando?

FERRANDO *e* GUGLIELMO: Richiamati da regio contrordine,
Pieni il cor di contento e di gaudio,
Ritorniamo alle spose adorabili,
Ritorniamo alla vostro amistà.

GUGLIELMO (*a* FIORDILIGI): Ma cos'è quel pallor, quel silenzio?

FERRANDO (*a* DORABELLA): L'idol mio, perchè mesto si stà?

DON ALFONSO: Dal diletto confuse ed attonite,
Mute, mute si restano là.

FIORDILIGI *e* DORABELLA (*a parte*): Ah, che al labbro le
voci mi mancano,
Se non moro, un prodigio sarà.

GUGLIELMO: Permittete che sia posto
Quel baul in quella stanza.
(GUGLIELMO *guarda sotto la tavola.*)
Dei! che veggio! un uom nascosto?
Un notajo? qui che fa?
(DESPINA *emerge, vestita come prima.*)

DESPINA: Non Signor non è un notajo,
E Despina mascherata,
Che dal ballo or è tornata,
E a spogliarsi, venne quà.

FIORDILIGI *e* DORABELLA: La Despina, la Despina!
Non capisco come và.

DESPINA: Una furba che m'agguagli
Dove mai si troverà!

FERRANDO *e* GUGLIELMO: Una furba uguale a questa,
Dove mai si troverà?

are whirling in my head. If they discover our deceit, whatever will become of us?

(DESPINA *hides under a table,* FERRANDO *and* GUGLIELMO *enter, dressed in their officer's uniforms.*)

FERRANDO *and* GUGLIELMO: Safe and sound, we joyously return to the embraces of our most faithful sweethearts, whose fidelity deserves this reward.

DON ALFONSO: Good heavens! Guglielmo! Ferrando! What joy! You've returned! Tell us how and when!

FERRANDO *and* GUGLIELMO: We were called back to Naples by the King's orders. Our hearts are full of joy and love, as we return to our adorable sweethearts and to you, our most beloved friend!

GUGLIELMO (*to* FIORDILIGI): But why are you so pale and so silent?

FERRANDO (*to* DORABELLA): My darling, why are you so sad?

DON ALFONSO: They're confused and bewildered by happiness.

FIORDILIGI *and* DORABELLA (*aside*): I simply can't speak. If I don't die here and now, it will be miraculous!

GUGLIELMO: Will you permit us to leave our baggage here? (GUGLIELMO *looks under the table.*)
Heavens, what's down there? A man in hiding! A lawyer! What is going on?
(DESPINA *comes out, dressed as before.*)

DESPINA: No, my Lord; I'm not a lawyer, but Despina, in disguise. I've just come home from a masked ball, and I was taking off my costume when you arrived.

FIORDILIGI *and* DORABELLA: The lawyer is Despina! I don't understand this at all!

DESPINA: Where on earth will you find anybody as clever as I am?

FERRANDO *and* GUGLIELMO: Where on earth will you find anybody as clever as Despina?

DON ALFONSO (*a parte a* FERRANDO *e* GUGLIELMO): Già
cadar lasciai le carte,
Raccoglietele con arte.

FERRANDO: Ma che carte sono queste?

GUGLIELMO: Un contratto nuziale?

FERRANDO *e* GUGLIELMO: Giusto ciel! voi qui scriveste,
Contradirci omai non vale,
Tradimento, tradimento,
Ah si faccia il scoprimento;
E a torrenti, a fiumi, a mari
Indi il sangue scorrerà!

FIORDILIGI *e* DORABELLA: Ah! Signor son rea di morte
E la morte io sol vi chiedo,
Il mio fallo tardi vedo,
Con quel ferro un sen ferite
Che non merita pietà!

FERRANDO *e* GUGLIELMO: Cosa fù?

FIORDILIGI *e* DORABELLA (*indicando* DON ALFONSO *e* DES-
PINA): Per noi favelli
Il crudel, la seduttrice.

DON ALFONSO: Troppo vero è quel che dice,
E la prova è chiusa lì!
(FERRANDO *e* GUGLIELMO *escono precipitosomente.*)

FIORDILIGI *e* DORABELLA: Dal timor io gelo, io palpito:
Perchè mai li discoprì!
(FERRANDO *entrando, senza la barba, ma coi vestiti del
suo travestito albanese.*)

FERRANDO (*a* FIORDILIGI): A voi s'inchina
Bella damina!
Il Cavaliere dell' Albania.
(GUGLIELMO, *entrando, col ritratto di* DORABELLA.)

GUGLIELMO (*a* DORABELLA): Il ritrattino
Pel coricino,
Ecco io le rendo
Signora mia.

FERRANDO *e* GUGLIELMO (*a* DESPINA): Ed al magnetico
Signor Dottore
Rendo l'onore
Che meritò.

FIORDILIGI, DORABELLA, DESPINA: Stelle! che veggo!
Al duol non reggo!

DON ALFONSO (*aside to* FERRANDO *and* GUGLIELMO): The contract is on the floor; pick it up, and read it aloud!

FERRANDO: What's this paper?

GUGLIELMO: A marriage contract?

FERRANDO *and* GUGLIELMO: Good Lord, you have both signed it! Your guilt is obvious!

FIORDILIGI *and* DORABELLA: Ah, I'm truly guilty, and I want you to kill me! I see my crime too late; kill me with your sword; I don't deserve your mercy!

FERRANDO *and* GUGLIELMO: Explain your betrayal!

FIORDILIGI *and* DORABELLA (*pointing to* DON ALFONSO *and* DESPINA): They beguiled us, that cruel man and that unprincipled girl!

DON ALFONSO: That's perfectly true, and you will find the proof hidden in the next room.

(FERRANDO *and* GUGLIELMO *rush out.*)

FIORDILIGI *and* DORABELLA: I'm shivering and shaking with terror— Why did he show them their hiding place?

(FERRANDO *enters, without his false beard, but with the clothing of his Albanian disguise.*)

FERRANDO (*to* FIORDILIGI): I bow to you, my sweet lady! I'm the noble Albanian lord!

(GUGLIELMO *enters with the portrait that he took from* DORABELLA.)

GUGLIELMO (*to* DORABELLA): I'll give you back my portrait in exchange for that little heart, my dear lady!

FERRANDO *and* GUGLIELMO (*to* DESPINA): And to the wonderful magnetic doctor let all honor be shown!

FIORDILIGI, DORABELLA, DESPINA: Heavens! This is dreadful! I cannot endure it!

FERRANDO, GUGLIELMO, DON ALFONSO (*a parte*): Son stupefatte!
Son mezze matte!

FIORDILIGI *e* DORABELLA (*indicando* DON ALFONSO): Ecco
là il barbaro che c'ingannò.

DON ALFONSO: V'ingannai, ma fu l'inganno
Disinganno ai vostri amanti,
Che più saggi omai saranno
Che faran quel ch'io vorrò.
Quà le destre, siete sposi,
Abbracciatevi e tacete.
Tutti quattro ora ridete,
Chi'io già risi e riderò.

FIORDILIGI *e* DORABELLA: Idol mio, se questo è vero,
Colla fede e coll' amore
Compensar saprò il tuo core,
Adorarti ognor saprò!

FERRANDO *e* GUGLIELMO: Te lo credo, gioja bella,
Ma la prova io far non vò.

DESPINA: Io non so se questo è sogno,
Mi confondo, mi vergogno:
Manco mal se a me l'han fatta,
Che a molt' altri
Anch'io la fò.

TUTTI: Fortunato l'uom', che prende
Ogni cosa pel buon verso,
E trai i casi, e le vicende
Da ragion guidar si fà.
Quel che suole altrui far piangere
Fia per lui cagion di riso,
E del mondo in mezzo i turbini,
Bella calma troverà.

FERRANDO, GUGLIELMO, DON ALFONSO (*aside*): They're amazed and stupefied! They're overwhelmed!

FIORDILIGI *and* DORABELLA (*pointing to* DON ALFONSO): You are the monster who deceived us!

DON ALFONSO: I only deceived you in order to free your lovers from their illusions. They will be wiser now, and I hope they'll follow my advice. Be reconciled: get married! Kiss each other and make it up! See the humor here; laugh, as I have laughed and will laugh again!

FIORDILIGI *and* DORABELLA: My darling, if this is true, I'll console your heart with faith and love; I will love you forever!

FERRANDO *and* GUGLIELMO: I believe you, my dearest— but this time I ask for no proof!

DESPINA: I don't know whether I'm awake or dreaming; I'm so confused and embarrassed. It seems that Don Alfonso has deceived me, when I thought that I was deceiving all the others!

ALL: Fortunate is the man who is able to make the best of all adversity! Through all vicissitudes he can let Reason be his guide. That which makes others weep will be a cause of laughter for him. And, even in the midst of a whirlwind, he will find a center of tranquillity!

THE
MAGIC
FLUTE

DIE
ZAUBERFLÖTE

*An opera
in two acts*

Music by
Wolfgang Amadeus Mozart
(K. 620)
Words by
Emanuel Schikaneder
and Carl Ludwig Giesecke

INTRODUCTION

The Magic Flute was first produced in September 1791, three months before Mozart's death at the age of thirty-five. To a great extent, the final form of Mozart's last opera was determined by the circumstances of its composition. The libretto was provided by Emanuel Schikaneder, an actor and singer who owned a popular theater in suburban Vienna. Well versed in the theatrical tastes of his day, Schikaneder took care to include many supernatural effects, much use of stage machinery and animals, and in Papageno, an eminently attractive role for himself. But *The Magic Flute* was intended to be something more than a fairy-tale entertainment. Mozart and Schikaneder were fellow Masons, and they attempted to write a popular Singspiel that would also glorify the fraternal order to which they belonged.

Since the Masons were (and are) a secret society, an air of mystery has always surrounded *The Magic Flute*. At first glance, it seems the classic tale of the noble prince, Tamino, who wins his princess, Pamina, through adherence to the tenets of virtue, while his humbler counterpart, Papageno, is, for his tribulations, likewise rewarded with a suitable bride. The folklike quality of much of the music, the supposedly magical instruments, the symbolic fire and waterfalls, all conspire to make the opera tremendously appealing, and yet its sheer delight is balanced by its spiritual seriousness.

It is true that *The Magic Flute* libretto contains much inconsistency; the course of the plot changes in midstream. Until the final scenes of the first act, when Sarastro becomes a universal benefactor, he is portrayed as an evil magician; the Queen of the Night is first good—it is she who orders the Ladies to give Tamino the magic flute so that he may save her daughter—and then, when she asks Pamina to murder Sarastro, she is portrayed as evil. Many critics have tried to explain this abrupt shift in the plot, but it is probable that Schikaneder came to a sudden decision to exalt the Masons, and had no time or inclination to change

398

the opening scenes. Other critics have conjectured that Sarastro represents Frederick the Great of Prussia, while the Queen of the Night is Maria Theresa, and Pamina symbolizes the people of Austria—such thoughts may have been in the authors' minds, but it is impossible to verify them.

Taking *The Magic Flute* as we find it, we see that it contains many elements of Masonic philosophy, combined not very skillfully with those devices that Schikaneder considered theatrically effective. Contrary to Mozart's usual practice, the characters become allegorical abstractions: Pamina is Purity; Tamino is Nobility; Sarastro is Good; and the Queen is Evil. One character, however, emerges as fully human and unique—Papageno.

Virtue for Tamino comes as naturally as breathing; without inner conflict or struggle, he rises to every trial and wins his princess. We admire him, but we do not sympathize with him. Papageno, however, is completely fallible, and therefore completely human. From the moment he boasts that it was he who killed the serpent, our sympathies are with him, and soon Papageno's quest for a wife has become as important to us as Tamino's search for Goodness and Truth—Papagena's long-awaited appearance provides the opera with its happiest moment. Papageno is basically unlike the philandering Don Giovanni, unlike the lustful Count in *The Marriage of Figaro,* or the amorous Cherubino in the same opera; he longs not for a variety of sexual experience, but only for a sympathetic wife and for children who will resemble him. It is his honest, unabashed acceptance of his own fears and appetites—and his freedom from pretentiousness—that gives human relevance and perspective to all the symbolic trials of the opera.

Unlike Mozart's other operas, which have to do mainly with the everyday world, *The Magic Flute* transports us to a supernatural realm. Each action of the characters is judged in terms of worthiness and unworthiness, of dignity and debasement, and although these ideas are symbolized rather than treated explicitly, Mozart has embellished them with music of such touching nobility that we do not demand detailed explanations. There is a sense in which the music of *The Magic Flute* is its own subject, for Mozart contemplates not the natural world, but a world of his own making, one where beauty is not an attribute but an essence.

Few other works of art transcend ordinary experience

as completely as does *The Magic Flute* and yet manage
fully to convince us and to carry us into their own auton-
omous realm. It is a measure of this opera's greatness
that a child can enjoy it spontaneously, while learned critics
never tire of interpreting its symbolism and the sublimity
of its harmonies.

ACT ONE

Tamino, a prince, being pursued by a serpent, is rescued by three Ladies, servants of the Queen of the Night, who kill the monster. A birdcatcher, Papageno, enters and boasts that it was he who killed the serpent; as punishment for his dishonesty, the Ladies seal his mouth with a padlock. They vanish, leaving Tamino with a portrait of the Queen's daughter, Pamina, whom the Queen has chosen to be the Prince's bride. The Queen appears, reassuring Tamino of this promise, on the condition that he free her daughter from bondage to Sarastro, whom she describes as an evil magician. The Ladies present Tamino with a magic flute that will protect him in any danger; to Papageno they give magic bells, and they remove the padlock from his mouth. The two young men then set off for Sarastro's palace.

In a room in the palace, Pamina is being threatened by a cruel Moor, Monostatos. Papageno appears suddenly, and Monostatos flees, frightened by the birdcatcher's feathered dress. Papageno tells Pamina of her impending rescue; they sing a duet in praise of love and depart to find Tamino.

Three Spirits lead Tamino to Sarastro's realm; he seeks admittance, and is informed by an old priest that this is the Temple of Wisdom, and that Sarastro took Pamina from her deceitful mother for reasons that cannot yet be revealed. Sarastro and his entourage enter, intercepting Pamina and Papageno, who are still seeking Tamino. Sarastro declares that he cannot yet set Pamina free and that Tamino (who has been brought in by Monostatos) and Papageno must undergo mysterious trials in the Temple of Proof.

ACT TWO

Papageno and Tamino wander through the darkness, conducted by the Speaker and another priest. Tamino is promised ultimate happiness, and Papageno is told that a wife will be his reward; first, however, each must demonstrate the virtues of silence and courage. In a sequence of scenes, the Queen appears to Pamina and gives her a dagger, instructing her to kill Sarastro; Papageno is harrassed by an old woman who insists that he marry her or forever renounce all pleasures of the world; and Tamino is forbidden to speak to Pamina, who is heartbroken at his seeming coldness when they meet. Finally, Pamina and Tamino are united; with the aid of the magic flute, they pass together through the trials of fire and water. Papageno, however, in despair, considers suicide, until the three spirits remind him of his magic bells. He plays and Papagena appears. His elderly bride has become the youthful Papagena; immediately the couple begins to plan a family. Tamino and Pamina are initiated into the joys of Isis and Osiris, and thus the wisdom of Sarastro and the power of sun and life triumph over the Queen of the Night and the forces of evil.

CHARACTERS

TAMINO, *an Egyptian prince*	*Tenor*
THREE LADIES, *servants of the* QUEEN OF THE NIGHT	
Sopranos, or Soprano, Mezzo-soprano, and Contralto	
PAPAGENO, *a birdcatcher*	*Baritone*
QUEEN OF THE NIGHT	*Soprano*
MONOSTATOS, *a Moor, a servant of* SARASTRO	*Tenor*
PAMINA, *daughter of the* QUEEN OF THE NIGHT	*Soprano*
THREE SPIRITS	*Sopranos, or Soprano, Soprano,*
	and Mezzo-soprano
TWO PRIESTS	*Baritones*
OLD PRIEST	*Baritone*
SARASTRO, *high priest of Isis and Osiris*	*Bass*
FIRST PRIEST	*Tenor*
SECOND PRIEST	*Bass*
OLD WOMAN (*later* PAPAGENA)	*Soprano*
TWO MEN IN ARMOR	*Tenor and Bass*
SPEAKER	*Speaking part*
THREE SLAVES *of* SARASTRO	*Speaking parts*
CHORUS *of priests, slaves, others*	

The action takes place in legendary times, in and around the Temple of Isis and Osiris, and in the realm of the QUEEN OF THE NIGHT.

DIE ZAUBERFLÖTE

I. Auftritt

Eine felsige Gegend, hie und da mit Bäumen überwachsen.
TAMINO *kommt im Jagdkleide von einem Felsen herunter mit einem Bogen, aber ohne Pfeil. Eine Schlange verfolgt ihn.*

1. Introduktion

TAMINO: Zu Hilfe! zu Hilfe! sonst bin ich verloren!
Der listigen Schlange zum Opfer erkoren!
Barmherzige Götter! Schon nahet sie sich!
Ach, rettet mich! Ach, schützet mich!
(*Er fällt in Ohnmacht. Die* DREI DAMEN *verschleiert, mit silbernen Wurfspiessen.*)

DREI DAMEN: Stirb, Ungeheuer, durch unsre Macht!
(*Sie stossen die Schlange entzwei.*)
Triumph! Triumph! Sie ist vollbracht,
Die Heldentat! Er ist befreit
Durch unsers Armes Tapferkeit.

ERSTE DAME: Ein holder Jüngling, sanft und schön!

ZWEITE DAME: So schön als ich noch nie gesehn!

DRITTE DAME: Ja, ja, gewiss zum Malen schön!

DREI DAMEN: Würd ich mein Herz der Liebe weihn,
So müsst es dieser Jüngling sein.
Lasst uns zu unsrer Fürstin eilen,
Ihr diese Nachricht zu erteilen.
Vielleicht dass dieser schöne Mann
Die vor'ge Ruhe ihr geben kann.

ERSTE DAME: So geht und sagt es ihr,
Ich bleib indessen hier.

ZWEITE DAME: Nein, nein! geht ihr nur hin,
Ich wache hier für ihn.

DRITTE DAME: Nein, nein! das kann nicht sein,
Ich schütze ihn allein.

ERSTE DAME: Ich bleib indessen hier!

ZWEITE DAME: Ich wache hier für ihn!

DRITTE DAME: Ich schütze ihn allein!

ERSTE DAME: Ich bleibe!

ZWEITE DAME: Ich wache!

ACT ONE

Scene I

A rocky region, overgrown with flowers. TAMINO *comes down from a cliff, dressed as a hunter, with a bow, but no arrows. He is pursued by a serpent.*

1. Introduction

TAMINO: Help me! Help me, or I am lost! The evil serpent pursues me. Gods, have mercy! Already it's upon me! Ah, rescue me! Protect me!
(*He falls into a swoon.* THREE LADIES *appear, with silver spears.*)

THREE LADIES: Die, monster, before our might!
(*They cut the serpent in two.*)
Triumph! Triumph! He is dead; our heroic deed is done! The young man is freed by the strength of our arms!

FIRST LADY: What a noble young man! So gentle and so beautiful!

SECOND LADY: I never saw such a handsome one before!

THIRD LADY: Certainly, he's pretty as a picture!

THREE LADIES: If I should give my heart in love, it would certainly be to this young man! Let's hurry to our queen to relate this information. Perhaps this handsome young man can restore her former peace.

FIRST LADY: Go and tell her about it. Meanwhile, I'll stay here.

SECOND LADY: No, no! you go instead. I'll watch in your place.

THIRD LADY: No, no! that won't do; I'll protect him by myself.

FIRST LADY: I'll stay here!

SECOND LADY: I'll watch here!

THIRD LADY: I'll protect him!

FIRST LADY: I'll stay!

SECOND LADY: I'll watch!

DRITTE DAME: Ich schütze!
DREI DAMEN: Ich! Ich! Ich!
Ich sollte fort? Ei, ei! Wie fein!
Sie wären gern bei ihm allein.
Nein, nein, das kann nicht sein!
Was wollte ich darum nicht geben
Könnt ich mit diesem Jüngling leben!
Hätt ich ihn doch so ganz allein!
Doch keine geht, es kann nicht sein!
Am besten ist es nun, ich geh—
Du Jüngling, schön und liebevoll,
Du trauter Jüngling, lebe wohl
Bis ich dich wieder seh. (*Sie gehen.*)

Dialog

TAMINO (*erwacht*): Wo bin ich? Ist's Phantasie, dass ich
noch lebe? oder hat eine höhere Macht mich gerettet? Wie?
—Die bösartige Schlange liegt tot zu meinen Füssen?
(*Man hört von hinten ein Waldflötchen.*)
Was hör' ich?—Ha, eine männliche Figur nähert sich dem
Tal.
(PAPAGENO *kommt einen Fussteig herunter, hat auf dem
Rücken eine grosse Vogelsteige, worin Verschiedene Vögel
sind. In der Hand hat er eine kleine Waldflöte.*)

2. Arie

PAPAGENO: Der Vogelfänger bin ich ja!
Stets lustig, heisa, hopsasa!
Ich Vogelfänger bin bekannt
Bei Alt und Jung im ganzen Land.
Weiss mit dem Locken umzugehn
Und mich aufs Pfeifen zu verstehn.
Drum kann ich froh und lustig sein,
Denn alle Vögel sind ja mein.
Der Vogelfänger bin ich ja—
Ein Netz für Mädchen möchte ich,
Ich fing sie dutzendweis für mich!
Dann sperrte ich sie bei mir ein,
Und alle Mädchen wären mein.
Wenn alle Mädchen wären mein,
So tauschte ich brav Zucker ein,
Die, welche mir am liebsten wär,
Der gäb ich gleich den Zucker her.
Und küsste sie mich zärtlich dann,
Wär sie mein Weib und ich ihr Mann.

THIRD LADY: I'll protect!

THREE LADIES: I! I! I! Shall I go? Well, well, how clever! Each one would like to remain with him alone—no, no, that cannot be! What wouldn't I give if I could only live with this young man! If I could have him all to myself—but they won't go—it cannot be! Now it is best for me to go. Trusty young man, farewell, until I see you again! (*They exit.*)

Dialogue

TAMINO (*regaining consciousness*): Where am I? Is it a dream that I'm still alive? Or has a higher power rescued me? What?—The evil serpent is lying dead at my feet! (*The sound of a wooden pipe is heard off-stage.*) What do I hear?— Something resembling a man approaches the valley.

(PAPAGENO *enters, dressed in feathers and carrying a bird-cage with a variety of birds in it. He has a little wooden flute in his hand.*)

2. Aria

PAPAGENO: I'm the famous birdcatcher. I'm always gay and happy, tra, la, la! Everyone throughout the countryside, young and old, everyone knows me. I lure the birds with my pipe and catch them with my net, and so I'm happy and gay, because they all are mine! I'm the famous bird-catcher— I would like to make a net for girls, and I would catch them by the dozens, like birds! Then I would keep them near me, and all the girls would be mine! And when all the girls were mine, I would find some delicious sugar and give it to the one I liked the best. Then she would kiss me tenderly if she were my wife and I her husband. She would sleep by my side and I would rock her to sleep like a child!

(*He blows his pipes, and goes toward the exit.*)

Sie schlief an meiner Seite ein,
Ich wiegte wie ein Kind sie ein.
(*Pfeift, will nach der Arie nach der Pforte gehen.*)

Dialog

TAMINO: He da!

PAPAGENO: Was da?

TAMINO: Sag mir, du lustiger Freund, wer du bist?

PAPAGENO: Wer ich bin? Dumme Frage!—Ein Mensch, wie du. Wenn ich dich nun fragte, wer du bist?

TAMINO: So würde ich dir antworten, dass ich aus fürstlichem Geblüte bin.

PAPAGENO: Das ist mir zu hoch. Musst dich deutlicher erklären, wenn ich dich verstehen soll!

TAMINO: Mein Vater ist ein Fürst, der über viele Länder und Menschen herrscht; darum nennt man mich Prinz.

PAPAGENO: Länder?—Menschen?—Prinz?—Sagst du mir zuvor: gibt's ausser diesen Bergen auch noch Länder und Menschen?

TAMINO: Viele Tausende!

PAPAGENO: Da liess sich eine Spekulation mit meinen Vögeln machen.

TAMINO: Wie nennt man eigentlich diese Gegend? Wer beherrscht sie?

PAPAGENO: Das kann ich dir ebenso wenig sagen, als ich weiss, wie ich auf die Welt gekommen bin.

TAMINO (*lacht*): Wie? Du wüsstest nicht, wo du geboren, oder wer deine Eltern waren?

PAPAGENO: Kein Wort! Ich weiss nur so viel, dass nicht weit von hier meine Strohhütte steht, die mich vor Regen und Kälte schützt.

TAMINO: Aber wie lebst du?

PAPAGENO: Von Essen und Trinken, wie alle Menschen.

TAMINO: Wodurch erhältst du das?

PAPAGENO: Durch Tausch—ich fange für die sternflammende Königin und ihre Jungfrauen verschiedene Vögel; dafür erhalte ich täglich Speise und Trank von ihr.

TAMINO: Sternflammende Königin? Sag mir, guter Freund, warst du schon so glücklich, diese Göttin der Nacht zu sehen?

PAPAGENO: Sehen? Die sternflammende Königin sehen?—

Dialogue

TAMINO: Come back!

PAPAGENO: Who is it?

TAMINO: Tell me, my happy friend, Who are you?

PAPAGENO: Who am I? Stupid question!— A man, like you! And if I asked you who you were?

TAMINO: Then I would answer that I am a prince of royal blood.

PAPAGENO: That's too complicated for me. You must explain that if I am to understand you!

TAMINO: My father rules over many men and lands; therefore, I am called a prince.

PAPAGENO: Lands?—Men?—Prince?—Tell me, Are there any other men and lands beside this one?

TAMINO: Many thousands!

PAPAGENO: Then perhaps I could sell some birds there.

TAMINO: What is this realm called? Who rules it?

PAPAGENO: That I can no more answer than I could tell you how I came into this world.

TAMINO (*laughing*): What? You don't know where you were born or who you parents were?

PAPAGENO: Not a word! I only know that not far from here is my thatched hut, which protects me from the rain and the cold.

TAMINO: But how do you live?

PAPAGENO: By eating and drinking, like all men.

TAMINO: How do you get it?

PAPAGENO: By trading— I catch birds for the star-flaming Queen and her ladies; in return I get food and drink from them.

TAMINO: Star-flaming Queen? Tell me, good friend, Have you been so fortunate as to see the Queen of the Night?

PAPAGENO: To see her? To see the star-flaming Queen!—

Welcher Sterbliche kann sich rühmen, sie je gesehn zu haben? (*für sich*) Wie er mich so starr anblickt! Bald fang ich an, mich vor ihm zu fürchten. (*laut*) Warum siehst du so verdächtig und schelmisch nach mir?

TAMINO: Weil—weil ich zweifle, ob du ein Mensch bist.

PAPAGENO: Wie war das?

TAMINO: Nach deinen Federn, die dich bedecken, halt ich dich—

PAPAGENO: Doch für keinen Vogel? Bleib zurück, sag ich, und traue mir nicht; denn ich habe Riesenkraft. (*für sich*) Wenn er sich nicht bald von mir schrecken lässt, so lauf ich davon.

TAMINO: Riesenkraft? Also, warst du wohl gar mein Erretter, der diese giftige Schlange bekämpfte?

PAPAGENO: Schlange! Ist sie tot oder lebendig?

TAMINO: Freund, wie hast du dieses Ungeheuer bekämpft? Du bist ohne Waffen.

PAPAGENO: Brauch keine! Bei mir ist ein starker Druck mit der Hand mehr als Waffen.

TAMINO: Du hast sie also erdrosselt?

PAPAGENO: Erdrosselt! Bin in meinem Leben nicht so stark gewesen, als heute.

(*Die* DREI DAMEN *erscheinen verschleiert.*)

DREI DAMEN: Papageno!

PAPAGENO: Aha, dass geht mich an! (*zu* TAMINO) Sieh dich um, Freund!

TAMINO: Wer sind diese Damen?

PAPAGENO: Wer sie eigentlich sind, weiss ich selbst nicht. Ich weiss nur so viel, dass sie mir täglich meine Vögel abnehmen, und mir dafür Wein, Zuckerbrot und süsse Feigen bringen.

TAMINO: Sie sind vermutlich sehr schön?

PAPAGENO: Ich denke nicht! Denn wenn sie schön wären, würden sie ihre Gesichter nicht bedecken.

DREI DAMEN: Papageno!

PAPAGENO: (*beiseite zu* TAMINO): Sei still! Sie drohen mir schon. (*laut*) Du fragst, ob sie schön sind, und ich kann dir darauf nichts antworten, als dass ich in meinem Leben nichts Reizenderes sah. (*für sich*) Jetzt werden sie bald wieder gut werden.

What mortal can say that he has seen her? (*to himself*) How he looks at me! Soon I shall begin to fear him! (*aloud*) Why do you look at me so strangely?

TAMINO: Because—because I was deciding whether you're a man.

PAPAGENO: Why?

TAMINO: From the feathers that cover you, I took you for—

PAPAGENO: For some kind of bird? Keep away, I tell you, and beware of me, because I have gigantic strength! (*to himself*) If I don't frighten him soon, I will have to run away.

TAMINO: Gigantic strength? Then it was you who rescued me from this evil serpent?

PAPAGENO: Serpent? Is it living or dead?

TAMINO: Friend, how did you fight this monster? You are without weapons.

PAPAGENO: I don't need any! With me, a strong squeeze of the hand is more than a weapon.

TAMINO: You choked it, then?

PAPAGENO: Choked it! I've never been so strong in my life as today.

(THREE LADIES *enter, veiled.*)

THREE LADIES: Papageno!

PAPAGENO: Ah, they're watching me. (*to* TAMINO) Be careful, my friend!

TAMINO: Who are these ladies?

PAPAGENO: Who they really are, not even I know. I only know that every day they take my birds and bring me wine, sugar bread, and sweet figs in exchange.

TAMINO: Are they really very beautiful?

PAPAGENO: I don't think so. If they were really beautiful, they wouldn't cover their faces.

THREE LADIES: Papageno!

PAPAGENO (*aside to* TAMINO): Be still! They want something of me. (*aloud*) You ask if they are beautiful, and I can only answer that I have never seen greater charm in my entire life. (*to himself*) That should keep them happy.

411

DREI DAMEN (*noch näher tretend, drohender*): Papageno!

PAPAGENO: Was muss ich denn heute verbrochen haben, dass sie so aufgebracht wider mich sind?—Hier, meine Schönen, übergeb ich euch meine Vögel.

ERSTE DAME (*reicht ihm ein Gefäss mit Wasser*): Dafür schickt dir unsere Fürstin heute zum ersten Mal statt Wein, reines, klares Wasser.

ZWEITE DAME: Und mir befahl sie, dass ich, statt Zuckerbrot, diesen Stein dir überbringen soll. Ich wünsche, dass er dir wohl bekommen möge.

PAPAGENO: Was? Steine soll ich fressen?

DRITTE DAME: Und statt der süssen Feigen, hab ich die Ehre, dir dies goldene Schloss vor den Mund zu schlagen. (*Sie hängt ihm das Schloss vor den Mund.*)

ERSTE DAME: Du willst vermutlich wissen, warum die Fürstin dich heute so wunderbar bestraft?
(PAPAGENO *bejaht es durch Nicken mit dem Kopf.*)

ZWEITE DAME: Damit du künftig nie mehr Fremde belügst.

DRITTE DAME: Und dass du nie dich der Heldentaten rühmest, die andere vollzogen haben.

ERSTE DAME: Sag an! Hast du diese Schlange bekämpft?
(PAPAGENO *verneint es, durch Schütteln mit dem Kopf.*)

ZWEITE DAME: Wer denn also?
(PAPAGENO *deutet an, dass er es nicht weiss.*)

DRITTE DAME (*zu* TAMINO): Wir waren's, Jüngling, die dich befreiten. Hier, dies Gemälde schickt dir die grosse Fürstin: es ist das Bildnis ihrer Tochter. "Findest du," sagte sie, "das diese Züge dir nicht gleichgültig sind, dann ist Glück, Ehr' und Ruhm dein Los!" Auf Wiedersehen. (*Geht ab.*)

ZWEITE DAME: Adieu, Monsieur Papageno! (*Geht ab.*)

ERSTE DAME: Fein nicht zu hastig getrunken!
(*Geht lachend ab.* PAPAGENO *eilt ab.*)

3. Arie

TAMINO (*blickt das Bildnis an*): Dies Bildnis ist bezaubernd schön,
Wie noch kein Auge je gesehn!
Ich fühl es, wie dies Götterbild
Mein Herz mit neuer Regung füllt.
Dies Etwas kann ich zwar nicht nennen,

THREE LADIES (*coming closer, in threatening tones*): Papageno!

PAPAGENO: What rule have I broken today to make them so angry?—Here, my beauties—here are my birds.

FIRST LADY (*giving him a jug of water*): For your birds, our Queen sends you today, instead of wine, pure, clear water.

SECOND LADY: And she ordered me, instead of sugar bread, to bring this stone to you. I hope it will bring you good health!

PAPAGENO: What? I must chew on stones?

THIRD LADY: And instead of sweet figs, I have the honor of locking your mouth with this golden padlock.
(*She locks his mouth, so that he cannot speak.*)

FIRST LADY: You would really like to know why our Queen punishes you so strangely today?
(PAPAGENO *nods his head.*)

SECOND LADY: So that you won't lie to strangers any more!

THIRD LADY: And so that you won't claim for yourself the heroic deeds of others.

FIRST LADY: Now continue! Papageno, was it really you who killed this serpent?
(PAPAGENO *denies it by shaking his head.*)

SECOND LADY: Who was it then?
(PAPAGENO *indicates that he does not know.*)

THIRD LADY (*to* TAMINO): We befriended you, young man! Here; this portrait was sent you by our great Queen; it's the picture of her daughter, Pamina. "If you find these features attractive," she says, "then joy, honor, and glory will be your reward." Good-by! (*Exits.*)

SECOND LADY: Adieu, Monsieur Papageno! (*Exits.*)

FIRST LADY: Don't drink too quickly!
(*Exits, laughing.* PAPAGENO *quickly exits.*)

3. Aria

TAMINO (*contemplating the portrait*): This portrait has a magical beauty—beyond what any human eyes have seen! I feel it—this image fills my heart with a new joy! It is past expression, but I sense it burning like a fire. Can this discovery be love? Yes, love is one; it is unique. Oh, if I could only find her now! Oh, if only she stood before me!

Doch fühl ich's hier wie Feuer brennen.
Soll die Empfindung Liebe sein?
Ja, ja die Liebe ist's allein!
O wenn ich sie nur finden könnte!
O wenn sie doch schon vor mir stände!
Ich würde, würde, warm und rein,
Was würde ich? Ich würde sie voll Entzücken
An diesen heissen Busen drücken,
Und ewig wäre sie dann mein!
(*Die* DREI DAMEN *erscheinen.*)

Dialog

ERSTE DAME: Rüste dich mit Mut und Standhaftigkeit, schöner Jüngling! Die Fürstin—

ZWEITE DAME: Hat mir aufgetragen, dir zu sagen—

DRITTE DAME: Dass der Weg zu deinem künftigen Glücke nunmehr gebahnt sei.

ERSTE DAME: Sie hat jedes deiner Worte gehört; sie hat—

ZWEITE DAME: Jeden Zug in deinem Gesichte gelesen—

DRITTE DAME: Hat beschlossen, dich ganz glücklich zu machen. "Hat dieser Jüngling," sprach sie, "auch so viel Mut und Tapferkeit, als er zärtlich ist, O, so ist meine Tochter ganz gewiss gerettet."

TAMINO: Kommt, Mädchen, führt mich! Sie sei gerettet! Das schwöre ich bei meiner Liebe, bei meinem Herzen! (*Kurzer starker Donner.*)
Ihr Götter, was ist das?
(*Es wird dunkel.*)

DREI DAMEN: Fasse dich!

ERSTE DAME: Es verkündet die Ankunft unserer Königin. (*Donner.*)

DREI DAMEN: Sie kommt!
(*Donner.*)
Sie kommt!
(*Donner.*)
Sie kommt!
(*Die Berge teilen sich, man erblickt einen Sternenhimmel und den Thron der* KÖNIGIN DER NACHT.)

4. Arie

KÖNIGIN DER NACHT: O zitt're nicht, mein lieber Sohn!
Du bist unschuldig, weise, fromm.
Ein Jüngling, so wie du, vermag am besten,

I would—I would—warmly and purely— What would I do? I would draw her gently to me, and eternally she would be mine!
(*The* THREE LADIES *re-enter.*)

Dialogue

FIRST LADY: Handsome youth, arm yourself with courage and strength! The Queen—

SECOND LADY: Has ordered me to tell you—

THIRD LADY: That the way to your future happiness is now open.

FIRST LADY: She has heard every word; she has—

SECOND LADY: Read every expression of your face—

THIRD LADY: She has decided to complete your happiness. "If this youth," she said, "is as brave and strong as he is tender, then my daughter will certainly be rescued!"

TAMINO: Come, ladies, lead me! I will rescue her! I swear that by my life, by my heart's salvation!
(*Thunder is heard.*)
God, what is that?
(*It becomes dark.*)

THREE LADIES: Do not fear!

FIRST LADY: Our Queen arrives!
(*Thunder.*)

THREE LADIES: She's coming!
(*Thunder.*)
She's coming!
(*Thunder.*)
She's coming!
(*The mountains part. The* QUEEN OF THE NIGHT *appears against a starry sky.*)

4. *Aria*

QUEEN OF THE NIGHT: Oh, do not tremble, my dear son. You are pure, wise, and brave. A youth like yourself would be the best person to entrust with my deep maternal sor-

Dies tiefbetrübte Mutterherz zu trösten.
Zum Leiden bin ich auserkoren,
Denn meine Tochter fehlet mir;
Durch sie ging all mein Glück verloren:
Ein Bösewicht entfloh mit ihr.
Noch sehe ich ihr Zittern
Mit bangem Erschüttern,
Ihr ängstliches Beben,
Ihr schüchternes Streben.
Ich musste sie mir rauben sehen:
Ach helft! ach helft! war alles, was sie sprach.
Allein vergebens war ihr Flehen,
Denn meine Hilfe war zu schwach.
Du wirst sie zu befreien gehen,
Du wirst der Tochter Retter sein.
Und werd ich dich als Sieger sehen,
So sei sie dann auf ewig dein.
(*Mit den* DREI DAMEN *ab. Das Theater verwandelt sich wieder, so wie es vorher war.*)

   Dialog

TAMINO (*nach einer Pause*): Ist's denn auch Wirklichkeit, was ich sah? O ihr guten Götter, täuscht mich nicht!
(*Er will sich entfernen,* PAPAGENO *tritt ihm in den Weg.*)

   5. Quintett

PAPAGENO (*deutet traurig auf das Schloss am Mund*): Hm, hm, hm, hm, hm!

TAMINO: Der Arme kann von Strafe sagen,
Denn seine Sprache ist dahin.

PAPAGENO: Hm, hm, hm, hm, hm, hm!

TAMINO: Ich kann nichts tun, als dich beklagen,
Weil ich zu schwach zu helfen bin.
(*Die* DREI DAMEN *erscheinen, und treten zwischen* TAMINO *und* PAPAGENO.)

ERSTE DAME: Die Königin begnadigt dich,
Erlässt die Strafe dir durch mich.
(*Sie nimmt ihm das Schloss vom Munde.*)

PAPAGENO: Nun plaudert Papageno wieder!

ZWEITE DAME: Ja, plaud're, lüge nur nicht wieder!

PAPAGENO: Ich lüge nimmermehr, nein, nein!

DREI DAMEN: Dies Schloss soll deine Warnung sein.

PAPAGENO: Dies Schloss soll meine Warnung sein.

416

row! Without my dear child I am forsaken in sadness. With her, all my happiness has vanished. A demon has stolen her from me! I can still see her trembling and overwhelmed. Her horror—her helpless resistance! I saw her taken from me. "Ah, help; ah, help," was all that she cried. But her pleading was in vain, and my efforts were too weak. Prince, you are sent to befriend her; you will be my daughter's savior! And when you have gained the victory, then she'll be forever yours.

(*She exits with the* THREE LADIES. *The theater changes back into the rocky landscape as before.*)

Dialogue

TAMINO (*after a pause*): Was that reality that I saw? O benevolent Gods, do not deceive me!

(*He starts to leave;* PAPAGENO, *entering, blocks his way.*)

5. Quintet

PAPAGENO (*pointing sadly to the padlock still in his mouth*): Hm, hm, hm, hm, hm!

TAMINO: This poor man is punished and cannot speak.

PAPAGENO: Hm, hm, hm, hm, hm, hm!

TAMINO: I can do nothing to relieve your suffering, for I am powerless.

(*The* THREE LADIES *enter, and step between* PAPAGENO *and* TAMINO.)

FIRST LADY: The Queen forgives you, and has bidden me to release you.

(*She unlocks the padlock.*)

PAPAGENO: Now Papageno will chatter once again!

SECOND LADY: Yes, chatter, but no more lying!

PAPAGENO: No, no, I'll never lie again!

THREE LADIES: This lock shall be your warning.

PAPAGENO: This lock shall be my warning!

417

ALLE: Bekämen doch die Lügner alle
Ein solches Schloss vor ihren Mund:
Statt Hass, Verleumdung, schwarzer Galle,
Bestünde Lieb und Bruderbund.

ERSTE DAME (*gibt* TAMINO *eine goldene Flöte*): O Prinz,
nimm dies Geschenk von mir!
Dies sendet unsre Fürstin dir.
Die Zauberflöte wird dich schützen,
Im grössten Unglück unterstützen.

DREI DAMEN: Hiermit kannst du allmächtig handeln,
Der Menschen Leidenschaft verwandeln:
Der Traurige wird freudig sein,
Den Hagestolz nimmt Liebe ein.

ALLE: O so eine Flöte ist mehr als Gold und Kronen wert,
Denn durch sie wird Menschenglück und Zufriedenheit
vermehrt.

PAPAGENO: Nun, ihr schönen Frauenzimmer,
Darf ich, so empfehl ich mich.

DREI DAMEN: Dich empfehlen kannst du immer,
Doch bestimmt die Fürstin dich,
Mit dem Prinzen ohn Velweilen
Nach Sarastros Burg zu eilen.

PAPAGENO: Nein, dafür bedank ich mich!
Von euch selber hörte ich,
Dass er wie ein Tigertier.
Sicher liess ohn alle Gnaden
Mich Sarastro rupfen, braten,
Setzte mich den Hunden für.

DREI DAMEN: Dich schützt der Prinz, trau ihm allein.
Dafür sollst du sein Diener sein.

PAPAGENO (*für sich*): Dass doch der Prinz beim Teufel
wäre!
Mein Leben ist mir lieb;
Am Ende schleicht, bei meiner Ehre,
Er von mir wie ein Dieb.

ERSTE DAME (*gibt* PAPAGENO *ein Glockenspiel*): Hier,
nimm dies Kleinod, es ist dein.

PAPAGENO: Ei, ei! Was mag darinnen sein?

DREI DAMEN: Darinnen hörst du Glöckchen tönen.

PAPAGENO: Werd ich sie auch wohl spielen können?

ALL: If every liar could be given such a lock for his mouth, then hatred and slander would turn to love and brotherhood!

FIRST LADY (*giving* TAMINO *a golden flute*): O Prince, accept the gift sent to you by our queen. This magic flute will protect you in the greatest danger.

THREE LADIES: Whenever you play it, sorrows will be transformed. The hateful heart will learn to love.

ALL: A flute like this is worth more than gold, for through it, one's goals may be attained.

PAPAGENO: Now, my lovely ladies, may I go?

THREE LADIES: No, you must obey us. The Queen asks you to hasten with the Prince to Sarastro's castle.

PAPAGENO: No, thank you! You've told me yourselves that he's fierce as a tiger, and that he will roast and cook me and feed me to his dogs!

THREE LADIES: The Prince will protect you; trust only him, and follow him as his servant.

PAPAGENO (*to himself*): I wish the Prince would go to the devil! My own life is too dear to me! At the crucial moment, he'll steal from my side like a thief!

FIRST LADY (*giving a box to* PAPAGENO): Here, take this little treasure; it's destined for you.

PAPAGENO: Well, then! What can be in it?

THREE LADIES: From inside you may hear the notes of bells.

PAPAGENO: Will I, too, be able to play them?

DREI DAMEN: O ganz gewiss, ja, ja gewiss!

ALLE: Silberglöckchen, Zauberflöten
Sind zu eurem Schutz vonnöten
Lebet wohl! Wir wollen gehn
Lebet wohl, auf Wiedersehn!

TAMINO: Doch, schöne Damen, saget an:—

PAPAGENO: Wie man die Burg wohl finden kann?

DREI DAMEN: Drei Knäbchen, jung, schön, hold und weise,
Umschweben euch auf eurer Reise;
Sie werden eure Führer sein,
Folgt ihrem Rate ganz allein

ALLE: So lebet wohl! Wir wollen geh'n
Lebt wohl, lebt wohl, auf Wiederseh'n! (*Alle ab.*)

II. Auftritt

Ein prächtiges ägyptisches Zimmer. MONOSTATOS *kommt,
mit* PAMINA. DREI SKLAVEN *tragen schöne Polster.*

6. *Terzett*

MONOSTATOS: Du feines Täubchen, nur herein!

PAMINA: O welche Marter, welche Pein!

MONOSTATOS: Verloren ist dein Leben!

PAMINA: Der Tod macht mich nicht beben,
Nur meine Mutter dauert mich;
Sie stirbt vor Gram ganz sicherlich!

MONOSTATOS: He, Sklaven, legt ihr Fesseln an!
Mein Hass soll dich verderben!

PAMINA: Lass mich lieber sterben,
Weil nichts, Barbar, dich rühren kann!
(*Sie sinkt ohnmächtig auf ein Sofa.*)

MONOSTATOS: Nun fort! Lass mich bei ihr allein!
(*Die* SKLAVEN *gehen ab.* PAPAGENO *von aussen am Fenster.*)

PAPAGENO: Wo bin ich wohl? Wo mag ich sein?
Aha! da find ich Leute.
Gewagt ich geh' hinein.
(*Geht herein.*)

Schön Mädchen, jung und fein,
Viel weisser noch als Kreide.
(MONOSTATOS *und* PAPAGENO *besehen sich; erschrecken
einer über den andern.*)

420

THREE LADIES: Oh, certainly!

ALL: Silver bells, a magic flute—are all that we need to protect us. Now we must depart. Farewell, until we meet again.

TAMINO: But, fair ladies, tell me first—

PAPAGENO: How can we find Sarastro's castle?

THREE LADIES: Three youthful spirits, gracious and wise, will guide you on your journey. Follow their advice alone.

ALL: Farewell, until we meet again! (*Exit.*)

Scene II

An elaborate Egyptian room in SARASTRO'S *castle.* MONO-STATOS *drags in* PAMINA. THREE SLAVES *enter, carrying embroidered pillows.*

6. Trio

MONOSTATOS: You sweet little dove, come with me!

PAMINA: Oh, what torture, what pain!

MONOSTATOS: Your life is ended!

PAMINA: Death doesn't frighten me, but I cannot endure my mother's sorrow; she'll die of grief!

MONOSTATOS: Slaves, bring irons and put them on her! My hatred shall destroy you!

PAMINA: Rather let me die! Will nothing calm you, monster?
(*She faints on the couch.*)

MONOSTATOS: Now, leave us! Let me be alone with her!
(*The* SLAVES *exit.* PAPAGENO *appears at the window.*)

PAPAGENO: Where am I now? What shall I do? Aha, there I see some people! Very well, I'll go inside.
(*He goes inside.*)

Pretty maiden, young and dainty, much whiter than chalk—
(*He sees* MONOSTATOS, *who notices him at the same time.*)

421

BEIDE: Hu! das ist der Teufel sicherlich!
Hab Mitleid! Verschone mich! Hu, hu, hu! (*Laufen beide ab.*)

Dialog

PAMINA (*spricht wie im Traum*): Mutter—Mutter—Mutter! Wie? Noch schlägt dies Herz? Zu neuen Qualen erwacht? O, das ist hart, sehr hart! Mir bitterer, als der Tod.

PAPAGENO (*tritt ein*): Bin ich nicht ein Narr, dass ich mich schrecken liess? Es gibt ja schwarze Vögel in der Welt, warum denn nicht auch schwarze Menschen? Ah, sieh da! Hier ist das schöne Mädchen noch. Du Tochter der nächtlichen Königin—

PAMINA: Nächtlichen Königin? Wer bist du?

PAPAGENO: Ein Abgesandter der sternflammenden Königin.

PAMINA: Meiner Mutter? O Wonne! Dein Name?

PAPAGENO: Papageno.

PAMINA: Papageno?—Papageno?—ich erinnere mich, den Namen oft gehört zu haben, dich selbst aber sah ich nie.

PAPAGENO: Ich dich ebenso wenig.

PAMINA: Du kennst also meine gute, zärtliche Mutter?

PAPAGENO: Wenn du die Tochter der nächtlichen Königin bist—ja!

PAMINA: O ich bin es.

PAPAGENO: Das will ich gleich erkennen.
(*Er sieht das Portrait an.*)
Die Augen schwarz—richtig, schwarz. Die Lippen rot—richtig, rot. Blonde Haare—blonde Haare. Alles trifft ein, bis auf Hände und Füsse. Nach dem Gemälde zu schliessen, sollst du weder Hände noch Füsse haben; denn hier sind keine angezegt.

PAMINA: Erlaube mir—Ja, ich bin's! Wie kam es in deine Hände?

PAPAGENO: Ich muss dir das umständlicher erzählen. Ich kam heute früh, wie gewöhnlich, zu deiner Mutter Palast mit meiner Lieferung—

PAMINA: Lieferung?

PAPAGENO: Ja, ich liefere deiner Mutter und ihren Jungfrauen schon seit vielen Jahren alle die schönen Vögel in den Palast. Eben als ich im Begriff war, meine Vögel

BOTH: Hoo! That certainly must be the devil! Have mercy! Spare me! Hoo, hoo, hoo! (*Both run out.*)

Dialogue

PAMINA (*speaking as though in a dream*): Mother, mother! What, is my heart still beating? Do I awaken to new grief? Oh, this is hard, so hard! It is more bitter to me than death!

PAPAGENO (*reappearing at the window*): Wasn't I stupid to be afraid? There are black birds in the world. Then, why not black men? Ah, look over there! the lovely maiden is still here. You, daughter of the Queen of the Night—

PAMINA: Queen of the Night? Who are you?

PAPAGENO: A messenger of the star-flaming Queen.

PAMINA: My mother? What joy! Your name?

PAPAGENO: Papageno.

PAMINA: Papageno! I have often heard that name, but I never actually saw you.

PAPAGENO: I never saw you either.

PAMINA: Then you know my good, tender mother?

PAPAGENO: If you are the daughter of the Queen of the Night—yes!

PAMINA: Oh, yes I am.

PAPAGENO: I'll confirm that at once.
(*He looks at the portrait that he carries.*)
The eyes are black— Right, black. The lips are red— Right, red. Blonde hair— Blonde hair. Everything is as it should be except for the hands and feet. According to the picture, you have none, for none are painted here.

PAMINA: Show it to me—yes, it is I. How did it come into your hands?

PAPAGENO: I must tell you a long story. Today, I came early, as usual, to your mother's palace for my delivery—

PAMINA: Your delivery?

PAPAGENO: Yes, I deliver to your mother and her young ladies in the palace, as many birds as I can catch. When I was there, I saw a young man who called himself a

423

abzugeben, sah ich einen Menschen vor mir, der sich Prinz nennen lässt. Dieser Prinz hat deine Mutter so eingenommen, dass sie ihm dein Bildnis schenkte und ihm befahl, dich zu befreien. Sein Entschluss war so schnell, als seine Liebe zu dir.

PAMINA: Liebe? Er liebt mich also? O, sage mir das noch einmal, ich höre das Wort Liebe gar zu gern.

PAPAGENO: Das glaube ich dir, du bist ja ein Mädchen. Wo blieb ich denn?

PAMINA: Bei der Liebe.

PAPAGENO: Richtig, bei der Liebe! Das nenn ich ein Gedächtnis haben! Komm, du wirst Augen machen, wenn du den schönen Jüngling erblickst.

PAMINA: Wohl denn, es sei gewagt! Aber wenn dies ein Fallstrick wäre—wenn dieser nun ein böser Geist von Sarastros Gefolge wäre?

PAPAGENO: Ich ein böser Geist? Wo denkst du hin? Ich bin der beste Geist von der Welt.

PAMINA: Vergib, vergib, wenn ich dich beleidigte! Du hast ein gefühlvolles Herz.

PAPAGENO: Ach, freilich habe ich ein gefühlvolles Herz! Aber was nützt mir das alles? Ich möchte mir oft alle meine Federn ausrupfen, wenn ich bedenke dass Papageno noch keine Papagena hat.

PAMINA: Armer Mann! Du hast also noch kein Weib?

PAPAGENO: Noch nicht einmal ein Mädchen, viel weniger ein Weib!—Und unsereiner hat doch auch bisweilen seine lustigen Stunden, wo man gern gesellschaftliche Unterhaltung haben möchte.

PAMINA: Geduld, Freund! Der Himmel wird auch für dich sorgen; er wird dir eine Freundin schicken, ehe du dir's vermutest.

PAPAGENO: Wenn er sie nur bald schickte!

7. Duett

PAMINA: Bei Männern, welche Liebe fühlen,
Fehlt auch ein gutes Herze nicht.

PAPAGENO: Die süssen Triebe mitzufühlen,
Ist dann der Weiber erste Pflicht.

BEIDE: Wir wollen uns der Liebe freu'n,
Wir leben durch die Lieb allein.

prince. This prince so pleased your mother that she gave him your picture and sent him to rescue you. His decision was as sudden as his love for you.

PAMINA: Love? Then he loves me? Oh, repeat that again! It makes me so happy to hear the word "love"!

PAPAGENO: That I can believe; you're a girl. Where was I?

PAMINA: You spoke of love.

PAPAGENO: That's right; I spoke of love. That's what I call having a memory! Come—you will stare when you see that handsome young prince.

PAMINA: Well, then, let's be going! But suppose this is another trick? Suppose you are only an evil spirit of Sarastro's?

PAPAGENO: I, an evil spirit? What are you thinking of? I'm always in the best of spirits.

PAMINA: Forgive me if I've offended you. You have a heart filled with good feelings.

PAPAGENO: Yes, of course I have a good heart. But what use is it to me? Often I want to tear out all my feathers when I think that Papageno still hasn't found a Papagena!

PAMINA: Poor man! Then you haven't a wife?

PAPAGENO: Not even a sweetheart, much less a wife!— And I long for the time when I will enjoy her company.

PAMINA: Patience, Friend! Heaven will take care of you; it will send you a wife sooner than you imagine.

PAPAGENO: If only it would send her soon!

7. Duet

PAMINA: A man who can feel love has goodness in his heart!

PAPAGENO: To share the sweet instinct is a woman's first duty!

BOTH: Then let us enjoy love; we are sustained by love alone!

PAMINA: Die Lieb versüsset jede Plage,
Ihr opfert jede Kreatur.

PAPAGENO: Sie würzet uns're Lebenstage,
Sie wirkt im Kreise der Natur.

BEIDE: Ihr hoher Zweck zeigt deutlich an,
Nichts Edlers sei, als Weib und Mann.
Mann und Weib, und Weib und Mann
Reichen an die Gottheit an. (*Beide ab.*)

III. Auftritt

*Ein Hain. Ganz im Hintergrunde der Bühne ist ein Tempel
worauf diese Worte stehen: Tempel der Weisheit. Dieser
Tempel führt mit Säulen zu zwei Tempeln, rechts auf dem
einen steht: Tempel der Vernuft. Links steht: Tempel der
Natur.* DREI KNABEN *führen* TAMINO *herein.*

8. Finale

DREI KNABEN: Zum Ziele führt dich diese Bahn,
Doch musst du, Jüngling, männlich siegen.
Drum höre unsre Lehre an:
Sei standhaft, duldsam und verschwiegen!

TAMINO: Ihr holden Knaben, sagt mir an,
Ob ich Pamina retten kann?

DREI KNABEN: Dies kund zu tun, steht uns nicht an:
Sei standhaft, duldsam und verschwiegen!
Bedenke dies; kurz, sei ein Mann,
Dann, Jüngling, wirst du männlich siegen. (*Gehen ab.*)

TAMINO: Die Weisheitslehre dieser Knaben
Sei ewig mir ins Herz gegraben.
Wo bin ich nun? Was wird mit mir?
Ist dies der Sitz der Götter hier?
Es zeigen die Pforten, es zeigen die Säulen,
Dass Klugheit und Arbeit und Künste hier weilen;
Wo Tätigkeit thronet und Müssiggang weicht,
Erhält seine Herrschaft das Laster nicht leicht.
Ich wage mich mutig zur Pforte hinein,
Die Absicht ist edel und lauter und rein.
Erzitt're, feiger Bösewicht!
Pamina retten ist mir Pflicht.
(*Er geht an die Pforte zur rechten Seite.*)

PRIESTER (*von innen*): Zurück!

TAMINO: Zurück? So wag ich hier mein Glück!
(*Er geht zur linken Pforte.*)

PAMINA: Love comforts every trouble; it exists in every creature.

PAPAGENO: It seasons all the days of our lives; it works in the whole realm of nature.

BOTH: The high goal is clearly revealed—there is nothing more noble than human love. Together man and wife can reach to godliness! (*Exit.*)

Scene III

A grove. In the background a temple inscribed with the words "Temple of Wisdom." This temple is connected by columns to two other temples. That on the right is inscribed "Temple of Reason"; that on the left, "Temple of Nature." THREE SPIRITS *enter, leading* TAMINO.

8. Finale

THREE SPIRITS: This road will lead you to your goal, but you must bear yourself like a man. First you must heed our teaching: be steadfast, patient, and silent!

TAMINO: But tell me, you gracious spirits, can I rescue Pamina?

THREE SPIRITS: That answer is not for us to give; be steadfast, patient, silent! Think of this—be a man, and you will conquer, as a man should! (*They exit.*)

TAMINO: May the wise counsel of these Spirits be ever engraved in my heart! Where am I now? What will happen to me? Is this place the seat of the Gods? There I see doors and pillars. Here wisdom and art dwell together harmoniously. Activity rules and idleness is banished, and thus this brotherhood is preserved free from wickedness. I boldly enter the gates! My purpose is noble and honorable and pure! Let evil tremble! To rescue Pamina is my duty! (*He goes toward portal at right.*)

PRIEST (*from within*): Go back!

TAMINO: Go back? Then I'll try my luck here! (*He goes toward left portal.*)

PRIESTER (*von innen*): Zurück!

TAMINO: Auch hier ruft man zurück.
Da seh ich noch eine Tür!
Vielleicht find ich den Eingang hier.
(*Er klopft, ein* ALTER PRIESTER *erscheint.*)

ALTER PRIESTER: Wo willst du, kühner Fremdling hin?
Was suchst du hier im Heiligtum?

TAMINO: Der Lieb und Tugend Eigentum.

ALTER PRIESTER: Die Worte sind von hohem Sinn!
Allein, wie willst du diese finden?
Dich leitet Lieb und Tugend nicht,
Weil Tod und Rache dich entzünden.

TAMINO: Nur Rache für den Bösewicht.

ALTER PRIESTER: Den wirst du wohl bei uns nicht finden.

TAMINO: Sarastro herrscht in diesen Gründen?

ALTER PRIESTER: Ja, ja! Sarastro herrschet hier.

TAMINO: Doch in dem Weisheitstempel nicht?

ALTER PRIESTER: Er herrscht im Weisheitstempel hier.

TAMINO: So ist denn alles Heuchelei!
(*Will gehen.*)

ALTER PRIESTER: Willst du schon wieder geh'n?

TAMINO: Ja, ich will geh'n, froh und frei,
Nie euren Tempel seh'n!

ALTER PRIESTER: Erklär dich näher mir,
Dich täuschet ein Betrug.

TAMINO: Sarastro wohnet hier,
Das ist mir schon genug!

ALTER PRIESTER: Wenn du dein Leben liebst,
So rede, bleibe da!
Sarastro hassest du?

TAMINO: Ich hass ihn ewig, ja!

ALTER PRIESTER: Nun gib mir deine Gründe an.

TAMINO: Er ist ein Unmensch, ein Tyrann!

ALTER PRIESTER: Ist das, was du gesagt, erwiesen?

TAMINO: Durch ein unglücklich Weib bewiesen,
Das Gram und Jammer niederdrückt.

ALTER PRIESTER: Ein Weib hat also dich berückt?
Ein Weib tut wenig, plaudert viel.

PRIEST (*from within*): Go back!

TAMINO: Here, too, they say "go back"? But I see another door. Perhaps I'll find an entrance here.
(*An* OLD PRIEST *appears at the center gate.*)

OLD PRIEST: What do you wish, bold Stranger? What do you seek in this holy place?

TAMINO: I seek the rights of love and virtue.

OLD PRIEST: Your words are inspired by a high purpose. Still, how will you find these things? You are not driven by love or virtue; you are impelled by death and vengeance.

TAMINO: Only with hatred for the scoundrel!

OLD PRIEST: You will not find such a man here.

TAMINO: Does Sarastro not rule this place?

OLD PRIEST: Yes, yes, Sarastro rules here.

TAMINO: Does he rule in Wisdom's temple?

OLD PRIEST: Yes, he rules in the Temple of Wisdom.

TAMINO: Then everything is hypocrisy.
(*He turns away.*)

OLD PRIEST: Will you leave us so soon?

TAMINO: Yes, I'll go happy and free, never again to see your Temple!

OLD PRIEST: Explain yourself more clearly. Perhaps you are mistaken.

TAMINO: Sarastro lives here. That is enough for me!

OLD PRIEST: If you love your life, explain yourself and do not go! Do you hate Sarastro?

TAMINO: Yes, I will hate him forever!

OLD PRIEST: Then give me your reasons.

TAMINO: He is a monster, a tyrant!

OLD PRIEST: Can you prove what you say?

TAMINO: Yes, by the misery and grief of an unhappy woman.

OLD PRIEST: That woman deceived you. Women do little although they chatter much. Do you believe such talk,

Du, Jüngling, glaubst dem Zungenspiel?
O legte doch Sarastro dir
Die Absicht seiner Handlung für!

TAMINO: Die Absicht ist nur allzu klar!
Riss nicht der Räuber ohn Erbarmen,
Pamina aus der Mutter Armen?

ALTER PRIESTER: Ja, Jüngling, was du sagst, ist wahr.

TAMINO: Wo ist sie, die er uns geraubt?
Man opferte vielleicht sie schon?

ALTER PRIESTER: Dir dies zu sagen, teurer Sohn,
Ist jetzt und mir noch nicht erlaubt.

TAMINO: Erklär dies Rätsel, täusch mich nicht!

ALTER PRIESTER: Die Zunge bindet Eid und Pflicht.

TAMINO: Wann also wird die Decke schwinden?

ALTER PRIESTER: Sobald dich führt der Freundschaft Hand
Ins Heiligtum zum ew'gen Band. (*Geht ab.*)

TAMINO: O ew'ge Nacht! Wann wirst du schwinden?
Wann wird das Licht mein Auge finden?

CHOR (*von innen*): Bald, bald, Jüngling, oder nie!

TAMINO: Bald, bald, bald sagt ihr, oder nie?
Ihr Unsichtbaren, saget mir,
Lebt denn Pamina noch?

CHOR: Pamina, Pamina lebet noch!

TAMINO: Sie lebt? sie lebt? Ich danke euch dafür.
O wenn ich doch im Stande wäre,
Allmächtige, zu eurer Ehre.
Mit jedem Tone meinen Dank
Zu schildern, wie er hier, entsprang.
(*Er spielt, sogleich kommen Tiere ihm zuzuhören.*)
Wie stark ist nicht dein Zauberton,
Weil, holde Flöte, durch dein Spielen
Selbst wilde Tiere Freude fühlen.
Doch nur Pamina bleibt davon!
Pamina, höre, höre mich!
Umsonst! Wo? Ach, wo find' ich dich?
(*PAPAGENO antwortet von innen mit seinem Flötchen.*)
Ha, das ist Papagenos Ton!
Vielleicht sah er Pamina schon,
Vielleicht eilt sie mit ihm zu mir!
Vielleicht führt mich der Ton zu ihr.
(*Er eilt ab.* PAPAGENO *und* PAMINA *eilen herbei.*)

BEIDE: Schnelle Füsse, rascher Mut

430

young man? If only you could understand the reason for Sarastro's actions!

TAMINO: The reason is all too clear. Did not the robber tear Pamina from her mother's arms?

OLD PRIEST: Yes, young man, what you say is true.

TAMINO: Where is Pamina, whom he has stolen from us? Has she been sacrificed yet?

OLD PRIEST: My dear son, I am not permitted to answer you at this time.

TAMINO: Explain this riddle; do not mystify me further!

OLD PRIEST: My tongue is bound by oath and duty.

TAMINO: But when can this veil be lifted?

OLD PRIEST: As soon as the hand of friendship leads you into the holiness of our order. (*Exits.*)

TAMINO: O everlasting night, will you never pass? When will my eyes discover the light?

CHORUS (*from within*): Soon, soon, young man, or never!

TAMINO: Soon or never, they say? You unseen ones, tell me— Does Pamina still live?

CHORUS: Pamina, Pamina, yes, she lives!

TAMINO: She lives? She lives? I thank you for telling me that! If only I were in a position to show you honor! My gratitude pours forth with every tone!

(*He plays the flute, and the animals of the forest come in to listen.*)

How compelling is the flute's melody! Magic flute, when I play upon you, even the wild beasts must feel joy! But Pamina does not appear! Pamina! Do you hear? In vain! Where is she? Will I ever find her?

(PAPAGENO'S *pipes are heard.*)

Ah—I hear Papageno's pipes! Perhaps he has seen Pamina; perhaps she is hurrying to me with him! Perhaps his call will lead me to her!

(*He exits.* PAMINA *and* PAPAGENO *enter.*)

BOTH: Nimble feet and rash courage may save us from

Schützt vor Feindes List und Wut.
Fänden wir Tamino doch,
Sonst erwischen sie uns noch!

PAMINA: Holder Jüngling!

PAPAGENO: Stille, stille, ich kann's besser!
(*Pfeift.*)

BEIDE: Welche Freude ist wohl grösser?
Freund Tamino hört uns schon!
Hieher kam der Flötenton.
Welch ein Glück, wenn ich ihn finde!
Nur geschwinde! Nur geschwinde!
(MONOSTATOS *tritt ihnen von dort her entgegen.*)

MONOSTATOS (*ihrer spottend*): Nur geschwinde! Nur ge-
schwinde!
Ha, hab ich euch noch erwischt!
Nur herbei mit Stahl und Eisen!
Wart, ich will euch Mores weisen!
Den Monostatos berücken!
Nur herbei mit Band und Stricken.
He, ihr Sklaven, kommt herbei!
(SKLAVEN *kommen, mit Fesseln.*)

PAMINA *und* PAPAGENO: Ach, nun ist's mit uns vorbei!

PAPAGENO: Wer viel wagt, gewinnt oft viel!
Komm, du schönes Glockenspiel,
Lass die Glöckchen klingen, klingen,
Dass die Ohren ihnen singen!
(PAPAGENO *spielt auf dem Glockenspiel. Sogleich tanzen
und singen* MONOSTATOS *und die* SKLAVEN.)

MONOSTATOS *und* SKLAVEN: Das klinget so herrlich, das
klinget so schön!
Larala la la larala la la larala!
Nie hab' ich so etwas gehört und geseh'n!
Larala la la larala la la larala! (*Ab.*)

PAMINA *und* PAPAGENO: Könnte jeder brave Mann
Solche Glöckchen finden!
Seine Feinde würden dann
Ohne Mühe schwinden,
Und er lebte ohne sie
In der besten Harmonie!
Nur der Freundschaft Harmonie
Mildert die Beschwerden;
Ohne diese Sympathie
Ist kein Glück auf Erden.

the fury and craft of our enemies. Let us find Tamino; even yet, we may be caught!

PAMINA: O noble young man!
PAPAGENO: Be quiet, I can call him better.
(*He blows his pipes.*)
BOTH: What joy can be greater? Tamino has heard us! The flute's tones are approaching! Now let us hurry!
(MONOSTATOS *enters, stepping in their path.*)

MONOSTATOS (*mocking them*): "Now let us hurry." Ha! I've caught you just in time. I'll put you both in chains! I'll teach you your manners! So you tried to deceive Monostatos! Slaves, bring me the ropes and irons!
(*The* SLAVES *bring in the chains.*)

PAMINA *and* PAPAGENO: Now we both are lost!
PAPAGENO: He who has daring often wins! Come save us, pretty bells! Ring and charm their ears!
(PAPAGENO *plays his bells.* MONOSTATOS *and the* SLAVES *dance to their sound.*)

MONOSTATOS *and* SLAVES: They ring so clearly and so beautifully! Tralala! Nothing I have ever heard can equal this! Tralala! (*They exit.*)

PAMINA *and* PAPAGENO: Oh, if every honest man could find bells like these, then his enemies would disappear, and without them he would live in greatest tranquillity. Only the harmony of friendship can banish grief; without such sympathy, there is no joy on earth.

433

CHOR (*von innen*): Es lebe Sarastro! Sarastro lebe!

PAPAGENO: Was soll das bedeuten? Ich zittre, ich bebe!

PAMINA: O Freund, nun ist's um uns getan,
Dies kündigt den Sarastro an!

PAPAGENO: O wär ich eine Maus,
Wie wollt ich mich verstecken!
Wär ich so klein wie Schnecken,
So kröch ich in mein Haus!
Mein Kind, was werden wir nun sprechen?

PAMINA: Die Wahrheit, wär sie auch Verbrechen!
(CHOR, SARASTRO *und Gefolge, kommen herein.*)

CHOR: Es lebe Sarastro! Sarastro soll leben!
Er ist es, dem wir uns mit Freuden ergeben!
Stets mög er des Lebens als Weiser sich freun,
Er ist unser Abgott, dem alle sich weihn.

PAMINA (*kniet*): Herr, ich bin zwar Verbrecherin,
Ich wollte deiner Macht entfliehn!
Allein, die Schuld ist nicht an mir;
Der böse Mohr verlangte Liebe;
Darum, o Herr, entfloh ich dir.

SARASTRO: Steh auf, erheitre dich, o Liebe!
Denn ohne erst in dich zu dringen,
Weiss ich von deinem Herzen mehr:
Du liebest einen Andern sehr.
Zur Liebe will ich dich nicht zwingen,
Doch geb ich dir die Freiheit nicht.

PAMINA: Mich rufet ja die Kindespflicht,
Denn meine Mutter—

SARASTRO: Steht in meiner Macht.
Du würdest um dein Glück gebracht,
Wenn ich dich ihren Händen liesse.

PAMINA: Mir klingt der Muttername süsse!
Sie ist es—

SARASTRO: Und ein stolzes Weib!
Ein Mann muss eure Herzen leiten,
Denn ohne ihn pflegt jedes Weib
Aus ihrem Wirkungskreis zu schreiten.
(MONOSTATOS *führt den* TAMINO *herein.*)

MONOSTATOS: Nun stolzer Jüngling, nur hieher!
Hier ist Sarastro, unser Herr.

CHORUS (*from within*): Long live Sarastro!

PAPAGENO: What does that noise mean? I'm trembling; I'm shivering!

PAMINA: O friend, it's all over for us. The voices herald Sarastro's arrival.

PAPAGENO: I wish I were a mouse; how quickly I would hide! Or if I were a snail, I would crawl into my shell. My dear girl, what shall we tell him now?

PAMINA: We must tell the truth. Only that will save us!
(CHORUS *appears, with* SARASTRO *and his following.*)

CHORUS: Long live Sarastro! We submit to his rule with joy! Forever may we rejoice in his wisdom! As our leader, we give him our devotion!

PAMINA (*kneeling*): My Lord! I have broken your laws! I wished to escape from your powers. But the guilt is not mine. The cruel Moor desired my love; therefore, my Lord, I ran away from you.

SARASTRO: Arise; take courage, my loved one! There is no need for you to tell me, for I know already what is in your heart. You love another deeply. I will not dictate whom you should love, but as yet, I cannot give you your freedom.

PAMINA: But a daughter's duty calls me to my mother—

SARASTRO: She is in my power. You would lose all chance of happiness if I gave you back into her hands.

PAMINA: But the name of mother is so sweet! She is—

SARASTRO: She is a proud woman! A man must lead your heart; without such guidance every woman strays beyond her allotted place.
(MONOSTATOS *enters, leading* TAMINO.)

MONOSTATOS: Now proud youth, come here! Here is our master, Sarastro.

PAMINA (*sieht* TAMINO): Er ist's!

TAMINO (*sieht* PAMINA): Sie ist's!

PAMINA: Ich glaub es kaum!
Es schling mein Arm sich um ihn her
Und wenn es auch mein Ende wär!

TAMINO: Es ist kein Traum!
Es schling mein Arm sich um sie her
Und wenn es auch mein Ende wär!
(*Sie umarmen sich.*)

CHOR: Was soll das heissen?

MONOSTATOS: Welch eine Dreistigkeit!
Gleich auseinander! Das geht zu weit!
(*Er kniet vor* SARASTRO.)
Dein Sklave liegt zu deinen Füssen:
Lass den verwegnen Frevler büssen!
Bedenk, wie frech der Knabe ist!
Durch dieses seltnen Vogels List
Wollt er Pamina dir entführen.
Allein ich wusst ihn auszuspüren.
Du kennst mich! Meine Wachsamkeit—

SARASTRO: Verdient, dass man ihr Lorbeer streut!
He, gebt dem Ehrenmann sogleich—

MONOSTATOS: Schon deine Gnade macht mich reich!

SARASTRO: Nur sieben und siebenzig Sohlenstreich!

MONOSTATOS: Ach Herr, den Lohn verhofft ich nicht!

SARASTRO: Nicht Dank, es ist ja meine Pflicht!

CHOR: Es lebe Sarastro, der göttliche Weise! Er lohnet und
strafet in ähnlichem Kreise.

SARASTRO: Führt diese beiden Fremdlinge
In unsern Prüfungstempel ein;
Bedecket ihre Häupter dann,
Sie müssen erst gereinigt sein.

CHOR: Wenn Tugend und Gerechtigkeit
Den Grossen Pfad mit Ruhm bestreut,
Dann ist die Erd' ein Himmelreich,
Und Sterbliche den Göttern gleich.

PAMINA (*seeing* TAMINO): It is he!

TAMINO (*seeing* PAMINA): It is she!

PAMINA: I can't believe it! I will embrace him, even though it may mean my death!

TAMINO: It's not a dream! I will embrace her, even though it may mean my death!
(*They embrace.*)

CHORUS: What does this mean?

MONOSTATOS: What impudence! Away from each other! You're going too far!
(*He kneels before* SARASTRO.)
Your slave lies here at your feet—let the insolent stranger be punished! Think of his impertinence! With this strange birdman, he would have stolen Pamina from you if I had not saved her. You know my watchfulness!

SARASTRO: You deserve laurels! Servants, give this worthy fellow—

MONOSTATOS: Already your graciousness makes me rich!

SARASTRO: Seventy-seven strokes of a whip!

MONOSTATOS: Ah, my Lord, I did not expect such a reward!

SARASTRO: No thanks; it is only my duty.

CHORUS: Long live Sarastro, the godly sage! He rewards and punishes with equal justice!

SARASTRO: Let these two strangers follow us into the Temple of Proof—let their heads be covered first—and there they will be purified.

CHORUS: When virtue and righteousness will strew the great path of life with glory, then will earth be as heaven, and mortals like gods!

ZWEITER AUFZUG

I. Auftritt

Der Wald. SARASTRO *und Priester kommen mit feierlichen Schritten.*

10. Arie mit Chor

SARASTRO: O Isis und Osiris, schenket
Der Weisheit Geist dem neuen Paar!
Die ihr der Wand'rer Schritte lenket.
Stärkt mit Geduld sie in Gefahr!

CHOR: Stärkt mit Geduld sie in Gefahr!

SARASTRO: Lasst sie der Prüfung Früchte sehen;
Doch sollten sie zu Grabe gehen,
So lohnt der Tugend kühnen Lauf,
Nehmt sie in euren Wohnsitz auf. (*Geht ab.*)

CHOR: Nehmt sie in euren Wohnsitz auf. (*Geht ab.*)

II. Auftritt

Ein kurzer Vorhof des Tempels. TAMINO *und* PAPAGENO, *verschleiert, werden vom* SPRECHER *und dem andern Priester hereingeführt. Die Priester lösen ihnen die Schleier ab und entfernen sich damit.*

Dialog

TAMINO: Eine schreckliche Nacht!—Papageno, bist du noch bei mir?

PAPAGENO: Ei, freilich!

TAMINO: Wo denkst du, dass wir uns nun befinden?

PAPAGENO: Wo? Ja, wenn's nicht finster wäre, wollt ich dir's schon sagen—aber so—
(*Donnerschlag.*)
O weh!

TAMINO: Was ist's?

PAPAGENO: Mir wird nicht wohl bei der Sache!

TAMINO: Du hast Furcht, wie ich höre.

PAPAGENO: Furcht eben nicht, nur eiskalt läuft's mir über den Rücken.
(*Starker Donnerschlag.*)
O weh!

438

ACT TWO

Scene I

A forest. SARASTRO *and* CHORUS *of priests solemnly march in.*

10. Aria with Chorus

SARASTRO: O Isis and Osiris, favor this new pair with wisdom's spirit! Guide the wanderers' steps; strengthen them with patience to meet all danger!

CHORUS: Strengthen them with patience to meet all danger!

SARASTRO: Let them see success in their task, but even if they should go to their graves, reward their virtue, and take them to your abode. (*Exits.*)

CHORUS: Take them to your abode. (*Exits.*)

Scene II

A small forecourt of the Temple. TAMINO *and* PAPAGENO, *veiled, are led in by the* SPEAKER *and another priest. The priests remove the veils and then depart.*

Dialogue

TAMINO: A terrible night!—Papageno, are you still with me?

PAPAGENO: I? Certainly.

TAMINO: Where do you think we are now?

PAPAGENO: Where? If it weren't so dark I might tell you, but like this—
(*A peal of thunder is heard.*)
O Gods!

TAMINO: What is it?

PAPAGENO: I don't like this whole affair.

TAMINO: I can see that you are afraid.

PAPAGENO: Not really afraid; I only have icy shivers running down my spine.
(*More thunder.*)
Help!

439

TAMINO: Was soll's?

PAPAGENO: Ich glaube, ich bekomme ein kleines Fieber.

TAMINO: Pfui, Papageno! Sei ein Mann!

PAPAGENO: Ich wollt, ich wär ein Mädchen!
(*Ein sehr starker Donnerschlag.*)
O! o! o! Das ist mein letzter Augenblick!
(SPRECHER *und der* ZWEITE PRIESTER *erscheinen mit Fackeln.*)

SPRECHER: Ihr Fremdlinge, was sucht oder fordert ihr von uns? Was treibt euch an, in unsere Mauern zu dringen?

TAMINO: Freundschaft und Liebe.

SPRECHER: Bist du bereit, sie mit deinem Leben zu erkämpfen?

TAMINO: Ja!

SPRECHER: Prinz, noch ist's Zeit zu weichen—einen Schritt weiter, und es ist zu spät.

TAMINO: Weisheitslehre sei mein Sieg; Pamina, das holde Mädchen, mein Lohn!

SPRECHER: Du unterziehst dich jeder Prüfung?

TAMINO: Jeder!

SPRECHER: Reiche mir deine Hand!

ZWEITER PRIESTER (*zu* PAPAGENO): Willst auch du dir Weisheitsliebe erkämpfen?

PAPAGENO: Kämpfen ist meine Sache nicht. Ich verlange auch im Grunde gar keine Weisheit. Ich bin so ein Naturmensch, der sich mit Schlaf, Speise und Trank begnügt; und wenn es ja sein könnte, dass ich mir einmal ein schönes Weibchen fange—

ZWEITER PRIESTER: Die wirst du nie erhalten, wenn du dich nicht unseren Prüfungen unterziehst.

PAPAGENO: Worin besteht diese Prüfung?

ZWEITER PRIESTER: Dich allen unseren Gesetzen zu unterwerfen, selbst den Tod nicht zu scheuen.

PAPAGENO: Ich bleibe ledig!

ZWEITER PRIESTER: Wenn nun aber Sarastro dir ein Mädchen aufbewahrt hätte, das an Farbe und Kleidung dir ganz gleich wäre?

PAPAGENO: Mir gleich? Ist sie jung?

ZWEITER PRIESTER: Jung und schön!

PAPAGENO: Und heisst?

TAMINO: What is it?

PAPAGENO: I think I am becoming a little feverish.

TAMINO: Oh, Papageno, be a man!

PAPAGENO: I wish I were a girl!
(*A third peal of thunder.*)
Oh! This is my last moment!
(*The* SPEAKER *and the* SECOND PRIEST *enter, with torches.*)

SPEAKER: Strangers, what do you seek from us? What brings you to our temple?

TAMINO: Friendship and love.

SPEAKER: Are you prepared to give your lives for these ideals?

TAMINO: Yes!

SPEAKER: Prince, now it is time to reconsider—one step farther and it will be too late.

TAMINO: Wisdom shall be my victory; Pamina, the holy maiden, my reward.

SPEAKER: Then you will endure every trial?

TAMINO: All of them!

SPEAKER: Take my hand!

SECOND PRIEST (*to* PAPAGENO): Will you also do battle for love of wisdom?

PAPAGENO: Doing battle is not one of my talents. Really, I don't need any wisdom. I'm a simple man who enjoys his food, sleep, and drink; and if I could only hope that some day I could catch a pretty wife—

SECOND PRIEST: You'll never find her without undergoing the trials!

PAPAGENO: But what are they?

SECOND PRIEST: You must follow our laws, even to the point of death.

PAPAGENO: I'll remain a bachelor!

SECOND PRIEST: If Sarastro has chosen a wife for you, just the same in color and dress as you are?

PAPAGENO: The same as I? Is she young?

SECOND PRIEST: Young and beautiful!

PAPAGENO: And she's called?

441

ZWEITER PRIESTER: Papagena!

PAPAGENO: Papagena? Die möcht ich aus blosser Neugierde sehen.

ZWEITER PRIESTER: Sehen kannst du sie!

PAPAGENO: Aber wenn ich sie gesehen habe, hernach muss ich sterben? Ja? Ich bleibe ledig!

ZWEITER PRIESTER: Sehen kannst du sie, aber bis zur verlaufnen Zeit kein Wort mit ihr sprechen. Wird dein Geist so viel Standhaftigkeit besitzen, deine Zunge in Schranken zu halten?

PAPAGENO: O ja!

ZWEITER PRIESTER: Deine Hand! Du sollst sie sehen.

SPRECHER (*zu* TAMINO): Auch dir, Prinz, legen die Götter ein heilsames Stillschweigen auf; ohne dieses seid ihr beide verloren. Du wirst Pamina sehen, aber nicht sie sprechen dürfen; dies ist der Anfang eurer Prüfungszeit.

11. Duett

ERSTER *und* ZWEITER PRIESTER: Bewahret euch vor Weibertücken:
Dies ist des Bundes erste Pflicht.
Manch weiser Mann liess sich berücken,
Er fehlte und versah sich's nicht.
Verlassen sah er sich am Ende,
Vergolten seine Treu mit Hohn.
Vergebens rang er seine Hände,
Tod und Verzweiflung war sein Lohn.
(*Beide* PRIESTER *ab. Plötzlich ist es dunkel.*)

Dialog

PAPAGENO: He, Lichter her! Lichter her!—Das ist doch wunderlich, so oft einen die Herren verlassen, sieht man mit offenen Augen nichts.

TAMINO: Ertrag es mit Geduld, und denke, es ist der Götter Wille.
(*Die* DREI DAMEN *erscheinen mit Fackeln.*)

12. Quintett

DREI DAMEN: Wie, wie, wie?
Ihr an diesem Schreckensort?
Nie, nie, nie
Kommt ihr glücklich wieder fort!
Tamino, dir ist Tod geschworen!
Du, Papageno, bist verloren!

SECOND PRIEST: Papagena!

PAPAGENO: Papagena? Then, I must see her, out of curiosity.

SECOND PRIEST: You may see her!

PAPAGENO: But if I've seen her, then must I die? Yes? Then I'll remain a bachelor.

SECOND PRIEST: You can see her, but you mustn't speak one word to her. Will your spirit be steadfast enough to control your tongue?

PAPAGENO: Oh, yes!

SECOND PRIEST: Your hand! You shall see her.

SPEAKER (*to* TAMINO): And you, Prince, the gods bind you to holy silence. Without this, you both are lost. You will see Pamina, but you are forbidden to speak to her. This is the beginning of your trial.

11. Duet

FIRST PRIEST *and* SECOND PRIEST: Beware of the deceptions of women: that is this brotherhood's first duty. Many a wise man who has not been prepared has fallen into this trap. In the end, he found himself forsaken; his fidelity rewarded with scorn. In vain did he wring his hands; death and despair were his reward.
(*Both* PRIESTS *exit; it becomes dark.*)

Dialogue

PAPAGENO: Hey! Lights here! Lights here!—It's strange; as soon as these gentlemen leave, it becomes black as night.

TAMINO: Bear it with patience; it is God's will.
(*The* THREE LADIES *appear, with torches.*)

12. Quintet

THREE LADIES: What are you doing in this dreadful place? You will never be able to leave! Tamino, you are doomed to death! Papageno, you too are lost!

PAPAGENO: Nein, nein, das wär zu viel!

TAMINO: Papageno, schweige still!
Willst du dein Gelübde brechen.
Nichts mit Weibern hier zu sprechen?

PAPAGENO: Du hörst ja, wir sind beide hin.

TAMINO: Stille, sag ich, schweige still!

PAPAGENO: Immer still, und immer still!

DREI DAMEN: Ganz nah ist euch die Königin.
Sie drang im Tempel heimlich ein.

PAPAGENO: Wie? Was? Sie soll im Tempel sein?

TAMINO: Stille, sag ich, schweige still!
Wirst du immer so vermessen
Deiner Eidespflicht vergessen?

DREI DAMEN: Tamino, hör, du bist verloren!
Gedenke an die Königin!
Man zischelt viel sich in die Ohren
Von dieser Priester falschem Sinn.

TAMINO: Ein Weiser prüft und achtet nicht.
Was der gemeine Pöbel spricht.

DREI DAMEN: Man sagt, wer ihrem Bunde schwört,
Der fährt zur Höll mit Haut und Haar.

PAPAGENO: Das wär beim Teufel unerhört!
Sag an, Tamino, ist das wahr?

TAMINO: Geschwätz von Weibern nachgesagt,
Von Heuchlern aber ausgedacht.

PAPAGENO: Doch sagt es auch die Königin.

TAMINO: Sie ist ein Weib, hat Weibersinn.
Sei still, mein Wort sei dir genug:
Denk deiner Pflicht und handle klug.

DREI DAMEN: Warum bist du mit uns so spröde?
Auch Papageno schweigt, so rede!

PAPAGENO: Ich möchte gerne—wohl—

TAMINO: Still!

PAPAGENO: Ihr seht, dass ich nicht kann das Plaudern lassen,
Ist wahrlich eine Schand für mich!

DREI DAMEN: Wir müssen sie mit Scham verlassen:
Es plaudert keiner sicherlich.

ALLE: Von festem Geiste ist ein Mann,
Er denket, was er sprechen kann.

PAPAGENO: No, that would be too much!

TAMINO: Papageno, be quiet! By speaking to these women, you are breaking your oath.

PAPAGENO: You heard them say that we both are lost?

TAMINO: Quiet, I say. Be quiet!

PAPAGENO: Always quiet; always quiet!

THREE LADIES: The Queen is nearby; she has forced her way secretly into the Temple.

PAPAGENO: What? She's in the Temple?

TAMINO: Quiet, I say! Do you insist on breaking your oath?

THREE LADIES: Tamino, listen—you are lost! Only think of the Queen. Many things are whispered about the false teachings of the priests.

TAMINO: A wise man judges for himself. He never believes vulgar gossip.

THREE LADIES: They say that he who joins this brotherhood goes immediately to hell, body and soul.

PAPAGENO: The devil's work! Tell me, Tamino, is this true?

TAMINO: It is the idle talk of women, conceived by hypocrites and spread by liars.

PAPAGENO: But the Queen says this also.

TAMINO: She is a woman, and has a woman's mind. Be quiet; my word should suffice for you. Think of your duty and be wise.

THREE LADIES: Why are you so cold to us? Papageno, you too are silent. Explain yourselves.

PAPAGENO: I'd like to very much, but—

TAMINO: Quiet!

PAPAGENO: You see, I'm not able to. I can't resist talking; it's really a disgrace for me!

THREE LADIES: We must reluctantly depart: neither of them will speak to us.

ALL: A man is strong of spirit. He considers his words before he speaks.

445

PRIESTER *und* CHOR (*von innen*): Entweiht ist die heilige Schwelle,
Hinab mit den Weibern zur Hölle!
(*Die* DREI DAMEN *wollen gehen.*)

PAPAGENO: O weh, o weh, o weh!
(*Er fällt zu Boden.* SPRECHER *und* ZWEITER PRIESTER *mit Fackeln treten ein.*)

Dialog

SPRECHER: Heil dir, Jüngling! Dein standhaft männliches Betragen hat gesiegt. Wir wollen also mit reinem Herzen unsere Wanderschaft weiter fortsetzen.
(*Er gibt ihm den Schleier um.*)
So! Nun komm!
(*Er geht mit* TAMINO *ab.*)

ZWEITER PRIESTER: Was seh ich! Freund, stehe auf! Wie ist dir?

PAPAGENO: Ich lieg in einer Ohnmacht!

ZWEITER PRIESTER: Auf! Sammle dich, und sei ein Mann!

PAPAGENO (*steht auf*): Aber sagt mir nur, meine Herren, warum muss ich denn alle diese Qualen und Schrecken empfinden? Wenn mir ja die Götter eine Papagena bestimmten, warum denn mit so viel Gefahren sie erringen?

ZWEITER PRIESTER: Diese neugierige Frage mag deine Vernunft dir beantworten. Komm! Meine Pflicht ist allein, dich weiterzuführen.
(*Er gibt ihm den Schleier um.*)

PAPAGENO: Bei so einer ewigen Wanderschaft möcht einem wohl die Liebe auf immer vergehen.
(ZWEITER PRIESTER *geht mit ihm ab.*)

III. Auftritt

Ein Garten im Mondschein. PAMINA *schlafend auf dem Sitz unter den Rosen.* MONOSTATOS *kommt.*

MONOSTATOS: Ha, da find ich ja die spröde Schöne! Welcher Mensch würde bei so einem Anblick kalt und unempfindlich bleiben? Das Feuer, das in mir glimmt, wird mich noch verzehren! Wenn ich wüsste—dass ich so ganz allein und unbelauscht wäre—Ein Küsschen, dächte ich, liesse sich entschuldigen.

13. Arie

Alles fühlt der Liebe Freuden,
Schnäbelt, tändelt, herzt und küsst;

alog

INA (*den Dolch in der Hand*): Morden soll ich? Götter,
ann ich nicht! Götter, was soll ich tun?

OSTATOS: Dich mir anvertrauen. Warum zitterst du?
meiner schwarzen Farbe, oder vor dem ausgedachten
d?

INA: Du weisst also?

OSTATOS: Alles. Du hast also nur einen Weg, dich und
e Mutter zu retten.

INA: Der wäre?

OSTATOS: Mich zu lieben! Ja oder nein!

INA: Nein!

OSTATOS: Nein?

ASTRO *tritt hinzu.* MONOSTATOS *erhebt den Dolch.*)
ahre denn hin!

ASTRO *schleudert* MONOSTATOS *zurück. Auf die Kniee*
nd.)
, ich bin unschuldig.

STRO: Ich weiss, dass deine Seele ebenso schwarz als
Gesicht ist. Geh!

OSTATOS (*im Abgehen*): Jetzt such ich die Mutter auf,
die Tochter mir nicht beschieden ist. (*Geht ab.*)

INA: Herr, strafe meine Mutter nicht! Der Schmerz
meine Abwesenheit—

STRO: Ich weiss alles. Du sollst sehen, wie ich mich an
er Mutter räche.

. Arie

iesen heil'gen Hallen
nt man die Rache nicht,
ist ein Mensch gefallen,
rt Liebe ihn zur Pflicht.
n wandelt er an Freundes Hand
gnügt und froh in's bess're Land.
iesen heil'gen Mauern,
Mensch den Menschen liebt,
n kein Verräter lauern,
l man dem Feind vergibt.
a solche Lehren nicht erfreun,
dienet nicht ein Mensch zu sein.
hen beide ab.)

50

PRIESTS *and* CHORUS (*from within*): Our sacred threshold
is profaned. Let these women be banished to hell!
(*The* THREE LADIES *rush out.*)

PAPAGENO: Oh, woe!
(*He falls to the ground. The* SPEAKER *and the* SECOND
PRIEST *enter, carrying torches.*)

Dialogue

SPEAKER: Hail, Prince! Your strong, manly behavior has
triumphed. And so we wish you to continue your wander-
ings with pure hearts.
(*He covers* TAMINO's *head with a veil.*)
So! Now come!
(*He exits with* TAMINO.)

SECOND PRIEST: What do I see? Friend, stand up! What
has happened to you?

PAPAGENO: I believe I have fainted!

SECOND PRIEST: Get up! Be a man!

PAPAGENO (*standing up*): But tell me now, my Lord, why
must I suffer these dangers and horrors? If the Gods are
willing to send me a Papagena, why must I work so hard
to get her?

SECOND PRIEST: Let your own intelligence answer that
question. Come! My duty is to lead you ahead.
(*He covers* PAPAGENO's *head with a veil.*)

PAPAGENO: After such everlasting wandering, one would
almost like to give up love forever!
(SECOND PRIEST *exits with him.*)

Scene III

A garden in the moonlight. PAMINA *is asleep beneath the
rosebushes.* MONOSTATOS *enters.*

MONOSTATOS: Ha, here I find the cold beauty! What man
could remain cold before such a charming sight? Now she
will feel the fire that burns within me. Since I am unobserved, a kiss, I think, would not be a crime!

13. Aria

Every being feels love's joy; every being bills and coos,
embraces and kisses. Shall I be deprived of love because

447

Und ich sollt die Liebe meiden,
Weil ein Schwarzer hässlich ist!
Ist mir denn kein Herz gegeben?
Bin ich nicht von Fleisch und Blut?
Immer ohne Weibchen leben
Wäre wahrlich Höllenglut!
Drum so will ich, weil ich lebe,
Schnäbeln, küssen, zärtlich sein!
Lieber guter Mond, vergebe:
Eine Weisse nahm mich ein.
Weiss ist schön, ich muss sie küssen:
Mond, verstecke dich dazu!
Sollt es dich zu sehr verdriessen,
O so mach die Augen zu!
(*Er schleicht langsam und leise zu* PAMINA *hin. Die* KÖNIGIN *kommt unter Donner aus der mittleren Versenkung, und so, dass sie gerade vor* PAMINA *zu stehen kommt.*)

Dialog

KÖNIGIN DER NACHT: Zurück!

PAMINA (*erwacht*): Ihr Götter!

MONOSTATOS: O weh! Die Göttin der Nacht.

PAMINA: Mutter! Mutter! meine Mutter!

MONOSTATOS: Mutter? Hm, das muss man von weitem belauschen.

KÖNIGIN DER NACHT: Verdank es der Gewalt, mit der man dich mir entriss, dass ich noch deine Mutter mich nenne. Siehst du hier diesen Stahl? Er ist für Sarastro geschliffen. Du wirst ihn töten.

PAMINA: Aber, liebste Mutter!

KÖNIGIN DER NACHT: Kein Wort!

14. Arie

Der Hölle Rache kocht in meinem Herzen,
Tod und Verzweiflung flammet um mich her!
Fühlt nicht durch dich Sarastro Todesschmerzen,
So bist du meine Tochter nimmermehr!
Verstossen sei auf ewig,
Verlassen sei auf ewig,
Zertrümmert sei'n auf ewig
Alle Bande der Natur,
Wenn nicht durch dich Sarastro wird erblassen!
Hört, Rachegötter, hört der Mutter Schwur!
(*Sie versinkt mitten in Donner und Blitz.*)

a black man is ugly? Is no heart given to me'
flesh and blood? To live without a wife foreve
horrible! I would be so kind! While I liv
to kiss and be tender! Dear good Moon, for
white girl has bewitched me. She is beautiful;
her! Moon, veil yourself, and if it makes you
rassed, then close your eyes!
(*He approaches* PAMINA *slowly and quietly.*
appears amid thunder and lightning and sta
PAMINA.)

Dialogue

QUEEN OF THE NIGHT: Go back!

PAMINA (*awakening*): O God!

MONOSTATOS: Oh, woe! The Queen of the Night

PAMINA: Mother! Mother! My mother!

MONOSTATOS: Mother? I will watch them from a

QUEEN OF THE NIGHT: I still consider myself you
despite the power that took you from me. You
dagger? It is sharpened for Sarastro—you must
with it!

PAMINA: But, beloved Mother!

QUEEN OF THE NIGHT: Not a word!

14. Aria

Hell's vengeance burns in my heart. Death anc
inflame me! Unless Sarastro feels the pangs
through you, you will never be my daughter an
I'll cast you out forever; I will forsake you! Every
nature will be severed unless Sarastro is destroyed
Hear! Gods of Wrath, witness a mother's curse!
(*She disappears amid thunder and lightning.*)

Dialogue

PAMINA (*the dagger in her hand*): Murder? Gods, I cannot! What shall I do?

MONOSTATOS: Confide in me! Why do you tremble? Because of my blackness, or because of the murder that you plan?

PAMINA: You know?

MONOSTATOS: Everything. There is only one way of escape for you and your mother.

PAMINA: What way?

MONOSTATOS: To love me! Yes, or no?

PAMINA: No!

MONOSTATOS: No?
(SARASTRO *enters.* MONOSTATOS *raises a dagger.*)
Then I will kill you!
(SARASTRO *holds* MONOSTATOS *back. He falls on his knees.*)
My Lord, I am not guilty.

SARASTRO: I know that your soul is as black as your face. Go!

MONOSTATOS (*leaving*): Now, I'll seek out the mother, since the daughter is not for me. (*Exits.*)

PAMINA: My Lord, don't punish my mother. The pain of my loss—

SARASTRO: I know all. You shall see how I avenge myself on your mother.

15. Aria

These sacred halls know no revenge. If a man should stray from the true path, love leads him back to his duty. Guided by friendship, one journeys to a better land. Within these holy halls where all men are united in love, no traitor can conceal himself; nor can he who rejects our teachings be worthy of manhood.
(*He exits with* PAMINA.)

IV. Auftritt

Eine kurze Halle. TAMINO *und* PAPAGENO *werden ohne Schleier von den zwei* PRIESTERN *hereingeführt.*

Dialog

SPRECHER: Hier seid ihr euch beide allein überlassen. Sobald die Posaune tönt, dann nehmt ihr euren Weg dahin. Prinz, lebt wohl! Noch einmal, vergesst das Wort nicht: Schweigen. (*Geht ab.*)

ZWEITER PRIESTER: Papageno, wer an diesem Ort sein Stillschweigen bricht, den strafen die Götter durch Donner und Blitz. Leb wohl! (*Geht ab.*)

PAPAGENO (*zu* TAMINO): Das ist ein lustiges Leben! Wär ich lieber in meiner Strohhütte, oder im Wald, so hört ich doch manchmal einen Vogel pfeifen! Mit mir selbst werd ich wohl sprechen dürfen; und auch wir zwei können zusammen sprechen, wir sind ja Männer. La la la—la la la! Nicht einmal einen Tropfen Wasser bekommt man bei diesen Leuten, viel weniger sonst was.

(TAMINO *geht ab. Ein altes hässliches* WEIB *kommt mit einem grossen Becher mit Wasser.*)
Ist das für mich?

ALTES WEIB: Ja, mein Engel!

PAPAGENO: Nicht mehr und nicht weniger als Wasser. Sag du mir, du unbekannte Schöne, werden alle fremden Gäste auf diese Art bewirtet?

ALTES WEIB: Freilich, mein Engel!

PAPAGENO: So, so!—Auf diese Art werden die Fremden auch nicht gar zu häufig kommen.

ALTES WEIB: Sehr wenig.

PAPAGENO: Kann mir's denken. Geh, Alte, setze dich her zu mir, mir ist die Zeit verdammt lange.

(WEIB *setzt sich zu ihm.*)
Sag du mir, wie alt bist du denn?

ALTES WEIB: Wie alt? Achtzehn Jahre und zwei Minuten.

PAPAGENO: Achtzig Jahre und zwei Minuten?

ALTES WEIB: Achtzehn Jahre und zwei Minuten!

PAPAGENO: Ha ha ha! Ei, du junger Engel! Hast du auch einen Geliebten?

ALTES WEIB: Ei, freilich!

PAPAGENO: Ist er auch so jung wie du?

Scene IV

A small hallway. TAMINO *and* PAPAGENO, *without veils, are led in by the* SPEAKER *and the* SECOND PRIEST.

Dialogue

SPEAKER: I leave you by yourselves. As soon as the trumpet sounds, go on your way. Prince, farewell! Once more, don't forget the word: Silence! (*Exits.*)

SECOND PRIEST: Papageno, he who breaks his silence in this place will be punished by the gods with thunder and lightning. Farewell! (*Exits.*)

PAPAGENO (*to* TAMINO): This is a gay life! I would rather be back in my straw hut, or in the woods, so that I could at least hear a bird sing. I am permitted to talk to myself, and also we can talk to each other, since we are both men. La la la—la la la! Not a drop of water do we get from these people, much less some food.
(TAMINO *exits. An old, ugly* WOMAN *appears, carrying a jug of water.*)
Is that for me?

OLD WOMAN: Yes, my angel!

PAPAGENO: Nothing better than water! Tell me, then, you mysterious beauty, is that how you entertain all strange guests?

OLD WOMAN: Certainly, my angel.

PAPAGENO: Well, well!—I imagine that strangers don't visit here too often?

OLD WOMAN: Hardly ever.

PAPAGENO: I should think so. Come on, old lady, sit beside me. Time passes very slowly here.
(*The* WOMAN *sits next to him.*)
Now tell me, how old are you?

OLD WOMAN: How old? Eighteen years and two minutes.

PAPAGENO: Eighty years and two minutes?

OLD WOMAN: Eighteen years and two minutes!

PAPAGENO: Ha, ha! You young angel! Have you a lover?

OLD WOMAN: Of course I have!

PAPAGENO: Is he as youthful as you are?

ALTES WEIB: Nicht gar, er ist um zehn Jahre älter.

PAPAGENO: Um zehn Jahre ist er älter als du? Das muss eine Liebe sein! Wie nennt sich denn dein Liebhaber?

ALTES WEIB: Papageno!

PAPAGENO: Papageno? Wo ist er denn, dieser Papageno?

ALTES WEIB: Da sitzt er, mein Engel!

PAPAGENO: Ich wär dein Geliebter?

ALTES WEIB: Ja, mein Engel!

PAPAGENO: Sag du mir, wie heisst du denn?

ALTES WEIB: Ich heisse—
(*Starker Donner, die* ALTE *hinkt schnell ab.* TAMINO *kommt wieder herein.*)

PAPAGENO: O weh! Nun sprech ich kein Wort mehr!
(*Die* DREI KNABEN *bringen Flöte und Glockenspiel.*)

16. Terzett

DREI KNABEN: Seid uns zum zweiten Mal willkommen,
Ihr Männer, in Sarastros Reich!
Er schickt, was man euch abgenommen,
Die Flöte und die Glöckchen euch.
Wollt ihr die Speisen nicht verschmähen,
So esset, trinket froh davon!
Wenn wir zum dritten Mal uns sehen,
Ist Freude eures Mutes Lohn.
Tamino, Mut! Nah ist das Ziel.
Du, Papageno, schweige still! (*Gehen ab.*)

Dialog

PAPAGENO: Tamino, wollen wir nicht speisen? Blase du nur fort auf deiner Flöte, ich will meine Brocken blasen. Herr Sarastro führt eine gute Küche. Auf die Art, ja, da will ich schon schweigen, wenn ich immer solche gute Bissen bekomme. Nun, ich will sehen, ob auch der Keller so gut bestellt ist.
(*Er trinkt.*)
Ha! das ist Götterwein!
(*Die Flöte schweigt.* PAMINA *eintretend.*)

PAMINA: Du hier? Gütige Götter! Dank euch! Ich hörte deine Flöte—und so lief ich pfeilschnell dem Tone nach. Aber du bist traurig? Sprichst nicht eine Silbe mit deiner Pamina? Liebst du mich nicht mehr?
(TAMINO *seufzt und winkt ihr fort.*)

OLD WOMAN: Not quite. He is ten years older.

PAPAGENO: Ten years older than you? That must be quite a love affair! What is your lover's name?

OLD WOMAN: Papageno.

PAPAGENO: Papageno? Where is he then, this Papageno?

OLD WOMAN: He's sitting here, my angel!

PAPAGENO: I am your lover?

OLD WOMAN: Yes, my angel!

PAPAGENO: Tell me, then, what is *your* name?

OLD WOMAN: My name is—

(*Loud thunder. The* OLD WOMAN *exits quickly.* TAMINO *comes in again.*)

PAPAGENO: Oh, woe! I won't utter another word.

(*The* THREE SPIRITS *enter, bringing the magic flute and bells.*)

16. Trio

THREE SPIRITS: For the second time we welcome you to Sarastro's realm! He returns your flute and bells to you. Accept this food; eat, drink, and be happy; for when you see us for the third time, joy will be your reward! Tamino, have courage; your goal is near! And you, Papageno, remain silent! (*They exit.*)

Dialogue

PAPAGENO: Tamino, shall we not eat? You can play on your flute, but I am going to have dinner. My lord Sarastro has a good cook! I'm glad to be silent when such a meal is before me! Now, let me see if his cellar is equally good. (*He drinks.*)

Ha! This wine is good!

(*He plays the flute.* PAMINA *enters.*)

PAMINA: You are here, Tamino? Good gods, I thank you. I heard your flute—and followed its tones. But why are you so sad? Won't you speak a word to your Pamina? Do you love me no longer?

(TAMINO *sighs and turns away from her.*)

455

Papageno, sage du mir, sag, was ist meinem Freund?
(PAPAGENO *hat einen Brocken in dem Munde, winkt ihr fortzugehen.*)
Wie? Auch du? O, das ist mehr als Tod! Liebster, einziger Tamino!

17. Arie

Ach, ich fühl's, es ist verschwunden,
Ewig hin der Liebe Glück!
Nimmer kommt ihr, Wonnestunden,
Meinem Herzen mehr zurück!
Sieh, Tamino, diese Tränen,
Fliessen, Trauter, dir allein!
Fühlst du nicht der Liebe Sehnen,
So wird Ruhe im Tode sein. (*Sie geht traurig ab.*)

V. Auftritt

Das Gewölbe von Pyramiden. CHOR *der Priester kommt mit* SARASTRO *herein.*

18. Chor

CHOR: O Isis und Osiris, welche Wonne!
Die düst're Nacht verscheucht der Glanz der Sonne.
Bald fühlt der edle Jüngling neues Leben,
Bald ist er unserm Dienste ganz ergeben.
Sein Geist ist kühn, sein Herz ist rein,
Bald wird er unser würdig sein.
(TAMINO *wird hereingeführt.*)

Dialog

SARASTRO: Prinz, dein Betragen war bis hierher männlich und gelassen; nun hast du noch zwei gefährliche Wege zu wandern. Schlägt dein Herz noch ebenso warm für Pamina, und wünschest du einst als ein weiser Fürst zu regieren, so mögen die Götter dich ferner begleiten. Deine Hand. Man bringe Pamina!
(*Zwei Priester bringen* PAMINA, *welche mit einem Schleier bedeckt ist.*)

PAMINA: Wo bin ich? Saget, wo ist mein Jüngling?

SARASTRO: Er wartet deiner, um dir das letzte Lebewohl zu sagen.

PAMINA: Das letzte Lebewohl?

SARASTRO: Hier!

PAMINA: Tamino!

TAMINO: Zurück!

Papageno, tell me— Why does my beloved spurn me?
(PAPAGENO, *his mouth full, gestures her to go away.*)
What? You also. Oh, this is worse than death! My love, my dear Tamino!

17. Aria

Ah, I feel it—all love has vanished; my happiness is gone. Never again will I enjoy those blissful hours; they are forever flown from my heart! See, Tamino, see, my tears flow, dearest, for you alone. If you no longer feel love's deep longing, then I can find peace only in death! (*Sadly, she exits.*)

Scene V

The vaults of the pyramids. The CHORUS *of priests enters, led by* SARASTRO.

18. Chorus

CHORUS: O Isis and Osiris, witness our joy! Dark night is pierced by the brilliance of the sun. Soon the noble youth will feel new life; soon he will be dedicated to our service. His spirit is bold; his heart is pure; soon he will be worthy of us.
(TAMINO *is led in.*)

Dialogue

SARASTRO: Prince, your deeds have been heretofore manly and prudent; now you have two last trials to undergo. If your heart still beats warmly for Pamina, and if you wish to rule as a wise king, then let the gods lead you onward. Your hand! Bring Pamina!
(*Two priests bring in* PAMINA, *who is veiled.*)

PAMINA: Where am I? Say, where is my loved one?
SARASTRO: He waits for you, to say his last farewell.

PAMINA: His last farewell?
SARASTRO: Here!
PAMINA: Tamino!
TAMINO: Go back!

457

19. Terzett

PAMINA: Soll ich dich, Teurer, nicht mehr seh'n?

SARASTRO: Ihr werdet froh euch wiederseh'n!

PAMINA: Dein warten tödliche Gefahren!

TAMINO *und* SARASTRO: Die Götter mögen mich ihn bewahren!

PAMINA: Du wirst dem Tode nicht entgehen,
Mir flüstert dieses Ahndung ein.

TAMINO *und* SARASTRO: Der Götter Wille mag geschehen,
Ihr Wink soll mir ihm Gesetze sein!

PAMINA: O liebtest du, wie ich dich liebe,
Du würdest nicht so ruhig sein.

TAMINO: Glaub mir, ich fühle gleiche Triebe,
Werd ewig dein Getreuer sein.

SARASTRO: Glaub mir, er fühlet gleiche Triebe,
Wird ewig dein Getreuer sein.
Die Stunde schlägt, nun müsst ihr scheiden!

PAMINA *und* TAMINO: Wie bitter sind der Trennung Leiden!

PAMINA: Tamino, muss nun wirklich fort!

TAMINO: Pamina, ich muss wirklich fort!

PAMINA *und* TAMINO: Lebewohl! Lebewohl!
Ach, gold'ne Ruhe, kehre wieder!

SARASTRO: Nun eile fort,
Dich ruft dein Wort!
Die Stunde schlägt!
Wir seh'n uns wieder!
(PAMINA *geht mit den Priestern ab,* SARASTRO *geht mit* TA-MINO.)

Dialog

PAPAGENO (*von aussen*): Tamino! Tamino! Willst du mich denn gänzlich verlassen?
(*Er kommt herein.*)
Wenn ich nur wenigstens wüsste, wo ich wäre. Tamino! Tamino! So lang ich lebe, bleib ich nicht mehr von dir! Nur diesmal verlass mich armen Reisegefährten nicht!
(*Er kommt an die Tür links vorn.*)

EINE STIMME (*ruft*): Zurück!
(*Donner und Feuer.*)

19. Trio

PAMINA: Shall I never see you again, my dearest?

SARASTRO: Your next meeting will be blessed with joy!

PAMINA: Your path is through deadly dangers!

TAMINO *and* SARASTRO: The gods will protect me (him)!

PAMINA: You won't escape; I have a premonition that you will die.

TAMINO *and* SARASTRO: Let the gods' will be done; their bidding shall be my (his) law!

PAMINA: If you loved as I do, you could not be so calm.

TAMINO: Believe me, I feel the same sadness and will always be true to you.

SARASTRO: Believe me, he feels the same sadness and will always be true to you. The hour strikes; now he must go!

PAMINA *and* TAMINO: How bitter are the sorrows of parting!

PAMINA: Tamino, must you really go away?

TAMINO: Yes, Pamina, I must go!

PAMINA *and* TAMINO: Farewell! Farewell! Ah, golden peace, when will you return to me?

SARASTRO: Now you must hurry; you must make good your word. The hour sounds your fate, but we shall meet again.

(PAMINA *is led away by the priests;* SARASTRO *exits with* TAMINO.)

Dialogue

PAPAGENO (*off-stage*): Tamino! Tamino! Will you leave me completely alone?
(*He enters.*)
If I only knew where I was! Tamino! Tamino! As long as I live I will never desert you again! For this one time, don't desert your poor fellow adventurer!
(*He comes to a door.*)

VOICE (*off-stage*): Go back!
(*Thunder and fire are seen.*)

PAPAGENO: Nun kann ich weder vorwärts noch zurück! Muss vielleicht am Ende gar verhungern! Schon recht! Warum bin ich mitgereist?

(*Der* SPRECHER *kommt herein.*)

SPRECHER: Mensch! Du hättest verdient, auf immer in finsteren Klüften der Erde zu wandern—die gütigen Götter aber entlassen dich der Strafe. Dafür aber wirst du das himmlische Vergnügen der Eingeweihten nie fühlen.

PAPAGENO: Je nun, es gibt noch mehr Leute meinesgleichen! Mir wäre jetzt ein gutes Glas Wein das grösste Vergnügen.

SPRECHER: Sonst hast du keinen Wunsch in dieser Welt?

PAPAGENO: Bis jetzt nicht.

SPRECHER: Man wird dich damit bedienen!

(*Ab. Sogleich kommt ein grosser Becher, mit rotem Wein angefüllt, aus der Erde.*)

PAPAGENO: Juchhe! da ist er schon!

(*Trinkt.*)

Herrlich! Himmlisch! Göttlich! Ha! ich bin jetzt so vergnügt, dass ich bis zur Sonne fliegen wollte, wenn ich Flügel hätte! Ha! Mir wird ganz wunderlich ums Herz! Ich möchte—Ich wünschte—ja, was denn?

20. Arie

Ein Mädchen oder Weibchen
Wünscht Papageno sich!
O so ein sanftes Täubchen
Wär Seligkeit für mich!
Dann schmeckte mir Trinken und Essen,
Dann könnt ich mit Fürsten mich messen,
Des Lebens als Weiser mich freun,
Und wie im Elysium sein!
Ein Mädchen oder Weibchen
Wünscht Papageno sich!
O so ein sanftes Täubchen
Wär Seligkeit für mich!
Ach, kann ich denn keiner von allen
Den reizenden Mädchen gefallen?
Helf eine mir nur aus der Not,
Sonst gräm ich mich wahrlich zu Tod!
Ein Mädchen oder Weibchen
Wünscht Papageno sich!
O so ein sanftes Täubchen

PAPAGENO: Now I can't go in either direction. Perhaps I'll starve to death here—very well! Why did I come here in the first place?

(SPEAKER *enters.*)

SPEAKER: Unhappy creature! You should be doomed to wander forever in the darkest abysses of the earth—but the good gods will spare you from punishment. However, you will never taste the heavenly pleasures of the elect.

PAPAGENO: That's all right. There are more people like me! Just a glass of good wine would give me greater pleasure.

SPEAKER: You have no other wish in this world?

PAPAGENO: No other.

SPEAKER: You shall be served!

(*He exits. A large goblet of red wine appears from the earth.*)

PAPAGENO: Aha! This is wonderful!

(*He drinks.*)

Splendid! Heavenly! I'm so happy that I could fly to the sun—if I had wings. Ha! Something strange is stirring in my heart! I wish—I want to—but what do I wish?

20. Aria

A sweetheart or a little wife is Papageno's wish! Oh, such a gentle dove would bring blessedness to me! Then eating and drinking, I would enjoy life like a sensible man; and happy as a prince, I would think myself in heaven. A sweetheart or a little wife— Ah, is there not one out of so many girls who might care for me? If no one will pity my sorrow, I'm certain I'll die of loneliness. A sweetheart or a little wife— If no one will choose me, my love will consume my being! But if a loving mouth would kiss me, then my suffering would be ended!

(*Enter the* OLD WOMAN, *dancing with the aid of her stick.*)

Die Zauberflöte

Wär Seligkeit für mich!
Wird keine mir Liebe gewähren,
So muss mich die Flamme verzehren;
Doch küsst mich ein weiblicher Mund,
So bin ich schon wieder gesund.

(*Das* ALTES WEIB, *tanzend, und auf ihren Stock dabei sich stützend, kommt herein.*)

Dialog

ALTES WEIB: Da bin ich schon, mein Engel!

PAPAGENO: Du hast dich meiner erbarmt?

ALTES WEIB: Ja, mein Engel!

PAPAGENO: Das ist ein Glück!

ALTES WEIB: Und wenn du mir versprichst, mir ewig treu zu bleiben, dann sollst du sehen, wie zärtlich dein Weibchen dich lieben wird.

PAPAGENO: Ei, du zärtliches Närrchen!

ALTES WEIB: O, wie will ich dich umarmen, dich liebkosen, dich an mein Herz drücken!

PAPAGENO: Auch ans Herz drücken?

ALTES WEIB: Komm, reich mir zum Pfand unseres Bundes deine Hand!

PAPAGENO: Nur nicht so hastig, lieber Engel! So ein Bündnis braucht doch auch seine Ueberlegung.

ALTES WEIB: Papageno, ich rate dir, zaudre nicht! Deine Hand, oder du bist auf immer hier eingekerkert.

PAPAGENO: Eingekerkert?

ALTES WEIB: Wasser und Brot wird deine tägliche Kost sein. Ohne Freund, ohne Freundin musst du leben, und der Welt auf immer entsagen.

PAPAGENO: Wasser trinken? Der Welt entsagen? Nein, da will ich doch lieber eine Alte nehmen, als gar keine. Nun, da hast du meine Hand mit der Versicherung, dass ich dir immer getreu bleibe (*für sich*) so lang' ich keine Schönere sehe.

ALTES WEIB: Das schwörst du?

PAPAGENO: Ja, das schwör ich!

(WEIB *verwandelt sich in ein junges Mädchen, welches ebenso gekleidet ist wie* PAPAGENO.)

Pa-Pa-Papagena!

(SPRECHER *kommt und nimmt sie bei der Hand.*)

Dialogue

OLD WOMAN: Here I am, my angel.

PAPAGENO: Then you pity me.

OLD WOMAN: Yes, my angel.

PAPAGENO: How fortunate I am.

OLD WOMAN: And if you swear fidelity to me, you will see that your little wife will love you tenderly!

PAPAGENO: Oh, you tender little fool!

OLD WOMAN: Oh, how I would hug you and kiss you and clutch you to my heart!

PAPAGENO: Clutch me to your heart?

OLD WOMAN: Give me your hand as a pledge of your oath!

PAPAGENO: Not so hasty, beloved angel! Such an oath needs some thought.

OLD WOMAN: I warn you, Papageno, don't delay! Your hand, or you will be detained here forever.

PAPAGENO: Forever?

OLD WOMAN: Water and bread will be your daily fare. Without a friend, without a sweetheart, you must live, and you must renounce the pleasures of the world!

PAPAGENO: Drink water! Renounce the world! No, I'd rather take an old woman than remain a bachelor. Now, you have my hand with my oath that I'll be true to you always (*aside*) until someone prettier comes along.

OLD WOMAN: You swear that?

PAPAGENO: Yes, I swear it.

(*The* OLD WOMAN *changes into a young girl, dressed like* PAPAGENO.)

Pa-pa-Papagena!

(SPEAKER *appears suddenly and steps between them.*)

463

SPRECHER: Fort mit dir, junges Weib! Er ist deiner noch nicht würdig! Zurück! sag ich.

PAPAGENO: Eh ich mich zurückziehe, soll die Erde mich verschlingen.
(*Er sinkt hinab.*)
O ihr Götter!
(*Er springt wieder heraus und läuft ab.*)

VI. Auftritt

Ein kurzer Garten. Die DREI KNABEN *fahren herunter.*

21. *Finale*

DREI KNABEN: Bald prangt, den Morgen zu verkünden,
Die Sonn auf goldner Bahn.
Bald soll der Aberglaube schwinden,
Bald siegt der weise Mann.
O holde Ruhe, steig hernieder,
Kehr in der Menschen Herzen wieder;
Dann ist die Erd ein Himmelreich,
Und Sterbliche den Göttern gleich.

ERSTER KNABE: Doch seht, Verzweiflung quält Paminen!

ZWEITER KNABE *und* DRITTER KNABE: Wo ist sie denn?

ERSTER KNABE: Sie ist von Sinnen!

DREI KNABEN: Sie quält verschmähter Liebe Leiden.
Lasst uns der Armen Trost bereiten.
Fürwahr, ihr Schicksal geht uns nah!
O wäre nur ihr Jüngling da!
Sie kommt, lasst uns beiseite gehn,
Damit wir, was sie mache, sehn.
(*Sie gehen beiseite.* PAMINA *halb wahnwitzig, mit einem Dolch in der Hand.*)

PAMINA: Du also bist mein Bräutigam!
Durch dich vollend ich meinen Gram!

DREI KNABEN: Welch dunkle Worte sprach sie da?
Die Arme ist dem Wahnsinn nah.

PAMINA: Geduld, mein Trauter, ich bin dein!
Bald werden wir vermählet sein!

DREI KNABEN: Wahnsinn tobt ihr im Gehirne,
Selbstmord steht auf ihrer Stirne. (*zu* PAMINA)
Holdes Mädchen, sieh uns an!

PAMINA: Sterben will ich, weil der Mann,
Den ich nimmermehr kann hassen,
Sein Traute kann verlassen! (*auf den Dolch zeigend*)
Dies gab meine Mutter mir.

SPEAKER: Away with you, young woman! He is not worthy of you! Go back, I say!

PAPAGENO: I won't go back, even if the earth should engulf me!

(*He sinks down.*)

O Gods!

(*He springs up again and runs out.*)

Scene VI

A small garden. The THREE SPIRITS *enter.*

21. Finale

THREE SPIRITS: Soon shines the morning in the golden path of the sun! Soon wise men shall triumph, and superstition shall disappear. O Holy Peace, descend with us; return to men's hearts, and earth will be a heavenly realm, and mortals will be like gods!

FIRST SPIRIT: But see—Pamina is torn by despair!

SECOND SPIRIT *and* THIRD SPIRIT: Where is she, then?

FIRST SPIRIT: She is out of her senses.

THREE SPIRITS: She suffers from the agonies of spurned love. Let us bring comfort to the poor girl. Truly, her fate concerns and grieves us! Oh, if only her prince were here! She comes; let us watch her for a moment.

(*They withdraw.* PAMINA *enters with a dagger in hand.*)

PAMINA: Then this dagger will be my bridegroom! With it, I shall end my grief!

THREE SPIRITS: What dark words does she speak? The poor girl is near madness.

PAMINA: Patience my darling, I am yours! Soon we will be united!

THREE SPIRITS: Darkness has obscured her mind. Suicide is written on her brow. (*to* PAMINA) Noble maiden, turn to us!

PAMINA: I wish to die, because the man whom I can never hate has forsaken me! (*indicating the dagger*) This was given to me by my mother.

465

DREI KNABEN: Selbstmord strafet Gott an dir!

PAMINA: Lieber durch dies Eisen sterben,
Als durch Liebesgram verderben!
Mutter, durch dich leide ich,
Und dein Fluch verfolget mich!

DREI KNABEN: Mädchen, willst du mit uns gehn?

PAMINA: Ha, des Jammers Mass ist voll!
Falscher Jüngling, lebe wohl!
Sieh, Pamina stirbt durch dich,
Dieses Eisen töte mich!

DREI KNABEN: Ha! Unglückliche, halt ein!
Sollte dies dein Jüngling sehen,
Würde er vor Gram vergehen;
Denn er liebet dich allein.

PAMINA: Was? Er fühlte Gegenliebe,
Und verbarg mir seine Triebe,
Wandte sein Gesicht von mir?
Warum sprach er nicht mit mir?

DREI KNABEN: Dieses müssen wir verschweigen,
Doch wir wollen dir ihn zeigen,
Und du wirst mit Staunen sehen,
Dass er dir sein Herz geweiht,
Und den Tod für dich nicht scheut.
Komm, wir wollen zu ihm gehn.

PAMINA: Führt mich hin, ich möcht ihn seh'n!

ALLE: Zwei Herzen, die vor Liebe brennen,
Kann Menschenohnmacht niemals trennen.
Verloren ist der Feinde Müh,
Die Götter selbsten schützen sie. (*Gehen alle ab.*)

VII. Auftritt

Zwei grosse Berge. ZWEI GEHARNISCHTE MÄNNER *führen* TA-
MINO *herein.*

ZWEI GEHARNISCHTE MÄNNER: Der, welcher wandert diese
Strasse voll Beschwerden,
Wird rein durch Feuer, Wasser, Luft und Erden:
Wenn er des Todes Schrecken überwinden kann,
Schwingt er sich aus der Erde himmelan.
Erleuchtet wird er dann im Stande sein,
Sich den Mysterien der Isis ganz zu weih'n.

466

THREE SPIRITS: Suicide is a sin against the gods!

PAMINA: I would rather die by this blade than perish from love's deep wound! Mother, I suffer, and your curse pursues me!

THREE SPIRITS: Maiden, will you go with us?

PAMINA: Ah, sorrow's cup is full! False youth, farewell! See, Pamina dies for you! This dagger will end my life!

THREE SPIRITS: Stop! Unhappy one, if your Prince could see you, he would die of grief, for he loves only you.

PAMINA: What? He returns my love, and is true to me? Then, why did he turn away his face? Why could he not speak one word?

THREE SPIRITS: We cannot tell you that. But we will take you to him, and you will see that he is risking death in devotion for you! Come, we will lead you to him.

PAMINA: I'll follow you. I must see him again!

ALL: Two hearts united in love cannot be separated by mortal power! All enemies threaten them in vain, for the gods will always protect them! (*Exit.*)

SCENE VII

Two large mountains. TWO MEN IN ARMOR *lead* TAMINO *in.*

TWO MEN IN ARMOR: Whoever journeys the dread path must be purified with fire, water, air, and earth. If he can conquer the fear of death, he will release himself from mundane bondage and will ascend from earth toward heaven. He will be worthy of consecration to the mysteries of Isis!

TAMINO: Mich schreckt kein Tod, als Mann zu handeln,
Den Weg der Tugend fortzuwandeln.
Schliesst mir die Schreckenspforten auf!
Ich wage froh den kühnen Lauf.

PAMINA (*von innen*): Tamino, halt! Ich muss dich sehn!

TAMINO: Was hör ich? Paminens Stimme?

ZWEI GEHARNISCHTE MÄNNER: Ja, ja, das ist Paminens
Stimme.

TAMINO: Wohl mir, nun kann sie mit mir geh'n,
Nun trennet uns kein Schicksal mehr,
Wenn auch der Tod beschieden wär!
Ist mir erlaubt, mit ihr zu sprechen?

ZWEI GEHARNISCHTE MÄNNER: Dir ist erlaubt, mit ihr zu
sprechen.

TAMINO: Welch Glück, wenn wir uns wiederseh'n,
Froh Hand in Hand in Tempel geh'n!
Ein Weib, das Nacht und Tod nicht scheut,
Ist würdig und wird eingeweiht.

ZWEI GEHARNISCHTE MÄNNER: Welch Glück, wenn wir euch
wiederseh'n,
Froh Hand in Hand in Tempel geh'n!
Ein Weib, das Nacht und Tod nicht scheut,
Ist würdig und wird eingeweiht.

(*Die Türe wird aufgemacht;* TAMINO *und* PAMINA *umarmen
sich.*)

PAMINA: Tamino mein! O welch ein Glück!

TAMINO: Pamina mein! O welch ein Glück!
Hier sind die Schreckenspforten,
Die Not und Tod mir dräu'n.

PAMINA: Ich werde aller Orten
An deiner Seite sein;
Ich Selbsten führe dich,
Die Liebe leitet mich!
Sie mag den Weg mit Rosen streu'n,
Weil Rosen stets bei Dornen sein.
Spiel du die Zauberflöte an;
Sie schütze uns auf unsrer Bahn.
Es schnitt in einer Zauberstunde
Mein Vater sie aus tiefstem Grunde
Der tausendjähr'gen Eiche aus,
Bei Blitz und Donner, Sturm und Braus.
Nun komm und spiel die Flöte an,
Sie leite uns auf grauser Bahn.

TAMINO: No death frightens me— I fear no pain that man can inflict. I must act like a man, and nobly face all dangers!

PAMINA (*off-stage*): Tamino, stop! I must speak to you.
TAMINO: What do I hear? Pamina's voice?
TWO MEN IN ARMOR: Yes, yes, that is Pamina's voice.

TAMINO: I am happy that she is permitted to accompany us! Now no fate can part us, even though death may await us here. May I speak to her?

TWO MEN IN ARMOR: Yes, you may speak to her.

TAMINO: What joy to see each other again! Hand in hand, we will enter the Temple. A woman who has no fear of death is worthy and will be ordained!

TWO MEN IN ARMOR: What joy to see each other again! Hand in hand, they will enter the Temple. A woman who has no fear of death is worthy and will be ordained!
(*The door opens.* TAMINO *and* PAMINA *embrace each other.*)

PAMINA: My Tamino! What happiness!
TAMINO: My Pamina! Oh, what happiness! But here before us are the fearful gates; danger and death are threatening.

PAMINA: My only wish is to be at your side. I will follow you. Love leads me on! Our path will be strewn with roses —but roses have sharp thorns. Play your magic flute as we go. It was carved in a witching hour by my father. His sorcery created it from ancient oak that had survived thunder, lightning, storm, and turmoil. Now, play upon it—its tones will protect us on our dreadful journey.

ALLE: Wir wandeln (Ihr wandelt) durch des Tones Macht
Froh durch des Todes düstre Nacht.
(*Die Türen werden nach ihnen zugeschlagen; man sieht*
TAMINO *und* PAMINA *wandern; man hört Feuergeprassel*
und Windgeheul. TAMINO *bläst seine Flöte. Sobald sie vom*
Feuer herauskommen, umarmen sie sich.)

PAMINA *und* TAMINO: Wir wandelten durch Feuergluten,
Bekämpften mutig die Gefahr.
Dein Ton sei Schutz in Wasserfluten,
So wie er es im Feuer war.
(TAMINO *bläst; man sieht sie hinuntersteigen und nach*
einiger Zeit wieder heraufkommen; sogleich öffnet sich
eine Türe; man sieht einen Eingang in einen Tempel, wel-
cher hell beleuchtet ist.)
Ihr Götter, welch ein Augenblick!
Gewähret ist uns Isis Glück!

CHOR (*von innen*): Triumph, Triumph, du edles Paar!
Besieget hast du die Gefahr,
Der Isis Weihe ist nun dein!
Kommt, tretet in den Tempel ein!
(*Alle ab.*)

VIII. Auftritt

Ein Garten mit einem Baum. PAPAGENO *allein, mit einem*
Strick umgürtet.

PAPAGENO: Papagena! Papagena! Papagena!
Weibchen! Täubchen! meine Schöne!
Vergebens! Ach, sie ist verloren,
Ich bin zum Unglück schon geboren!
Ich plauderte, und das war schlecht,
Und drum geschieht es mir schon recht!
Seit ich gekostet diesen Wein,
Seit ich das schöne Weibchen sah,
So brennt's im Herzenskämmerlein,
So zwickt es hier, so zwickt es da.
Papagena! Herzensweibchen!
Papagena, liebes Täubchen!
's ist umsonst, es ist vergebens!
Müde bin ich meines Lebens!
Sterben macht der Lieb ein End,
Wenn's im Herzen noch so brennt.
(*nimmt einen Strick von seiner Mitte*)
Diesen Baum da will ich zieren,
Mir an ihm den Hals zuschnüren,

ALL: We (they) travel without fear through death's dark night!

(TAMINO *and* PAMINA *pass through one of the portals into the Cave of Fire.* TAMINO *plays his flute. They emerge and embrace one another.*)

PAMINA *and* TAMINO: We have passed through the fire unscathed; we have withstood the danger. And the flute that protected us from fire will now save us from water, as well. (*They pass through another portal into a waterfall. Again* TAMINO *plays his flute. When they emerge, an entrance to the Temple shines brightly before them.*)
O God! how sudden and profound are the joys of Isis!

CHORUS (*off-stage*): You have triumphed, noble pair! You have mastered the trials! You are now worthy to enter the Temple with us. The power of Isis is yours!
(*All exit.*)

Scene VIII

A garden with a large tree. PAPAGENO *is alone, he has a rope around him.*

PAPAGENO: Papagena! My dear little wife! My beautiful dove! I give up! She is lost to me. I am born to misfortune! I chattered, and for that I was justly repaid. Since I tasted that wine, since I saw that pretty little woman, my heart has been aflame. It tweaks me here, it tweaks me there. Papagena, wife of my heart! Papagena, my sweet dove! All is lost; it is in vain. I am weary of my life, and if I die, it will end love's torment, and no longer will my heart ache. (*taking the rope*) I'll hang myself on this tree—for the world has treated me cruelly. Good night, then, you deceitful world! Since you gave me no sweetheart, I may as well die. Pretty girls, remember me! Won't anyone pity me? Must I hang without a word of sympathy? Call to me—yes or no? Nobody hears me, all is quiet; it is the will of the gods. Papageno, quickly—end your life! Now, I'll do it! But first—I'll count to three. One—two—

Weil das Leben mir missfällt;
Gute Nacht, du falsche Welt!
Weil du böse an mir handelst,
Mir kein schönes Kind zubandelst,
So ist's aus, so sterbe ich;
Schöne Mädchen, denkt an mich!
Will sich eine um mich Armen,
Eh ich hänge, noch erbarmen,
Wohl, so lass ich's diesmal sein!
Rufet nur: ja, oder nein!
Keine hört mich; alles stille!
Also ist es euer Wille?
Papageno, frisch hinauf!
Ende deinen Lebenslauf!
Nun, ich warte noch, es sei!
Bis man zählet: eins, zwei, drei!
Eins!—Zwei!—Drei!
Nun wohlan, es bleibt dabei,
Weil mich nichts zurücke hält,
Gute Nacht, du falsche Welt!

(*Will sich hängen. Die* DREI KNABEN *fahren herunter.*)

DREI KNABEN: Halt ein, o Papageno! und sei klug,
Man lebt nur einmal, dies sei dir genug!

PAPAGENO: Ihr habt gut reden, habt gut scherzen;
Doch brennt es euch wie mich im Herzen,
Ihr würdet auch nach Mädchen gehn.

DREI KNABEN: So lasse deine Glöckchen klingen;
Dies wird dein Weibchen zu dir bringen.

PAPAGENO: Ich Narr vergass der Zauberdinge!
Erklinge, Glockenspiel, erklinge!
Ich muss mein liebes Mädchen seh'n!
Klinget, Glöckchen, klinget!
Schafft mein Mädchen her!
Klinget, Glöckchen, klinget!
Bringt mein Weibchen her.

(*Die* DREI KNABEN *bringen* PAPAGENA *heraus.*)

DREI KNABEN: Nun, Papageno, sieh dich um!
(PAPAGENO *sieht sich um.*)

PAPAGENO: Pa—pa—pa—pa—pa—pa—Papagena!

PAPAGENA: Pa—pa—pa—pa—pa—pa—Papageno!

PAPAGENO: Bist du mir nun ganz gegeben?

PAPAGENA: Nun, bin ich dir ganz gegeben!

three! Nobody comes; it's still the same; nobody will prevent me. Then, false world, good night!
(*He starts to hang himself. The* THREE SPIRITS *enter.*)

THREE SPIRITS: Stop, Papageno, stop and be wise! Man lives only once; that should be enough for you!

PAPAGENO: I understand that, but if your hearts ached like mine, you too would seek comfort.

THREE SPIRITS: Then let your bells ring out—for they will bring your wife to you.

PAPAGENO: How stupid I am to forget the magic bells! Ring, magic bells, ring out! I must see my sweetheart; bring her to me!
(*The* THREE SPIRITS *make* PAPAGENA *appear.*)

THREE SPIRITS: Now, Papageno, look around!
(PAPAGENO *turns around and sees her.*)

PAPAGENO: Pa-pa-pa-Papagena!

PAPAGENA: Pa-pa-pa-Papageno!

PAPAGENO: Are you really mine?

PAPAGENA: I am really yours!

PAPAGENO: Nun, so sei mein liebes Weibchen!

PAPAGENA: Nun, so sei mein Herzenstäubchen!

BEIDE: Welche Freude wird das sein,
Wenn die Götter uns bedenken,
Unsrer Liebe Kinder schenken,
So liebe, kleine Kinderlein!

PAPAGENO: Erst einen kleinen Papageno—

PAPAGENA: Dann eine kleine Papagena—

PAPAGENO: Dann wieder einen Papageno—

PAPAGENA: Dann wieder eine Papagena—

PAPAGENO: Papageno!

PAPAGENA: Papagena!

PAPAGENO: Es ist das höchste der Gefühle,
Wenn viele Papageno,
Der Eltern Segen werden sein.

PAPAGENA: Es ist das höchste der Gefühle,
Wenn viele, viele Papagena
Der Eltern Segen werden sein.

(*Sie gehen ab.*)

IX. Auftritt

Vor dem Tempel. MONOSTATOS, *die* KÖNIGIN *mit allen ihren* DAMEN, *kommen von beiden Versenkungen.*

MONOSTATOS: Nur stille, stille, stille,
Bald dringen wir im Tempel ein.

ALLE: Nur stille, stille, stille,
Bald dringen wir im Tempel ein.

MONOSTATOS: Doch, Fürstin, halte Wort! Erfülle—
Dein Kind muss meine Gattin sein.

KÖNIGIN DER NACHT: Ich halte Wort; es ist mein Wille,
Mein Kind soll deine Gattin sein.

DREI DAMEN: Ihr Kind soll deine Gattin sein.

MONOSTATOS: Doch still, ich höre schrecklich Rauschen
Wie Donnerton und Wasserfall.

KÖNIGIN DER NACHT *und* DREI DAMEN: Ja, fürchterlich ist
dieses Rauschen,
Wie fernen Donners Widerhall!

MONOSTATOS: Nun sind sie in des Tempels Hallen.

ALLE: Dort wollen wir sie überfallen,
Die Frömmler tilgen von der Erd
Mit Feuersglut und mächt'gem Schwert.

PAPAGENO: You are my dear little wife!

PAPAGENA: You are my heart's dove!

BOTH: What joy it will be, when the gods bless us with lovely children!

PAPAGENO: First a little Papageno!

PAPAGENA: Then a little Papagena!

PAPAGENO: Then another Papageno!

PAPAGENA: Then another Papagena!

PAPAGENO: Papageno!

PAPAGENA: Papagena!

PAPAGENO: It will be the height of joy when many little Papagenos bless their parents with happiness!

PAPAGENA: It will be the height of joy when many little Papagenas bless their parents with happiness!
(*They exit.*)

Scene IX

Before the Temple. Enter MONOSTATOS, *the* QUEEN OF THE NIGHT, *and the* THREE LADIES.

MONOSTATOS: We must be silent! Soon we shall be in the Temple!

ALL: We must be silent! Soon we shall be in the Temple!

MONOSTATOS: Queen, keep your word—remember that your daughter must be my wife!

QUEEN OF THE NIGHT: I keep my word; it is my will! My daughter will be your wife!

THREE LADIES: Her daughter will be his wife.

MONOSTATOS: But listen— I hear a terrible roaring, like the thunder of a waterfall.

QUEEN OF THE NIGHT *and* THREE LADIES: The sound is fearful, like the peal of faraway thunder!

MONOSTATOS: Now they are all in the Temple's halls.

ALL: There we shall fall upon them. We shall extirpate them from the earth with fire's flames and mighty sword.

DREI DAMEN *und* MONOSTATOS: Dir, grosse Königin der Nacht,
Sei uns'rer Rache Opfer gebracht.
(*Man hört Donner, Blitz, Sturm.*)
ALLE: Zerschmettert, zernichtet ist unsere Macht,
Wir alle gestürzet in ewige Nacht!
(*Sie sinken alle in die Erde.*)

X. Auftritt

Tempel der Sonne. SARASTRO *steht erhöht;* TAMINO, PAMINA, *beide in priesterlicher Kleidung. Die* DREI KNABEN *halten Blumen.*

SARASTRO: Die Strahlen der Sonne vertreiben die Nacht,
Zernichten der Heuchler erschlichene Macht.
CHOR: Heil sei euch Geweihten! Ihr dränget durch Nacht.
Dank sei dir, Osiris, dank dir, Isis, gebracht!
Es siegte die Stärke, und krönet zum Lohn
Die Schönheit und Weisheit mit ewiger Kron.

THREE LADIES *and* MONOSTATOS: Through you, great Queen of the Night, our revenge shall be accomplished!
(*There is loud thunder and lightning.*)

ALL: Destroyed is our power; we are all plunged into everlasting night!
(*They sink into the earth.*)

Scene X

The Temple of the Sun. SARASTRO *stands elevated above* TAMINO *and* PAMINA, *who are dressed in priestly clothing. The* THREE SPIRITS *carry large sunflowers.*

SARASTRO: The rays of the sun have conquered the night, destroying the deceiving powers of darkness!

CHORUS: Hail, leader and guide! You have rescued the worthy ones from the threat of night! Homage to Isis and Osiris, you who have watched over all of us! The strength of justice has prevailed, and as a reward, all worthiness will be crowned with everlasting beauty and wisdom!

RECOMMENDED RECORDINGS

THE ABDUCTION FROM THE SERAGLIO

Beecham, Marshall, Hollweg, Simoneau (Angel; monaural and stereophonic).

The dash and sparkle of Beecham's highly individual concept of the score, brilliantly realized by an able cast.

Fricsay, Stader, Häfliger (Decca).

A charming performance, more intimate and lyrical, but not as incisive as the Beecham recording; also, for the most part, well-sung.

THE MARRIAGE OF FIGARO

Busch, Glyndebourne Festival Opera Company (Victor).

A superbly integrated performance, vitalized by Busch's authoritative leadership. Although here, as in all the Glyndebourne sets, the sound is not comparable to that of newer recordings, definitive qualities make the album well worth searching for. In this particular opera, virtually all the recitative is cut; the purchaser must decide for himself how much of a drawback this is.

Guilini, Schwarzkopf, Moffo, Taddei, Wächter (Angel; monaural and stereophonic).

A scintillating performance, both funny and touching, sparked by fine conducting and a cast that thoroughly knows and relishes its comedic manners.

Kleiber, Siepi, Gueden, Della Casa, Corena, Danco (London; monaural and stereophonic).

A solid, clear-sounding, nearly uncut performance, including an aria or two rarely encountered in the opera house. Kleiber's sense of style overcomes certain moments of heaviness on the part of the generally competent soloists.

Leinsdorf, Della Casa, Peters, London, Tozzi (Victor; monaural and stereophonic).

Leinsdorf leading a cast of Metropolitan favorites through a cheerful, spirited, and agreeable rendition of the score. The singing is a bit uneven, but the performance moves briskly.

478

DON GIOVANNI

Busch, Glyndebourne Festival Opera Company (Victor; re-issued by Electrola).
Universally accepted as one of the finest operatic recordings ever made. See comment on Busch's *Figaro* recording. A cast without stars is admirably qualified to bring out all the sweep and subtlety of the score.

Guilini, Wächter, Sutherland, Schwarzkopf, Taddei (Angel; monaural and stereophonic).
An almost ideal cast performing superbly under a firm and understanding baton; brilliant singing, and a concept whose attention to detail equals its concern for the large outlines of the score. This album is worthy to stand beside the earlier Busch album, with vastly improved sound.

Moralt, London, Zadek, Simoneau (Epic).
A beautifully paced, thoughtful performance. A cast well-suited to the opera's requirements invariably succeeds in conveying the spirit of the music, particularly in the recitative.

Leinsdorf, Nilsson, Price, Siepi, Valetti, Corena (Victor; monaural and stereophonic).
Capricious tempos and a somewhat debatable cast detract from the effectiveness of the singing and the undeniable sweep of the performance as a whole.

Krips, Siepi, Danco, Dermota (London; monaural and stereophonic).
A heavy, serious rendition that includes some intelligent singing.

COSÌ FAN TUTTE

Busch, Glyndebourne Festival Opera Company (Victor).
Again, the standard by which all subsequent and brighter-sounding sets must be judged. Busch, allowing no hint of sogginess to invade his crisp, airy presentation of the score, achieves a true Mozartean ensemble rather than a hastily assembled and rehearsed collection of stars.

Von Karajan, Schwarzkopf, Merriman (Angel).
A rather small-scaled conception, with singers whose performances are, generally, not quite equal to the arias, but who make the most of the many ensembles.

Stiedry, Steber, Thebom, Tucker (Columbia).
For those who enjoy opera in English. Steber's fine singing

479

and Stiedry's understanding of the score may balance other deficiencies.

THE MAGIC FLUTE

Beecham, Berger, Lemnitz, Hüsch (Victor; reissued by Electrola).
A brilliant, magnificently sung performance, replete with breadth and vitality. The sound is inferior to that of newer recordings.

Fricsay, Stader, Häfliger, Fischer-Dieskau (Decca).
A charming performance, flexible and lyrical, well-sung and clearly recorded.